The Knopf Collector's Guide
to American Antiques

W9-BTF-913

Robert Bishop & William C. Ketchum, Jr.
Series Consultants

A Chanticleer Press Edition

Glass Bottles, Lamps & Other Objects

Jane Shadel Spillman

With photographs by Raymond Errett

Alfred A. Knopf, New York

This is a Borzoi Book
Published by Alfred A. Knopf, Inc.

Prepared and produced by
Chanticleer Press, Inc., New York.

Color reproductions by Nievergelt Repro AG, Zurich,
Switzerland. Type set in Century Expanded by Dix Type Inc.,
Syracuse, New York. Printed and bound by Dai Nippon Printing
Co., Ltd., Tokyo, Japan.

First Printing

Library of Congress Catalog Number: 83-47986
ISBN: 0-394-71541-1

Contents

Acknowledgments

Many people have assisted in the preparation of this book.
Special thanks are due to all the institutions and individuals who
made their collections available to us. I am most grateful to
Dwight Lanmon, Director of The Corning Museum of Glass, for
permission to photograph the museum's collection; to both Mary
Kay Ingenthron, Deputy Director of Public Affairs, and Susan
Williams, Curator of Household Accessories and Tablewares, at
The Margaret Woodbury Strong Museum for their willing
cooperation; and to Osna Fenner, Elizabeth Brill, Donald Hall,
and G. Eason Eige, Chief Curator of Collections at the
Huntington Galleries, Inc., for loaning objects from their
collections. I especially want to thank Burton Spiller not only for
providing bottles to be photographed, but also for reading the
bottle manuscript and for helping William C. Ketchum, Jr.,
to determine the bottle prices. I owe a debt of gratitude to
Helen McKearin and Kenneth M. Wilson, without whose careful
research on bottles and flasks the first part of this book could not
have been written.
At Corning, Raymond Errett, assisted by Nicholas Williams,
spent months photographing almost all of the objects in this
book, and Patricia Driscoll and Priscilla Price helped in the
preparations for photography. In New York City, William C.
Ketchum, Jr., reviewed the entire manuscript, making many
helpful suggestions, and compiled the Price Guide. Robert
Bishop also read the manuscript and gave invaluable support.
Amelia Weiss skillfully copy-edited the text. At home, I am
grateful to Don, Beth, and Sam, who managed without me for
many weekends while I typed and who encouraged me when I grew
weary.
My appreciation goes to Paul Steiner and his staff at Chanticleer
Press: Gudrun Buettner and Susan Costello, who developed the
idea for this series; Jane Opper, who, with the help of Lori Renn,
edited and coordinated the project; Michael Goldman and Cathy
Peck, who provided editorial assistance in the final stages; Carol
Nehring, who supervised the art and layouts; and Helga Lose,
who directed the production of the book. Finally, I want to thank
Charles Elliott, Senior Editor at Alfred A. Knopf, for his
encouragement and support.

About the Author, Photographer, and Consultants

Jane Shadel Spillman
Curator of American Glass at The Corning Museum of Glass, author Jane Shadel Spillman is a leading authority on American antique glass and has lectured widely on the subject. She has written *American and European Pressed Glass in The Corning Museum of Glass*, *Glassmaking: America's First Industry*, *The Knopf Collectors' Guide to Glass Tableware, Bowls & Vases*, and *Pressed Glass 1825–1925* for the 1983 special summer exhibition she organized at The Corning Museum of Glass. Mrs. Spillman is also coauthor of *The Complete Cut & Engraved Glass of Corning*, *The Cut & Engraved Glass of Corning, 1868–1940*, and *M'Kee Victorian Glass: Five Complete Catalogs from 1859/60 to 1871*.

Raymond Errett
Photographer Raymond Errett is Conservator-Photographer at The Corning Museum of Glass and has specialized in photographing glass for 20 years. His photographs have been featured in many national publications and appear in *Masterpieces of Glass* by Robert J. Charleston and, most recently, *Glass Tableware, Bowls & Vases* by Jane Shadel Spillman.

William C. Ketchum, Jr.
Consultant and author of the Price Guide, William C. Ketchum, Jr., is a member of the faculty of The New School for Social Research. He is also a guest curator at the Museum of American Folk Art in New York City and a consultant to several major auction houses. Dr. Ketchum has written 18 books, including *A Treasury of American Bottles*, *The Catalog of American Antiques*, and *The Knopf Collectors' Guide to Pottery & Porcelain*. He is an associate editor at *Antique Monthly*.

Robert Bishop
Director of the Museum of American Folk Art in New York City, consultant Robert Bishop is author of more than 30 books, among them *American Decorative Arts, 1620–1980* and *The Knopf Collectors' Guide to Quilts*. He established the first master's degree program in folk art studies at New York University. Dr. Bishop is on the editorial boards of *Art & Antiques*, *Horizon Magazine*, and *Antique Monthly*.

Preface

The incredible variety of American glass—from tableware to bottles, lamps, and paperweights—has made glass collecting one of the most popular fields in American antiques. This volume, a companion to *The Knopf Collectors' Guide to Glass Tableware, Bowls & Vases*, features flasks, bottles, jars, candlesticks, lamps, paperweights, and toy glassware. Since collectors often discover and want to identify a wide assortment of other glass objects, such pieces as animal figurines, doorknobs, target balls, windows, and unusual pressed-glass patents are also included here.

Spurred by an interest in American history, people have been collecting and studying figured flasks since the 1920s, identifying the portraits on them, researching the factory names and political events that inspired the designs and inscriptions, and categorizing rare colors and patterns. But only since the 1960s have other types of bottles been avidly pursued. Whiskey, gin, medicine, milk, perfume, pickle, ink, and many other kinds of bottles find a home today in someone's collection. And a collection need not be limited to a particular type of bottle, but may be devoted to early pontiled examples, bottles in a favorite color, or those produced by a particular glasshouse. Become a bottle collector and join the hardy breed that enjoys the search almost as much as the treasure, whether it leads to a dump, an old factory site, or even underwater. There are now more than a hundred books on bottles and dozens of regional bottle clubs throughout the country.

Antique candlesticks and lamps have been collected for at least fifty years, not only for their graceful shapes but also as reminders of bygone eras. Enthusiasts can trace the history of American lighting through their collections. Similarly, people have been collecting paperweights since the 1950s, seeking especially beautiful and rare examples that can be attributed to a particular factory or maker. In contrast, collecting toy glassware is a relatively new field; many miniatures can be linked with early 19th-century glasshouses.

This book completes the coverage of virtually every type of glass made in America from Colonial times to 1950. To help collectors recognize and identify the wide variety of objects they find, we have organized this guide by shape rather than by chronology, method of manufacture, or decorative style. The text accompanying each illustration describes a representative object, tells how, where, and when it was made, provides historical background, and gives practical hints.

To help you determine the prices you can expect to pay, the Price Guide lists current values for the types of glass shown. Many of the pieces are quite inexpensive, indicating that collecting antique bottles, lamps, and other glass objects can be within everyone's means. Using this guide, it is possible to build a distinctive collection of fine American antique glass.

A Simple Way to Identify Bottles, Lamps, and Other Glass Objects

Valued in their day for their utility, beauty, and craftsmanship, antique bottles, lamps, and other glass objects are appreciated today as documents of our American heritage. Among the oldest examples are crude windowpanes and bottles blown in some of the country's first glasshouses; the most elegant examples include skillfully made candlesticks, lamps, and paperweights created in 19th- and 20th-century factories.

Visual Organization

To help collectors identify, date, and assess the value of the examples they find, we have chosen 346 representative types for full picture-and-text coverage. In presenting the diversity of American glass, this volume includes not only the most common examples available but also rare and outstanding pieces; familiarity with the whole spectrum of glass types is important for a complete understanding of the American glass industry. So that the object you want to find can be located quickly, the color plates and accompanying text are organized visually according to shape. This organization is further explained in the Visual Key. Experienced collectors who want to refer directly to a specific bottle brand or manufacturer can turn to the index.

The introductory essay on how antique bottles, lamps, and other glass objects were made provides essential background information. Detailed drawings of bottles, candlesticks, and lamps, as well as an illustrated chart of pontil marks, make it easier to recognize and analyze glass types. Each of the three major groups of color plates is preceded by an essay that gives an historical overview of the examples covered.

Identification Tools

To help collectors identify specific pressed and cut patterns on candlesticks and lamps, there are detailed pattern lists in the index under these two categories. Furthermore, since most glass lighting devices were produced by tableware factories, and some even matched popular tableware sets, collectors may refer to the illustrated Pressed Pattern Guide and Cut Motif Guide in the companion volume *The Knopf Collectors' Guide to Glass Tableware, Bowls & Vases.* The Cut Motif Guide will also help in identifying the designs on perfume bottles and dresser accessories. Finally, the up-to-date Price Guide lists price ranges for all of the types of glass objects in this volume. Using these tools—photographs, descriptions, essays, and drawings—both beginning collectors and connoisseurs will find that this book makes collecting bottles, lamps, and other glass objects more enjoyable and rewarding.

How Antique Bottles, Lamps, and Other Glass Objects Were Made

During the late 18th and throughout the 19th centuries, the manufacture of most glass objects involved the same raw materials and at least one of three methods: free-blowing, mold-blowing, and pressing.

Raw Materials and Colors

The basic raw material for glass was silica, usually in the form of sand. Other substances were sometimes added to color or purify the glass or to make it melt faster. Sometimes broken fragments, known as cullet, were also added to speed the melting process. This combination of raw materials was called a batch.

Colors

Most silica contains iron impurities, which give the glass a natural green, brown, amber, or aquamarine color. This crude type of glass, referred to by glassmakers as green glass, was cheap to produce and used for bottles, jars, windows, and rarely, tableware. Each color varied from light to dark, depending on the amount and type of iron impurities, the temperature of the furnace, and how long the glass was heated.

Colorless glass, called white glass by glassmakers, was used primarily for tableware, perfume bottles, and medical and chemical containers. It required purer sand and a limited amount of manganese as a decolorizer. All types of glass could be artificially colored by adding metallic oxides. Blues were achieved by adding cobalt or copper; purple by adding manganese; yellow-green by adding uranium; red by adding gold or copper; and opaque white glass required tin or another mineral as an opacifier.

Molten Glass

Once all the ingredients had been mixed, the batch was shoveled into ceramic pots within a furnace and heated for about 24 hours at a temperature of 1000° F or more. When the glass reached a nearly liquid, or molten, state, it was ready to be worked. (Since the early 20th century, glass has been melted in huge tanks that can hold a ton or more, and then drawn off into machines that automatically blow or press it into the desired shape at high speeds.)

Bottles

Until the end of the 19th century, bottles were shaped by free-blowing or mold-blowing. In free-blowing, the glassblower took a four-to-six-foot hollow iron rod, called a blowpipe, and dipped it into the pot of molten glass, gathering a glob onto the end of the rod. This glob, or gather, was then rolled into a symmetrical form on a polished metal or stone slab, called a marver, so that the sides of the bottle would be of uniform thickness. To expand the gather, the head glassblower, or gaffer, blew into the pipe to make a small bubble. He gradually enlarged the bubble and shaped the bottle, taking care to keep it centered on the blowpipe.

Shaping Free-blown Bottles

When the basic bottle shape was completed, another workman brought the gaffer a small amount of molten glass on the end of a solid iron rod called the pontil rod (usually dubbed "punty"). He pressed the end of the glass-coated rod to the bottom of the bottle on the side opposite the blowpipe. As soon as the half-finished bottle adhered to the molten glass, the blowpipe was

cracked off by dripping a drop or two of water onto the end of the blowpipe. The gaffer then finished the neck where the blowpipe had been removed. The lip could be left plain, or an extra small gather could be applied to the neck of the bottle to form a collar or a ring below the lip. After about 1840 a lipping tool, a sort of pliers, occasionally was used to squeeze the small extra gather into the type of collar desired. A handle could also be added at this stage.

From the moment the initial gather for the bottle was taken from the pot, the glass gradually cooled, so it was often necessary to briefly warm the bottle in the furnace. Since the glass was still quite soft during the entire shaping process, it tended to sag to one side. To counteract this tendency, the blower had to keep turning the blowpipe or pontil rod. If he worked too slowly and had to warm the bottle too often, the repeated heating and cooling could cause the half-finished bottle to crack or fall off the blowpipe.

Finishing the Bottle

When the bottle was completely formed, the pontil rod was broken off, leaving a sharp scar, called the pontil mark, on the base. Finally, the finished bottle was gradually cooled, or annealed, in an annealing oven. Annealing was absolutely necessary in order to remove tensions from the glass that might cause it to break.

Beginning in the mid-19th century in the United States, a tool called the snap case gradually replaced the pontil rod. The snap case resembled a cage on the end of a pole; it held a bottle securely while the neck was finished. Since the bottle and the snap case were not fastened together, when the snap case was removed, it did not leave a mark. Although by the 1870s the snap case was widely used in bottle factories, the pontil rod was preferred in tableware factories and is still employed today.

Mold-blowing Bottles

The second method of shaping a bottle was to blow the marvered gather into a mold, usually metal, thereby eliminating much of the initial hand shaping. The simplest mold type, called the dip mold, consisted of one or two parts. Although some dip molds were plain, most had a pattern, such as ribs or diamonds. To produce vertical ribs, a workman pushed the marvered gather into a one-piece vertically ribbed dip mold to create a pattern on the outside of the gather. When the glass was expanded and shaped in the usual way, the rib pattern remained clearly molded, although slightly spread out. If any pattern other than ribs was desired, it was necessary to use a two-part dip mold so that it could be opened to withdraw the gather without spoiling the pattern.

Another kind of mold, the full-size mold, had the advantage of completely shaping and patterning the body of the bottle. A workman inserted the marvered gather into the mold, which was closed around the gather. Then the gaffer inflated the gather until it took the shape of the mold. When the mold was opened, only the neck and lip needed finishing. Full-size molds had two, three, four, or even five parts, depending on the shape of the bottle.

Not only did full-size molds ensure uniform size, they could also emboss the name of the manufacturer, the contents, or an advertising message onto every bottle blown in that mold. Some molds had interchangeable elements, called slug plates, that could be slipped in and out; each plate bore a different inscription, allowing the same mold to be used for many customers.

Because of the variety of molds used in bottle making, mold seams may be found running either up the sides of the bottle to the shoulders, or around the base or shoulders. Mold seams will seldom help date a bottle, since these marks are more a characteristic of the type of mold than a bottle's age. Sometimes mold marks were removed by fire-polishing the bottle, accomplished by holding it briefly in the furnace.

Candlesticks and Lamps
From the late 18th through 19th centuries, most candlesticks and lamps were made in glass factories specializing in tableware. Since attractiveness was much more important for candlesticks and lamps than it was for bottles, they were usually made of a colorless, often heavy, sparkling lead glass that was purer than the green glass used for bottles. If the lamps and candlesticks were colored, the colors were carefully mixed, in contrast to the greens and ambers haphazardly produced in bottle factories. After annealing, candlesticks and lamps were embellished with engraved, acid-etched, or enameled decoration, all of which had to be executed by specialized craftsmen.

Blowing and Pressing
Some candlesticks and lamps were free-blown or mold-blown in much the same way as bottles were formed, but others were pressed or else partly pressed and partly blown. The process of free-blowing candlesticks and lamps was more complicated than blowing bottles, since each separate gather for the separate parts had to be shaped individually.

All or part of a candlestick or lamp could also be formed by mold-blowing or by the new method of pressing. For pressing, a gather of molten glass was dropped into a heavy multipiece mold supported by a large machine. When a lever was pulled, the plunger pressed into the glass-filled mold, and, within seconds, the object was decorated and usually fully shaped. The mold was then opened and the piece removed, ready to be annealed or attached to another part. Since it was impossible to press a closed piece, however, the lamp font had to be first pressed in an open cup shape, then tooled shut. Unless fire-polished or further tooled after removal from the mold, the pressed object did not have a pontil mark.

Candlesticks and lamps were often made in two parts, with the bottom part pressed and the top part blown, or both parts pressed. Before annealing, a flat disk of hot glass was inserted between the parts, which were then pressed together to ensure a firm bond. The disk was rarely omitted, because without it the object was greatly weakened.

About mid-19th century, glass lamp fonts were connected to brass stems and stone bases by metal screws. Later, brass collarlike connectors, usually fastened with plaster, were used to join the font and base, although some connectors were still screwed in place. By the mid-1870s, some candlesticks and lamps were pressed in one piece. For a lamp, however, the mold had to be made in such a way that two plungers worked simultaneously, one to press the font and one to press the base.

Paperweights
Many of the antique paperweights collected today have enclosed decoration and were made by a combination of blowing and a process known as lampworking. Instead of starting with a batch

of raw materials, lampworking used already manufactured glass, which was remelted over a very hot flame. The colored glass designs formed by this process were then encased in a dome of colorless glass and the finished weight was annealed.

Creating Enclosed Designs

To make an enclosed design, the paperweightmaker bundled together a large bunch of glass rods of various colors so that a pattern—possibly a flower, animal, human face, date, or initial—was formed in cross-section within the bundle. The design could be very detailed, since at this stage it was fairly large. Next the maker fused the rods, known as canes, by heating them at the furnace, and drew out the bundle of rods so as to elongate it without losing the pattern. Now several feet in length but only about a quarter-inch or less in cross-section, the bundle of canes was sliced. Every slice from a bundle had the same miniature pattern. These slices were then combined into a wide variety of designs. For example, in scrambled millefiori weights, the slices were jumbled together in a dense mass, and, in concentric millefiori weights, they were assembled in closely spaced concentric circles. Sulphide paperweights had an enclosed ceramic figure, most often of a person's profile or an animal. Cased paperweights, often called overlay weights, were made of several layers of glass fused together, with the layers cut away in a pattern to expose the underlying design.

American floral paperweights usually contained a single large flower or an arrangement of small flowers. The small flowers were made of individually lampworked petals and leaves put together on a prepared ground and carefully covered with colorless glass that was then shaped into a dome. Large single flowers were formed by forcing molten glass in the desired colors into a colorless gather, using a tool called a crimp. As the crimp pushed the colored glass inside the colorless ball, it shaped a three-dimensional flower. A particular paperweightmaker's designs may sometimes be recognized by similarities resulting from the use of the same crimp.

Windows

In the 18th and 19th centuries, two European blowing techniques were used to make window glass: the crown method and the cylinder method. By the end of the 19th century, the casting of plate glass, which produced larger, heavier, and clearer panes, supplemented the two earlier techniques.

Crown Method

Using the crown method, the glassblower gathered molten glass from the pot onto his blowpipe, rolled or marvered it, then blew a bubble two feet or more in diameter. Next the bubble was attached to a pontil rod and the blowpipe removed. Now the workman spun the pontil rod rapidly between his hands. Centrifugal force caused the bubble to flap open around the large hole left by the blowpipe. The result was the crown, or table, a flat circular sheet of glass three feet or more in diameter. After annealing, the sheet was cut into small panes; the one at the center had a large knob where the pontil rod had been attached and was called the bull's-eye pane. Except for the bull's-eye, crown glass was quite clear and free from distortion, but the individual panes were relatively small.

Cylinder Method

With the cylinder method, the glassblower tooled the bubble into a cylinder three to six feet in length. During the late 19th century, the glassblower stood on a raised platform and swung the cylinder into a pit to elongate the glass. Next the cylinder was detached from the blowpipe. After both ends were cut off, the cylinder was cut open down its length and flattened into a rectangular sheet. This sheet was then annealed and cut into individual panes. Although the panes were much larger than crown panes, the flattening process wrinkled the glass surface.

Casting Plate Glass
In contrast to the two earlier methods, the casting of plate glass did not require any blowing. A pot of molten glass was poured onto a steel bed and then flattened with long tools before annealing. Since contact with the steel and the flattening tools made the glass surface uneven, the upper and lower surfaces had to be ground smooth before the sheet was cut into panes. Panes of practically any size could be made by this technique. Until the introduction of automatic machinery, the casting of plate glass was prohibitively expensive because the smoothing process had to be completed by hand.

Making Stained Glass and Beveled Glass
Most glass used in 19th- and early 20th-century stained-glass windows was blown by the cylinder method and then cut into small pieces. However, special patterns had to be cast. A stained glass workshop usually contained long rows of bins, filled with flat pieces of glass in different solid hues or multicolored, marbleized, and layered pieces. For each window, an artist made a full-size drawing or a cartoon indicating the colors; the more expensive the window, the more elaborate the coloring. Next, workmen cut the colored glass into the right shapes and sizes and assembled the design with lead channels. In less costly windows made up of larger pieces, design details were given a stained-glass effect through a process similar to enameling. During the early 20th century, beveled glass was made by cutting the edges of cast plate glass into flat facets or bevels. Since the panes were usually fairly small, the bevels acted as prisms reflecting the light.

Toy Tableware and Other Glass
Most toy glassware was pressed in the same manner as the full-size tableware of the period, although some of the earliest miniatures were free-blown or mold-blown, and, starting in the mid-19th century, some pieces were formed by lampworking. Similarly, the miscellaneous glass objects included in this book were made by the various methods already described.

Parts of Bottles

Flask

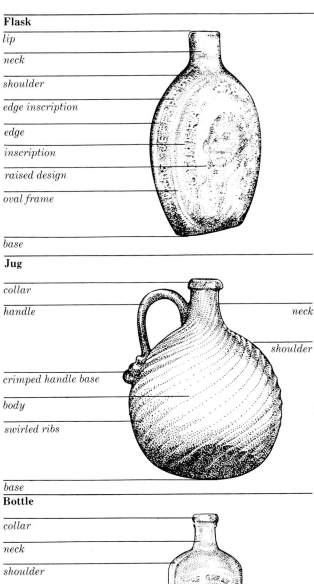

lip

neck

shoulder

edge inscription

edge

inscription

raised design

oval frame

base

Jug

collar

handle

neck

shoulder

crimped handle base

body

swirled ribs

base

Bottle

collar

neck

shoulder

inscription

side

front

base

Pontil Marks on Antique Bottles

Rough Pontil

The rough pontil is the most widely found pontil mark on bottles made before 1850; bottles made later only occasionally have rough pontils. After the body of the bottle had been blown and shaped, either by using a mold or by free-blowing, a pontil rod containing a glob of molten glass was attached to the bottom of the bottle so that the neck and lip could be finished. When the pontil rod was broken away, it left a rough, solid, circular scar. Since this scar sometimes protruded and could be quite sharp, the bottom of the bottle was often pushed slightly into the body.

Iron or Graphite Pontil

The iron or graphite pontil is characteristic of certain kinds of bottles and flasks made during the 1845–70 period, especially soda and mineral water bottles. Instead of coating the tip of the pontil rod with hot glass, a red-hot, bare iron rod was sometimes used. When the rod was removed from the bottle, some of the iron flaked off, leaving a smooth, circular depression with black or reddish-brown markings that look like graphite pencil rubbings.

Ring Pontil

Never particularly common, the ring pontil is found on bottles made before 1850. This pontil is believed to have been created when a blowpipe was used as a pontil rod.

Molds, Lips, Burners, and Stems

Bottle Molds
part-size plain dip mold   *part-size ribbed dip mold*   *full-size 2-piece mold*

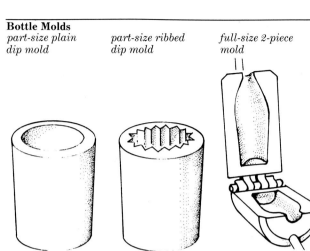

Bottle Lips and Collars
plain lip   *folded lip*   *ring below lip*

Lamp Burners
whale-oil drop burner   *screw-in whale-oil burner*   *screw-in burning-fluid burner*

Candlestick and Lamp Stems
spindle   *baluster*   *baluster*

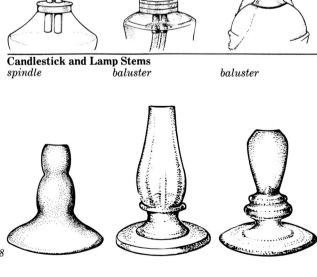

full-size 3-piece mold

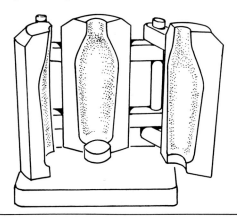

rounded collar   *flanged lip*   *flat collar*

 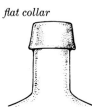

screw-in kerosene burner

multiknopped   *columnar*   *realistic-form*

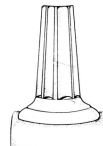 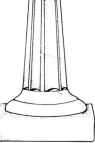 

Parts of Candlesticks

One-piece Candlestick

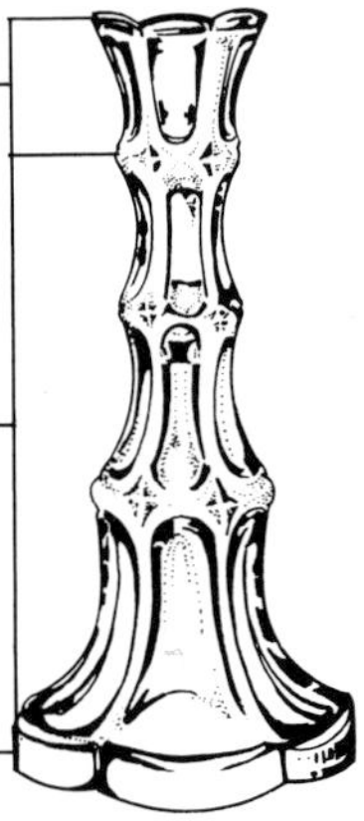

socket

stem

base

Two-piece Candlestick Joined with Disk

socket

disk

stem with base

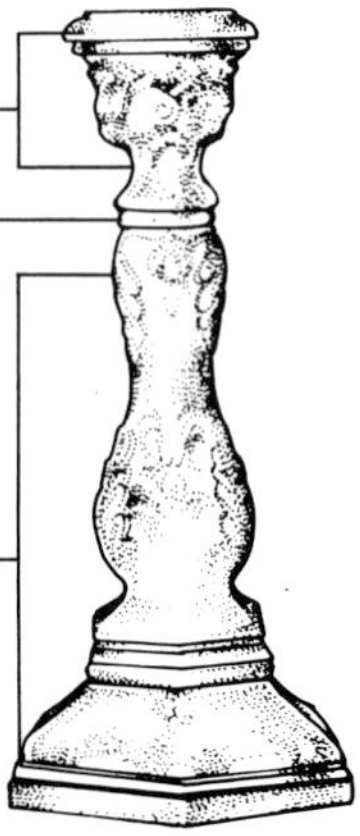

Three-piece Candlestick Joined with Disks

socket

disks

stem

disks

foot

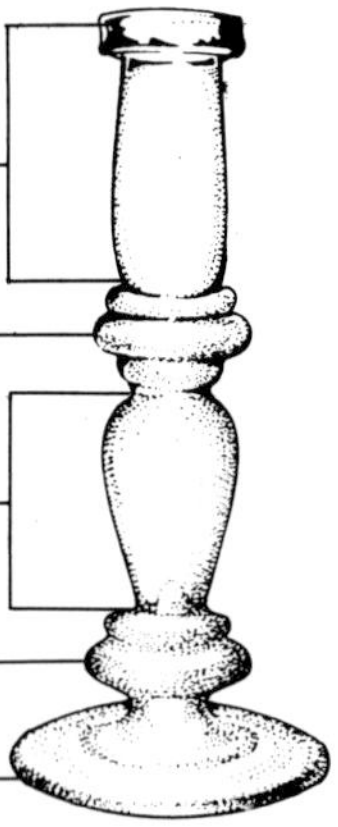

Parts of Lamps

Whale-oil Lamp

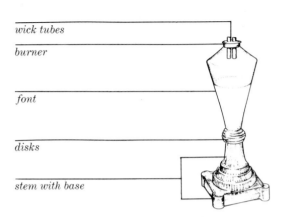

wick tubes

burner

font

disks

stem with base

Kerosene Lamp

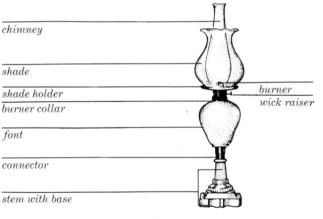

chimney

shade

shade holder

burner collar

font

connector

stem with base

burner

wick raiser

Electric Lamp

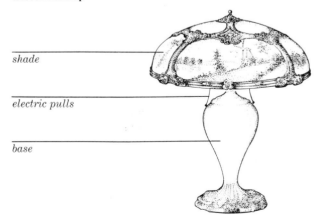

shade

electric pulls

base

How to Use This Guide

Identifying and evaluating antique American bottles, lamps, and other glass objects requires a combination of many skills: an understanding of how these pieces were made, an appreciation of decorative techniques, a knowledge of glass types and forms, and an awareness of current market activity. The simple steps outlined below will help you acquire these skills.

Preparation

1. Turn to the Visual Key to become acquainted with how glass objects in this book are organized. Based on shape, the 346 color plates are divided into sixteen groups; similar pieces within each division are grouped together.
2. Read the brief paragraph about the group that interests you; this discusses the forms illustrated in that group.

Using the Color Plates to Identify Your Piece

1. Compare the object you wish to identify with the drawings in the Visual Key. Find the drawing that most closely resembles your piece and then turn to the entries listed above the drawing.
2. Continue the visual comparison by narrowing your choice to a single color plate. Remember that your piece may not match it exactly; for example, your bottle may not have the same inscription as the one illustrated. The text account lists the variations most often encountered.
3. Read the text account to check your identification. Here you will find a detailed description of the piece shown, common variations, and hints on how to recognize reproductions.
4. After you have verified your identification, look in the Price Guide under the entry number for an estimate of the current market value of the piece. The introduction to each group explains many of the factors that can affect price.

Developing Expertise

1. Begin by reading the essay How Antique Bottles, Lamps, and Other Glass Objects Were Made. Then turn to the historical essays at the beginning of the three major sections: Bottles and Flasks, Miscellaneous Glass, and Candlesticks and Lamps. Within these divisions, each of the sixteen groups is preceded by a brief discussion of the shapes and designs as well as the period and method of manufacture of the objects included in that group.
2. Familiarize yourself with the basic terminology. The Glossary defines glass terms. Drawings on pages 15 and 18 through 21 point out parts of typical bottles, candlesticks, and lamps. The illustrated chart on pages 16 and 17 explains the different types of pontil marks found on antique bottles.
3. If you are interested in the works of a particular glass manufacturer or a specific bottle type or brand, consult the Index. Candlestick and lamp patterns are indexed under these two glass types.
4. Collectors who specialize in candlesticks, lamps, perfume bottles, or dresser accessories may find further information on pressed patterns and cut motifs in the companion volume *The Knopf Collectors' Guide to Glass Tableware, Bowls & Vases.* Learning to recognize tableware patterns and styles will help you identify and date other glass objects with similar decoration.
5. Check the Permanent Antique Glass Collections and the Organizations for Collectors sections for other resources.
6. Consult the Bibliography for important books and periodicals.
7. The essays Where to Look for Antique Glass; How to Select Bottles, Lamps, and Other Glass Objects; and Care and Display provide guidelines for acquiring and maintaining a collection.

Information-at-a-Glance

Each color plate in this book is accompanied by a full text description. At a glance, you can find an illustration that matches the type of object you would like to identify and then read the information you need to evaluate and date it. The entry number is repeated in the Price Guide.

Description
The description covers the general shape of an object, its decoration, and such secondary features as handles and lids. Inscriptions, trademarks, and pontil marks are also noted. Pontil marks are unpolished, unless otherwise indicated. All documented colors of an object are listed as well as the kind of glass (transparent, opaque, opalescent, or iridescent); clear glass is referred to as colorless. For figured flasks, the McKearin number is also provided. Technical terms are defined in the Glossary, and illustrations on pages 15 through 21 point out the parts of typical bottles, candlesticks, and lamps.

Variations
This category indicates common variations for the type of object illustrated, such as differences in shape, inscriptions, trademarks, or color. For figured flasks, the number of variants for the type shown is given first, counting the one illustrated; the description of a flask's variants includes size but not color because there are only a few standard sizes but many possibilities for colors.

Type and Dimensions
Here you will learn how the piece shown was made and decorated and its dimensions. Unless otherwise indicated, all molds are full size and multipiece. Such features as inscriptions, neck rings, or lips were formed in the mold unless they are described as "applied" or "finished." The expression "pressed in mold" refers to the 19th-century mechanical press that predated automated machinery. (Basic bottle molds are illustrated on pages 18 and 19.) Measurements are made to the highest and widest points, and height includes the lid on jars and the chimney on lamps.

Locality and Period
This section tells where and when glass of the type shown was made. The locality and period of variants are listed only when this information differs from the object illustrated. For glass made before about 1890, the term "Midwest" designates the area of western Pennsylvania, West Virginia, Ohio, and Kentucky; before this time, few glasshouses existed further west.

Comment
The history of the type of object pictured is related here, including its use, popularity, and influence. Information drawn from such contemporary sources as catalogues and price lists is frequently provided.

Hints for Collectors
These tips point out how to identify and date glass of the type illustrated, which features to look for and which to avoid, and how to recognize reproductions.

Visual Key

The glass objects included in this guide have been divided into 16 groups. For each group, a symbol appears on the left along with a brief explanation of the types of objects in that group. Drawings of representative pieces in the group are shown on the right, with plate numbers indicated above them. Similarly shaped objects occasionally appear in different groups. To help you find these pieces, their plate numbers have an asterisk (*). The group symbol is repeated on the opening page of the section concerning that group and again in the Price Guide.

Figured Flasks (*Plates 1–40*)
All of these bottles are flattened on the front and reverse sides and bear a raised, molded design or inscription. Most are either oval or oblong with rounded or sloping shoulders. Other forms include squares with rounded corners, rectangles with angled shoulders, pear shapes, and circles.

Round and Oval Bottles (*Plates 41–50*)
These bottles range from more or less globe-shaped calabashes, carboys, and demijohns to oval flasks and single-handled whiskey bottles. Unlike many of the representational designs on figured flasks, the designs on the flasks included here have overall swirled ribs or a diamond pattern.

Cylindrical Bottles (*Plates 51–65*)
One of the most common bottle shapes, cylindrical bottles have been used for centuries to hold a variety of liquids. Bottles for wine and carbonated drinks have a long or medium-length, narrow neck, while milk and cream bottles typically have a short, wide neck. Cylindrical or oblong bottles with an even wider mouth have been used to hold pickles, medicines, and glue.

Rectangular Bottles (*Plates 66–85*)
The rectangular bottle is a standard shape used for all kinds of liquids, such as proprietary medicines and shoe blacking, as well as for such solids as pickles, snuff, and druggists' powders. Rectangular shapes vary from wide-mouthed jars to taller, thinner bottles with a relatively short neck and rounded or sloping shoulders. Also included here are other flat-sided bottles, both hexagonal and oblong, and wrapped bottle packages.

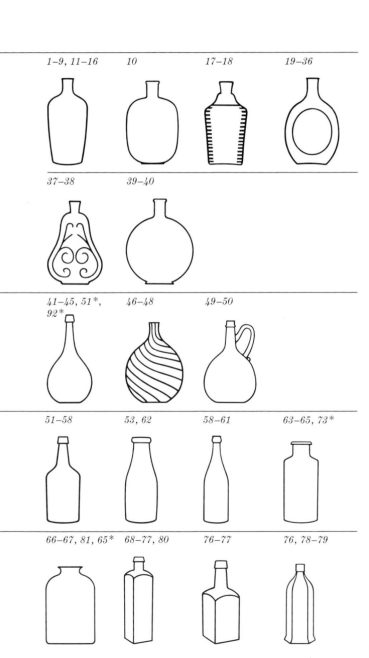

1–9, 11–16   10   17–18   19–36

37–38   39–40

41–45, 51*, 92*   46–48   49–50

51–58   53, 62   58–61   63–65, 73*

66–67, 81, 65*   68–77, 80   76–77   76, 78–79

Rectangular Bottles (*Plates 66–85*)
Continued.

Figural Bottles (*Plates 86–116*)
All of these bottles have unusual shapes. Many are in the form of log cabins, people, or animals. Others resemble barrels, ears of corn, hearts, or piled-up cannonballs. The small candy containers are especially fanciful; marketed as souvenirs and children's toys, these include animal, clock, train, and car shapes.

Ink Bottles and Inkwells (*Plates 117–127*)
Usually little more than 2″ tall, these ink bottles and inkwells were used on desks. The most common bottles are conical with plain sides or with flat panels around the sides. Unusual forms range from bottles resembling a snail, teakettle, or turtle to those in the form of a house or barrel. Inkwells tend to be blocklike geometric shapes. Most are square, rectangular, conical, or cylindrical. Small oval nursing bottles are also included in this section.

Jars (*Plates 128–141*)
Preserving jars hardly vary in shape. All are cylindrical with a wide mouth. Although some jars have slightly sloping or rounded shoulders, most have no shoulders below the threaded mouth. Lids range from screw-on zinc caps to glass lids with metal clamps or wire bails. A few storage jars have a more loosely fitting, plain or knobbed glass lid.

Drug, Perfume, and Other Fancy Bottles (*Plates 142–169*)
Most of these containers are ornamental, designed to be displayed on a shelf or table or carried in a lady's purse. Many have a glass stopper or pewter top as well as an intricate pattern. The larger bottles range from tall cylinders and corset-shaped or multisided forms to bulging pear shapes and globes with a long neck. Some have a foot but others rest on a flat base. Purse-size perfume bottles are oval, conical, or even spirals or violin shapes, and many cannot stand upright.

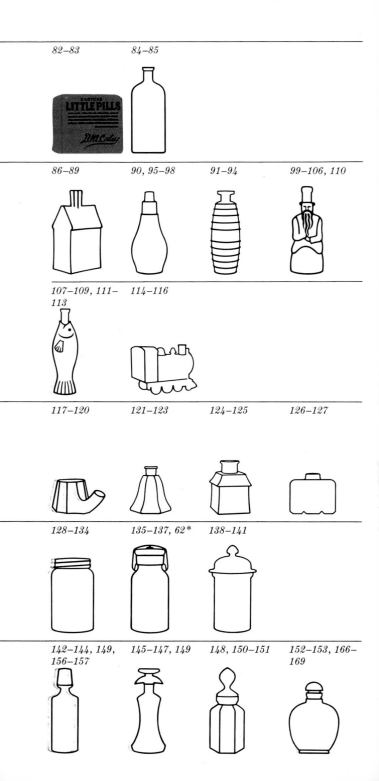

82–83   84–85

86–89   90, 95–98   91–94   99–106, 110

107–109, 111–   114–116
113

117–120   121–123   124–125   126–127

128–134   135–137, 62*   138–141

142–144, 149,   145–147, 149   148, 150–151   152–153, 166–
156–157   169

Drug, Perfume, and Other Fancy Bottles (*Plates 142–169*)
Continued.

Dresser Sets, Bells, and Other Ornamental Glassware
(*Plates 170–185*)
All of these diverse objects are essentially decorative. Cologne
and perfume bottles, powder jars, humidors, ointment boxes,
and letter holders bear fancy enameled, gilt, cut, engraved, or
molded designs. Bells and trumpets are graceful, tapered forms,
while string holders, garden bells, and smoke bells are dome-
shaped. Fishbowls and banks tend to be more globe-shaped.

Toy Glassware (*Plates 186–203*)
Miniatures included in this section may be divided into 3 basic
types: toy tableware such as cups, saucers, tureens, and bowls;
bottles and decanters; and other miniatures such as candlesticks
and flatirons. Most of this glass is about 2″ to 4″ tall or smaller.

Miscellaneous Objects (*Plates 204–230*)
This eclectic assortment includes an automobile vase, eyecup,
powder horn, flytrap, and many other novel items. Some objects
are bell-shaped like funnels. Others, including stocking darners,
pipes, and rolling pins, have a handle or stem. Still others, such
as canes and pens, are long and thin. Some articles are in the
form of a shoe, book, or animal.

Knobs, Balls, and Paperweights (*Plates 231–255*)
Many of these objects are disklike or globe-shaped. Except for
the balls, most are elaborately decorated. Paperweights come in
a variety of forms ranging from relatively simple, low spheres or
half-spheres to tall forms with a stem or pedestal-like base.
Realistic shapes include buildings, animals, and fruit.

154–155, 158–159
160–163
164–165

170–171, 180–185
172–173
174–176
177–179

186, 203
187–189
189–202

204–207
208–210
211–215
216–218

219–220
221–223, 229–230
224–228

231–234
235–241
242–245, 251–255
246–250

Windows (*Plates 256–263*)
Both functional and ornamental, antique windows are usually rectangular or square. The earliest blown panes are plain and often bubbly, while pressed examples have floral or geometric designs. Stained-glass windows, made of numerous small sections connected by lead channels, are prized for their vivid colors and rippled or shaded hues.

Candlesticks (*Plates 264–286*)
Most candlesticks are tall, single candleholders, although some are low or multibranched. The simplest tall forms have spindle-shaped stems. Among the many other stem variations are baluster shapes, tiered forms, and even figures. Simple candlestick sockets with a plain rim are relatively rare; the majority have a wide, flanged lip. The candlestick base varies from a circular foot to a stepped, square plinth.

Hand Lamps, Miniature Night Lamps, and Lanterns
(*Plates 287–304*)
Hand lamps have a handle and usually a small flat-bottomed font or fuel reservoir. Miniature night lamps, rarely more than 12″ tall, have a shade, a font, a brass kerosene burner and shade holder, and often a chimney. The lanterns are usually taller and have a metal top with a handle and a metal bottom containing the burner. Peg lamps used in candlesticks and an electric light bulb cover are also included.

Table Lamps (*Plates 305–346*)
Most lamps in this section are oil lamps designed to burn whale oil, burning fluid, or kerosene. They usually have simply a font on a stem and base; few survive with their original chimney. More elaborate examples have a chimney and shade and sometimes also dangling prisms. Some later electric lamps have a broad shade and a proportionately tall stem and base unit. Hanging shades are also shown here as well as a hurricane shade meant to protect a candle from drafts.

256–260   261–263

264–265, 269   266–274, 277,   275–277   278–280
                 281–282

283–285   286

287–292, 301   293–300   302   303–304

305–306   307–310   311–316, 318–   317, 324–332
                                  323

333–336   337–339   340–344   345–346

Bottles and Flasks

The colorful history of glassmaking in America has its roots in the very first colony established in Jamestown, Virginia, in 1607. Only a year after the first settlers had landed, a small factory financed by English investors and staffed by a handful of German and Polish glassblowers began operations in the wilderness. Yet by the end of 1609, when no more than a sample of goods had been shipped back to England, the ill-fated venture came to an abrupt end. Despite efforts to revive the Jamestown factory and to build other glasshouses in the Colonies, most glass had to be imported from England, France, and Holland until at least the mid-18th century.

Bottles numbered high on the import list. The need for glass containers rapidly increased as more settlers arrived and as wine and spirits merchants began to bottle these beverages instead of selling them in large barrels or casks. The English government, however, discouraged all new industries, expecting the fledgling territory to supply raw materials to companies in England and then buy back the finished products. Since the materials had to make a round trip across the ocean, the colonists paid a high price for all manufactured items.

The Pioneer Bottle Factories

One of the first successful glasshouses was begun by Caspar Wistar, who had immigrated to Philadelphia from Germany. A manufacturer of brass buttons, Wistar also sold bottles and other glass in his store. In 1738 Wistar signed an agreement with four German glassmakers in which he promised to provide the site for a factory as well as the supplies if the glassmakers would teach him and his son the secrets of glassblowing. The factory opened in 1739 in Wistarburgh, southern New Jersey, not far from Philadelphia, and operated quite profitably until it was forced to close during the American Revolution. In 1765 the glasshouse advertised, among other items, "most sorts of bottles, gallon,

Detail of a figured flask.

half gallon and quart, . . . snuff and mustard bottles." Since none were signed or otherwise marked, only a few bottles that remained in the Wistar family can be positively attributed to the Wistar factory.

Between 1763 and 1774 Henry William Stiegel, another German immigrant, started three separate glasshouses in Pennsylvania, one at Elizabeth Furnace and two at Manheim. Two factories made bottles and window glass, but Stiegel's ambition to produce fine tableware at the third and largest glasshouse proved his undoing and led to bankruptcy in 1774. Several types of colored pocket flasks with diamond or rib patterns have been attributed to Stiegel's third factory because fragments with those patterns were discovered at the site. Some flasks have also been found in Lancaster County, Pennsylvania. At best Stiegel attributions can only be based on this circumstantial evidence.

A third major glassmaking venture was started in 1784 by John Frederick Amelung, a German backed by a group of German investors, at New Bremen, Maryland. Unlike Wistar and Stiegel, Amelung left a substantial group of signed and dated pieces, including an engraved pocket flask and an engraved set of bottles.

From the middle to late 18th century, a few other glasshouses were started in New England and Pennsylvania, but none operated as long or as successfully as the three pioneer companies.

Bottle Manufacturing in the 19th Century

It was not until the War of 1812 temporarily removed British competition from the market that the American glass industry began to prosper. Bottle glasshouses gradually spread through southern New Jersey, upstate New York, Connecticut, New Hampshire, and Vermont. A few bottlemakers established themselves in Maryland, and several opened factories on the

Detail of a proprietary medicine bottle.

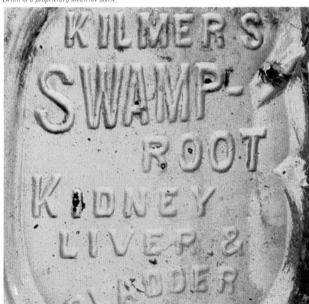

frontier, clustered in western Pennsylvania, Ohio, and the part of Virginia later called West Virginia. Until the late 19th century, glass manufacturing scarcely existed in the South or on the West Coast.

All of the early 19th-century factories produced the same types of bottles, ranging from those for wine, gin, porter, and whiskey to household containers and jars for snuff, mustard, shoe blacking, and ink. The first of these bottles, made from the end of the 18th century to about 1830, were either free-blown or blown in part-size pattern molds. Bottles produced by either method were rarely of uniform size or exactly the same pattern, so unless the bottles bear identifying marks, it is nearly impossible to know in which factory or even which area they were made. In the 1820s, when full-size molds became widely used, bottle designs became more distinct because neither size nor pattern was altered after the bottle was removed from the mold, and some designs can be traced to specific glasshouses or regions.

To flask collectors, one of the most important New England factories is the Keene-Marlboro-Street Glass Works, which operated in Keene, New Hampshire, from 1815 until 1841. Although the glasshouse manufactured some tableware, it is known for its large output of all kinds of bottles.

The Kensington Glass Works, established in a suburb of Philadelphia in 1816, is another major early bottle glasshouse. While at first not very successful, the company prospered under the direction of Thomas W. Dyott, a Philadelphia druggist, who became owner in 1821. By 1833 Dyott operated five factories between Philadelphia and Kensington (to which at least 21 flask types have been attributed), and had founded the model factory community at Dyottville. Unfortunately, he overextended himself and in 1838 was sentenced to prison for bankruptcy.

Detail of a pickle jar.

A Thriving Bottle Industry

By about 1850 new bottle factories had spread throughout the East and Midwest. Patent and proprietary medicines, promoted by self-proclaimed doctors, were selling like hotcakes. Most of these nostrums, including bitters, were not really medicines but herbal tonics containing alcohol or traces of addictive drugs. Although collectors call these patent and proprietary medicines, the formulas were neither disclosed nor in most cases patented, and only the brand names were registered with the U.S. Patent Office. The thousands of different glass containers ranged from conventional cylindrical and rectangular bottles to such novelty shapes as log cabins and fish. The bottle industry was further expanded by the bottling of beer, mineral water, and milk.

With such a diversified market, the retailers who ordered bottle molds were anxious to have distinctive, immediately recognizable bottles for their brands of bitters, whiskey, or even cologne. Most glasshouses did not make their own molds, but purchased them from moldmakers in large cities. In some cases the molds actually belonged to the customers; if a customer became dissatisfied with one glasshouse, he could take his mold to another.

Toward the end of the 19th century, the gradual introduction of automatic bottle-blowing machines forced some old-fashioned factories to close, and bottle and jar making was eventually consolidated in a few large companies. Some of these can trace their origins back to the beginnings of the industry. For instance, the Glassboro, New Jersey, plant of the enormous Owens-Illinois Inc. goes back to Solomon Stanger's glasshouse, founded in 1780.

Detail of a whiskey bottle seal.

Figured Flasks

Collectors generally call any bottle that is flattened on the front and reverse sides a flask. Although some flasks from the late 18th and early 19th centuries were free-blown or blown in part-size pattern molds, most flasks were made in the 19th century in full-size molds and bear raised designs on one or both sides. All of the examples illustrated in this section are of the type blown in full-size molds and are known collectively as figured flasks.

Immensely popular from the mid-1820s through the 1870s, figured flasks were sold as promotional novelties by rum, gin, and whiskey distributors and retailers, and may have been given away by politicians as a means of luring voters. The standard figured flask sizes are the pocket-size half-pint and pint. Quart flasks, made in smaller quantities, were probably designed for home use or for easy packing in store crates and boxes. Gallon-size flasks are unusual. Like other bottles of the period, most flasks were closed with corks.

Flask Designs

Large-scale production of flasks is an American phenomenon, although some engraved or enameled free-blown examples were made in northern Europe during the 18th and 19th centuries. The earliest American figured flasks were probably the sunburst and Masonic designs made in Keene, New Hampshire, before 1820. These were followed in the 1820s and 1830s by a great outpouring of flask designs, with about 400 introduced before 1850, and several hundred others dating from the 1850–80 period. Flask molds made after about 1850 tended to be simpler than the earliest, sharply detailed patterns.

Collectors often divide figured flasks into two categories: historical flasks and pictorial flasks. In the historical group are portraits of politicians and heroes, such as George Washington, the Marquis de Lafayette, Benjamin Franklin, Andrew Jackson, William Henry Harrison, and Zachary Taylor; national symbols, such as the figure Columbia or the American eagle; and Masonic emblems, such as the square and compass and the all-seeing eye. The purely decorative designs in the pictorial group include scrolls, cornucopias, corn, trees, sunbursts, sloops, and deer.

McKearin Numbers

Before World War II, flask collectors had begun to divide flask designs into groups according to their subject matter. One collector, George S. McKearin, with the help of his daughter Helen, codified the groups giving each group the letter G (for group) and a Roman numeral, and each flask within that group an Arabic numeral. The flask chart they published in *American Glass* in 1948 permitted hundreds of collectors to correspond about the same flask by using its number. McKearin continued his charts in the 1950s, and the last revision, by Helen McKearin with Kenneth Wilson, was published in 1978. It lists 15 flask groups and more than 760 different designs.

In the entries that follow, the McKearin numbers are given at the end of each description. Since the molds used to make flasks formed the body only up to the shoulder or partway up the neck, the mouths had to be finished by hand. Therefore, flasks from the same mold (thus with the same McKearin number) could have different lips or collars. Some bear pontil marks, while others do not. Because of the many possible lip finishes and pontils, only those features on the variation illustrated appear in the description.

1 American eagle/anchor flask

Description
Flattened oblong bottle with rounded shoulders. Raised design on each side. Plain edge. Ring below lip. No pontil mark. Front has small American eagle facing left; row of 13 stars arched above. Reverse side has anchor and rope with inscriptions "RAVENNA" above and "GLASS/COMPANY" below; 1st and 3rd words enclosed by narrow frames. Colors: transparent aquamarine, dark blue-green, green, olive-yellow, olive-amber, and dark amber. McKearin Number: GII–37.

Variations
4 varieties in similar shapes. 1 illustrated. 2 have different perched eagle, and 1 has flying eagle; reverse sides have "NEW LONDON/GLASS WORKS" with anchor. Half-pint, pint, and quart.

Type and Dimensions
Blown in full-size 2-piece mold for pattern and shape. Neck finished; ring applied. Pint.

Locality and Period
Ravenna Glass Works, Ravenna, Ohio. 1857–69. Variants from New London Glass Works, New London, Connecticut.

Comment
There are 4 flask types marked "RAVENNA" and 4 unmarked types that can be attributed to the same glasshouse on the basis of similarities. Founded in about 1857, the factory changed hands and names several times until it closed in 1880.

Hints for Collectors
One of the most common of the eagle flasks, examples in aquamarine are easy to find in the Midwest. This type comes in a much greater variety of colors than most late flasks.

2 Horseman/dog flask

Description
Flattened oblong bottle with rounded shoulders. Raised design on each side. Plain edge. Ring below lip. With or without pontil mark on base. Front has horseman wearing cap, tight coat, and breeches; riding bareback to right; horse with flying mane and tail. Reverse side has dog walking right. Colors: transparent amber, aquamarine, olive-green, yellow-green, and purplish-brown. McKearin Number: GXIII–17.

Variations
3 varieties in similar shapes. 1 illustrated. 1 has soldier on horseback on front and dog on reverse; 1 has horseman losing cap on front and running dog on reverse. Half-pint and quart.

Type and Dimensions
Blown in full-size 2-piece mold for pattern and shape. Neck finished; ring applied. Pint.

Locality and Period
The East or Midwest. c. 1870–90.

Comment
This flask can be dated based on its shape, but nothing in its design makes a glasshouse attribution possible. Although some soldier flasks were made in Baltimore, these could have come from the Midwest, Philadelphia, New Jersey, or New York.

Hints for Collectors
Some rare examples of the type illustrated have handles.
In the early days of flask collecting—the 1920s through the 1950s —most collectors turned up their noses at any post-Civil War design. However, rising prices and scarcity have made these later pictorial flasks as popular as the earlier ones. The later flasks can be found at bottle swap shows and through clubs.

3 Pike's Peak/hunter flasks

Description
Flattened oblong bottle with rounded shoulders. Raised design on each side. Plain edge. Ring below lip. No pontil mark. Front (right) has prospector walking right with hat on head, bag over shoulder, and walking stick; inscription "FOR PIKE'S PEAK" arched above. Reverse side (left) has hunter facing right and firing gun at deer. Colors: (right) transparent olive-green and aquamarine; (left) transparent light to dark amber, aquamarine, and olive-yellow. McKearin Numbers: GXI–51 (front); GXI–50 (reverse).

Variations
9 varieties in same shape with hunter on reverse. Most have slight mold differences, but 1 has "E.KAUFFELD" below hunter on reverse, and 1 shows prospector walking left, with "FOR PIKE'S PEAKE" above, and hunter on reverse facing left. Half-pint, pint, and quart.

Type and Dimensions
Blown in full-size 2-piece mold for pattern and shape. Neck finished; ring applied. Pint.

Locality and Period
Probably Pittsburgh or Ohio. 1859–c. 1875.

Comment
Unlike most other late flasks, the 9 examples with a hunter on the reverse side are rectangular in cross section rather than elliptical; probably one shop supplied molds for all 9.

Hints for Collectors
Pike's Peak/hunter flasks are harder to find than the Pike's Peak/American eagle examples. The 2 bottles illustrated are the most common of this type.

American eagle/Willington flasks

Description
Flattened oblong bottle with rounded shoulders. Raised design on each side. Plain edge. Flat or rounded collar. No pontil mark. Front (left) has American eagle facing left and perched on laurel wreath, with "LIBERTY" arched above. Reverse side (right) has inscription "WILLINGTON/GLASS, Co/WEST WILLINGTON/CONN" with 1st and 3rd lines curved. Colors: (both) transparent green, dark olive-green, amber, and olive- and reddish-amber. McKearin Number: GII–61 (front and reverse).

Variations
6 varieties in similar shapes. 5 have slight mold differences; 1 has "WESTFORD/GLASS/Co/WESTFORD/CONN" on reverse. Half-pint and pint.

Type and Dimensions
Blown in full-size 2-piece mold for pattern and shape. Neck finished; collar applied. Quart.

Locality and Period
Willington Glass Company, West Willington, Connecticut. c. 1850–70. 1 variant from Westford Glass Company, Westford, Connecticut.

Comment
Willington Glass made primarily bottles from 1815 until 1872. Bottles for gin, porter, ale, schnapps, wine, ink, oil, shoe blacking, snuff, and mineral water, as well as demijohns, are all listed in the company account book from 1865 through 1872.

Hints for Collectors
The flasks illustrated and the pint-size flask almost exactly like them are the most common American eagle flasks. The other Willington and Westford flasks are comparatively scarce.

American eagle/anchor flasks

Description
Flattened oblong bottle with rounded (left) or sloping shoulders (right). Raised design on each side. Plain edge. Plain lip or narrow collar. Pontil mark on base. Front (left) has American eagle facing left and perched on laurel wreath, with 7 stars above. Reverse side (right) has anchor and rope; 1 pennant above inscribed "NEW LONDON" and 1 below has "GLASS WORKS." Colors: (left) transparent light and dark green; (right) transparent aquamarine, amber, yellow-green, olive-green, and yellow-green shading to amber. McKearin Numbers: GII–66 (front); GII–67 (reverse).

Variations
4 varieties in similar shapes. 2 illustrated. 1 has flying eagle on front; 1 has different perched eagle on front and "RAVENNA/GLASS COMPANY" with anchor on reverse. Pint.

Type and Dimensions
Blown in full-size 2-piece mold for pattern and shape. Neck and lip finished; collar applied. Left: quart. Right: half-pint.

Locality and Period
New London Glass Works, New London, Connecticut. 1856–c. 1865. Ravenna variant from Ravenna Glass Works, Ravenna, Ohio.

Comment
It is easy to date these flasks because the New London Glass Works was in business for a comparatively short time. Except for these flasks and 1 other type marked "UNION GLASS WORKS/NEW LONDON," little is known of the firm's output.

Hints for Collectors
An early 20th-century adaptation depicts a sailing ship instead of the anchor.

6 American eagle flask

Description
Flattened oblong bottle with sloping shoulders, narrower toward base. Raised design on each side. Edge has 1 narrow vertical rib. Ring below lip. No pontil mark. Front has sketchy American eagle facing left with pennant. Below eagle, faint inscription "CUNNINGHAM/& CO/PITTSBURGH" in oval frame. Reverse side has similar eagle with "GLASS/MANUFACTURERS." Colors: transparent light blue and aquamarine. McKearin Number: GII–111.

Variations
58 varieties in similar shapes with slight mold differences. Eagle faces left or right; many inscriptions, some just "PITTSBURGH/PA" or another glasshouse; some lack inscription; a few have blank reverse. Half-pint, pint, and quart.

Type and Dimensions
Blown in full-size 2-piece mold for pattern and shape. Neck finished; ring applied. Pint.

Locality and Period
Cunningham & Company, Pittsburgh. c. 1875–86. Most variants from Pittsburgh area.

Comment
Four marked varieties of eagle flasks are definitely attributable to the Cunningham firm, but the company probably also made similar unmarked flasks with the characteristic oblong shape and eagle with pennant design. From 1845 to 1930, Cunningham produced a great variety of bottles, jars, and other glass containers.

Hints for Collectors
Late eagle flasks like this one are much easier to find than the earlier kind with a more detailed and realistic eagle.

Clasped hands/eagle flasks

Description
Flattened oblong bottle with sloping shoulders. Raised design on each side. Plain edge. Ring below lip. No pontil mark. Front (left) has large shield with 13 stars arched above and laurel branch on either side; shield encloses clasped hands in frame in upper part and blank oval frame in lower part. Reverse side (right) has flying eagle facing right with pennant in beak and blank oval frame below. Colors: (left) transparent yellow-green; (right) transparent golden amber. McKearin Numbers: GXII–5 (front); GXII–6 (reverse).

Variations
45 varieties in similar shapes, most with "UNION" on front above shield. Of these, on reverse 35 have flying eagle, 8 have cannon, cannonballs, and flag, and 2 have oval frame with laurel wreath. Half-pint, pint, and quart.

Type and Dimensions
Blown in full-size 2-piece mold for pattern and shape. Neck finished; ring applied. Quart.

Locality and Period
Probably Pittsburgh or Ohio. c. 1865–75.

Comment
The clasped hands and Union shield design was undoubtedly inspired by the Civil War. It was produced either before the war ended or afterward to commemorate the heroic struggle to preserve the Union.

Hints for Collectors
Do not be confused by reproductions of this common flask. A whiskey decanter made in the 1960s has a sunburst design on the reverse side instead of the eagle. A European reproduction of a quart flask has a blank reverse side.

8 Duck flask

Description
Flattened oblong bottle with rounded shoulders. Raised design on 1 side. Edge has broad, flat band. Ring below lip. No pontil mark. Front has inscription "WILL YOU TAKE" arched above "A DRINK?/WILL A" and duck in water with "SWIM?" below. Reverse side blank. Colors: transparent aquamarine and light yellow-green. McKearin Number: GXIII–27.

Variations
5 varieties in same shape with slight mold differences in lettering and ducks. Half-pint, pint, and quart.

Type and Dimensions
Blown in full-size 2-piece mold for pattern and shape. Neck finished; ring applied. Quart.

Locality and Period
Lockport Glass Works, Lockport, New York. c. 1860–80. Variants possibly from Pittsburgh area and from some unknown factories.

Comment
Duck flasks poke fun at the temperance movement, in full swing at the time. Although it is unlikely that the Lockport Glass Works made all of the variants, a quart and a half-pint size were both made there and so, probably, was one of the pints. Similar pint and half-pint molds were used in another factory, perhaps located near Pittsburgh, since many late flasks are from that area.

Hints for Collectors
Although the 2 half-pint flasks with the duck design are rare, the pint size is readily available. More of these flasks were probably made.

9 Traveler's Companion flask

Description
Flattened oblong bottle with rounded shoulders. Raised design on each side. Edge has 1 vertical mold seam. Flat collar. No pontil mark. Front has 8-pointed star with inscription "TRAVELER'S" arched above and "COMPANION" in semicircle below. Reverse side has star with "LANCASTER" arched above and "ERIE.CO.N.Y." in semicircle below. Colors: transparent amber, bluish-aquamarine, blue-green, and olive-yellow. McKearin Number: GXIV–5.

Variations
9 varieties in similar shapes. 1 illustrated. Of 4 others with similar fronts, 2 have "RAVENNA/GLASS Cº" on reverse, and 1 has grain. 3 lack star on front; on reverse, 1 has star, 1 has "RAILROAD/GUIDE," and 1 is blank. 1 has duck on front and "LOCKPORT/GLASS/WORKS" on reverse. Half-pint, pint, and quart.

Type and Dimensions
Blown in full-size 2-piece mold for pattern and shape. Neck finished; collar applied. Pint.

Locality and Period
Lancaster Glass Works, Lancaster, New York. c. 1860–75. Variants from Lockport, New York; Ravenna, Ohio; and unknown factories.

Comment
Located near Buffalo, the Lancaster glasshouse produced a tremendous quantity of bottles and flasks as well as free-blown tableware from 1849 to 1908.

Hints for Collectors
This rare flask marked with the maker's name is considered highly desirable by collectors.

Description
Flattened square bottle with rounded corners and oblong base.
Raised design on 1 side. Plain edge. Double rounded collar. No
pontil mark. Front has full face of Columbus turned slightly left
and wearing broad-brimmed hat; inscription "COLUMBIAN
EXPOSITION" arched above head and "1893/A.E.M. BROS & CO." below.
Reverse side has "PENNSYLVANIA/PURE RYE/BAKER/WHISKEY,"
with 1st and 4th words curved. Color: transparent amber.
McKearin Number: GI–128.

Variations
2 Columbus varieties. 1 illustrated. 1 other, in flattened oval
shape, has half-length portrait with "COLUMBUS" in semicircle
below; pint. Many plain pumpkinseed flasks; half-pint and pint.

Type and Dimensions
Blown in full-size 2-piece mold for pattern and shape. Neck
finished; collar applied. Pint.

Locality and Period
Probably the Midwest. 1893. Oval variant from unknown firm.

Comment
The flask shown is a souvenir of the famous Columbian
Exposition, a world's fair held in Chicago in 1893. Although
scheduled for 1892, the 400th anniversary of the discovery of
America, the fair was not organized in time and had to be
postponed.

Hints for Collectors
Collectors call this shape a pumpkinseed flask. Pumpkinseed
flasks in many sizes and colors are very common and usually
inexpensive. Most are plain, but some have a few words to
identify their contents. All date from the 1880s and 1890s. The
limited-edition Columbus flask illustrated is rare.

Pike's Peak/American eagle flasks

Description
Flattened oblong bottle with sloping shoulders. Raised design on each side. Plain edge. Ring below lip. No pontil mark. Front (left) has prospector walking left with hat on head, bag over shoulder, and walking stick in hand; inscription "FOR PIKE'S PEAK" arched above and "OLD RYE" in rectangular frame below. Reverse side (right) has sketchy American eagle facing right with pennant; oval frame below with "PITTSBURGH PA." Colors: (both) transparent aquamarine and yellow-green. McKearin Numbers: GXI–9 (front); GXI–10 (reverse).

Variations
39 varieties in similar shapes. Decoration varies: prospectors differ greatly, with or without inscription; eagles vary slightly, facing right or left; oval frame with or without glasshouse name. Of these, 6 have blank reverse; 1 has prospector. Half-pint, pint, and quart.

Type and Dimensions
Blown in full-size 2-piece mold for pattern and shape. Neck finished; ring applied. Left: pint. Right: half-pint.

Locality and Period
Pittsburgh. 1859–c. 1875.

Comment
Gold prospectors who ventured westward in 1858–59 adopted the slogan "Pike's Peak or bust." The thought of gold generated such tremendous excitement around the country that merchants made fortunes selling all sorts of gold-rush mementos.

Hints for Collectors
The 2 flasks illustrated, like most of the Pike's Peak flasks, are relatively easy to find.

12 Sailor/banjo player and soldier/dancer flasks

Description
Flattened oblong bottles with rounded shoulders. Raised design on each side. Plain edge. Plain lip. No pontil mark. Front of sailor type (right) has sailor dancing a hornpipe, with inscription "CHAPMAN" in narrow rectangular frame below. Reverse side of soldier type (left) has ballet dancer facing front wearing ruffled skirt, with "CHAPMAN" in narrow rectangular frame below. Colors: (right) transparent aquamarine and olive-green; (left) transparent amber, aquamarine, dark green, and light yellow-green. McKearin Numbers: GXIII–10 (front); GXIII–11 (reverse).

Variations
3 varieties of sailor/banjo player flask in same shape; reverse sides have man on bench playing banjo; half-pint. 4 varieties of soldier/dancer flask in same shape; fronts have soldier holding rifle; pint. Varieties of both types have frame below figure, blank or with "BALT.MD." or "CHAPMAN."

Type and Dimensions
Blown in full-size 2-piece mold for pattern and shape. Neck and lip finished. Left: pint. Right: half-pint.

Locality and Period
Chapman's Maryland Glass Works, Baltimore. c. 1850–62.

Comment
John Lee Chapman, a druggist, built the Maryland Glass Works in 1847 or 1848. The business closed in 1862 when Chapman was elected mayor of Baltimore.

Hints for Collectors
While the soldier/dancer flasks are common, the sailor/banjo player type is comparatively scarce.

13 Masonic/American eagle flask

Description
Flattened rectangular bottle with sloping shoulders, narrower
toward base. Raised design on each side. Edge has 5 vertical
ribs. Folded-out lip. Pontil mark on base. Front has Masonic
symbols: pillars, arch, mosaic pavement, all-seeing eye, square
and compass, triangle, beehive, crossed level and plumb line,
trowel, skull and crossbones, sun and moon, and Jacob's ladder.
Reverse side has American eagle facing left and holding banner
with inscription "E PLURIBUS UNUM"; below eagle, oval frame with
"HS." Colors: transparent light and dark green, blue-green, olive-
green, and olive-amber. McKearin Number: GIV–2.

Variations
36 varieties in similar shapes with eagle on reverse; oval below
eagle may be plain or have initials, star, "KEENE," or "1829." 2
others have Masonic design on reverse. 25 different Masonic
flasks have other designs. Half-pint and pint.

Type and Dimensions
Blown in full-size 2-piece mold for pattern and shape. Neck and
lip finished. Pint.

Locality and Period
Keene-Marlboro-Street Glass Works, Keene, New Hampshire.
1815–17. Variants also from elsewhere in New England.
c. 1815–30.

Comment
Masonic flasks were made to appeal to Freemasons, a powerful
social and political force in 18th- and 19th-century America.

Hints for Collectors
Do not be confused by a reproduction of a variant marked "IP."
Copies bear the initials "JP" and some are stamped "OLD
STURBRIDGE VILLAGE."

Masonic flask

Description
Flattened rectangular bottle has sloping shoulders. Raised design on each side. Edge has 1 heavy vertical rib. Plain lip. With or without pontil mark. Front has large 6-pointed star enclosing eye; inscription "A D" near base. Reverse side has 6-pointed star enclosing bent arm with emblem below; "G R J A" near base. Colors: shades of transparent amber, olive-amber, and olive-green. McKearin Number: GIV–43.

Type and Dimensions
Blown in full-size 2-piece mold for pattern and shape. Neck and lip finished. Pint.

Locality and Period
Possibly Stoddard, New Hampshire. c. 1840–60.

Comment
George McKearin originally placed the flask pictured in Group X, the miscellaneous group, but further research led his daughter Helen to classify it with other Masonic flasks. The initials apparently stand for the Alexander Delta Arch and the Grand Royal Jerusalem Arch, which are associated with the rituals of the Royal Arch Masons, an advanced level of Masonry. The stars and eye are the Star of David and the all-seeing eye of God. But the meanings of both the raised arm and the emblem below the arm are unknown.

Hints for Collectors
This common flask is often overlooked by collectors of Masonic memorabilia because the symbolism is not as obvious as that on other flasks.

15 Girl with bicycle flask

Description
Flattened rectangular bottle with sloping shoulders. Raised design on 1 side. Edge has broad, flat band. Ring below lip. No pontil mark. Front has girl in long skirt on old-fashioned bicycle facing left; from her lips, pennant with inscription "NOT FOR JOE." Reverse side blank. Colors: transparent dark amber and aquamarine. McKearin Number: GXIII–1.

Variations
3 varieties in similar shapes and same size. 1 illustrated. 1 has same design, but smaller; 1 lacks pennant and reverse has American eagle above oval frame, with "A & DH.C."

Type and Dimensions
Blown in full-size 2-piece mold for pattern and shape. Neck finished; ring applied. Pint.

Locality and Period
Probably Pittsburgh area. c. 1870–80. 1 variant from A. & D.H. Chambers, Pittsburgh.

Comment
Whimsical flask designs like the one illustrated are expressions of pure Americana. Since the bottle manufacturer is unknown, both the song title and the bicycle can be used as clues for dating this flask. The song "Not for Joe" was a music-hall favorite of the 1870s, popularized by the English entertainer Arthur Lloyd. Similarly, bicycling became an especially fashionable sport during the 1870–80 period.

Hints for Collectors
The 3 flasks with the girl on her bicycle are all relatively scarce despite their late date.

16 Lettered flask

Description
Flattened rectangular bottle with sloping shoulders. Raised design on 1 side. Edge has broad, flat band. Ring below lip. No pontil mark. Front has double elliptical frames enclosing inscription "ZANESVILLE/CITY/GLASS WORKS." Reverse side blank. Colors: transparent amber, aquamarine, and purplish-red. McKearin Number: GXV–28.

Variations
34 varieties in similar shapes, most with glasshouse names. Half-pint, pint, and quart.

Type and Dimensions
Blown in full-size 2-piece mold for pattern and shape. Neck finished; ring applied. Pint.

Locality and Period
Zanesville City Glass Works, Zanesville, Ohio. 1867–c. 1875. Variants from the East and Midwest.

Comment
The Zanesville glasshouse that made the flask pictured here was in operation from about 1842 until about 1923, longer than most other glasshouses. Its founder, George W. Kearns, was a glassblower from Pittsburgh, who with several others took over the White Glass Works in Zanesville.

Hints for Collectors
Flasks that lack pictorial designs have not attracted much attention among collectors. As a result, although some are rare, most are quite inexpensive. The unusual purplish-red variant is a find for bottle collectors. In the more common aquamarine, a flask of identical design would appear much less interesting.

Lafayette flasks

Description
Flattened rectangular bottle with rounded shoulders, narrower
toward base. Raised design on each side. Edge has many
horizontal ribs, several around base and shoulder. Plain lip.
Pontil mark on base. Front (right) has profile of Lafayette facing
right, with inscription "LA FAYETTE" arched above and "S & C"
below. Reverse side (left) has profile of Clinton facing right, with
"DE WITT CLINTON" arched above and "COVENTRY/C–T" below.
Colors: (right) transparent light and dark olive-green, olive-
amber, and amber; (left) transparent olive-amber and amber.
McKearin Numbers: GI–81 (front); GI–80 (reverse).

Variations
7 varieties in same shape and sizes. 2 illustrated and 1 other have
Clinton on reverse; 4 have Masonic symbols. 3 varieties in similar
shapes have liberty cap on pole on reverse.

Type and Dimensions
Blown in full-size 2-piece mold for pattern and shape. Neck and
lip finished. Left: pint. Right: half-pint.

Locality and Period
Thomas Stebbins's glasshouse, Coventry, Connecticut. 1824–25.
Variants also from Mt. Vernon Glass Works, Vernon, New York.

Comment
Lafayette toured this country in 1824–25, the same year DeWitt
Clinton, governor of New York, pushed the Erie Canal to
completion. Both events are commemorated on the flask shown.

Hints for Collectors
Lafayette flasks are likely to turn up at flask and bottle auctions
in New England, although none are really common.

Sunburst flask

Description
Flattened rectangular bottle with angled shoulders, narrower toward base. Raised design on each side. Edge has many horizontal ribs, several around base, neck, and shoulders. Plain lip. Pontil mark on base. Front has oval sunburst of 28 rays, with inscription "KEEN" running vertically from base to top of small central oval. Reverse side has "P & W" in center of sunburst. Colors: transparent dark olive-green and olive-amber. McKearin Number: GVIII–8.

Variations
25 varieties in similar shapes. 1 illustrated and 2 others have "KEEN"; 9 others have horizontal ribs at neck and base; 20 lack central oval; 2 have blank central oval; on some, rays are uneven lengths. Half-pint and pint.

Type and Dimensions
Blown in full-size 2-piece mold for pattern and shape. Neck finished; collar applied. Pint.

Locality and Period
Keene-Marlboro-Street Glass Works, Keene, New Hampshire. c. 1820–30. Variants also from elsewhere in New England.

Comment
Like the Masonic flasks, the sunbursts from Keene, New Hampshire, are among the earliest decorative flasks made.

Hints for Collectors
This common flask type is still easy to find in New England. But beware of a Mexican reproduction. It lacks an inscription, is much lighter in weight, and was made in light blue-green, dark blue, purple, and possibly aquamarine, none of which were colors used for the original flasks.

Sunburst flask

Description
Flattened oval bottle, narrower toward base. Raised design in oval frame on each side. Edge has 3 vertical ribs. Plain lip. Pontil mark on base. Front and reverse sides have sunburst with 36 rays and 5 ovals in center. Colors: transparent light aquamarine and colorless with purple tint. McKearin Number: GVIII–21.

Variations
6 varieties in similar shapes. 5 have slight mold differences; 1 has central ovals in flower design. Half-pint and pint.

Type and Dimensions
Blown in full-size 2-piece mold for pattern and shape. Neck and lip finished. Pint.

Locality and Period
Probably Pennsylvania, Maryland, or Ohio. c. 1820–35.

Comment
The oval sunburst is a common motif on furniture of the Federal period and appears on pressed glass as well as on flasks. One flask of the type illustrated was found with a leather sheath and strap, suggesting that these flasks may have been used as canteens by soldiers or farmers.

Hints for Collectors
Although sunburst flasks with vertical edge ribs have not been reproduced, there is at least 1 adaptation of the design, a 4-ounce bottle made by the Imperial Glass Company in the 1930s. Perhaps intended for perfume, it has "IG" on the base for Imperial Glass, and the inscription "MOTHER'S/DAY/GREETINGS" on 1 side.

Description
Flattened oval bottle. Raised design in oval frame on each side.
Edge has many fine vertical ribs. Plain lip. Pontil mark on base.
Front (right) has stag facing right with inscription "GOOD GAME"
below and up side. Reverse side (left) has weeping willow.
Colors: (right) transparent aquamarine; (left) transparent
aquamarine and light green. McKearin Numbers: GX–2 (front);
GX–1 (reverse).

Variations
4 varieties in same shape with stag on 1 side. 2 illustrated.
2 have "COFFIN & HAY/HAMMONTON" around stag and eagle on
reverse. 1 flattened rectangular flask has hunter on reverse.
Half-pint and pint.

Type and Dimensions
Blown in full-size 2-piece mold for pattern and shape. Neck and
lip finished. Left: pint. Right: half-pint.

Locality and Period
Possibly Coffin & Hay, Hammonton, New Jersey. c. 1835–40.
2 eagle variants from same; other probably from the Midwest.

Comment
Because 2 flasks with "COFFIN & HAY" show a similar stag, the
"GOOD GAME" stag variants have been attributed to the same firm.
Judging by their shape, they appear to be from the same period,
but specific attribution is uncertain.

Hints for Collectors
The 2 stag/willow flasks are comparatively scarce. Because there
are so few stag flasks, they are not a particularly popular type.
Most flask collectors prefer to specialize in a large design group
or an area, such as the Midwest.

Railroad flask and reproduction

Description
Flattened oval bottle. Raised design in oval frame on each side. Edge has 3 vertical ribs. Plain lip. Pontil mark on base. Front and reverse sides have horse pulling cart on rail; cart filled with kegs. Inscription "SUCCESS TO THE RAILROAD" arched around horse and cart. Authentic colors: transparent aquamarine, amber, olive-amber, and dark olive-green. McKearin Number: GV–3.

Variations
13 varieties in same shape. 1 illustrated and 6 others have horse-drawn railroad on both sides: placement of inscription differs slightly, and 2 lack inscription. 4 have eagle on reverse; of these, 2 have "RAILROAD/LOWELL" on front. 2 have early locomotive and "SUCCESS . . ." on both sides. 1 more angular variant has locomotive, lacks inscription, and has winged figure on reverse. Half-pint and pint.

Type and Dimensions
Blown in full-size 2-piece mold for pattern and shape. Neck and lip finished. Pint.

Locality and Period
Keene-Marlboro-Street Glass Works, Keene, New Hampshire. c. 1830–35. Variants from New York and Connecticut. c. 1830–50.

Comment
Capitalizing on the tremendous popularity of the railroad, bottlemakers produced 14 varieties of railroad flasks in the 1830s and 1840s. Most show the horse-drawn railway, but 2 depict an early steam locomotive. The Granite Railway, begun at Quincy, Massachusetts, in 1826, was the first horse-drawn railway in this country. Nearly 200 more lines were planned, chartered, or built

Authentic flask

in the following decade. Railroad flasks were made in Keene, New Hampshire; Vernon and Saratoga, New York; Coventry, Connecticut; and a few other glasshouses.

Hints for Collectors

The type of railroad flask shown on the left is quite common and relatively inexpensive. Unfortunately, the railroad flask is one of the most often reproduced flasks, and at least 4 different reproductions in the same sizes as authentic flasks can be found on the market today. Two reproductions created in the 1930s or 1940s have much less detail. One in transparent aquamarine and light blue has thinner letters and a horse with very thin legs and a nearly invisible mane. The other in transparent yellow-green also has thin letters, but both the horse's mane and the cart are better defined. The oldest reproduction was manufactured in Czechoslovakia in the 1920s for a shop in Boston. These flasks come in transparent aquamarine, amber, olive-amber, dark olive-green, medium and dark green, yellow-green, and very dark brown or green that appears black. They are easy to spot if you examine the mane of the horse: It will be quite spiky, nothing at all like the mane on the genuine flasks. In other respects this reproduction is true to the original.

The most recent reproductions are those made by Clevenger Brothers in New Jersey from the 1940s or 1950s through the 1970s. Many of these originally had paper labels identifying them as part of Clevenger's Glass Master line. They were intended to be sold in gift shops strictly as reproductions. Clevenger copies are of poor quality, bubbly glass made in a great variety of purely 20th-century colors, such as the purple illustrated, bright green, and bright blue. Many also have fluted lips, totally unlike those on authentic flasks. With care, none of the 4 reproductions should deceive an observant collector.

Reproduction

Description
Flattened oval bottle. Raised design in oval frame on each side. Edge has 3 vertical ribs. Plain lip. Pontil mark on base. Front has sloop with pennant blowing toward left and water beneath. Reverse side has inscription "BRIDGETOWN/NEW JERSEY" running clockwise inside frame. Colors: transparent dark olive-amber and light aquamarine. McKearin Number: GX–7.

Variations
7 varieties in similar shapes. 1 illustrated. 4 have flower or star on reverse; 1 has "FELLS" above and "POINT" below sloop, with Baltimore Washington Monument on reverse; 1 has Kossuth with "BRIDGETON./NEW JERSEY" on reverse. Half-pint and pint.

Type and Dimensions
Blown in full-size 2-piece mold for pattern and shape. Neck and lip finished. Half-pint.

Locality and Period
Bridgeton Glass Works, Bridgeton, New Jersey.
1846–c. 1855. Variants also from Baltimore Glass Works.

Comment
The glass factory in Bridgeton, which operated well into the 20th century, made all kinds of bottles, from fruit jars, druggists' ware, and carboys to bottles for beer and wine. On some flasks, Bridgeton is spelled with a "w."

Hints for Collectors
In mid-century the Bridgeton factory was still small and did not produce any designs in great numbers. As a result, these flasks are comparatively scarce. The horizontal bar on the front of the flask shown is a fault in the glass.

Baltimore Battle Monument flask

Description
Flattened oval bottle. Raised design in oval frame on each side.
Plain edge. Plain lip. Pontil mark on base. Front has Baltimore
Battle Monument with statue. Reverse side has grape wreath
around inscription "A/LITTLE/MORE/GRAPE/CAP^T BRAG." Colors:
transparent dark brownish-pink, purplish-red, light aquamarine,
and light olive-green. McKearin Number: GVI–1.

Variations
4 varieties in similar shapes. 1 illustrated and 1 other have grape
wreath on reverse; 1 has "BALTIMORE" above monument and
"LIBERTY & UNION" on reverse; 1 has "BALTIMORE GLASS WORKS"
above monument and portrait of Washington on reverse. 3 other
varieties have grape wreath on reverse, but front has cannon and
"GEN^L TAYLOR NEVER SURRENDERS." Half-pint and pint.

Type and Dimensions
Blown in full-size 2-piece mold for pattern and shape. Neck and
lip finished. Half-pint.

Locality and Period
Baltimore Glass Works, Baltimore. 1847–48.

Comment
The monument honors those who fell in defense of Baltimore
during the War of 1812, while the motto "A little more grape,
Captain Bragg" figured in Zachary Taylor's presidential
campaign of 1848.

Hints for Collectors
To distinguish Baltimore Battle and Baltimore Washington
monument flasks, look for faint bands on the monument. Those
with bands are the scarcer Battle Monument flasks; Washington
Monument flasks lack bands.

Description
Flattened oval bottle. Raised design in oval frame on each side.
Edge has 3 vertical ribs. Plain lip. Pontil mark on base. Front
(right) has upright cornucopia curving left filled with produce;
raised dot above end. Reverse side (left) has 2-handled urn also
filled with produce. Colors: (right) transparent dark olive-green,
green, and blue-green; (left) transparent amber and olive-amber.
McKearin Numbers: GIII–11 (front); GIII–8 (reverse).

Variations
19 varieties in same shape. 2 illustrated. 15 have slight mold
differences; 2 have cornucopia on reverse. 26 cornucopia/eagle
types in similar shapes. Half-pint, pint, and 1½ pints.

Type and Dimensions
Blown in full-size 2-piece mold for pattern and shape. Neck and
lip finished. Half-pint.

Locality and Period
Left: the East. Right: Vernon and Saratoga, New York.
c. 1820–50.

Comment
The cornucopia brimming with flowers or produce was a familiar
symbol of prosperity in the early 1800s. It derives from a Greek
myth in which Zeus gave his nurse a cow's horn that was
magically filled with everything the owner wished.

Hints for Collectors
Beware of reproductions of this common flask. One fake made
around 1900 is reddish-amber, an inauthentic color. Another copy
from the 1960s is of new-looking, bubble-free glass. An Old
Sturbridge Village adaptation features a grasshopper on the
reverse side.

25 Baltimore Washington Monument/corn flask

Description
Flattened oval bottle. Raised design in oval frame on each side. Plain edge. Ring below lip. No pontil mark. Front has Baltimore Washington Monument with statue; inscription "BALTIMORE" below. Reverse side has large ear of corn with "CORN FOR THE WORLD" arched above. Colors: transparent purple, brownish-pink, green-blue, light blue, aquamarine, green, amber, and olive-yellow. McKearin Number: GVI–4.

Variations
5 varieties in same shape with slight mold differences. 1 lacks "BALTIMORE." Half-pint, pint, and quart.

Type and Dimensions
Blown in full-size 2-piece mold for pattern and shape. Neck finished; ring applied. Quart.

Locality and Period
Baltimore Glass Works, Baltimore. c. 1840–50.

Comment
Like other bottles with the ear of corn design, the one illustrated probably commemorates Baltimore's extensive trade in grains during the period. Four other flask types also feature the Baltimore Washington Monument but without the statue; 3 of these have portraits on the reverse side, and 1 has a sloop. Most likely, these versions were made in the 1820s before the monument was completed.

Hints for Collectors
The flask shown here is common, although some variations are quite rare, including the one without the inscription "BALTIMORE."

Tree flask

Description
Flattened oval bottle. Raised design in oval frame on each side.
Plain edge. Flat collar. Pontil mark on base. Front and reverse
sides have large tree with leaves nearly filling frame. Colors:
transparent aquamarine, blue, amber, and olive-yellow.
McKearin Number: GX–17.

Variations
5 varieties in similar shapes. 1 illustrated. 1 other has oval frame
on each side; "SUMMER" above tree with foliage and "WINTER"
above bare tree. Of 3 without frame, 2 have tree with foliage on
1 side and bare tree on other, and 1 has tree with foliage on both
sides. Half-pint, pint, and quart.

Type and Dimensions
Blown in full-size 2-piece mold for pattern and shape. Neck
finished; collar applied. Pint.

Locality and Period
The East or Midwest. c. 1840–60.

Comment
The designs of middle and late 19th-century flasks tend to be
more varied than those on earlier examples and are rarely
related to political or historical figures and events. Subjects
taken from nature had great popular appeal.

Hints for Collectors
Note that the designs on flasks made after the 1840s are not
nearly as detailed as those on earlier bottles. The more intricate
molds took more time to make, and consequently the flasks made
from them were more expensive. All tree flasks are quite
common, although the variant illustrated is the hardest to find.

Washington/Farmers' Arms flask

Description
Flattened oval bottle. Raised design in oval frame on each side.
Plain edge. Flat collar. Pontil mark on base. Front has profile of
Washington wearing plain toga and facing left. Reverse side has
sheaf of grain on top of crossed pitchfork and rake. Color:
transparent aquamarine. McKearin Number: GI–58.

Variations
3 varieties in same shape. 1 illustrated. 1 has detailed toga; 1 has
sheaf of grain only on reverse. Half-pint, pint, and quart.

Type and Dimensions
Blown in full-size 2-piece mold for pattern and shape. Neck
finished; collar applied. Pint.

Locality and Period
Probably Dyottville Glass Works, Philadelphia. c. 1848–60.
Variants probably from the Midwest.

Comment
Similar to the many Washington/Taylor flasks, the one illustrated
here was probably produced for Zachary Taylor's presidential
campaign of 1848, when supporters wanted to compare his
leadership abilities to Washington's. The crossed pitchfork and
rake were known as the Farmers' Arms, and represented a
subtle appeal for rural support.

Hints for Collectors
Because this flask was made only in aquamarine and is quite
common, it is less interesting and less expensive than many
others. Unlike several of the Washington/Taylor flasks, the
example shown here has not been reproduced.

Description
Flattened oval bottle. Raised design in oval frame on each side.
Plain edge. Plain lip. Pontil mark on base. Front (right) has
profile of Washington wearing toga and facing left, with
inscription "THE FATHER OF HIS COUNTRY" arched above. Reverse
side (left) has profile of Taylor in uniform facing left, with "I HAVE
ENDEAVOUR,D TO DO MY DUTY" arched above. Colors: (right)
transparent purple, green, yellow-green, aquamarine, blue,
olive-yellow, and colorless; (left) transparent brownish-pink,
shades of green, aquamarine, and blue. McKearin Numbers:
GI–42 (front); GI–43 (reverse).

Variations
17 varieties in same shape. Inscriptions above Taylor vary: "GEN.
TAYLOR NEVER SURRENDERS," "A LITTLE MORE GRAPE CAPTAIN
BRAGG," or "GEN.Z.TAYLOR"; some lack inscription; 2 have
"DYOTTVILLE GLASS WORKS, PHILAD.ᴬ" above oval frame. 2 other
Washington flasks have blank reverse. Half-pint, pint, and quart.

Type and Dimensions
Blown in full-size 2-piece mold for pattern and shape. Neck and
lip finished. Quart.

Locality and Period
Probably Dyottville Glass Works, Philadelphia. 1846–c. 1850.
Variants also possibly from the Midwest.

Comment
On campaign flasks of the type shown, most inscriptions stress
Taylor's participation in the Mexican War of 1846–48.

Hints for Collectors
Reproductions of the "DYOTTVILLE" and "GEN.Z.TAYLOR" flasks
have bumpy surfaces and are often bright blue and purple.

Taylor/corn flask

Description
Flattened oval bottle. Raised design in oval frame on each side. Edge has 3 vertical ribs. Plain lip. Pontil mark on base. Front has profile of Taylor in uniform facing right, with inscription "ZACHARY TAYLOR" arched above and "ROUGH & READY" in semicircle below. Reverse side has stalk of corn with "CORN FOR THE WORLD" arched above. Colors: transparent brownish-pink, dark olive-green, purple, blue, aquamarine, and amber. McKearin Number: GI–74.

Variations
2 varieties in same shape and size. 1 illustrated. Other 1 has slight mold differences and plain edge.

Type and Dimensions
Blown in full-size 2-piece mold for pattern and shape. Neck and lip finished. Pint.

Locality and Period
Baltimore Glass Works, Baltimore. c. 1845–50.

Comment
The inscription "CORN FOR THE WORLD" appears on only a few flasks made in Baltimore. Although some scholars suggest that the motto may have been inspired by the repeal of the Corn Laws in England in 1846, it is more likely a reference to the corn whiskey inside. The more typical Taylor portrait flasks have Washington on the other side.

Hints for Collectors
Both Taylor/corn flasks are extremely rare, quite costly, and best sought from dealers and collectors who specialize in historical flasks. Blue and purple flasks are the most unusual; amber is scarce, and aquamarine the most common.

Washington/classical bust flask

Description
Flattened oval bottle. Raised design in oval frame on each side.
Edge has 1 vertical rib. Plain lip. Pontil mark on base. Front has
profile of Washington wearing toga and facing right. Reverse
side has classical bust facing right, with inscription "BALTIMORE x
GLASS. WOKS." arched above. Colors: transparent dark brownish-
pink, purple, aquamarine, yellow, amber, light olive-green, and
light green. McKearin Number: GI–23.

Variations
3 varieties in similar shapes and same size. 1 illustrated. 1 has
"BALTIMORE x GLASS. WORKS.," with every "s" reversed; 1 has
"BRIDGETOWN NEW JERSEY" above bust on both sides.

Type and Dimensions
Blown in full-size 2-piece mold for pattern and shape. Neck and
lip finished. Quart.

Locality and Period
Baltimore Glass Works, Baltimore. 1832–45. 1 variant from
Bridgeton, New Jersey.

Comment
The bust on the reverse side is usually identified as Zachary
Taylor because his portrait appears on most Washington flasks of
this shape. However, the likeness more closely resembles known
portraits of the Kentucky senator Henry Clay.

Hints for Collectors
The variant from Bridgeton, New Jersey, is the most common
of the 3 flasks. Because the name of the town is spelled as
Bridgetown, the flask appeals to collectors who feel alternate
spellings have a folk charm.

Jackson/American eagle flasks

Description
Flattened oval bottle. Raised design in oval frame on each side.
Edge has vertical rib and horizontal beading. Plain lip. Pontil
mark on base. Front (left) has ¾ view of Jackson in uniform
facing left, with inscription "GENERAL JACKSON." arched above.
Reverse side (right) has American eagle facing right, and
perched on oval frame with "J.R." in frame and "LAIRD. S.C. PITT."
below. Colors: (left) transparent blue-green, aquamarine, and
light green; (right) transparent olive-yellow, yellow-green, and
colorless with purple tint. McKearin Numbers: GI–65 (front);
GI–66 (reverse).

Variations
5 varieties in same shape and size. 2 illustrated. 2 others have
eagle on reverse, and 1 has flowers. 2 other Jackson flasks have
Masonic symbols.

Type and Dimensions
Blown in full-size 2-piece mold for pattern and shape. Neck and
lip finished. Pint.

Locality and Period
Probably James Taylor & Company, Brownsville, Pennsylvania.
1824–28. Variants from Pittsburgh area. Masonic types from
Wheeling, West Virginia, and Mantua, Ohio.

Comment
The Jackson flasks were probably made during Andrew Jackson's
presidential campaigns against John Quincy Adams. Jackson lost
in 1824 but won a resounding victory in 1828.

Hints for Collectors
A nearly identical Adams/American eagle flask was also made in
James Taylor's glasshouse. It is rarer than the type shown.

Description
Flattened oval bottle. Raised design in oval frame on each side.
Edge has 3 vertical ribs. Plain lip. Pontil mark on base. Front
(left) has ¾ view of Franklin facing left, with inscription
"BENJAMIN FRANKLIN" arched above and edge inscriptions
"ERIPUIT COELO FULMEN./SCEPTRUMQUE TYRANNIS." and
"KENSINGTON GLASS/WORKS, PHILADELPHIA." Reverse (right) has ¾
view of Dyott facing right, with "T.W.DYOTT,M.D." arched above
and no edge inscription. Colors: (left) transparent dark green,
aquamarine, purple, and colorless; (right) transparent
aquamarine. McKearin Numbers: GI–96 (front); GI–95 (reverse).

Variations
5 varieties in similar shapes and same sizes. 2 illustrated. 2
others have Dyott on reverse; of these, 1 has plain edge and 1
has edge inscriptions "WHERE LIBERTY DWELLS/THERE IS MY
COUNTRY" and "KENSINGTON . . . ." 1 has "WHEELING GLASSWORKS"
above Dyott.

Type and Dimensions
Blown in full-size 2-piece mold for pattern and shape. Neck and
lip finished. Left: quart. Right: pint.

Locality and Period
Kensington Glass Works, Philadelphia. 1824–28. Variants also
from Wheeling Glass Works, Wheeling, West Virginia.

Comment
Thomas W. Dyott, a self-styled M.D. and patent-medicine
vendor, also produced bottles from 1818 until 1837.

Hints for Collectors
The Latin translates: "He snatches from the sky the thunderbolt
and the scepter from tyrants." In the early 1800s more people
would have been able to read the inscription.

Description
Flattened oval bottle. Raised design in oval frame on each side. Edge has 1 vertical rib. Plain lip. Pontil mark on base. Front has ¾ view of Washington in uniform facing left, with inscription "GENERAL WASHINGTON" arched above. Reverse side has American eagle facing right perched on oval frame; "T.W.D." inside frame and "E.PLURIBUS UNUM" arched above eagle. Edge inscription "ADAMS & JEFFERSON/JULY 4.A.D.1776/KENSINGTON GLASS/ WORKS PHILADELPHIA." Colors: transparent aquamarine, dark blue, green, dark yellow-green, golden yellow, and dark amber. McKearin Number: GI–14.

Variations
18 varieties in similar shapes and same size. Some lack inscriptions on front, reverse, or edge. May have "G.GEO." or "G.G.WASHINGTON"; 2 have Washington facing right; eagle and initials vary; 1 has "PITTSBURGH" above eagle.

Type and Dimensions
Blown in full-size 2-piece mold for pattern and shape. Neck and lip finished. Pint.

Locality and Period
Kensington Glass Works, Philadelphia. 1826. Variants from Pittsburgh area. c. 1820–30.

Comment
The edge inscriptions refer to the fact that John Adams and Thomas Jefferson both died on July 4, 1826, the 50th anniversary of the signing of the Declaration of Independence.

Hints for Collectors
Relatively common in aquamarine, this flask type has special historical appeal because of the July 4th date.

Description
Flattened oval bottle. Raised design in oval frame on each side.
Edge has 3 vertical ribs. Plain lip. Pontil mark on base. Front
(left) has American eagle facing right perched on oval frame,
with arrows in 1 claw and olive branch in other; rays around
eagle's head. Reverse side (right) has upright cornucopia curving
left filled with produce. Colors: (left) transparent aquamarine,
dark blue, light and dark amber, and dark olive-green; (right)
transparent aquamarine and colorless. McKearin Numbers:
GII–16 (front); GII–17 (reverse).

Variations
25 varieties: 23 in similar shapes, 2 more angular. Eagle may lack
rays; cornucopia may be upside down or curving right; edge may
be plain, beaded, or with "KENSINGTON GLASS/WORKS
PHILADELPHIA." Half-pint and pint.

Type and Dimensions
Blown in full-size 2-piece mold for pattern and shape. Neck and
lip finished. Half-pint.

Locality and Period
Probably Pittsburgh area. c. 1820–40. Variants also from
Philadelphia. Angular flasks from Connecticut.

Comment
Chosen as a national emblem in 1782, the eagle has been used as
a decorative motif in every material from silver to wood. It often
appears with a shield, arrows, and olive branch.

Hints for Collectors
Beware of a crudely blown reproduction made in the 1930s or
1940s. It has an unusual, textured surface.

35 Taylor/Ringgold flask

Description
Flattened oval bottle, narrower toward base. Raised design in oval frame on each side. Edge has 3 vertical ribs. Plain lip. Pontil mark on base. Front has profile of Taylor in uniform facing left, with inscription "ROUGH AND READY" in semicircle below. Reverse side has profile of Ringgold in uniform facing left, with "MAJOR" arched above and "RINGGOLD." in semicircle below. Colors: transparent purple, green, dark blue-green, blue, aquamarine, translucent light green, and colorless. McKearin Number: GI–71.

Variations
2 varieties in same shape and size. 1 illustrated. 1 has plain edge.

Type and Dimensions
Blown in full-size 2-piece mold for pattern and shape. Neck and lip finished. Pint.

Locality and Period
Probably Baltimore Glass Works, Baltimore. 1846–48.

Comment
Major Samuel Ringgold was a Baltimore hero who fought in the Mexican War and died during the Battle of Palo Alto in May 1846. A number of Ringgold souvenirs were made, among them this flask, pressed-glass cup plates, and lithographs.

Hints for Collectors
Relatively common today, these flasks must have been produced in large quantities. You can find them in the Northeast, although they are most available in the mid-Atlantic states. Aquamarine is easy to locate but other colors are rare.

Description
Flattened oval bottle, narrower toward base. Raised design in oval frame on each side. Edge has 1 broad, vertical rib. Plain lip. Pontil mark on base. Front has profile of Columbia wearing liberty cap and facing left, with 13 stars above, and inscription "KENSINGTON" below; vertical ribbing below inscription. Reverse side has American eagle facing right, with "UNION.Cº" below; vertical ribs at base. Color: transparent aquamarine. McKearin Number: GI–117.

Variations
5 varieties in same shape. 1 illustrated and 2 others have "KENSINGTON" on front and "UNION.Cº" on reverse; 1 has "ASHTON" and "HOUGH"; 1 lacks inscriptions. 2 varieties more oval and lack ribs at base. 1 has "B&W" in script below eagle; 1 lacks inscription. Half-pint, ¾ pint, and pint.

Type and Dimensions
Blown in full-size 2-piece mold for pattern and shape. Neck and lip finished. Pint.

Locality and Period
Union Glass Company, Kensington, Pennsylvania. c. 1820–29. More oval variants from unknown glasshouse.

Comment
In the 19th century, Columbia was used to symbolize the United States in the same way that John Bull represented England. She is usually shown wearing the liberty cap, another popular 19th-century symbol of freedom.

Hints for Collectors
Columbia flasks are scarce. An Historical Bottle Collectors Guild reproduction is marked "OI 1974" on the base.

Kossuth cologne bottle

Description
Flattened pear-shaped bottle. Raised design on each side. Plain
edge. Folded-in lip. Pontil mark on base. Front has Kossuth in
uniform facing front with 5-petaled flower above and inscription
"L.KOSSUTH" in semicircle below. Reverse side has 5-petaled
flower above scrolls and blank rectangle. Colors: transparent
aquamarine and colorless.

Variations
Many varieties in similar shapes. 1 type has leaves and flowers
on both sides; this variant sometimes purplish-blue and may have
paper label printed "EAU/DE/COLOGNE." 1 type has portrait of child
and "CHARLEY ROSS."

Type and Dimensions
Blown in full-size 2-piece mold for pattern and shape. Neck and
lip finished. Height: 5¾". About 6 ounces.

Locality and Period
Probably New Jersey. 1850–51. Ross variant 1875–76.

Comment
Louis Kossuth, the Hungarian patriot who led his people against
the Austrian empire, became a hero throughout western Europe
and America in the mid-19th century. Kossuth appealed to the
U.S. Congress in 1851 for aid, but despite widespread popular
support, he received no help from the government. Charley
Ross, whose portrait appears on a variation, was kidnapped in
1875 and never found. The search for the kidnappers and the
trial were greatly publicized.

Hints for Collectors
Both the Kossuth and Ross bottles are very rare, and Kossuth
examples the scarcest of all. The variant with leaves and flowers
on both sides is the easiest to find.

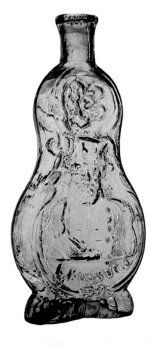

Scroll flask and reproduction

Description
Flattened pear-shaped bottle with oblong base. Raised design
on each side. Edge has 1 vertical rib. Plain lip. Pontil mark on
base. Front and reverse sides have 2 pairs of scrolls and 2 stars,
1 near center and 1 on shoulder. Authentic colors: transparent
aquamarine, amber to olive-amber, purplish-blue, and
translucent grayish-white with pink tint; other colors reported
but not verified. McKearin Number: GIX–2.

Variations
73 varieties in similar shapes, all with matching scroll design on
both sides. 4 have "LOUISVILLE KY" on 1 side and "GLASS WORKS"
on other; 1 has "S.M'KEE." on 1 side; 1 has "ROUGH" on 1 side and "&
READY" on other; 1 has "BP & B" on 1 side; and 2 have "J.R. & S[ON]."
on 1 side. 20 have fleur-de-lis in design; 2 have anchors. Half-
pint, pint, quart, 2 quarts, and 1 gallon.

Type and Dimensions
Blown in full-size 2-piece mold for pattern and shape. Neck and
lip finished. Quart.

Locality and Period
Probably the Midwest. c. 1840–55.

Comment
There is a wide range of scroll flasks, all with pear-shaped bodies
and stylized designs. Although the examples bearing the initials
of Bakewell, Page & Bakewell and John Robinson & Son
probably date from the early 1830s, most scroll flasks were made
in the 1840s and early 1850s, and all were produced in the
Midwest. The flasks marked "LOUISVILLE KY" are the only
marked products from the Louisville Glass Works, which
operated from 1855 to 1873. Many collectors call the factory
midwestern because the men who ran it probably moved to

Authentic flask

Kentucky from western Pennsylvania, West Virginia, or Ohio; at the time that area was considered the Midwest. There were no glass factories in the South until the end of the 19th century.

Hints for Collectors

Many scroll flasks are easily found today at bottle and flask auctions as well as bottle shows and glass sales. Be careful, however, because 3 different scroll reproductions are on the market. The earliest reproduction is of very bubbly green or yellow-green glass, as illustrated here on the right. Note that the glass surface is somewhat uneven compared with older flasks and the base is slightly concave. Made from the 1950s to the present, this reproduction lacks the pontil mark of authentic flasks, and many pieces are marked on the base with the initials "CB" for Clevenger Brothers. The second reproduction is of better quality glass (with fewer bubbles) in light amber, dark blue, purple, dark red, and possibly other colors. This reproduction has a slightly rough pontil mark and was made in West Virginia, perhaps as early as 1950, possibly by the Blenko factory in Milton. At the time, Blenko was making reproductions for Colonial Williamsburg and the Jamestown, Virginia, glasshouse. Despite the quality of this reproduction, the uncharacteristic colors are inauthentic and easy to spot. The third reproduction, in light purple and dark blue, differs only slightly from the second, and here, too, the colors give it away as a fake. An adaptation of a scroll flask also exists in greenish-yellow, but it is not a true reproduction since the bottle holds only a quarter-pint. Machine-made, this adaptation was probably a cologne bottle.

Reproduction

Bryan/coin flask

Description
Circular bottle with oblong base. Raised design in circular frame
on each side. Edge milled like a coin. Rounded collar. No pontil
mark. Front has profile of Bryan facing left, with inscription "IN
SILVER WE TRUST" arched above and "BRYAN 1896 SEWALL"
in semicircle below. Reverse side has American eagle above laurel
wreath; "UNITED DEMOCRATIC TICKET" arched over "WE SHALL
VOTE" above eagle and "16 TO 1" near base. Colors: transparent
amber and colorless. McKearin Number: GI–126.

Variations
2 varieties in same shape and size. 1 illustrated. Other 1 has
McKinley on front, with "SOUND MONEY AND PROTECTION" arched
above and "McKINLEY & HOBART" in semicircle below. Reverse has
honeybee, with "IN GOLD WE TRUST" arched above and "1896" near
base.

Type and Dimensions
Blown in full-size 2-piece mold for pattern and shape. Neck
finished; collar applied. Half-pint.

Locality and Period
Probably the Midwest. 1896.

Comment
Campaign souvenirs for the presidential election of 1896 when
Democrat William Jennings Bryan ran and lost to Republican
William McKinley, flasks like the one shown bear slogans
supporting the silver standard and no import tariffs. These were
popular causes among the working class.

Hints for Collectors
Although scarce, coin campaign flasks can turn up at flea markets
and bottle swap shows.

Bininger's regulator flask

Description
Circular bottle with oblong base. Raised design on 1 side.
Rounded collar. No pontil mark. Front has clock dial with Roman
numerals and hands set at 11:00, with inscription "BININGER'S"
arched above and "REGULATOR" in semicircle below. "19 BROAD S͞T"
curved at left edge and "NEW YORK" at right edge. Reverse side
and edge blank. Colors: transparent amber and colorless.
McKearin Number: GXIII–87.

Variations
3 varieties. 1 illustrated. 2 others more square in shape. 1 has
hands set at 7:12 with "REGULATOR" only; 1 has hands set at 4:55,
lacks inscription, and has sunburst on reverse; both colorless.
Half-pint and pint.

Type and Dimensions
Blown in full-size 2-piece mold for pattern and shape. Neck
finished; collar applied. Pint.

Locality and Period
Probably Whitney Glass Works, Glassboro, New Jersey; possibly
New Jersey or New York. 1861–64.

Comment
Bottles made for A.M. Bininger & Company, a tea, wine, and
spirits merchant in New York City, are relatively easy to date
because several, including the one illustrated, bear the company
address of 19 Broad Street, where the firm was located only from
1861 to 1864. The flask probably contained whiskey, promoted as
a "regulator" of the internal system.

Hints for Collectors
The 2 colorless clockface variants are probably from the 1880s
and are somewhat more common than the Bininger flask.

Round and Oval Bottles

Some of the oldest American bottles are round or oval forms dating from the late 18th and early 19th centuries. Because most of these early bottles were free-blown or blown in part-size pattern molds, they tend to be somewhat irregularly shaped. All originally had cork stoppers.

Pattern-molded Flasks
Among the earliest bottles were the flattened oval flasks made in the 1770s by European glassblowers in the first American glasshouses. Ribbed and diamond-patterned flasks were produced by such pioneer glasshouses as Stiegel's factory in Manheim, Pennsylvania, and Amelung's glasshouse in New Bremen, Maryland, as well as in several other early factories in the East and Midwest. Their small size, often less than a half-pint, made the flasks especially handy for carrying in a pocket. After 1830 pattern-molded flasks generally went out of fashion, replaced by the more uniform figured flasks produced in full-size molds.

Chestnut Bottles, Carboys, and Demijohns
Named for their often flattened globe shape, chestnut bottles also date from the late 18th and early 19th centuries. Since the form of these free-blown bottles depended on the whim and skill of the glassblower, they range from flattened ovals to completely round globes. Some have fairly long necks for easy handling. Carboys and demijohns are also globe-shaped with long necks. Dating from the mid-19th century, most of these huge free-blown bottles have capacities of five to ten gallons.

Whiskey Jugs and Calabash Bottles
Called handled whiskeys by collectors, whiskey jugs are usually globe-shaped with applied handles. These forms were made from 1815 to 1875 and used both as containers for store-bought whiskey and as decanters at home. Calabash bottles, named for their long-necked calabash gourd shape, are also included in this section, although some collectors group them with historical flasks because they bear the same designs and were made in the same factories during the mid-19th century.

Louis Kossuth calabash

Description
Globe-shaped bottle with long neck. Vertical ribs from shoulder to flat collar. Narrow shoulder ring. Front has profile of Kossuth facing right with inscription "KOSSUTH" arched above. Reverse side has tree with foliage. Pontil mark on circular base. Colors: transparent olive-yellow, aquamarine, and yellow-green. McKearin Number: GI–113.

Variations
4 calabash varieties in same size; portraits vary greatly. 1 illustrated. On reverse, 1 has Jenny Lind and 2 have ship and all or part of "U.S.STEAM FRIGATE/MISSISSIPPI/S.HUFFSEY." Pint-size, flattened oval flask has Kossuth with "NEW JERSEY/BRIDGETON."; sloop on reverse.

Type and Dimensions
Blown in full-size multipiece mold for pattern and shape. Neck finished; collar applied. About 1½ quarts. Height: 10½".

Locality and Period
The East; possibly New Jersey or Philadelphia. 1851–52.

Comment
The calabash bottle is an unusual flask form that dates from about 1850 to 1855. The more typical flattened flask shape was made from about 1815 to 1880. Louis Kossuth, who appears on the front of the calabash shown here, was a Hungarian statesman. He defied the Austrian emperor and briefly governed Hungary as an independent republic from 1848 to 1849.

Hints for Collectors
The bottle illustrated is easier to find than the variations with the ship *Mississippi*. Most calabashes have a ring pontil mark or, rarely, an iron pontil mark.

Description
Globe-shaped bottle with long neck. Vertical ribs from shoulder to flat collar. Narrow shoulder ring. Front (right) has ¾ view of Lind facing left encircled by wreath, with inscription "JENNY LIND" arched above. Reverse side (left) has glasshouse with "GLASS WORK'S" arched above and "S.HUFFSEY" below. Pontil mark on circular base. Colors: (right) transparent aquamarine; (left) transparent aquamarine, blue, and blue-, yellow-, and olive-green. McKearin Numbers: GI–100 (front); GI–99 (reverse).

Variations
10 calabash varieties; 2 illustrated. On reverse, flask at left and 7 others have glasshouse with or without inscriptions; 1 has tree. Reverse of front illustrated has Kossuth. Of these, 5 have many vertical ribs from base to shoulder. 3 violin-shaped flasks have Lind on both sides. Calabash: 1–1½ quarts. Violin shape: pint and quart.

Type and Dimensions
Blown in full-size multipiece mold for pattern and shape. Neck finished; collar applied. About 1½ quarts. Left height: 10½″. Right height: 10¼″.

Locality and Period
Probably Isabella Glass Works, New Brooklyn, New Jersey. 1851–52. Variants from New Jersey and the Midwest.

Comment
Jenny Lind, the Swedish Nightingale, took America by storm when P.T. Barnum promoted her concert tour in 1851. The flask shown was made for Samuel Huffsey, a Philadelphia retailer.

Hints for Collectors
A calabash reproduction made in the 1930s has a glasshouse with "FISLERVILLE GLASS WORKS" on the reverse side.

43 Carboy

Description
Globe-shaped bottle with long neck. Ring below lip. Pontil mark on circular base slightly pushed into body. Colors: transparent blue-green, dark olive-green, green, and dark amber.

Variations
Body may be flattened or more cylindrical. May have flat or rounded collar. May be in wicker tub with 2 handles.

Type and Dimensions
Free-blown, then tooled into shape; or blown in dip mold, then expanded and tooled into shape after removal from mold. Ring applied. Height: 16¾".

Locality and Period
New England, southern New Jersey, and the Midwest. Europe; widely exported to the United States. c. 1825–70.

Comment
Carboys were used during the 19th century for bulk shipping of acids and other strong chemicals. They were usually set into tubs, or baskets, of heavy wicker that covered the sides to the shoulders and had 2 carrying handles. This protection guarded against breakage and made these heavy bottles easier to carry. It is unusual to find a carboy still in its wicker tub.

Hints for Collectors
The earliest carboys are globe-shaped and have what is called a string rim—a thread of glass applied just below the rim. A cover that helped to hold the cork in place was tied on under the rim. Later examples are more cylindrical, with rounded or flat collars. The bottle illustrated dates from a middle period and has a chipped lip, which lessens its value slightly.

Demijohn

Description
Flattened globe-shaped bottle with long neck. Flat collar. Pontil mark on circular base slightly pushed into body. Colors: transparent blue-green, dark olive-green, green, and dark amber. Encased up to collar in wicker basket with 2 handles.

Variations
Shape may be rounder. May have ring below lip or rounded collar. May lack basket.

Type and Dimensions
Blown in dip mold, then expanded and tooled into shape after removal from mold. Collar applied. Height: 11″.

Locality and Period
New England, southern New Jersey, and the Midwest. Europe; widely exported to the United States. c. 1840–60.

Comment
In the 17th and 18th centuries, demijohn and carboy were interchangeable terms for storage bottles with a capacity of a gallon or more. (Five gallons was the usual size, but bottles could contain up to 10 gallons; the example illustrated could hold 1 gallon.) At first, demijohn was the more common term, but by the 19th century the 2 terms were differentiated: Carboy indicated a very large container for corrosive liquids, while demijohn was a smaller but similarly shaped bottle for spirits, wine, oil, honey, or other noncorrosive liquids.

Hints for Collectors
Even if the wicker is in bad shape, a bottle with a casing is more interesting and valuable to a collector than one without it.

Chestnut or Ludlow bottles

Description
Oval bottle with medium-length or long neck. Flanged or plain
lip. Pontil mark on oval base slightly pushed into body. Colors:
shades of transparent green, brown, and amber; sometimes
aquamarine and colorless.

Variations
Neck length varies. Body varies from a flatter oval to nearly
globe-shaped. May have ring below lip.

Type and Dimensions
Free-blown, then tooled into shape. Height: 3–7″.

Locality and Period
Vermont, New Hampshire, Massachusetts, Connecticut, New
York, southern New Jersey, Pennsylvania, and Ohio. Europe;
widely exported to the United States. c. 1780–1830.

Comment
One of the most common bottle types of the late 18th and early
19th centuries, these oval shapes were named chestnut bottles
by a collector who thought they resembled a chestnut. Other
collectors, believing the bottles had been blown in Ludlow,
Massachusetts, dubbed them Ludlow bottles. Actually, bottles
and flasks in this shape were made by every bottle manufacturer
at the time and came in a wide variety of sizes and colors. Many,
including the Pitkin and midwestern types, were blown in
pattern molds, but more were free-blown, as shown. Although
some bottles were imported during the 18th century, the
majority in this shape were manufactured here. They became
such an important commodity that a premium was offered for
their return. It was not until the middle of the 19th century,
when enough bottles were manufactured cheaply in the United
States, that distillers and brewers stopped buying used bottles.

Early Americans drank a wide variety of beverages. Some, such as cider and perry (made from pears), were traditional in England; others, like beer, porter, and ale, were common in the Germanic countries as well. During this period, wine was usually imported in barrels and casks and bottled for resale. Whiskey, gin, and rum were usually made by commercial distillers, and milder drinks, such as cider, perry, ale, and beer, were often homebrewed for a 6-month or year's supply. At this time, people seldom drank water unless nothing else was obtainable, and milk, which was rarely consumed by adults, was not bottled. All bottles were especially scarce on the western frontier when it was first being settled in the 1810s. One late 18th-century traveler noted that in Philadelphia alone so much porter was being produced that it would take the output of an entire glasshouse to meet the demand for bottles.

Hints for Collectors

Since it is impossible to tell in which glasshouse or even in which country a bottle of the type shown was made, attribution in no way affects value. Because they are rare, however, the large and small bottles are considered more desirable.

Pitkin-type flasks

Description
Flattened oval bottle with short neck. Plain lip. Double layer of glass from base to shoulder with broken-swirl ribs. Pontil mark on oval base slightly pushed into body. Colors: (left) transparent olive-amber, olive-green, and dark green; (right) transparent light and dark green, light and dark amber, and aquamarine.

Variations
Always even number of ribs, from 16 to 36; rarely 44. Ribs may be swirled to right or left. Body may be more globe-shaped.

Type and Dimensions
Free-blown and partially expanded; coated with 2nd gather up to the shoulder, then blown in vertically ribbed dip mold and swirled; redipped in same mold for broken-swirl ribs. Expanded and tooled into final shape after removal from mold. Left height: 6⅝". Right height: 6¾".

Locality and Period
Left: Massachusetts, Connecticut, and New Hampshire; possibly Clementon, New Jersey. c. 1790–1830. Right: Mantua and probably other Ohio factories. c. 1810–30.

Comment
These flasks are blown from a double gather of glass, the second layer covering the first up to the shoulder. This technique, called the German half-post method, was commonly used in Europe to make case bottles and flasks in the 17th and 18th centuries. In this country the double gather was employed primarily for flasks. Collectors often call the flasks pictured, with the double gather and 2 sets of ribs, Pitkin or Pitkin-type flasks. All were thought to have been made in the Pitkin family glasshouse in East Hartford, now Manchester, Connecticut, from about 1783 to 1830. This has not been proved, but they were also produced

in other New England and midwestern glasshouses.

The 2 distinct regional types are illustrated here. Eastern Pitkin-type flasks (left) are lightweight and generally narrower than midwestern examples. They are widest from front to back toward the base. The ribbing, which is narrow and closely spaced, is either a single set of swirled ribs or 2 superimposed sets, called broken-swirl ribs; the ribs are seldom straight. Most eastern flasks have 32 or 36 ribs. In contrast, midwestern Pitkin-type flasks (right) are heavier, and the glass is slightly thicker. Most midwestern flasks have a wide, flattened globe shape, widest from front to back at the shoulder. Some, however, are flattened ovals resembling the eastern Pitkin types, and others are bulbous. The ribs are generally broken-swirl, and the number varies considerably—16, 20, 24, 26, 30, 32, 36, or rarely 44. Not all Pitkin-type flasks fit exactly into either category. For both types, however, the pint size is most common.

Hints for Collectors

Like other early glassware, Pitkin-type flasks are rarely available in the average antiques shop, but they can be found in shops that specialize in old glass or at many of the smaller auction houses that sell glass. These flasks are higher priced than the common late 19th-century bottles, but far less expensive than the rarest historical flasks. Color does not greatly affect desirability, but condition is very important. The closer a bottle is to perfect, the better. Cracked or chipped bottles are less valuable, but a lip that has been ground down to mask a chip is far worse than having the chip.

Description
Flattened oval bottle with short neck. Plain lip. Primarily diamond patterns: diamonds with 4 dots (below left), diamonds over flutes (below right), diamonds (opposite left), diamonds with daisies (opposite middle), or hexagons with daisies (opposite right). Pontil mark on oval base slightly pushed into body. Colors: transparent blue, light and dark purple, light green, and colorless.

Variations
Body may have 12- or 15-diamond rows or vertical or swirled ribs.

Type and Dimensions
Blown in part-size 2-piece mold for pattern, then expanded and tooled into shape after removal from mold. Height: 4¾–6″.

Locality and Period
Below left: J.F. Amelung's New Bremen Glassmanufactory, New Bremen, Maryland. 1785–95. Below right and all opposite: H.W. Stiegel's American Flint Glass Works, Manheim, Pennsylvania. 1770–74. Similar flasks from Albert Gallatin's New Geneva Glass Works, New Geneva, Pennsylvania. 1797–c. 1810.

Comment
These 18th-century flasks from some of America's earliest glasshouses are all exceptionally rare. Fragments of the diamond flask with 4 dots, a pattern known as checkered diamonds, have been found in both purple and colorless glass at the site of Amelung's glasshouse during archaeological excavations by the Smithsonian Institution and the Corning Museum of Glass in 1962 and 1963. The other 4 flasks illustrated, usually found in light and dark purple and rarely in blue or colorless glass, are attributed to Stiegel's third factory, built in Manheim in 1770,

but the evidence is purely circumstantial. Similar flasks in light green glass with diamonds or diamonds over flutes are associated with Gallatin's New Geneva Glass Works.

Since Stiegel did not mark any of his glass, it is difficult to make positive attributions. In 1914 Frederick Hunter, a collector, did some digging at the site of Stiegel's Manheim glasshouse. Since he was not a trained archaeologist, he assumed that every shard of glass that he found on the site must have been made there. In fact, quite a lot of the glass was probably either German or English.

Hints for Collectors

Stiegel-type flasks are generally found at auctions or with specialized dealers; once or twice a lucky collector has spotted one in a junk shop for a few dollars. One of the Amelung flasks was found in a box of miscellaneous 19th-century bottles at a country auction outside of Washington, D.C., in 1981. However, these highly desirable flasks are usually expensive and should only be purchased from a reputable dealer, especially since there are many reproductions of several Stiegel patterns.

A variant diamond-daisy mold was used in the 1920s to make flask reproductions, but they have shorter necks and squatter bodies than the originals. Several taller, more oval flask copies have also been found in the diamond-daisy pattern. During the 1930s the glassblower Emil Larsen, a Swedish immigrant who had worked for the Dorflinger, Pairpoint, and Durand companies, set up his own small factory in Vineland, New Jersey, where he blew a number of reproductions. Among them are Stiegel-type ribbed and diamond-patterned flasks of inauthentic bright purple, blue, green, and very rarely red, a color not made originally. Today even Larsen flasks are sought by collectors.

Midwestern pattern-molded flasks

Description
Flattened oval to globe-shaped bottle with short neck. Plain lip.
Diamonds (below left), vertical ribs (below right, opposite left),
broken-swirl ribs (opposite middle), or swirled ribs (opposite
right). Pontil mark on oval or circular base slightly pushed into
body. Colors: shades of transparent green, aquamarine, amber,
and brown; rarely transparent purple, blue, and colorless.

Type and Dimensions
Blown in part-size 2- or 3-piece mold for pattern, then expanded
and tooled into shape after removal from mold. Height: 5⅛–
8¼″.

Locality and Period
Western Pennsylvania, West Virginia, and Zanesville, Mantua,
and Kent, Ohio. c. 1800–40.

Comment
The distinctive products of the early glasshouses in Ohio and
western Pennsylvania are among the rarest and most prized
glass collected today. Known as midwestern glass, the bottles,
flasks, and tableware made in these factories are easily
recognized by their ribbed, swirled, or diamond patterns, usually
in a wide range of ambers and greens. All were made using
pattern molds.
Similar molds must certainly have been known in the East, but
they were not used as extensively, and the color range of eastern
flasks is not as great. Although it is difficult to make definite
attributions, a 16-diamond mold as well as 16- and 20-rib molds
have been traced to the New Geneva Glass Works near
Pittsburgh because they survived in the family of a New Geneva
glassblower. However, the molds may also have been used in
other nearby glasshouses before or after New Geneva. A 24-rib
mold and a 10-diamond mold are attributed to Zanesville; 15-

diamond and 16- and 32-rib molds are associated with the Mantua factory; and a 20-rib mold was used at the Kent factory. In the 1920s, Harry Hall White, a glass collector, excavated numerous glass fragments with these characteristics at the Mantua and Kent sites. However, the molds used in all of the midwestern factories were probably also employed in more than one place, since it was a common practice to sell molds from factory to factory.

Zanesville had 2 glasshouses: the Zanesville Glass Manufacturing Company (1815–51), commonly called the White Glass Works because it produced white hollow ware; and the Muskingum Green Glass Works (1816–49), a bottle glasshouse. The Mantua Glass Works operated from 1822 to 1829, while the Parks, Edmunds & Parks Company at Kent was open from 1824 to 1834. Other frontier glass factories were operated for brief periods in Cincinnati, Moscow, Portage, and Painesville, Ohio; Maysville, Kentucky; and several West Virginia towns.

Hints for Collectors

Collectors call large flasks "grandfather flasks," and the slightly smaller ones "grandmother flasks." Both are rarer than the medium-size ones. Ambers, greens, and blues are associated with Zanesville; ambers, greens, and purples with Mantua; and ambers and greens with Kent. One of the greatest difficulties in collecting midwestern pattern-molded glass is that Mexican glassware of the late 19th and early 20th centuries is extremely similar. The Mexican glass was made in greens, amber, and blue in many of the same shapes and patterns as the early 19th-century Ohio glass. The Metropolitan Museum of Art in New York City has sold midwestern and Stiegel-type reproductions for the past 20 years, but these are all marked "MMA" on the base.

Handled whiskey bottles

Description
Flattened oval or globe-shaped bottle with medium-length or short neck and ear-shaped handle. Ring below lip or rounded collar. Without or with swirled ribs. Pontil mark on oval or circular base slightly pushed into body. Colors: transparent light and dark brown, light and dark amber, and green.

Variations
Neck length varies. Type of lip varies. Body may be more pear-shaped or cylindrical with sloping shoulders. Pattern may be diamonds or vertical ribs. Side may have molded inscription, applied seal, or paper label with name of distiller.

Type and Dimensions
Left: free-blown, then tooled into shape; ring and handle applied. Height: 7⅜". Right: blown in part-size 2-piece mold for pattern, then expanded, swirled, and tooled into shape after removal from mold; collar and handle applied. Height: 6¼".

Locality and Period
New York, New Jersey, Pennsylvania, and Ohio. c. 1815–50.

Comment
Jugs of this type with handles may have been designed as decanters. The swirled ones are certainly related to the tableware produced in Ohio factories in the second quarter of the 19th century. The plain free-blown ones, however, are products of bottle factories, and were probably intended as commercial containers. Many had paper labels giving the name and manufacturer of the contents.

Hints for Collectors
The swirled Ohio bottles are harder to find than the plain ones. Examples with labels, inscriptions, or seals are considered the most interesting.

Handled whiskey bottles

Description
Conical or flattened globe-shaped bottle with short to medium-length neck and ear-shaped handle. Rounded collar with pouring lip (left) or ring below lip (center, right). With or without vertical ribs. Applied seal or molded mark: left seal has "STAR WHISKEY/ NEW YORK/W.B.CROWELL"; center seal has "CHESNUT GROVE/ WHISKEY/C.W."; right mark has "CHESNUT GROVE/WHISKEY/C.W." Pontil mark on circular or oval base slightly pushed into body. Colors: transparent amber, brown, and green.

Variations
Seals or marks have names of many other distillers and sellers. Bottle may lack seal or mark. May have flat collar.

Type and Dimensions
Left: blown in vertically ribbed dip mold, then expanded and tooled into shape after removal from mold. Collar, handle, and seal applied. Height: 8¾". Center and right: blown in full-size 2-piece mold for pattern and shape. Neck finished; ring and handle applied; seal applied (center). Height: 8".

Locality and Period
New York and New Jersey. c. 1840–75. Variants probably from New England and the Midwest.

Comment
The initials on handled whiskey jugs usually refer to the distiller, but sometimes they name the whiskey retailer.

Hints for Collectors
Handled jugs are rarer than ordinary whiskey bottles both because fewer were made and because handles tend to break.

Cylindrical Bottles

The cylindrical bottle is the most common bottle form, readily identified with wine, beer, and soda. Free-blown and mold-blown examples have been made in the United States since the late 18th century and possibly as early as mid-century.

Wine and Medicine Bottles

The first free-blown wine bottles made in this country were usually cylindrical with long necks, although even earlier European imports were squat and round. Later 19th-century mold-blown American wine bottles, which were taller and thinner, resembled the classic Bordeaux bottles we know today. Some of the first American-made medicine bottles were also cylindrical, but these bottles were shorter and had wide, short necks.

Beer, Ale, Mineral Water, and Coca-Cola Bottles

When beer, ale, and mineral water began to be bottled in the mid-19th century, the cylindrical shape proved to be the strongest, able to withstand the pressure of the carbonated beverage inside. A cylinder with sloping shoulders and a medium-length neck became the standard form and is still in use. The most durable bottle shape was the torpedo-shaped cylinder with a rounded bottom, used for mineral water from 1860 to 1890. Since corners are the weak points in a bottle, a rounded base proved stronger against internal pressure. These bottles were even better suited to shipping than rectangular bottles. Unable to stand upright, they had to be packed horizontally. This position kept the liquid in constant contact with the cork, which expanded to fit tightly in the bottle neck and prevented the bottle from leaking. By the late 19th century, carbonated drinks such as Coca-Cola and other flavored sodas were sold for home use and also distributed in cylindrical bottles.

Household and Milk Bottles

Solid foods like pickles as well as household products such as glue were bottled commercially after about 1850, often in cylindrical containers. When bottles for milk and cream were introduced toward the turn of the century, they were also cylindrical with wide necks. Huckleberry bottles, like Mason jars, were sold empty for home preserving.

Corks, Stoppers, and Other Closures

Most of the bottles included in this section were sealed with corks. To keep the corks on bottles containing carbonated drinks, a wire was usually tied over the top of the cork and then twisted around the neck of the bottle. These improvised closures were replaced in the late 19th century by toggle-type stoppers held in place by wire loops. For example, the Lightning stopper, patented in 1875, combined a metal and rubber lid and a wire bail and lever. For sanitary purposes, most early milk bottles used Lightning-type closures and later tin caps with wire bails. These lids were eventually replaced after 1889 by paper caps that rested on a groove inside the bottle neck.

Early 18th-century wine bottles

Description
Hexagonal or round, squat bottle with wide shoulders and long, sloping neck. Ring below lip. Right: circular seal impressed with "N/Green/1724." Pontil mark on hexagonal or circular base pushed into body. Colors: transparent dark green and dark olive-green.

Variations
Shape may be nearly conical, tapering from wide shoulders to narrow base. Neck length varies.

Type and Dimensions
Left: blown in dip mold, then expanded and tooled into shape after removal from mold; ring applied. Height: 8″. Right: free-blown, then tooled into shape; ring and seal applied. Height: 6⅝″.

Locality and Period
England; widely exported to the United States. Left: c. 1735–1800. Right: c. 1720–50.

Comment
English bottles were used in the Colonies before the American glass industry was able to supply locally made ware. The earliest examples, from about 1630, were squat with disproportionately long necks. Gradually, the neck was shortened, and the body evolved from conical to round and then cylindrical.

Hints for Collectors
Many English wine bottles bear the owner's seal, but it is unusual to find an 18th-century American bottle with a seal. Since the 1950s, Colonial Williamsburg has sold an authentic-looking copy of an 18th-century English seal bottle.

Description
Cylindrical bottle with rounded shoulders and long neck. Narrow collar. Pontil mark on circular base pushed into body. Colors: transparent green, dark green, olive-green, and dark amber.

Variations
Neck length varies.

Type and Dimensions
Free-blown, then tooled into shape. Collar applied. Height: 9–9½".

Locality and Period
England; widely exported to the United States. Possibly Massachusetts, Connecticut, New York, southern New Jersey, Pennsylvania, and Maryland. c. 1780–1800.

Comment
Until at least 1830, far more wine bottles were made in England and exported to America than were made here, and so any bottle of this early date is probably English. The bottles illustrated are midway in the shape evolution from squat to cylindrical. Like modern wine bottles, they were closed with a cork that was withdrawn with a corkscrew, invented around 1680. All early bottles bear the pushed-in pontil mark typical of inexpensive 18th-century glass.

Hints for Collectors
Both of these bottles came from shipwrecks, and they still have iridescent surfaces with scaly residue. The example on the left was found on a British ship sunk in Yorktown harbor, Virginia, in 1781. The bottle on the right is from a ship discovered in the Bay of Fundy, Canada.

53 Saratoga mineral water bottles

Description
Cylindrical bottle with rounded shoulders and long or short neck (left, right), or sloping shoulders and wide, short neck (center). Flat collar. 1 side has inscription: "D.A.KNOWLTON/SARATOGA/N.Y." (left), "LYNCH & CLARKE/NEW YORK" (center), and "CONGRESS & EMPIRE SPRINGS CO/HOTCHKISS & SONS/CW/NEW YORK/SARATOGA, N.Y." (right). Circular base without pontil mark (left, right) or with pontil mark and slightly pushed into body (center). Colors: transparent light and dark green, light and dark amber, brown, and aquamarine.

Variations
Inscriptions of other firms, such as Star Spring Company, High Rock Springs, Aetna Spring, and Champion Spring.

Type and Dimensions
Blown in full-size multipiece mold for pattern and shape. Neck finished; collar applied. Left height: 9½". Center height: 7¼". Right height: 7".

Locality and Period
Saratoga Mountain Glass Works, Mt. Pleasant, 1844–c. 1870; Saratoga Congressville Glass Works, Congressville, c. 1870–90; and other New York glasshouses, c. 1840–1900. Possibly New England and New Jersey. c. 1840–1900.

Comment
Saratoga with its natural springs became a European-style spa in the 19th century and attracted thousands of visitors. For those who could not afford the trip, the water was sold in half-pint, pint, and quart bottles beginning in 1826.

Hints for Collectors
Early Saratoga bottles are rare; most date from after 1850.

Oak Orchard Acid Springs bottle

Description
Cylindrical bottle with sloping shoulders and long neck. Flat collar. Inscription "OAK ORCHARD/ACID SPRINGS. G.W.MERCHANT/LOCKPORT N.Y." around shoulder. Circular base slightly pushed into body; no pontil mark. Colors: transparent light and dark blue-green, light and dark amber, and green.

Variations
Shoulder may have "OAK ORCHARD/ACID SPRINGS H.W.BOSTWICK AGT NO 574." Outer edge of base may have "GLASS FROM F.HITCHENS FACTORY LOCKPORT N Y."

Type and Dimensions
Blown in full-size multipiece mold for pattern and shape. Neck finished; collar applied. Height: 8⅝".

Locality and Period
Lockport Glass Works, Lockport, New York. c. 1850–70.

Comment
The Oak Orchard Acid Springs Company, established in the 1840s, bottled spring water from several springs near Alabama Center in Genesee County, New York. Each produced water with a slightly different taste, and the different colors of the bottles indicated from which spring the water came. All of the Oak Orchard bottles were made at the Lockport Glass Works, founded in 1843 and in operation until the 1880s. In 1849 alone, the spring water company used 25,000 Lockport bottles. Francis Hitchens bought the bottle factory in 1850 and enlarged production to include medicine and perfume bottles.

Hints for Collectors
These spring water bottles were made in such quantities that they are relatively easy to find in the Northeast.

19th-century wine bottles

Description
Cylindrical bottle with rounded or sloping shoulders and long neck. Flat collar or ring below rounded lip. With mold seams and base rim inscriptions: "DYOTTVILLE GLASS WORKS PHIL^A" (below left), "WHITNEY GLASS WORKS" (below right), and "WILLINGTON GLASS WORKS" (opposite left). With impressed seal: "MT VERNON/MSM/GLASS CO" (opposite right). Circular base pushed into body with (opposite right) or without pontil mark (below, opposite left). Colors: shades of transparent green, brown, and amber.

Variations
Bottles with mold seams may have other inscriptions: "WEEKS & GILSON SO STODDARD N.H."; "ELLENVILLE GLASS WORKS"; "CUNNINGHAM & IHMSEN"; "W McCULLY & CO"; or "BUSHWICK GLASS WORKS." Seal may have "JH," "JL," "TRL," or "WB."

Type and Dimensions
Below and opposite left: blown in full-size multipiece mold for pattern and shape. Neck finished; collar applied. Height: 11½".
Opposite right: blown in dip mold, then expanded and tooled into shape after removal from mold. Ring and seal applied. Height: 9¼".

Locality and Period
Below and opposite left: New Hampshire, Massachusetts, New York, New Jersey, and Pennsylvania. c. 1850–80. Opposite right: Mt. Vernon Glass Works, Vernon, New York. 1810–25.

Comment
With their dark colors and cylindrical shape, the 4 bottles illustrated are typical 19th-century American wine bottles. The shortest example represents the earliest type of mold-blown bottle. Its body was blown in a 1-piece dip mold; the shoulder and neck were formed by hand. A thick, rounded ring of glass

was applied to the rim of the lip so that a waxed cloth could be tied on over the mouth. The other 3 bottles were made at least 40 years later in 3-piece molds. One part, or piece, of the mold formed the body below the shoulder, and the other 2 pieces were used to form the shoulder and neck, usually leaving a horizontal mold seam around the bottle below the shoulder. After the bottle was removed from the mold, the neck and lip were finished by hand. Similarly shaped bottles were also made in full-size 2-piece molds and thus bear mold seams on each side of the body. This 2-piece mold was used to make flasks by at least 1815, although it may not have been used for bottles until the 1840s. Glassmakers did not employ the 3-piece mold until the mid-19th century. Probably all 3 later bottles once held wine, although they may also have been used for other popular drinks, such as porter, beer, ale, and cider. Their broad, flat collars are characteristic of the 1850–70 period and are also seen on flasks from about 1850 to 1880.

Hints for Collectors
Examine the base rim of a wine bottle: An inscribed company name will help you date it. If the base has no inscription but the body has mold seams similar to those on the bottles illustrated, the bottle probably dates from the late 19th century. Many of these bottles can still be found today. The Mt. Vernon wine bottle is quite rare, and can only be located through dealers, if at all.

Porter bottle

Description
Cylindrical bottle with sloping shoulders and long neck. Flat collar. 1 side has inscription "PHILADELPHIA/X X/PORTER & ALE/ UNION GLASS WORKS." Other side has "D.L./ORMSBY/NEW YORK." Pontil mark on circular base slightly pushed into body. Colors: transparent brown, light and dark green, blue, aquamarine, and light and dark amber.

Variations
May lack "D.L./ORMSBY/NEW YORK." Inscriptions of other firms or brands. Sizes 6½–9".

Type and Dimensions
Blown in full-size multipiece mold for pattern and shape. Neck finished; collar applied. Height: 6¾".

Locality and Period
Union Glass Works, Philadelphia. c. 1840–60. Variants from other factories in Pennsylvania, New England, New York, and New Jersey. c. 1845–75.

Comment
Bottles for porter, ale, and beer were virtually interchangeable before 1850, but in glass-company advertisements they were usually referred to as porter bottles. Often dark in color, they were made in a great number of glasshouses, and taverns as well as breweries bottled their own products. Around mid-century, bottles embossed with the names of ales or porters began to appear. Most closely resembled soda water bottles.

Hints for Collectors
The earliest porter bottles were free-blown or mold-blown; those with "PORTER" or "ALE" usually date from 1845 to 1875. Since they are sturdy, many have survived.

Mineral water bottles

Description
Cylindrical (left, right) or 10-sided (center) bottle with sloping shoulders and medium-length neck. Flat or rounded collar. Inscription on 1 or 2 sides: "TAYLOR/NEVER/SURRENDERS" and "UNION GLASS WORKS/PHILAD^A" (left), "PREMIUM/SODA OR/MINERAL/WATER/ALBANY/Wm.W.LAPREUS" (center), and "SEYMOUR/& CO/BUFFALO/N.Y." (right). Pontil mark on circular or 10-sided base slightly pushed into body. Colors: transparent blue, aquamarine, brown, green, and amber.

Variations
Inscriptions of many other firms or brands, such as Haskins Spring Company, Martin & McCarthy, and John Matthews.

Type and Dimensions
Blown in full-size multipiece mold for pattern and shape. Neck finished; collar applied. Left and center height: 7½″. Right height: 7¼″.

Locality and Period
Union Glass Works, Philadelphia, and other factories in Pennsylvania, New York, and New Jersey. c. 1840–70.

Comment
First produced in England around 1800, carbonated water was made and sold on the East Coast by 1812. But it was not until the 1830s that large-scale distribution began. Because the contents were under pressure, the bottles had thick walls.

Hints for Collectors
Early soda bottles like those shown here are more popular than later, thin-walled examples. The bottle at the left is particularly interesting since it is probably a souvenir of Taylor's presidential campaign of 1848.

Description
Cylindrical bottle with sloping or rounded shoulders and long or medium-length neck. Rounded collar. Designs and inscriptions on 1 side. Left: warrior with banner "EXCELSIOR," with inscription "THE GEORGE BECHTEL BREWING CO." above and "BOTTLED AT BREWERY/STAPLETON/STATEN ISLAND" below. Center: portrait of Washington with "WASHINGTON BREWERY COMPANY" above and "TRADE/MARK/REGISTERED/WASHINGTON D.C." below. Right: "D.CRONK GIBBONS & CO/SUPERIOR ALE/BUFFALO/N.Y." Circular base without (left, center) or with pontil mark (right). Colors: transparent aquamarine, blue, light and dark green, and brown. Left: Lightning stopper.

Variations
Shape and size vary slightly; other firm or brand names.

Type and Dimensions
Blown in full-size multipiece mold for pattern and shape, including collar (left, center); neck finished and collar applied (right). Left height: 9¼". Center height: 9½". Right height: 7".

Locality and Period
Left and center: throughout the United States. c. 1895–1910. Right: the East and Midwest. c. 1845–75.

Comment
After 1870, most beer was made by commercial brewers and sold locally because it did not travel well. Each brewery had its own bottle, resulting in hundreds of designs. The Lightning stopper on the Bechtel bottle was invented in 1875 to replace the cork.

Hints for Collectors
Beer bottles with the word beer on them usually date after 1871. To pin down the date, check brewery names in old city directories.

Coca-Cola bottles

Description
Cylindrical bottle with sloping shoulders and medium-length
neck. Rounded collar. 1 side has inscription "Coca-Cola/
TRADEMARK REGISTERED" (both), and "BOTTLING CO. WATERBORO SC
PROPERTY OF COCA COLA" near circular base (right). Colors:
transparent aquamarine and colorless.

Variations
Lower body may be ribbed and slightly indented. Shoulders may
be flat. Inscription may be embossed in white. Bottle may have
diamond-shaped paper label.

Type and Dimensions
Blown in automatic bottle-blowing machine for pattern and
shape. Height: 7".

Locality and Period
Probably the Midwest; possibly Root Glass Company, Terre
Haute, Indiana. 1899–c. 1916.

Comment
Coca-Cola was perfected by Dr. John S. Pemberton, an Atlanta
pharmacist, in 1886. It was originally dispensed as a soda
fountain drink, but in 1894 was bottled and sold for home use.
The original formula contained traces of cocaine, which were
removed with improved refining methods. Bottles in the shape
illustrated were used from 1899 until about 1916, when the more
familiar Coke-bottle shape was introduced.

Hints for Collectors
Many of the earliest flat-shouldered bottles have been found in
the South; later ones are more evenly distributed throughout the
United States. A bottle with the name embossed in red or yellow
dates from after 1933.

Description
Cylindrical bottle with sloping shoulders and medium-length neck. Flat collar. Inscription "SEE THAT EACH CORK IS BRANDED/ CANTRELL & COCHRANE DUBLIN & BELFAST" near rounded base; no pontil mark. Colors: transparent aquamarine, blue, green, light and dark brown, and light and dark amber.

Variations
Inscriptions of other firms or brands, such as "F.GLEASON/ ROCHESTER/N.Y." Shape may be more oval.

Type and Dimensions
Blown in full-size multipiece mold for pattern and shape. Neck finished; collar applied. Height: 9½".

Locality and Period
Ireland; widely exported to the United States. c. 1860–90. Variants from the East and Midwest.

Comment
Round-bottomed bottles are often called torpedo or egg bottles. They were made that way so the bottles could be packed in a horizontal position; keeping the contents in contact with the cork prevented it from drying out. Nearly all once contained soda or mineral water. As with most soda bottles, the cork was wired on below the collar. Round-bottomed beer bottles are much less common because at that time beer was not sent any great distance from where it was bottled.

Hints for Collectors
The bottles marked "CANTRELL & COCHRANE" were used for exporting mineral water from Ireland to England and the United States. They are quite common in this country, while American torpedo bottles are difficult to find.

Description
Cylindrical bottle with sloping shoulders and wide, medium-length neck. Rounded collar. Vertical panels around body. Circular base slightly pushed into body; no pontil mark. Colors: transparent brown and amber.

Variations
Sides may be plain. Collar may be flat.

Type and Dimensions
Blown in full-size multipiece mold for pattern and shape. Neck finished; collar applied. Height: 11¼″.

Locality and Period
Westford Glass Company, Westford, Connecticut. 1857–73. Willington Glass Works, West Willington, Connecticut. 1840–75. Possibly other New England factories.

Comment
These bottles are commonly called huckleberry bottles in New England, where some elderly residents can still remember when they were used for preserving fruit, probably cranberries, blueberries, and huckleberries. Because liberal amounts of sugar were used to prevent the fruit from spoiling, it was not necessary to boil the bottles, as was done in canning. The usual seal was a cork with wax or perhaps a waxed cloth tied over the cork. The bottle illustrated was found with several others early in this century in Connecticut; a few bottles still contained preserves.

Hints for Collectors
Huckleberry bottles are much rarer than some of the beer, wine, and spirits bottles in similar shapes. The wide neck is a clue that it was meant to contain solids, not liquids.

Description
Cylindrical bottle with steeply sloping shoulders and wide, short neck. Rounded collar. Designs and inscriptions. Left: 1 side has cow's head with "AHS" below; 1 has "MASS R SEAL/ONE QUART LIQUID/ALTA CREST FARMS/SPENCER MASS./REED W. 184"; base has "PATENTED MAY 28, 1929, NO.78623 34." Center: 1 side has "BIG ELM/DAIRY/COMPANY/REED 2"; 1 has "ONE QUART/LIQUID/REGISTERED/52925"; base has "B34." Right: 1 side has "HALF PINT" above circular frame enclosing cow's head and "HAMPDEN/REGISTERED/CREAMERY CO."; 1 has "MASS. SEAL/TR."; base has "H.E.WRIGHT & SONS BOSTON." Circular base. Colors: colorless; rarely transparent green and amber. Right: tin cap and wire bail closure.

Variations
Many dairy names. May have tin handle attached to tin band.

Type and Dimensions
Blown in automatic bottle-blowing machine for pattern and shape. Left height: 9½". Center height: 9". Right height: 5½".

Locality and Period
Throughout the United States. c. 1910–40.

Comment
One of the first glass milk bottles was patented in 1884 by Dr. Henry Thatcher, said to have been horrified to see a milkman dip from a can into which a child had dropped a dirty rag doll. Thatcher's Common Sense Milk Jar of 1889 became the industry standard: It had a waxed paper cap that fit into a groove inside the neck.

Hints for Collectors
Pre-1890 bottles with bail closures and metal caps are scarce. Most antique milk bottles available today are machine-made.

63 Pickle bottle

Description
Cylindrical bottle with rounded shoulders and wide, medium-length neck. Flat collar. 1 side has oval frame enclosing design of Bunker Hill Monument below inscription "TRADE MARK"; around frame, "SKILTON, FOOTE & CO'S/BUNKER HILL PICKLES." Circular base without pontil mark. Color: transparent amber.

Variations
May lack inscription. Shape may be rectangular. Variants transparent aquamarine, amber, and colorless.

Type and Dimensions
Blown in full-size multipiece mold for pattern and shape. Mouth fire-polished before annealing. Height: 8″.

Locality and Period
Probably the East Coast; possibly New England. 1864–c. 1890. Variants c. 1860–90.

Comment
Many of the food companies just getting started in the late 19th century, such as Heinz in Pittsburgh and French in Rochester, New York, are still in business. Skilton, Foote & Company, founded in 1864 in Somerville, Massachusetts, was well known in its day and prospered until the turn of the century. It began by manufacturing vinegar, but soon branched out into pickles and other condiments, selling them in pint and quart bottles.

Hints for Collectors
Since it is from a firm little-known today, the bottle illustrated should not be expensive. It is typical of the simple pickle jar and bottle designs of the late 19th century. Earlier pickle bottles had elaborate Gothic arch designs.

Glue bottle

Description
Oblong bottle with rounded shoulders and wide, long neck.
Flanged lip. 1 side has inscription "USE/BOILING/HOT/AND/
QUICKLY"; 1 has "IMPERIAL/CEMENT." Oval base without pontil
mark. Colors: transparent aquamarine and colorless.

Variations
Inscriptions of other brands. Bottle may be square or
rectangular. May have pontil mark.

Type and Dimensions
Blown in full-size multipiece mold for pattern and shape. Neck
and lip finished. Height: 3″.

Locality and Period
Throughout the United States. c. 1870–1900.

Comment
It was not until the mid-19th century that store-bought glue was
available for home use. Before then, paste or glue was made at
home whenever it was needed. Spaulding's glue was probably
the earliest to be marketed, since the small cylindrical bottles
that contained it usually bear pontil marks, an early finishing
technique that was abandoned by the 1870s. Pontiled glue bottles
are rare, however, and the great majority date from between
1870 and 1900.

Hints for Collectors
Since similarly shaped bottles without an identifying inscription
could have been meant for either ink or glue, it is quite likely
that bottles once used to hold glue are now in collections of plain
ink bottles. Glue bottles may be picked up relatively easily and
inexpensively and are a good starting point for a beginning
collector.

Early medicine and essence bottles

Description
Cylindrical or rectangular bottle with wide, short neck. Flanged lip. Pontil mark on square base (right) and on circular base slightly pushed into body (left). Colors: transparent aquamarine, green, and colorless.

Variations
Neck length varies. Shape may be more oval.

Type and Dimensions
Left: free-blown, then tooled into shape. Height: 5½″. Right: blown in dip mold, then expanded and tooled into shape after removal from mold. Height: 5″.

Locality and Period
The East. c. 1800–50.

Comment
Plain bottles like the examples illustrated are earlier than the bitters and medicine bottles with elaborate mold-blown decoration. Glass medicine vials were offered for sale in the Colonies as early as the mid-18th century, suggesting that they were reused rather than thrown away when empty. At the time there were at most 2 glass factories in operation, and it was not until the American glass industry was well established, after the War of 1812, that bottles were easily obtainable by doctors and apothecaries.

Hints for Collectors
As with all early bottles, it is pointless to try to make a factory or even specific regional attribution. However, the bottles shown here are fairly easy to date since they have the flanged lip and pontil mark characteristic of bottles from the first half of the 19th century.

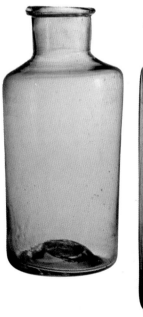

Rectangular Bottles

Although many rectangular bottles once contained gin or proprietary medicines, a wide variety of products, ranging from druggists' powders to pickles, ink, and shoe blacking, have been sold in rectangular bottles of varying proportions throughout the decades.

Case and Gin Bottles

Rectangular bottles were probably first used because of the ease in shipping them. The shape was ideal for transporting gin in compartmentalized wooden cases from England to the Colonies. From the early packing crates was developed the 18th-century traveling liquor chest with its set of six to twelve flat-sided bottles, complete with matching wineglasses and tumblers. No well-to-do gentleman traveled without a liquor chest in his carriage. When not in use during travel, the case was a convenient place to keep the supply of household spirits, and the bottles served as decanters. Most traveling sets were probably imported from Europe. However, gin bottles, also known as case bottles, became staples of American glasshouses beginning in the late 18th century. To this day gin is recognized by the shape of its container, although now the bottles are colorless rather than the green or amber of most early gins.

Snuff Bottles

Another early product of American glasshouses, the snuff jar was advertised by Caspar Wistar's factory in 1765 and probably made even earlier. These small, mold-blown, rectangular or square bottles with wide, short necks were manufactured up to the end of the 19th century when taking snuff was no longer considered fashionable.

Patent and Proprietary Medicine Bottles

Throughout the second half of the 19th century and into the early 20th, vendors of patent and proprietary medicines captivated the American public with their nonprescription cure-alls, whose main ingredient was usually alcohol. Marketed as bitters, sarsaparilla, and healthful tonics, the thousands of formulas required a vast supply of glass bottles. Manufacturers used the rectangular bottle to their advantage: The flat sides offered plenty of room for embossed inscriptions or paper labels with alluring claims and designs.

By 1906 more than 50,000 patent and proprietary medicines were on the market, with 365 million bottles made a year and annual sales of over 80 million dollars. These days of glory came to an abrupt end in January 1907 with the signing of the Pure Food and Drug Act, which required registering the contents of all purported medicines; 240 brands contained so much alcohol that they needed to be sold in liquor stores, and many others incorporated addictive drugs such as opium and morphine. The surviving patent medicines were radically altered to reduce their alcohol or drug content.

Corks, Caps, and Labels

All of the bottles shown in this section were closed with corks, although some later 20th-century patent medicine bottles had screw-on caps. Patent and proprietary medicine bottles had paper labels; most of these have been lost. Some bottles may still be found in their original paper wrappings.

Description
Square jar with rounded shoulders and short neck. Wide mouth with flanged lip. Pontil mark on square base slightly pushed into body. Colors: transparent light and dark green; rarely light and dark amber.

Variations
Height and width vary slightly. May have paper label.

Type and Dimensions
Blown in dip mold, then expanded and tooled into shape after removal from mold. Height: 5".

Locality and Period
Probably southern New Jersey. Possibly England. c. 1760–1850.

Comment
Snuff, a preparation of tobacco, is named for the way it is used: A person sniffs it up the nostrils to produce a sneeze. Not simply powdered tobacco, snuff was treated with a liquid containing aromatic substances plus salt and then fermented for several months. Snuff was introduced in Europe shortly after tobacco was discovered in North America, and its use was confined mainly to the aristocracy. By the 18th and early 19th centuries, snuff taking was virtually regarded as an art. People prepared their own mixture and kept it in elegant, often jeweled, snuffboxes. When the middle class began to use snuff in the mid-18th century, they bought it in square or rectangular glass jars with cork stoppers.

Hints for Collectors
It is impossible to know for certain whether an early snuff jar was made in America or imported from England. Both are of equal value.

Snuff jar

Description
Rectangular jar with beveled corners and rounded shoulders.
Short neck. Wide mouth with flanged lip. Pontil mark on square
base slightly pushed into body. Colors: transparent light and
dark green; rarely light and dark amber.

Variations
Height and width vary slightly. May have "LORILLARD" on base
or other inscription on front. May have paper label.

Type and Dimensions
Blown in dip mold, then expanded and tooled into shape after
removal from mold. Height: 7¼".

Locality and Period
Probably southern New Jersey; possibly New England, New
York, and Pennsylvania. Possibly England. c. 1760–1850.

Comment
By the mid-18th century, bottled snuff was imported into the
Colonies. Although it was also made here, advertisements
suggest that users preferred the imported variety. Several
American glasshouses probably made snuff jars, including a
factory in Germantown, Massachusetts. Demand for jars must
have been considerable as Stiegel's glasshouse in Manheim,
Pennsylvania, produced more than a thousand in February 1767,
alone. Snuff jars were made into the late 19th century, although
the practice of taking snuff had dwindled.

Hints for Collectors
Collectors consider pontiled snuff jars with labels or inscriptions
the most desirable. If the base inscription is "LORILLARD," the
bottle was made in New York in the middle to late 19th century;
it will not have a pontil mark. The giant tobacco company
Lorillard is still in operation today.

Gin or case bottles

Description
Rectangular bottle with rounded shoulders. Straight sides (left) or sides narrower toward base (right). Short neck. Flanged lip or flat collar. Square base with or without pontil mark. Colors: transparent light to dark green and light to dark amber; these colors with corks; occasionally colorless with glass stopper.

Variations
Sizes 8–16″; sizes illustrated are most common. Colorless bottles may have engraved, gilt, or enameled decoration. May have plain lip. May have seal.

Type and Dimensions
Free-blown and tooled into shape; or blown in dip mold, then expanded and tooled into shape after removal from mold. Right: collar applied. Left height: 10⅞″. Right height: 11½″.

Locality and Period
The East. Europe; widely exported to the United States. c. 1760–1850.

Comment
Rectangular bottles like those illustrated here are often referred to as either gin or case bottles. Since the 17th century they have been used to hold gin. Their boxlike shape was ideal for shipping inside wooden cases, usually with 12 or 16 compartments. Most colorless bottles in this shape are decanters that were part of traveling liquor chests used by the wealthy.

Hints for Collectors
The earliest case bottles have a pontil mark and a plain lip. Later examples have mold marks on the base and may lack the pontil mark. While most European bottles are indistinguishable from American examples, Dutch bottles often bear a seal with the initials of the manufacturer.

Dr. Townsend's Sarsaparilla bottle

Description
Rectangular bottle with rounded shoulders and short neck. Flat collar. 1 side has inscription "DR TOWNSEND S"; 1 side has "SARSAPARILLA"; and 1 has "ALBANY/N.Y."; 4th side blank. Pontil mark on square base. Colors: transparent blue-green, green, amber, and brown.

Variations
More than 20 varieties; arrangements of lettering and type of collar vary. Inscription may be "OLD DR TOWNSEND S"; "DR S P TOWNSEND"; or "OLD DR J TOWNSEND"; locality may be "NEW YORK."

Type and Dimensions
Blown in full-size multipiece mold for pattern and shape. Neck finished; collar applied. Height: 9⅝".

Locality and Period
The East. 1849–c. 1900.

Comment
Dr. Townsend's Sarsaparilla may have been the earliest sarsaparilla marketed; Samuel P. Townsend of New York City and Albany started advertising as early as 1849. His product was nothing more than whiskey flavored with sassafras bark and molasses, but it sold like hotcakes and made its proprietor a millionaire. Jacob Townsend, an unrelated competitor, cashed in on S.P. Townsend's advertising by using similar bottles for his own sarsaparilla and claiming that he was the original Dr. Townsend.

Hints for Collectors
All of the colors can be found easily. Jacob Townsend and Samuel P. Townsend bottles are equally valuable.

Description
Rectangular bottle with rounded shoulders and short neck. Flat collar. 1 side has inscription "MONK'S OLD/BOURBON/WHISKEY"; 1 has "FOR/MEDICINAL/PURPOSES"; 1 has "WILSON FAIRBANKS & CO./SOLE AGENTS"; 4th side blank. Pontil mark on square base. Colors: transparent aquamarine and light and dark amber.

Variations
Inscriptions of other whiskeys and distillers or retailers, such as "THE DUFFY MALT WHISKEY COMPANY/ROCHESTER, N.Y. USA."

Type and Dimensions
Blown in full-size multipiece mold for pattern and shape. Neck finished; collar applied. Height: 8".

Locality and Period
The East. c. 1850–70. Variants c. 1850–1900.

Comment
Because of the strong influence of the temperance movement during the second half of the 19th century, manufacturers of whiskey tried to sell their beverages as medicinal products, as seen on the bottle illustrated here. Some manufacturers even had double advertising for the same product, emphasizing the alcohol content for the saloon and the medicinal properties for use in the home.

Hints for Collectors
Rectangular and cylindrical whiskey bottles are much more common than figural whiskeys or handled jugs. Collectors often search for them in dump piles. These classic forms are also widely available at bottle swap shows and flea markets.

Dr. Hostetter's Bitters bottle

Description
Rectangular bottle with rounded shoulders and short neck. Flat
collar. 1 side has inscription "DR. J. HOSTETTER'S/STOMACH
BITTERS"; other 3 sides blank, 1 with paper label printed
"HOSTETTER'S Celebrated STOMACH BITTERS." with directions for
use and testimonials below. Square base without pontil mark.
Colors: transparent amber; rarely olive-green.

Variations
5 varieties with slight variations in lettering and labels.

Type and Dimensions
Blown in full-size multipiece mold for pattern and shape. Neck
finished; collar applied. Height: 9″.

Locality and Period
Probably Pittsburgh. 1856–1902.

Comment
David Hostetter and George Smith manufactured one of the most
popular bitters ever concocted in America. They began
operations in New England in the 1850s, near the beginning of
the bitters craze, advertising a remedy that was nearly 50
percent alcohol. The highly successful team even convinced the
United States government that their tonic was a necessary
stimulant for soldiers to use before battle. During the Civil War,
the Union Army is said to have consumed carloads of the stuff
during every campaign. Ironically, Hostetter died in 1888 of a
liver ailment. By then he was a wealthy man.

Hints for Collectors
Of all bitters bottles, Hostetter's is among the easiest to find
today. Examples with their labels still intact, like the bottle
shown here, are especially interesting.

72 L.Q.C. Wishart's Pine Tree Cordial bottle

Description
Rectangular bottle with flat shoulders and medium-length neck. Flat collar. 1 side has inscription "L.Q.C. WISHART'S"; 1 has pine tree with "PATENT" above and "1859" below; 1 has "PINE TREE/TAR CORDIAL/PHILᴬ"; 4th side with handwritten paper label. Circular depression on square base; no pontil mark. Colors: transparent amber, light and dark green, and yellow-, olive-, and blue-green. Cork stopper with wax on top.

Variations
May have pine tree on 4th side with "TRADE" above and "MARK" below; may have pine tree and "PATENT/1859" on 2 sides; may have "PINE/TREE/CORDIAL/PHILᴬ." Most lack label.

Type and Dimensions
Blown in full-size multipiece mold for pattern and shape. Neck finished; collar applied. Height: 8¼".

Locality and Period
Lancaster Glass Works, Lancaster, New York, and Whitney Brothers Glass Company, Glassboro, New Jersey. Possibly other New York, New Jersey, and Pennsylvania firms. 1859–c. 1880.

Comment
Lucius Q.C. Wishart was a grocer in Philadelphia until he developed the Pine Tree Cordial formula that marked his entry into the field of patent medicines in the late 1850s. Since the trademark was patented in 1873, all bottles with the pine tree and the words "TRADE/MARK" date from after that year.

Hints for Collectors
Wishart's Cordial bottles come in several sizes (about 11, 16, and 25 ounces), colors, and designs and would make an attractive small collection in themselves.

Early medicine bottles

Description
Rectangular bottle with sloping shoulders or cylindrical bottle with flat shoulders. Short neck. Flat collar or flanged lip. Front has paper label printed "DR. STAFFORD'S VEGETABLE COMPOSITION." or "DR. BEACH'S VEGETABLE COMPOSITION," with directions for use below. Pontil mark on rectangular or circular base. Colors: transparent aquamarine, light green, and colorless. Cork stopper with wax on top.

Variations
Shape may be square.

Type and Dimensions
Left: blown in full-size multipiece mold for pattern and shape. Neck finished; collar applied. Height: 5". Right: blown in dip mold, then expanded and tooled into shape after removal from mold. Height: 4¼".

Locality and Period
Canada Glass Works, Como, Quebec, and St. John's Glass Works, St. John's, Quebec. c. 1850–56. Similar bottles from the East and Midwest. c. 1830–60.

Comment
The bottles shown here predate the era of mass-produced medicine bottles. C.W. Harris of Manchester, Quebec, prepared the powders for both Dr. Stafford and Dr. Beach. Since Harris was in business for a short period, the bottles can be dated. The glassworks are also known because only 2 operated in Quebec at that time. Similar bottles were made in the United States.

Hints for Collectors
Early bottles with the original labels and contents are much rarer than the later mass-produced patent medicine bottles, yet they are generally overlooked by collectors.

Hood's Sarsaparilla bottle

Description
Rectangular bottle with rounded shoulders and short neck.
Rounded collar. 1 side has inscription "HOOD'S/COMPOUND/
EXTRACT/SARSA/PARILLA"; 1 has "C I HOOD & CO"; 1 has "LOWELL
MASS"; 4th side blank. Rectangular base without pontil mark.
Colors: transparent aquamarine; very rarely purple.

Variations
8 or 9 varieties of Hood's bottle; some lack "COMPOUND/EXTRACT";
others have minor differences in placement of letters; 4th side
may have "APOTHECARIES." Other brands include "SAND'S,"
"BROWN'S," and "DANA'S"; neck length varies slightly according to
brand.

Type and Dimensions
Blown in full-size multipiece mold for pattern and shape. Neck
finished; collar applied. Height: 8¾".

Locality and Period
Probably the East. 1876–1912. Variants c. 1870–1920.

Comment
In the early 19th century, sarsaparilla was a popular patent
medicine derived from roots and herbs, primarily sassafras, and
hence considered a natural tonic. Its popularity grew markedly
between 1850 and 1880, when the compound was mixed with
alcohol, and at least 100 varieties appeared on the market. After
passage of the Pure Food and Drug Act of 1907, the alcohol was
removed, and sarsaparilla evolved into a soft drink.

Hints for Collectors
Blown examples like the one shown here are earlier than
machine-blown bottles, which have mold marks from base to lip.
Hood's Sarsaparilla bottles are still readily available.

Dr. Kilmer's Swamp Root Cure bottle

Description
Rectangular bottle with rounded shoulders and short neck.
Rounded collar. 1 side has inscription "THE GREAT" above kidney-
shaped frame with "DR./KILMER'S/SWAMP–ROOT/KIDNEY/LIVER&/
BLADDER/CURE" and "SPECIFIC" below; others blank. Rectangular
base without pontil mark. Color: transparent aquamarine.

Variations
Inscriptions of other firms or brands.

Type and Dimensions
Blown in full-size multipiece mold for pattern and shape. Neck
finished; collar applied. Height: 8″.

Locality and Period
Probably New Jersey. c. 1880–1910.

Comment
Although Dr. S.A. Kilmer of Binghamton, New York, developed
the original Swamp Root Cure, it was his nephew Willis S.
Kilmer who built the family fortune through clever marketing of
the product in liquid, pill, and powder forms. At the time,
upstate New York was a fertile area for patent medicines: H.H.
Warner and Asa Soule had large companies in Rochester; Kilmer
and S.T. Drake manufactured their products in Binghamton; and
several other vendors operated out of Lockport, near Buffalo,
including the famous seven Sutherland sisters, who marketed a
hair-growing tonic.

Hints for Collectors
Dr. Kilmer's bottles were made in tremendous quantities and are
easy to find today. Many antique bottles are found at dumps or
by digging at old outhouse or rubble heap sites. Some may need
a thorough scrubbing, but avoid harsh cleansers that will scratch
the surface of the glass.

Description
Left: flattened rectangular bottle with rounded shoulders and medium-length neck. Flat collar. Front has inscription "TRICOPHEROUS/FOR THE SKIN/AND HAIR"; reverse side has "DIRECTIONS/*IN THE*/PAMPHLET"; 1 edge has "BARRY'S" and other has "NEW YORK." Rectangular base without pontil mark. Center: octagonal bottle with flat shoulders and medium-length neck. Rounded collar. 1 side has "W.T.BAIRD"; others blank. Pontil mark on octagonal base. Right: equal-sided rectangular bottle with flat shoulders and medium-length neck. Flanged lip. "D.EVANS/CAMOMILE/PILLS," 1 word per 3 sides; 4th side blank. Square base without pontil mark. Colors: transparent aquamarine and colorless.

Variations
Neck length and lip treatment vary. Inscriptions may be of other firms or brands.

Type and Dimensions
Blown in full-size multipiece mold for pattern and shape. Neck and lip finished; collar applied. Left height: 6¼". Center height: 5½". Right height: 3½".

Locality and Period
The East and Midwest. c. 1860–95.

Comment
The 3 bottles illustrated here are the standard shapes for mass-produced medicine bottles from the second half of the 19th century. The bottle with the pontil mark is probably the earliest of the 3, while the flattened one is the most common.

Hints for Collectors
Both bottles without pontil marks were made using the snap tool, which leaves no mark and was introduced in the 1850s.

G.W. Merchant bottles

Description
Flattened rectangular bottle with flat shoulders and medium-length or long neck. Flat collar. Left: front has inscription "G.W. MERCHANT/CHEMIST" with edge inscriptions "FROM THE LABORATORY OF" and "LOCKPORT, N.Y." Right: front has inscription "G.W.MERCHANT/LOCKPORT/N.Y." Other sides blank. Pontil mark on each rectangular base slightly pushed into body. Colors: transparent aquamarine and light and dark green.

Variations
Inscriptions may be "FROM THE/LABORATORY/OF G.W.MERCHANT/CHEMIST" and/or "GARGLING OIL/LOCKPORT, N.Y."

Type and Dimensions
Blown in full-size multipiece mold for pattern and shape. Neck finished; collar applied. Left height: 5½". Right height: 5".

Locality and Period
Lockport Glass Works, Lockport, New York. 1843–c. 1870.

Comment
The glassworks in Lockport was started in 1843 and operated under a variety of owners until the end of the 19th century. Among its best local customers was the chemist Dr. George W. Merchant, who in 1833 began to make the medicine soon known all over the country as Lockport Gargling Oil. The bottles came in 4 sizes, ranging from 4 to 10 ounces, and the formula was 44 percent alcohol with 1 grain of opium per fluid ounce. The paper labels recommended it as an invaluable remedy for "Horses, Cattle and Human Flesh."

Hints for Collectors
Because Merchant bottles are not as common as Hostetter's Bitters bottles, they often sell for 3 times the price.

Master ink bottle

Description
Hexagonal bottle with sloping shoulders and short neck. Flat collar and narrow neck ring. Same design on each side: quatrefoil in circle inside large Gothic arch. Panels around base have inscription "CA/RT/ER." Hexagonal base without pontil mark. Color: transparent dark blue.

Variations
Shape may be cylindrical or rectangular. May lack arches and have inscription of other ink manufacturer: "HARRISON'S COLUMBIAN INK"; "S.S.STAFFORD'S"; "J.M.BUTLER"; or "E.WATERS, TROY." May have pontil mark. Variants in light blue and aquamarine.

Type and Dimensions
Blown in automatic bottle-blowing machine for pattern and shape. Height: 8″.

Locality and Period
New England. c. 1900–20. Variants from the East and Midwest. c. 1850–90. Throughout the United States. c. 1890–1920.

Comment
Collectors call bulk ink containers like the one shown here master inks to distinguish them from the smaller, wide-based bottles used on the desk. The hexagonal shape of Carter's ink bottles was so distinctive that the label "CARTER'S/RYTO/PERMANENT/BLUE-BLACK/INK" was scarcely necessary. Master inks from other companies have plainer shapes.

Hints for Collectors
Ranging from a half-pint to a gallon, master inks larger than a quart are extremely rare. Although the bottle shown was machine-made, earlier bottles were mold-blown and finished by hand. These earlier examples are more valuable.

Cathedral pickle bottles

Description
Rectangular bottle with sloping shoulders and wide, short neck.
Flanged lip and rounded neck ring. Each side has ornate Gothic
arch. Square base with or without pontil mark. Colors:
transparent green and aquamarine; rarely transparent dark
amber.

Variations
Bottle may have 6 or 8 sides. Gothic arch design varies and may
extend only over lower part of bottle.

Type and Dimensions
Blown in full-size multipiece mold for pattern and shape. Neck
and lip finished. Left height: 12″. Center height: 11″. Right
height: 9½″.

Locality and Period
The East and Pittsburgh area. c. 1840–80.

Comment
Although pickles were undoubtedly sold commercially in jars or
bottles before 1840, it is not clear what the earliest pickle jars
looked like. Collectors call wide-mouthed pickle bottles with the
Gothic arch design cathedral pickle jars. These became popular
around the mid-19th century before the use of simpler cylindrical
or rectangular bottles. They were made in a wide variety of
patterns and sizes in basically the same shape but in a limited
color range. None are signed, so that it is generally impossible to
make definite factory attributions. In 1847, however, the
Coventry Glass Works in Coventry, Connecticut, advertised
pickle jars in quart and half-gallon sizes, and fragments have
been found at several New Jersey sites.

Hints for Collectors
Complex designs, like the ones shown, are especially desirable.

Doyle's Hop Bitters bottle

Description
Rectangular bottle with angled shoulders and short neck. Flat
collar. Design of hop berries and leaves in rectangular panel on 2
sides. Front panel has paper label with hop berries design and
"HOP/BITTERS" printed at top and "HOP BITTERS/Manufacturing Co/
ROCHESTER, N.Y." at bottom. Inscriptions on 4 shoulder panels:
"DOYLE'S" on panel above label and single word "HOP," "BITTERS,"
and "1872" on each of 3 others. Square base without pontil mark.
Colors: transparent light to dark amber; rarely green.

Variations
Placement of hop berries and size of inscriptions vary. May have
"DR SOULE," with or without "S" reversed, in place of "DOYLE'S."

Type and Dimensions
Blown in full-size multipiece mold for pattern and shape. Neck
finished; collar applied. Height: 9½".

Locality and Period
New York or western Pennsylvania. 1872–c. 1900.

Comment
This brand of bitters was patented in 1872 by J.D. Doyle of
Rochester, New York. He marketed his own product and also
sold the rights to Asa Soule, another self-taught pharmacist, who
advertised the same formula in a nearly identical bottle. The
bottles were probably purchased from many factories.

Hints for Collectors
Few examples of this common bottle type retain their original
paper labels. If you are lucky enough to find a labeled bottle,
store it in a dry place and, above all, do not wash it. The variant
with the backwards "S" in Soule is an interesting find.

81 Shoe blacking bottle

Description
Rectangular bottle with rounded shoulders and wide, short neck.
Plain lip. Plain sides, each with paper label: front label has
"EXTRA FINE/JAPAN SPONGE/BLACKING,/Water Proof./Manufactured
by THOMAS HOLLIS,/Druggist & Chemist,/No. 30, Union street,/
BOSTON."; other 3 sides have slightly different wording and
include directions for use. Pontil mark on square base. Color:
transparent dark olive-green.

Variations
Shape may be cylindrical or multisided. May have paper labels of
other firms or brands; may lack label.

Type and Dimensions
Blown in full-size multipiece mold for shape. Neck and lip
finished. Height: 4½".

Locality and Period
The East; probably New Jersey and Pennsylvania. c. 1800–50.

Comment
In the early 19th century, members of the upper class were
considered unkempt if their boots were not properly black and
shiny. This was, to some extent, a heritage from the military.
Shoe blacking was sold in cakes in the 18th century, but became
available in liquid form in the early 1800s. A blacking bottle
resembles other small bottles; only the paper label distinguishes
its former contents.

Hints for Collectors
Blacking bottles are collected mainly by those who seek out early
blown bottles for their age rather than their beauty. The ones
with paper labels are usually the most popular.

Description
Flattened oblong bottle with sloping shoulders and medium-length neck. Folded lip. Front has Indian wearing feathered headdress and facing left, with inscription "INDIAN/CLEMENS TONIC/PREPARED BY/GEO. W. HOUSE" arranged around him. Other side blank. Pontil mark on oval base. Color: transparent aquamarine.

Variations
Similar bottles with Indian have inscription "Dr. Morgridge's VEGETABLE/FAMILY/MEDICINES" or "JACKSONS ABORIGINAL/AMERICAN MEDICINES/J.P.GOLDBOROUGH SOLE PROPRIETOR."

Type and Dimensions
Blown in full-size multipiece mold for pattern and shape. Neck and lip finished. Height: 5¾".

Locality and Period
Probably Pittsburgh area. c. 1845–55.

Comment
Sold at a dollar per bottle, Clemens Indian Tonic was supposed to cure discomfort and fever, with the recommended adult's dosage of a large tablespoonful every hour. In a period when a dollar might represent a laborer's weekly wages, this tonic was expensive. Nevertheless, "Indian" medicines elicited a great following; the Indian symbolized the natural man and herbal cures were deemed the ideal health tonics.

Hints for Collectors
Clemens Indian Tonic bottles are rare. The example illustrated is especially valuable since it is enclosed in its original paper wrapper.

83 J.B. Wheatley's Spanish Pain Destroyer bottle

Description
Cylindrical bottle with rounded shoulders and short neck. Rounded collar. 1 side has inscription "J.B.WHEATLEY'S SPANISH PAIN DESTROYER, DALLASBURGH, KY." Pontil mark on circular base. Color: transparent aquamarine.

Variations
Inscription "J.B.WHEATLEY'S COMPOUND SYRUP DALLASBURGH KY."

Type and Dimensions
Blown in full-size multipiece mold for pattern and shape. Neck finished; collar applied. Height: 5".

Locality and Period
Pittsburgh area. Possibly Louisville, Kentucky. c. 1850–70.

Comment
J.B. Wheatley's Spanish Pain Destroyer was packaged in six-packs, probably for the druggist rather than for home use. Its popularity reflects the lure of supposedly foreign medicines. The tonic was only 50 cents a bottle. Like many other proprietary medicines, the outer paper wrapper makes extravagant miracle claims: "This remedy will cure the Pains and Aches of the Human Family; let them be either internal or external diseases. It will cure Cramp, Cholic, Cholera, Cholera Morbus, Burns, Summer Complaint, Corns, Rheumatism, Sore Throat, Dysentery, Headache, Toothache, and Earache, Chapped or Cracked Hands . . . and many other diseases of Man and Beast."

Hints for Collectors
Because these 6 bottles are still in the original wrapping, they are exceptionally desirable. Even the unwrapped bottles are not easy to find, since not many have survived.

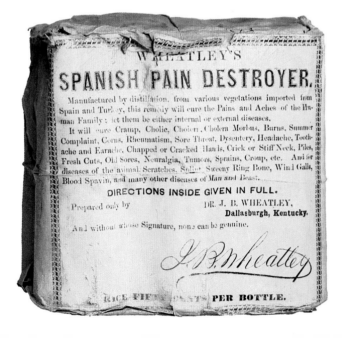

84 Lydia Pinkham's Vegetable Compound bottle

Description
Flattened oblong bottle with sloping shoulders and short neck. Rounded lip. Front has inscription "LYDIA E PINKHAM'S/ VEGETABLE COMPOUND"; reverse side blank. Oval base without pontil mark. Color: transparent aquamarine.

Type and Dimensions
Blown in full-size multipiece mold for pattern and shape. Lip fire-polished before annealing. Height: 7".

Locality and Period
New England. c. 1875–1900. Machine-made c. 1900–20.

Comment
One of the most famous 19th-century patent medicines, Lydia Pinkham's Vegetable Compound is the only widely successful formula invented and marketed by a woman. When her family neared bankruptcy in 1873, Mrs. Pinkham of Lynn, Massachusetts, decided to sell her home remedy for "women's ailments." By the turn of the century, Pinkham's company employed about 450 people to manufacture and bottle the medicine, informally advertised by the slogan, "A baby in every bottle." After about 1900 the bottles were machine-made. Despite her enthusiastic support of the temperance movement, Pinkham saw nothing illogical in the fact that her compound, like many others, was mostly alcohol. She wrote an accompanying pamphlet discussing female medical problems in franker terms than those used by most doctors, and after 20 years the original 4-page flyer had become a hefty booklet.

Hints for Collectors
Collecting the various editions of the pamphlet is a fascinating adjunct to a Pinkham bottle collection.

Warner's safe medicine bottle

Description
Flattened oblong bottle with sloping shoulders and short neck.
Rounded collar. Front has large safe, with inscription "WARNER'S/
SAFE/KIDNEY & LIVER/CURE" above and "ROCHESTER N.Y." below.
Reverse side blank. Oval base without pontil mark. Color:
transparent amber. Cork stopper.

Variations
Inscription may read "WARNER'S SAFE BITTERS"; "WARNER'S SAFE
TONIC BITTERS"; "WARNER'S SAFE LIVER CURE"; "WARNER'S SAFE
DIABETES CURE"; or "WARNER'S NERVINE." On any of these, safe
door may be inscribed "TRADE/MARK."

Type and Dimensions
Blown in full-size multipiece mold for pattern and shape. Neck
finished; collar applied. Height: 9″.

Locality and Period
Probably Pittsburgh area. 1879–c. 1900.

Comment
At one time Hulbert Harrington Warner of Rochester, New
York, sold safes, but in the 1870s he began to produce a line of
proprietary medicines. Warner adopted a safe as his trademark
in 1879, and most of his medicines bear this symbol. An astute
businessman, Warner had offices in Europe and Australia in the
1890s. He built an opulent mansion in Rochester and funded
the city's observatory.

Hints for Collectors
Most Warner bottles are quite easy to collect today. Another of
Warner's products was marketed in a bottle shaped like a log,
but the safe bottles are more common and somewhat less
expensive.

Figural Bottles

Ranging in shape from log cabins and barrels to an ear of corn, a baby, and a pig, figural bottles are one of the most diversified areas of bottle collecting, overlapping many other specialized fields. Here a bottle is valued primarily for its unusual form, and its original contents or use is of secondary importance. The smallest figurals are candy, perfume, and smelling salts bottles, many with capacities of fractions of an ounce, while the largest whiskeys hold up to a gallon. Unlike copies of most other bottles, some figural reproductions are also collected.

Advertising Ploys
During the 19th century, long before federal laws regulated the manufacture of alcohol, locally brewed whiskeys were sold throughout the country. The use of eye-catching bottles became an excellent means of outselling rivals. Not only would the distinctive shape attract customers, but the immediately recognizable form would become identified with the product. By the 1860s and 1870s, the overwhelming success of patent and proprietary medicines, many of which contained as much alcohol as the whiskeys, further intensified the competition, and the variety of bottles multiplied.

Popular Shapes
A uniquely American symbol, the log cabin is one of the oldest figural bottles, dating to William Henry Harrison's presidential campaign against Martin Van Buren in 1840. The design inspired several 19th-century copies and numerous 20th-century reproductions, including a syrup jug and glass bank made in the past 20 years. The barrel is another favorite, used for at least a dozen bitters bottles, as well as a few whiskey and smelling salts bottles and even a fire extinguisher. Some collectors specialize in figures. Among those illustrated are a bust of Grover Cleveland, an Uncle Sam catsup container, and an Indian squaw bitters bottle.

Candy Containers
Made as souvenirs for the Philadelphia Centennial Exposition of 1876, the first known figural candy containers are small bottles in the form of the Liberty Bell and Independence Hall. By the end of the century, other figural candy bottles were being marketed for sale to travelers. Containers shaped like railroad lanterns were sold at railroad stations and on trains, while hotels offered mementos in the form of suitcases or clocks with the name of the hotel embossed or painted on the front. Political candidates wooed voters by distributing hat-shaped candy containers filled with rainbow-colored nuggets. But it was not until the era of the automatic bottle-blowing machine that figural candy containers were mass-produced, and by the 1930s the market was flooded with a tremendous assortment. Many shapes were made expressly for children, such as bottles in the form of dogs, rabbits, hens, horns, whistles, telephones, guns, cars, trains, and airplanes.

Corks and Other Closures
Most of the early toiletry, medicine, and beverage bottles illustrated here were sealed with corks, but some had wire bail closures. The later food containers bore screw-on tin lids. Candy containers with necks or mouths often used cork stoppers or pewter or tin screw-on lids, whereas less bottlelike candy containers may be found with slide-off metal or cardboard closures.

Jacob's Cabin Tonic Bitters bottle

Description
Bottle in form of house with shingled gable roof beveled at ends of ridge. Short neck. Folded-out lip. Front has arched door and 3 windows. Front of roof and 1 side have inscription "JACOB S/CABIN TONIC/BITTERS"; other side has "LABORATORY/PHILADELPHIA." Reverse side including roof blank. Pontil mark on rectangular base slightly pushed into body. Colorless. McKearin Number: GVII–6.

Variations
5 varieties with shingled roof in same shape and size. 1 illustrated. 4 others in light or dark green, or light or dark amber have "E.G.BOOZ'S/OLD CABIN/WHISKEY."

Type and Dimensions
Blown in full-size multipiece mold for pattern and shape. Neck and lip finished. About 1 quart. Height: 7½".

Locality and Period
Probably Whitney Glass Works, Glassboro, New Jersey. c. 1860–70.

Comment
The bottle illustrated is attributed to the Whitney Glass Works because of its striking similarity to the Booz bottle, undoubtedly made there. One of the oldest and largest glasshouses in New Jersey, Whitney was founded in 1813. The plant was purchased by the Owens Bottle Company in 1918 and still operates as part of Owens-Illinois, Inc.

Hints for Collectors
The Jacob's Cabin bottle was reproduced by the Historical Bottle Collectors Guild, a division of Owens-Illinois, using both an original mold and 19th-century blowing techniques. All 792 copies are marked "OI 1974" on the base.

87 Log cabin bottle

Description
Bottle in form of log cabin with gable roof. Short neck. Flanged lip. Horizontal ribs resembling logs around body. Front and reverse sides have door and 2 windows, with cider barrel to right of door and inscription "TIPPECANOE" above. Pontil mark on rectangular base. Color: transparent dark olive-green. McKearin Number: GVII–2.

Variations
2 varieties in same size with loglike ribs. 1 illustrated. 1 has hip roof and "NORTH BEND" on reverse.

Type and Dimensions
Blown in full-size multipiece mold for pattern and shape. Neck and lip finished. About 1 pint. Height: 6″.

Locality and Period
Mt. Vernon Glass Works, Vernon, New York. 1840.

Comment
Made for William Henry Harrison's presidential campaign of 1840 against Martin Van Buren, this log cabin bottle and its variant delivered a subtle message. Harrison was accused of being content to sit in his cabin and drink cider all day, but his supporters turned this criticism to his favor. The cabin stood for his frontiersmanlike ways, while the cider barrel indicated his generosity and American "folk" background. The example illustrated is probably slightly earlier than its variant, since the slogan "Tippecanoe and North Bend" emerged later in the campaign. "Tippecanoe and Tyler too," a better-known slogan from the same campaign, does not appear on any bottle.

Hints for Collectors
Both the Tippecanoe and North Bend log cabin bottles are extremely rare.

88 Booz's Old Cabin Whiskey bottle and adaptation

Description
Bottle in form of house with shingled gable roof beveled at ends of ridge. Short neck. Flat collar. Front has arched door and 3 windows. Front of roof and 1 side have inscription "E.G.BOOZ'S/ OLD CABIN/WHISKEY."; other side of bottle has "120 WALNUT S$^{\underline{T}}$/ PHILADELPHIA"; reverse of roof has "1840." Circular depression on rectangular base; no pontil mark. Authentic color: transparent dark amber. McKearin Number: GVII–4. Wire bail closure.

Variations
5 varieties with shingled roof in same shape and size. 1 illustrated. 1 in light green has beveled roof with 2 periods under "T" in "ST"; 2 in amber, dark amber, or dark green have unbeveled roof, and 1 of these also has 2 periods under "T"; 1 colorless bitters bottle has "JACOB S/CABIN TONIC/BITTERS."

Type and Dimensions
Blown in full-size multipiece mold for pattern and shape. Neck finished; collar applied. About 1 quart. Height: 7¾".

Locality and Period
Whitney Glass Works, Glassboro, New Jersey. 1860–75.

Comment
Edmund G. Booz, importer and dealer in wines and spirits, had a shop on 120 Walnut Street in Philadelphia between 1860 and his death in 1870, which helps to date the bottles accurately. The date on the roof is probably a reference to the age of the whiskey, although similarly shaped bottles were associated with William Henry Harrison's "log cabin and cider barrel" campaign of 1840. Some Booz bottles have a stopper with the inscription "PATENTED/REIS$^{\underline{D}}$/3 JUN. 1871/JAN 5 1875," indicating when the patent was reissued to the Whitney Glass Works.

Authentic bottle

Hints for Collectors

The Booz bottle was reproduced or had its design adapted many times, perhaps because of the easily recognizable shape. The earliest reproduction, made in the 1930s, has an unbeveled roof. There are 2 periods under the "T" in "ST" and no period after the word "WHISKEY" both on the right side of the bottle and on the roof. The base has a diagonal mold seam running from corner to corner. This copy was first made by Clevenger Brothers in New Jersey only in amber glass, but was later produced in a wide variety of colors, including bright blue, purple, and bright green. Clevenger also manufactured a reproduction of the Booz bottle with the beveled roof corners from at least the 1940s to the 1970s. On this copy, more of the corners is cut away than on the original; "1840" is smaller; and there is no period after "WHISKEY" on the right side of the bottle. There are several adaptations of the cabin design, some without inscriptions on the sides. The one shown here, with a paper label on the blank reverse side, has the molded door and windows but no inscriptions on the front. It was probably made in the 1950s.

Adaptation

Drake's Plantation Bitters bottle

Description
Rectangular bottle in form of log cabin with hip roof. Short neck. Flat collar. Horizontal ribs around body; front and reverse sides have blank rectangular panel. Front of roof has inscription "S.T./ DRAKE'S/1860/PLANTATION/X/BITTERS"; reverse has "PATENTED 1862." Square base without pontil mark. Colors: transparent amber, shades of green-amber, and light and dark brown.

Variations
17 varieties. Of these, 8 are Drake's bottles, with minor differences in size and placement of letters. 9 are other brands in similar shapes: "AMERICAN LIFE BITTERS"; "HOLTZERMAN'S BITTERS"; "KELLY'S OLD CABIN BITTERS"; "OLD CABIN BITTERS"; "O.K. PLANTATION BITTERS"; "OLD HOMESTEAD BITTERS"; "DR. PETZOLD'S BITTERS"; "PRAIRIE BITTERS"; and "WOODGATE'S BITTERS."

Type and Dimensions
Blown in full-size multipiece mold for pattern and shape. Neck finished; collar applied. Height: 10″.

Locality and Period
New Jersey and the Midwest. 1862–c. 1890.

Comment
Drake's Plantation Bitters bottles, patented in 1862, are the earliest bottles made in this shape. The blank spaces on the front and reverse of the bottle once held paper labels, but the bottle's distinctive design was intended for easy recognition even by illiterate buyers. Although 9 competing bitters companies copied the log cabin bottle, only Drake used rum in his bitters formula.

Hints for Collectors
Most Drake's bottles are very common, but similar bottles by other companies are rare.

McKeever's Army Bitters bottle

Description
Cylindrical bottle in form of military drum with pyramid of
cannonballs on top. Medium-length neck with neck ring. Flat
collar. Inscription "McKEEVER'S ARMY BITTERS" around body.
Circular depression on circular base; no pontil mark. Color:
transparent reddish-amber.

Type and Dimensions
Blown in full-size multipiece mold for pattern and shape. Neck
finished; collar applied. Height: 10½".

Locality and Period
The East or Midwest. c. 1860–70.

Comment
McKeever's Army Bitters is not nearly as common as other
bitters preparations such as Doyle's Hop Bitters, but the bottle
is much more interesting. The Civil War probably motivated
bottlemakers to produce designs such as the drum and
cannonballs pictured here and a cannon-barrel shape for whiskey.
When the government introduced sales taxes at about the same
time, the bitters business was given an unexpected boost: Bitters
and other medicinal products were taxed at a much lower rate
than alcoholic beverages, even though most bitters contained at
least as much alcohol as many whiskeys.

Hints for Collectors
The McKeever's Army Bitters bottle is relatively rare, probably
because it was made for only a short period around the time of
the Civil War. After that, it is likely that the manufacturers
found a less warlike bottle design easier to sell.

Description
Flattened barrel-shaped bottle with flat shoulders. Medium-length neck. Flat collar. Overall design of hoops and staves. Front (left) has rectangular panel with profiles of Cleveland and Stevenson; inscription "OUR CHOICE" above and "CLEVE&STEVE/ NOVEMBER 8TH 92/MARCH 4TH 93" below. Reverse side (right) has small rooster facing right. Circular depression on oblong base; no pontil mark. Colors: (left) transparent aquamarine and colorless; (right) transparent amber and very light purple. McKearin Numbers: GI–123a (front); GI–124 (reverse).

Variations
3 varieties. 2 illustrated; reverse of front shown has rooster facing left. 1 oblong variant has Cleveland on front and blank reverse side; pint.

Type and Dimensions
Blown in full-size multipiece mold for pattern and shape. Neck finished; collar applied. Left: pint. Height: 7″. Right: half-pint. Height: 5¾″.

Locality and Period
The East or Midwest. 1892.

Comment
The flasks illustrated here were made as campaign souvenirs for the 1892 presidential election, when Grover Cleveland and Adlai Stevenson, grandfather of the 1952 candidate, ran on the Democratic ticket and won. During that period the presidential term started in March; this explains the second date on the flask.

Hints for Collectors
It has been suggested that the half-pint flask may have been for cologne rather than spirits, but this is unlikely.

Basket-weave and barrel-shaped smelling salts bottles

Description
Globe- or barrel-shaped bottle. Medium-length or short neck.
Folded-in lip. Basket-weave pattern with blank oval on 1 side
(left) or sketchy barrel hoop-and-stave design (right). Circular
base with or without pontil mark. Colors: transparent light
aquamarine, light green, and colorless.

Variations
Basket-weave variants may be more cylindrical; may have ear-
shaped handle; may have plain lip.

Type and Dimensions
Blown in full-size multipiece mold for pattern and shape. Neck
and lip finished. Height: about 3″.

Locality and Period
The East; probably New England south to southern New Jersey.
c. 1830–70.

Comment
Small basket-weave bottles, ranging from an ounce to a half-pint,
were probably formed in imitation of the larger wicker-covered
demijohns and carboys. Most had a paper label that identified the
contents—hair oil, smelling salts, cologne, or another toiletry.
Several glass factories in southern New Jersey, including
Solomon Stanger's Glass Works and Williamstown Glass Works,
manufactured barrel-shaped cologne bottles, as did the nearby
Dyottville Glass Works in Philadelphia. In Massachusetts the
Boston & Sandwich Glass Company, Thomas Cains's Phoenix
Glass Works, and New England Glass Company may also have
produced barrel-shaped colognes.

Hints for Collectors
Cologne bottles in simple shapes are easier to find than the
fancier figural colognes.

93 Bourbon whiskey bitters bottle

Description
Barrel-shaped bottle with flat shoulders. Short neck. Flanged lip. Horizontal ribs around upper and lower body. Unpatterned area in between ribs with inscription "BOURBON WHISKEY/BITTERS" on 1 side and blank on other. Circular base without pontil mark. Colors: transparent light and dark amber.

Variations
Other inscriptions are "OLD SACHEM/BITTERS/AND/WIGWAM TONIC"; "GREELEY'S BOURBON BITTERS"; "GREELEY'S BOURBON WHISKEY BITTERS"; "HIGHLAND BITTERS/AND/SCOTCH TONIC"; "KEYSTONE BITTERS"; "ORIGINAL/POCAHONTAS/BITTERS/W. FERGUSON"; "HALL'S BITTERS. E.E.HALL, NEW HAVEN"; or "SMITH'S DRUID BITTERS."

Type and Dimensions
Blown in full-size multipiece mold for pattern and shape. Neck and lip finished. Height: 9¼".

Locality and Period
New England or New Jersey. c. 1880–95. Most variants c. 1873–90.

Comment
An extremely popular design, the barrel-shaped bottle originated in the 1860s. Most of the bitters bottles listed here were made between 1873 and 1890, except for Keystone Bitters, produced as late as 1908. All were made in a great variety of colors, including aquamarine, light green, and brownish-pink, which collectors call puce. The bottle illustrated may have contained Greeley's Bitters since others like it have been found with a Greeley's paper label.

Hints for Collectors
Amber and aquamarine are the most common colors for barrel-shaped bottles. The Pocahontas Bitters is the hardest to find.

Bourbon whiskey bottle

Description
Barrel-shaped bottle with flat shoulders. Short neck. Rounded
collar. Horizontal ribs around both upper and lower body.
Unpatterned area in between with inscription "OLD KENTUCKY/
1849/RESERVE/BOURBON" around circle on 1 side; "DISTILLED IN 1849"
around shoulder; and "A.M.BININGER & CO. 19 BROAD ST. NY." near
base. Circular base without pontil mark. Colors: transparent
light and dark brown and amber.

Variations
Number and placement of ribs vary. Inscription may be name of
another whiskey distiller. May have pontil mark.

Type and Dimensions
Blown in full-size multipiece mold for pattern and shape. Neck
finished; collar applied. Height: 9⅝".

Locality and Period
The East; probably New Jersey. 1861–64.

Comment
A.M. Bininger, the New York City retailer who commissioned
the bottle shown here, sometimes had inventively shaped bottles
made to order. Bininger's name appears on several unusual
designs, including a cannon-shaped bottle for Great Gun Gin, a
handled bottle for Day Dream Whiskey, and a circular clock-
shaped bottle inscribed "REGULATOR." Bininger also advertised
Wine Bitters and Knickerbocker Wine Bitters, although bottles
for these have not been identified.

Hints for Collectors
Many whiskey bottles have a date molded into the side, which
often misleads beginning collectors. The date refers to the
purported age of the whiskey, not to the year the bottle was
made and the whiskey bottled.

Description
Triangular, pear-shaped bottle with rounded front surface. Short neck. Plain lip. Front has quilted pattern and horseshoe-shaped panel with inscription "PERFECTION HAND GRENADE" around edge, and "PAT D/BY/A JONES/1885" in center; other 2 sides are blank. Triangular base without pontil mark. Colors: transparent amber and colorless.

Variations
Bottle may be barrel- or globe-shaped; either shape may have diamond pattern, vertical ribs, floral design, or plain front. Inscription may be "HARDEN'S HAND FIRE EXTINGUISHER" or "HNS." Variants also transparent blue and green and possibly opaque white. May have metal cap.

Type and Dimensions
Blown in full-size multipiece mold for pattern and shape, neck and lip finished; or blown in automatic bottle-blowing machine for pattern and shape. Height: 8″.

Locality and Period
Throughout the United States. 1871–c. 1910. Variants from Hayward Company, New York City, and Harden Hand Fire Extinguisher Company, Chicago.

Comment
Fire grenades contained carbon tetrachloride. When thrown at a fire, the bottle broke and produced a fire-extinguishing foam. The first device of this kind was patented in 1871 by the Harden Company. This firm and the Hayward Company made the majority of glass fire grenades.

Hints for Collectors
Because these bottles were meant to be broken, few survive today. Those remaining are often intact with cap and contents.

Description
Bottle in form of heart set on rectangular base. Medium-length neck. Rounded collar. Both edges have inscription "JOHN HART & CO." No pontil mark. Color: transparent reddish-amber.

Variations
May lack inscription and be several inches shorter.

Type and Dimensions
Blown in full-size multipiece mold for pattern and shape. Neck finished; collar applied. Height: 7".

Locality and Period
Glasshouse unknown; the East or Midwest. c. 1870–1900.

Comment
The heart-shaped bottle shown here is the only figural design to be found among bottles for hair preparations. It contained Hart's Hair Restorer for ladies. All kinds of hair lotions were popular at the time, since most women had long hair. After a girl reached 16 or 18 she was expected to put her hair up, either in the pompadour or some related style, and for these styles, the more hair the better. Ladies with less than luxuriant tresses used puffs of cotton or hair, called rats, to fill out their hairdos while they waited for Hall's Hair Restorer or Ayer's Hair Vigor to do its work. Gentlemen were also encouraged to take care of their hair, although in their case color not abundance seems to have been most important; a number of hair dyes were marketed exclusively for men.

Hints for Collectors
The Hart bottle appeals both to collectors of figural bottles and to collectors of cosmetics containers.

Description
Cylindrical bottle in form of cannon barrel. Short neck. Rounded collar. 1 side has inscription "J.T.GAYEN/ALTONA" (left) or "BUCHANAN'S/EXTRACT/OF SUGAR CORN" (right). Circular base without pontil mark. Colors: shades of transparent amber and brown.

Variations
Inscription may be "GENL SCOTTS/NEW YORK/ARTILLERY BITTERS" or "A.M.BININGER & CO/19 BROAD ST/N.Y."

Type and Dimensions
Blown in full-size multipiece mold for pattern and shape. Neck finished; collar applied. Left height: 14". Right height: 8¾".

Locality and Period
The East. c. 1855–70.

Comment
Although the source of the 2 bottles illustrated is unknown, both were almost certainly made during the Civil War, when cannon-shaped bottles were very popular. The bottle produced by the Bininger company was used for Great Gun Gin from 1861 to 1864. The General Scott's Bitters bottle was named for Winfield Scott, a hero of the Mexican War and the general in charge of the Union army at the beginning of the Civil War.

Hints for Collectors
The Bininger cannon is fairly scarce, but the General Scott bottle is the rarest of all bitters bottles; only a few examples have been found. The whiskey bottles illustrated are somewhat more available.

Description
Cylindrical bottle in form of ear of corn. Short neck. Flat collar.
1 side has blank oval above rectangular panel with inscription
"NATIONAL/BITTERS"; blank oval with paper label (left) or without
label (right). Circular base has "PATENT 1867" and no pontil mark.
Colors: transparent light to dark amber; sometimes aquamarine
and brownish-pink.

Variations
Base may lack inscription.

Type and Dimensions
Blown in full-size multipiece mold for pattern and shape. Neck
finished; collar applied. Height: 12¾".

Locality and Period
Probably Pittsburgh area. 1867–74.

Comment
National Bitters was produced by John H. Kurtz, who owned a
liquor warehouse in Pittsburgh in the 1860s. In 1869 Kurtz sold
his interest to Henry Schlichter, who moved the business to
Philadelphia. Kurtz bought the business back in 1873, but went
bankrupt the following year. The name National Bitters was
calculated to sound official and sell well; Kurtz had no connection
with the government.

Hints for Collectors
This is an easy bottle to find in amber, but aquamarine is quite
rare. Examples are most likely obtained from a private collector
or dealer who specializes in bitters bottles.

Indian Queen Bitters figural bottle

Description
Bottle in form of woman wearing crown, feathered dress, and leggings, and holding shield. Short neck. Folded-in lip. Shield has inscription "BROWN'S/CELEBRATED/INDIAN HERB BITTERS." Circular base without pontil mark. Colors: shades of transparent brown, amber, and green, and colorless.

Variations
May be marked "PATENTED/FEB 11/1868" at lower back edge of dress, or "PATENTED/1867" in slanting arc on back of figure; "CELEBRATED" may lack "R." 1 variant has shield held up against body with "MOHAWK WHISKEY/PURE/RYE." Another has shield near base with "H.PHARAZYN/PHIL^A/RIGHT SECURED."

Type and Dimensions
Blown in full-size multipiece mold for pattern and shape. Neck and lip finished. Height: 12".

Locality and Period
The East. 1867–c. 1890.

Comment
There was a great deal of interest in "Indian" remedies in the mid-19th century since the Indian medicine men were believed to be good doctors. However, most so-called Indian medicines had nothing to do with Indians, little to do with medicine, and were usually more than half alcohol.

Hints for Collectors
Popularly referred to as Indian Queens, bottles like the one shown here are among the most sought-after bitters bottles. Green and colorless examples are much rarer than brown and amber and are likely to be more expensive. Several Indian Queens are sold yearly at auction houses, but they are also available from flask and bottle dealers.

Flaccus Brothers Catsup figural bottle

Description
Bottle in form of Uncle Sam wearing suit with cutaway coat. Top hat forms short neck with screw thread at bottom. Plain lip. Circular base has inscription "PAT APL'D FOR" and pontil mark. Colorless.

Variations
Cylindrical bottle may have either design of cow's head and "FLACCUS BROS. STEERS HEAD TABLE DELICACIES," or cow's or deer's head design with flowers and no inscription. This shape also transparent amber and green and opaque white.

Type and Dimensions
Blown in full-size multipiece mold for pattern and shape. Neck and lip finished. Height: 9¾".

Locality and Period
Probably West Virginia. 1898–c. 1910.

Comment
E.C. Flaccus was a food broker and manufacturer in Wheeling, West Virginia. Although Flaccus Brothers was first listed in the Wheeling directories in 1892, its trademark application indicates that it had been in business since 1880. After 1892 the company split into 2 independent operations, E.C. Flaccus and Flaccus Brothers. Most Flaccus containers are wide-mouthed jars with either a glass stopper or a glass screw-on lid; they contained such condiments as mustard and pickles as well as fruit. The design of the figural bottle illustrated was registered in 1898.

Hints for Collectors
All Flaccus containers are popular, but the Uncle Sam bottle is particularly prized because it is the only figural. It can be found at a bottle show and sale or from private collectors.

Poland Spring Water figural bottle

Description
Bottle in form of old man holding rod and sitting on barrel. Short neck. Flat collar. Front has inscription "Poland/ water" vertically near base. Reverse side has "H.RICKER & SONS PROPRIETORS" and monogram "PSW" within a circle formed by words "POLAND MINERAL SPRING WATER." Circular base without pontil mark. Colors: colorless; occasionally transparent light aquamarine; rarely amber.

Type and Dimensions
Blown in full-size multipiece mold for pattern and shape. Neck finished; collar applied. Height: 9″.

Locality and Period
New England, New York, and Pennsylvania. c. 1885–1905.

Comment
The water of Poland Springs, Maine, made the town prosperous for at least 40 years, since demand for the water supported a large hotel as well as a bottling business. According to local tradition, the bottles were originally purchased from a glass factory near Hartford, Connecticut. In the 1890s the Union Glass Company of Somerville, Massachusetts, is said to have made the bottles, and in the early 20th century, Cunningham & Company of Pittsburgh supplied them. The design remained the same, however, until the early 20th century, when the figural bottle was discontinued. The figure represents Moses about to strike the rock on Horeb.

Hints for Collectors
This bottle has been reproduced several times in the 20th century. Some but not all have the inscription "FACSIMILE OF THE ORIGINAL" on the reverse side.

Little girl figural cologne bottle

Description
Bottle in form of girl wearing coat and hat and holding a muff.
Short neck. Narrow, flat collar. Circular base without pontil
mark. Colorless.

Variations
Other human figures include court jester, baby, standing man,
and figure labeled "Billikin." Great variety of colors, including
transparent aquamarine, amber, and green; opalescent bluish-
white; and opaque white, blue, and green.

Type and Dimensions
Blown in full-size multipiece mold for pattern and shape. Neck
finished; collar applied. Height: 6⅜".

Locality and Period
The East. c. 1880–1900.

Comment
Figural colognes are not as common as figural whiskey and
bitters bottles, but they are equally popular. The bottle
illustrated has no space for a paper label, but the small size and
feminine appearance suggest that is was meant to contain a
toiletry for ladies.

Hints for Collectors
Bottles like this were usually lovingly saved, even after they
were empty, and seldom thrown away with the trash. For this
reason they are not likely to be found at dumps as are liquor and
bitters bottles. The best sources are specialized dealers and
other collectors. Advertisements in collectors' magazines will
often provide a lead to a specific bottle.

Golfer figural bottle

Description
Bottle in form of man wearing flat cap, loose shirt, knickers, knee socks, and flat shoes, and holding a putter. Man stands on flat, square base. Short neck. Plain lip. Base has inscription "JOLLY GOLFER" on front and "PATENT APPLIED FOR" underneath. Glass cap fits into neck. Colors: frosted dark blue and green.

Variations
Other male figures include coachman in greatcoat and top hat, prizefighter, and representation of W.C. Fields.

Type and Dimensions
Bottle blown in automatic bottle-blowing machine for pattern and shape. Cap pressed. Acid-treated for frosted finish after annealing. Height: 11½″.

Locality and Period
Glasshouse unknown; the United States. c. 1915–35.

Comment
The former contents of the bottle illustrated are a matter of conjecture, since there is neither a label nor inscription. Probably the bottle contained Scotch: The golfer is clearly Scottish, with his tam and tartan socks, and golf had its origins in Scotland.

Hints for Collectors
Unlike other fields of bottle collecting in which age and country of origin are important, many figural bottle collectors are more interested in design. For this reason, European and American examples are deemed equally collectible. Some machine-made figurals are also prized, particularly those in unusual intense colors, such as the bottle shown here.

Washington figural bottle reproduction

Description
Bottle in form of upper torso of Washington in uniform on circular base. Short neck. Flat collar. Flat circle on front. Pontil mark on base. Authentic colors: transparent aquamarine and light and dark amber. Reproduction colors: transparent blue, colorless, and possibly others.

Variations
Reproduction may have faint inscription "SIMONS CENTENNIAL BITTERS" on front and "TRADE MARK" on reverse side. Authentic bottle has same inscription.

Type and Dimensions
Blown in full-size multipiece mold for pattern and shape. Neck finished; collar applied. Height: 9⅞".

Locality and Period
Glasshouse unknown; the United States. c. 1950–70.

Comment
The original Washington bust bottle on which this copy is based was made in 1876 for Simon's Centennial Bitters, and is the earliest figural bottle that can be reliably dated. Although advanced collectors prefer authentic figurals, 20th-century reproductions appeal to beginners because they are more available and considerably less expensive.

Hints for Collectors
To distinguish a genuine old bottle from a reproduction, check the color carefully: Authentic bottles were never made in the blue illustrated. Some reproductions and all authentic bottles have an inscription, but only on authentic examples are the letters clearly molded. The authentic bottles were made in the size of the reproduction pictured here; copies also come in smaller sizes.

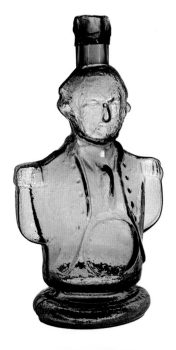

Description
Bottle in form of bust of Cleveland on circular pedestal base. Short neck. Flanged lip. Base has inscription "CLEVELAND" on front and no pontil mark underneath. Frosted colorless bust; neck and base clear.

Variations
Similar busts include Garibaldi, the Italian patriot (1807–82); Victor Hugo, the French novelist (1802–85); Charles Parnell, the Irish statesman (1846–91); and Daniel Webster, the American statesman (1782–1852). May have faint pontil mark.

Type and Dimensions
Blown in full-size multipiece mold for pattern and shape. Neck and lip finished. Acid-treated for frosted finish after annealing. Height: 9¾".

Locality and Period
Glasshouse unknown; the United States. 1884–92.

Comment
Grover Cleveland is the only American president to have served 2 nonconsecutive terms. President from 1885 to 1889, he lost the 1888 election to Benjamin Harrison, then ran again in 1892, winning a second term. This bottle was probably made during one of the campaigns. The very similar bottles depicting Garibaldi, Hugo, and Parnell may have been made around the same time, since all died during this period. Even though Webster had been dead for some time, the Webster bottle is probably also contemporary.

Hints for Collectors
The Grover Cleveland bottle is somewhat easier to find than the others. Since Cleveland was a popular American president, it is likely that more were made.

Crying baby figural bottle

Description
Bottle in form of baby's head and shoulders on circular base.
Short neck. Narrow, flat collar. Base has inscription "T.P.S.&CO"
and no pontil mark. Colors: transparent aquamarine and
colorless.

Variations
Base may lack initials, or may have initials with either "JUNE 9 '74"
or "JUNE 2 '74." Bottle may be painted.

Type and Dimensions
Blown in full-size multipiece mold for pattern and shape. Neck
finished; collar applied. Height: 6⁵⁄₁₆″.

Locality and Period
Probably New York or New Jersey. 1874–c. 1885.

Comment
Popularly called the Crying Baby Bottle, this design was
patented by Thomas P. Spencer of New York City on June 9,
1874. Patent specifications indicate that the bottle was intended
for "perfumery," but there is no logical space for a paper label
and no molded inscription naming the contents. It may have
contained syrup or some other medicine for children.

Hints for Collectors
Some examples are painted. If any paint remains, it is wise to
leave it alone even if incomplete; the closer a bottle is to its
original state, the better most collectors like it. Some bottles
have the incorrect date of June 2. These are just as common as
bottles with the correct date; both are of equal value.

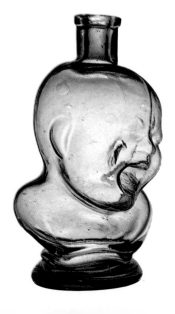

Elephant figural cologne bottle

Description
Bottle in form of elephant on rectangular platform base. Long, ornate neck. Flanged lip. Design of saddlecloth and howdah on back; trunk curled over basket of flowers. Vertical ribs on 3 sides of platform; pontil mark on base. Colors: transparent aquamarine and colorless.

Variations
Bottle may be in form of monument, shell, column, fountain, or building with seated Buddha, standing Indian, or other figure between columns. These bottles are in opaque white and opaque or transparent blue.

Type and Dimensions
Blown in full-size multipiece mold for pattern and shape. Neck and lip finished. Height: 4¾".

Locality and Period
Probably Massachusetts or New Jersey. Possibly France or Bohemia. c. 1840–60. Variants c. 1830–60.

Comment
A number of figural cologne and smelling salts bottles were made in the mid-19th century. Two bottles in the shape of the Pantheon in Paris and another in the shape of a Parisian fountain were probably imported to this country from France since French perfumes were already greatly favored here. The other figural bottles could be either American or European; all have similar figures, scrolls, and flowers.

Hints for Collectors
Figural cologne bottles in exotic shapes with ornate patterns are especially popular with collectors and therefore hard to find. Bright blue ones are the most expensive.

Description
Bottle in form of fish. Medium-length neck protrudes from open mouth. Flat collar. Belly has flat oval for label. Circular base without pontil mark. Authentic colors: transparent amber; rarely colorless, sometimes with purple tint, and yellow-green; very rarely blue. Adaptation colors: colorless; also green, pink, and other transparent colors not originally made.

Variations
Authentic bottles have inscription around each eye: "W.H.WARE PAT 1866" on 1 side and either "THE FISH BITTERS" or "DOCTOR FISCH'S BITTERS" on other. May have "PAT 1866" on base.

Type and Dimensions
Blown in full-size multipiece mold for pattern and shape. Neck finished; collar applied. Height: 14".

Locality and Period
Probably Europe. c. 1930–50. Authentic bottles from New York or New Jersey. 1866–c. 1900.

Comment
The design of a fish-shaped bottle for bitters was patented by W.H. Ware of Philadelphia on December 4, 1866. All Ware Bitters bottles are marked and most are amber. Ever since Ware, the fish-shaped bottle has been copied by many firms.

Hints for Collectors
This 20th-century adaptation was probably blown in Italy or France to be sold in gift stores. The pharmaceutical firm Eli Lilly & Company used a machine-made copy of Ware's design without the inscription for its cod-liver oil from 1922 to 1933. Made by the Mount Glass Works of Indianapolis, these bottles came in 3, 6¼, and 10" sizes.

Oyster figural bottle

Description
Bottle in form of oyster shell. Short neck with screw threads. No base or pontil mark. Colorless. Metal screw-on cap.

Variations
May be painted in natural colors of the oyster shell. May be in form of clam or scallop.

Type and Dimensions
Blown in full-size multipiece mold for pattern and shape. Height: 5¼″.

Locality and Period
Probably the East. 1891–c. 1910.

Comment
The oyster bottle design was patented by William T. Murphy of New York City on January 6, 1891. All of the bottles were supposed to be painted to resemble oysters. Murphy also patented a clam-shaped bottle on December 27, 1892. Although a patent has not been found for the similar scallop-shell bottle, it is probably also one of Murphy's designs. The original contents of these bottles is a mystery. It is unlikely that they contained perfume, since shellfish are not usually associated with pleasant odors. Possibly the bottles held liquor or a sauce for fish.

Hints for Collectors
All of the shell bottles are common, although 19th-century examples are scarcer than those made in the early 20th century. Collectors of figural bottles usually start with the easily obtainable 1940s and 1950s bottles and work back to the earlier, rarer ones.

Baby-in-a-basket figural bottle

Description
Bottle in form of baby lying in oval basket made of leaves. Short neck. Narrow, flat collar. Flat base without pontil mark. Colorless.

Variations
Bottle may be in form of crying child or child's head.

Type and Dimensions
Blown in full-size multipiece mold for pattern and shape. Neck finished; collar applied. Height: 4⅝″.

Locality and Period
The East. c. 1870–90.

Comment
The maker of this interesting bottle has never been identified, since the design was not patented and the bottle lacks an inscription. Probably the bottle contained some infant-related product, perhaps a soothing syrup for crying babies. Yet the small size also suggests that the bottle could have been intended for a lady's dressing table and may have contained hair oil or perfume. Since there is no place for a paper label bearing the name of the product, consumers must have recognized it through newspaper advertising and word of mouth. Collectors call the figure illustrated Moses in the Bulrushes or Baby in a Cabbage Leaf.

Hints for Collectors
One of the most popular figural bottles, examples like this one are becoming increasingly hard to find. For many collectors, the chase is part of the fun, and they enjoy searching out rarities.

Pig figural bottle

Description
Bottle in form of pig with feet folded underneath body. Short
neck forms tail. Rounded collar. 1 side has inscription "SUFFOLK
BITTERS"; 1 has "PHILBROOK & TUCKER/BOSTON." No base or pontil
mark. Color: transparent amber.

Variations
Inscription "BERKSHIRE BITTERS/A MANN & CO/CINCINNATI, O." or
"SOMETHING GOOD/IN A HOG'S."

Type and Dimensions
Blown in full-size multipiece mold for pattern and shape. Neck
finished; collar applied. Length: 10″.

Locality and Period
Probably New Jersey. c. 1860–80. Variants possibly from the
Midwest: Berkshire Bitters 1873–78; other variant c. 1870–1900.

Comment
The pig figural bottle appeals to collectors of both bitters and
figurals, as well as to any collector who finds a shape like the one
illustrated amusing. Both pig-shaped bitters bottles are fairly
rare, especially the one for Berkshire Bitters, produced for only
5 years. The bottle marked "SOMETHING GOOD/IN A HOG'S" probably
contained whiskey; some whiskey is made from corn, and corn is
used to feed hogs. There is no such connection between bitters
and corn, but bitters manufacturers were always looking for
unusual shapes that could be easily recognized.

Hints for Collectors
Look for this type of figural at auctions, at specialized bottle and
flask shops, or more rarely at collectors' club bottle swap shows.

Bear grease jars

Description
Jar with lid in form of bear sitting on haunches, with paws in front of chest and muzzle on nose. Plain lip. Base has inscription "X BAZIN PHILADA" (left) or "PHALEN & SON N.Y." (right). Lid sits on top of jar. Colors: opaque white; light and dark blue; and dark purple, which may appear black.

Variations
Bear may be plain and lack base inscription; larger bears with chain and no muzzle. Similar jar in form of short, squat man, with large hat for a lid.

Type and Dimensions
Jar and lid pressed in separate molds for pattern and shape. Height: 3⅞″.

Locality and Period
Probably Boston & Sandwich Glass Company, Sandwich, Massachusetts; possibly New England Glass Company, Cambridge, and other New England manufacturers. c. 1850–70.

Comment
Bear-shaped jars like the ones shown here are thought to have contained bear grease, a men's hair preparation popular in the second half of the 19th century. Bazin and Phalen are the names of firms that sold men's and ladies' toiletries. Both must have commissioned similar molds and possibly asked the same factory to make the jars.

Hints for Collectors
These rare jars are much sought after by collectors of New England glass. A similar man-shaped jar is known as the Little Cavalier.

113 Rabbit candy container

Description
Container in form of rabbit sitting on haunches, with forepaws close to chest and ears straight up. Inscription "¾ OZ AVOR." and "USA" on either side of tail. Gilt on upper body; green paint near base. Base with screw threads. Colorless. Tin screw-on cap.

Variations
Rabbit may be eating carrot, emerging from eggshell, pushing a wheelbarrow or cart, carrying basket, or holding basket and sitting on dome; may be crouching instead of sitting; may have forepaws extended in front.

Type and Dimensions
Pressed in mold for pattern and shape. Gilded and painted after annealing. Height: 5″.

Locality and Period
Victory Glass Company, Jeannette, Pennsylvania. 1919– c. 1930. Variants from western Pennsylvania, West Virginia, and Ohio. c. 1920–50.

Comment
Colorless glass candy containers were a specialty of the Victory Glass Company, which produced some of the most popular figural candy containers. More than 65 designs are marked; others like the unmarked rabbit pictured here can be identified through similarities to marked examples.

Hints for Collectors
Victory used a "VG" trademark from about 1919 to 1933, "V.G.CO." and "Victory Glass Co." in the 1930s, and "Victory Glass Inc." in the 1940s and 1950s. Since the periods for some marks overlap, this method of dating can only be approximate.

Clock candy container

Description
Container in form of dome-shaped mantel clock with hands set at
11 o'clock. Scrolls on front around face, on edges, and on reverse
side. Gilt trim on clock face and scrolls. Colors: opaque white and
colorless. Tin slide-off base.

Variations
Clock may be rectangular or triangular; may have pink and green
enameled floral decoration below face; sides may be ruby-stained;
top may be enameled "Souvenir of" with a town name.

Type and Dimensions
Pressed in mold for pattern and shape. Gilded after annealing.
Height: 3⅛".

Locality and Period
Western Pennsylvania, West Virginia, and Ohio. 1908–12.

Comment
One of the most beloved candy containers, this clock was
advertised by jobbers as early as 1908. After the Pure Food and
Drug Act was amended in 1912, most toy candy containers were
marked with the weight of the contents, usually "1 OZ AVOR" or
some fraction or multiple. The fact that this clock bears no
markings suggests an earlier date. Since most candy containers
were made in the same area from 1890 to 1930, it is also safe to
assume that this unmarked example came from the same region.

Hints for Collectors
Westmoreland Glass Company of Grapeville, Pennsylvania, made
reproductions of this clock in 1973, but since they are colored
glass they should not confuse anyone.

Train candy container

Description
Container in form of steam locomotive with cowcatcher, smokestack, and bell. Front has inscription "PRR/666." Colorless. Lithographed tin slide-off closure at rear depicts cab interior with controls, stoker, and engineer.

Variations
4 variants with lithographed closures at rear and various railroad initials, including "N.Y.C.," "M.C.R.R.," and "B.&O.RR." May be marked underneath "WEST BROS CO/GRAPEVILLE PA." 23 others have different closures without lithograph.

Type and Dimensions
Pressed in mold for pattern and shape. Height: 3".

Locality and Period
Probably Westmoreland Specialty Company, Grapeville, Pennsylvania. c. 1925–30. Variants from western Pennsylvania, West Virginia, and Ohio.

Comment
The most interesting toy train container is a 3-car train, patented in 1925. The engine, similar to the one shown here, has a glass coupling that enables it to be hooked to a coal tender and a gondola car. Glass candy containers were most popular in the 1890–1930 period, and many of them also functioned as toys. Glass companies sold the toys to jobbers, who filled them with small round candies and then resold them to stores. In the 1940s plastic began to replace glass, and by the mid-1960s glass candy containers were no longer being made.

Hints for Collectors
The 3-car train is extremely rare, but the locomotives are quite easy to find. Trains, cars, and airplanes are especially popular with collectors.

Amos 'n' Andy in a taxicab candy container

Description
Container in form of open automobile, with driver bent over steering wheel and passenger leaning back. 1 side has inscription "VICTORY GLASS CO./JEANNETTE, PA," and 1 has "1 OZ AVOR." Colors: colorless; wheels and parts of car painted yellow; figures painted black, driver's coat blue, passenger's suit red. Tin slide-off base painted red.

Variations
4 other open cars and 24 closed cars, mostly pre-World War I models. No other cars have passengers.

Type and Dimensions
Pressed in mold for pattern and shape. Painted after annealing. Height: 2⅝".

Locality and Period
Victory Glass Company, Jeannette, Pennsylvania. 1929. Variants from western Pennsylvania, West Virginia, and Ohio. c. 1910–40.

Comment
"Amos 'n' Andy," the popular radio show that became an American institution, was created by Charles Correll and Freeman Gosden in 1928 and continued until the 1950s. This candy container appeared on the market only a year after the show first aired. Since the molds had to be specially made, it required a certain amount of business acumen to produce a toy like this so quickly.

Hints for Collectors
All memorabilia connected with early radio personalities, such as Amos and Andy, and Edgar Bergen and Charlie McCarthy, are very popular today and likely to rise in value.

Ink Bottles and Inkwells

Ink containers are among the earliest bottles manufactured in America. One of Henry William Stiegel's glasshouses in Manheim, Pennsylvania, advertised inks in 1772, and by about 1810 several factories listed them in their inventories. Until about 1820, when American companies began to manufacture ink and sell it in bottles, ink was either prepared by local apothecaries or imported from England.

Ink Bottle Types
The first ink bottles were probably plain and, except for their paper labels, indistinguishable from other bottles. As commercial ink became more common, the low broad-based shape gradually evolved.

Tall bulk-storage bottles, now called master inks by collectors, were filled with ink and sold to schools and offices. Most held a pint or a quart, and occasionally two quarts to a gallon; the ink was either ready for use or concentrated. Since master inks were used to fill smaller bottles and inkwells, many have pouring lips.

The smaller bottles were intended for use on the desk. Before the invention of the fountain pen, the quill and later the steel nib were used for writing. Since both required frequent redipping in ink, the ink container had to be sturdy. After the 1880s, fountain pens with ink reservoirs, which needed to be filled only occasionally, replaced the dip point, and round and square bottles became the standard forms.

Ink Bottle Shapes
Most of the inks pictured in this section are individual desk bottles with capacities of one to several ounces. The basic 19th-century ink is the conical bottle with plain sides or eight to sixteen flat panels. Collectors call the paneled bottles umbrella inks.

Manufactured from the 1860s to 1900, more plain and paneled conical inks were probably made than any other type. During the presidential campaign of 1840, ink containers were sold in the form of log cabins and barrels in imitation of the larger whiskey bottles. By the 1870s, bottle shapes ranged from domed turtle inks and conical teakettle inks with a spout to those in the form of banks, trains, and schoolhouses. Most were closed with corks, but some had screw-on caps.

Inkwells
Unlike ink bottles, inkwells were usually sold empty; they were intended for redipping the pen and not for storage. Mold-blown inkwells were made as early as 1815 at bottle factories in Connecticut and New Hampshire. During the second half of the 19th century, inkstands and desk sets became the fashion. Each set included a container for sealing wax, a seal, a candle (for melting the wax), and a shaker for sand (to scatter over the ink for drying). Turn-of-the-century sets featured boxes for stamps, sponges, blotters, letter openers, and letter racks. The fanciest sets, many of which were imported, came in every conceivable color, and some combined glass with silver, brass, or ceramic.

Nursing Bottles
Because of their somewhat similar shape and small size, 19th-century nursing bottles are included in this section. Most had corks and rubber nipples or tubes. Relatively few early examples were made since, until the late 19th century, most women breast-fed their babies. Later nursing bottles are generally available today.

Nursing bottles

Description
Flattened oval bottle with short neck and rounded collar or plain lip. With or without neck ring. Below left: inscription "TYER RUBBER COMPANY/ANDOVER MASS/NURSER" on 1 side and "TYRIAN NURSER" with measured increments on other. Below right: large opening on 1 side (top) and "THE FAVORITE/PATENTED OCT 21TH/ 1890/MCKINNON & CO/NEW YORK" on other (bottom). Opposite left: "THE QUEEN CITY/FEEDERS/CERITY & MORRELL" enclosed in trefoil on 1 side and "FEEDERS" on other. Opposite right: "FLUID OZ" with measured increments on 1 side and other side blank. Each has oval base without pontil mark. Colorless. Below left: cork stopper with glass and rubber tubes and rubber mouthpiece. Below right: metal cap.

Variations
Inscriptions of other firms or brands.

Type and Dimensions
Blown in full-size multipiece mold for pattern and shape. Below left length: 5⅛". Below right length: 6". Opposite left height: 5¾". Opposite right length: 6¼".

Locality and Period
Throughout the United States. c. 1870–1910.

Comment
Infant and invalid feeders are among the oldest bottles, found in pottery as early as 1500 B.C. Since then nursing bottles have been made in all sorts of materials, ranging from pottery and glass to wood, stone, silver, and other metals. By the 19th century, however, glass nursing bottles superseded those made from other materials because they were cheaper to produce and easier to clean.

In 1841 Charles M. Windship of Roxbury, Massachusetts, was the first American to receive a patent for a nursing bottle. Windship's bottle was intended to be held against the mother's breast in an effort to deceive the baby. The first rubber nipple used in this country was patented by Elijah Pratt of New York City in 1845, but it was not until the early 20th century that a practical rubber nipple was perfected. The Tyrian nurser illustrated has a cork stopper with a glass tube, which was connected to a rubber tube with a nipplelike mouthpiece at the end (opposite left foreground). These devices were popular for a while, but as with all the early rubber products, the tube and mouthpiece deteriorated rapidly and were difficult to keep sanitary.

Both the Tyer nursing bottle and the McKinnon feeder with the large opening on top are less common than the other 2 standard types pictured here. The upright bottle in widespread use today was developed after the turn of the century.

Hints for Collectors

Most collectors of nursing bottles look for all types and collect both American and European examples, including related advertisements and the original boxes. As unusual as this specialty may seem, there is considerable interest in nursing bottles and an active society that distributes the newsletter "Keeping Abreast." Extensive public and private nursing bottle collections are often displayed at annual meetings. One of the best collections on public view is at the Museum of the History of Medicine of the Academy of Medicine in Toronto.

Description
Set with 2 flattened circular bottles, each with spout at 1 side. Ring below lip. No pontil mark. Colors: transparent aquamarine and dark blue, opaque white, and colorless. Cast-iron stand has flat rectangular base with 4 feet, 3-armed rack with crossbar, and 2 circular plates, each forming cap for 1 bottle.

Variations
Stand varies in design; may be marked "CLIPPER," with patent dates of March 12 and October 8, 1878, or January 14 and November 25, 1879. Stand may hold only 1 bottle or rarely 3 bottles. Bottle may rest on glass or ironstone saucer.

Type and Dimensions
Blown in full-size multipiece mold for shape. Bottle diameter: about 2¾". Stand length: 7¾". Height: 4".

Locality and Period
Bottles: the Pittsburgh area. Stand: the East and Midwest. c. 1870–90.

Comment
These inkwells in their swivel stand are typical desk accessories from the late 19th century, when inventive manufacturers marketed gimmicks to attract buyers. The set pictured here offered self-closing bottles: Placed upright, each bottle is open; pushed against the crossbar, the bottle is closed. Several similar devices were patented between 1875 and 1885, as indicated by dates on other stands.

Hints for Collectors
Although opaque white and transparent dark blue bottles are the most desirable, even the other colors are prized.

Teakettle ink bottle

Description
Bottle in form of teakettle with flat top. 8 flat panels around
body, and spout at 1 side. Plain lip. Octagonal base without
pontil mark. Colors: transparent amber, purple, aquamarine, and
blue; opaque light green, light blue, and white; and colorless.

Variations
Body may have molded geometric or floral design, or gilt or cut
decoration; patterns vary widely. May have inscription with
manufacturer's name or trademark. Base may have pontil mark.
Spout may have metal cap.

Type and Dimensions
Blown in full-size multipiece mold for shape. Spout and lip
finished. Height: 2″.

Locality and Period
The East. Europe; widely exported to the United States.
c. 1840–1900.

Comment
One of the most popular ink bottle designs, the teakettle ink was
made in a wide variety of glass colors and patterns as well as in
white ceramic. Glass examples with elaborate embossed floral
patterns and gilt decoration were probably made in Europe.
Teakettle inks in opaque glass may be American or French.

Hints for Collectors
The European examples often cost slightly less than their
American counterparts, since American collectors prefer glass
that was made in this country. However, unless the teakettle
inks bear manufacturers' trademarks, there is no way to
distinguish the two.

Turtle ink bottle

Description
Circular bottle with domed top and short neck set off center.
Plain lip. Top has design of bird on branch. Circular base without
pontil mark. Colors: transparent aquamarine; rarely amber, blue,
and green.

Variations
Top may lack bird. More than 20 unpatterned variants with
inscriptions. Top may have inscription "A & F" or "INK CARTER'S";
lower edge may have "J.J.BUTLER CIN.O," "DAVIDS," or "DESSAUER'S
JET BLACK INK"; base may have "F.D.A." Shape may be octagonal
with "HARRISON'S COLUMBIAN INK" around lower edge. Names of
other firms or brands as inscriptions or labels.

Type and Dimensions
Blown in full-size multipiece mold for pattern and shape. Neck
and lip finished. Height: 1½".

Locality and Period
The East. 1865–c. 1900.

Comment
Collectors call the domed ink bottle with an offset neck a turtle
ink. This shape was patented in 1865 by J. & I.E. Moore of
Warren, Massachusetts, and was made for this company and
many others for about 30 years. A very popular design in its day,
the bottle was often used in schools.

Hints for Collectors
Inks of this type predate the age of the automatic bottle-blowing
machine and were finished using a snap tool, which leaves no
mark. Beware of turtle inks reproduced by Clevenger Brothers
in the 1950s. They were made in purple, an unusual color for
19th-century inks in this shape, and were blown in an old mold
marked "HOVER PHILAD."

Harrison's Columbian Ink bottles

Description
Cylindrical or octagonal bottle with angled shoulders and short neck. Folded-in lip. Inscription "HARRISON'S/COLUMBIAN/INK" around body. Pontil mark on circular or octagonal base. Colors: transparent dark blue, aquamarine, and green.

Variations
Cylindrical and octagonal bottles may be tall, with inscription running vertically. Also tall bottle with 12 panels.

Type and Dimensions
Blown in full-size multipiece mold for pattern and shape. Neck and lip finished. Left height: 2⅛". Right height: 1¾".

Locality and Period
Whitney Brothers, Glassboro, New Jersey, and other factories in the East. 1847–77.

Comment
Apollos W. Harrison of Philadelphia manufactured black, blue, and red ink from 1847 until 1877. He used hundreds of bottles in sizes from an ounce to a gallon to sell his product. Widely distributed in the 19th century, Harrison's bottles are found throughout the United States, even on the West Coast.

Hints for Collectors
Because the Harrison company was in business for such a long time and used a number of different molds, it is possible to assemble a sizable collection of Harrison's Columbian Ink bottles in several colors and shapes, and in many sizes including the taller master inks used for bulk storage.

Umbrella ink bottle reproduction

Description
Conical bottle with 8 flat panels around body and short neck. Thick flange at rim. Octagonal base. Authentic colors: transparent amber, amber-green, amber-olive, olive-green, and aquamarine; rarely purple, blue, and brownish-pink. Reproduction colors: transparent purple, green, and blue.

Variations
Body may have 8–16 panels. May have shoulder ring.

Type and Dimensions
Blown in automatic bottle-blowing machine for shape. Height: 2¾″.

Locality and Period
Throughout the United States. c. 1970–present.

Comment
Collectors call the original conical inks with 8 to 16 panels around the sides umbrella inks. They were manufactured from about 1865 until 1900. The reproduction shown here was probably made to be sold in gift shops. Like other bottles of this type, the copy comes in brighter colors than the original. Somewhere along the line it fell into inexperienced hands and wound up in an antiques shop for sale among older bottles. This happens all too often with unmarked copies of old designs.

Hints for Collectors
Always examine a bottle carefully before purchasing it. If the mold marks go all the way up to the lip, the bottle was not hand finished and may be machine-made. On most old bottles the lip was hand finished, and consequently the mold marks go up only to the shoulder or part way up the neck. Additionally, most reproductions look very new unless they have been artificially weathered.

Conical ink bottle

Description
Conical bottle with short neck. Rounded collar. Thick shoulder ring. Circular base has inscription "CARTER" and no pontil mark. Colors: shades of transparent aquamarine, blue, light and dark green, light and dark amber, and colorless.

Variations
Base may lack inscription or have numbers and letters. Bottle may have plain lip, pontil mark, narrow shoulder ring, or any combination of these.

Type and Dimensions
Blown in full-size multipiece mold for pattern and shape. Neck and collar finished. Height: 2½".

Locality and Period
The East. c. 1865–1900.

Comment
In 19th-century America, ink was a source of prestige. Only those who could read and write were likely to use this expensive commodity, and at a time when only half the population was literate, this ability was an important distinction. The cone is the most common ink bottle shape. Before the invention of the fountain pen, writing required dipping frequently into the ink bottle, and a sturdy container with a wide base like the one seen here was especially desirable.

Hints for Collectors
Conical and umbrella ink bottles are more plentiful and usually less expensive than most teakettle and schoolhouse inks. They are found in the greatest variety of colors. Do not confuse older bottles with reproductions in vivid blues, purples, and greens that are brighter than the originals.

Schoolhouse ink bottle

Description
Bottle in form of schoolhouse with hip roof and short neck in place of chimney. Narrow, flat collar. Front has door and 3 windows; each side has 1 window; reverse side blank. Roof has inscription "S.I.COMP." Square base without pontil mark. Colors: transparent aquamarine and colorless; rarely opaque white.

Variations
At least 14 house-shaped ink bottles; inscriptions and placement of windows and doors vary considerably. May have "NE PLUS ULTRA FLUID" or "S.F.CAL INK CO" on roof or "PATD MAR 14 1871" on base; may lack inscription. House may resemble log cabin, with "HARRISON" and "TIPPECANOE" on roof.

Type and Dimensions
Blown in full-size multipiece mold for pattern and shape. Neck and collar finished. Height: 2¾".

Locality and Period
Probably New Jersey. c. 1880–1900.

Comment
The design pictured was made for the Senate Ink Company of Philadelphia, and the bottles were probably purchased from a factory in nearby New Jersey. The earliest of the house-shaped inks is the log cabin example, which was undoubtedly made for Harrison's presidential campaign of 1840. Most of the house-shaped inks, however, date from the last quarter of the 19th century.

Hints for Collectors
Do not be fooled by a machine-made reproduction in blue that is marked "JAPAN" on the base.

Barrel-shaped ink bottle

Description
Horizontal barrel-shaped bottle with 2 braces underneath to keep bottle from tipping. Short neck. Plain lip. Ribs around body. 1 side has partial paper label. Base has inscription "PAT OCT 17 1865" and no pontil mark. Color: transparent dark amber, which may appear black. Cork stopper.

Variations
Inscriptions vary greatly. May have "PAT MARCH" on 1 side and "1870" on other; may have "PETROLEUM P B & CO" on 1 side and "WRITING FLUID" on other; may have "TIPPECANOE EXTRACT" on 1 side and "HARD CIDER" on other; may have patent date of March 1, 1870 on base; may have "OPDYKE BROS FRENCH TOWN NEW JERSEY" on label or inscription "OPDYKE BROS INK" on base; may lack inscription. May have diamond pattern. Cork stopper may be marked "S.I.CO." May be upright barrel with or without inscription. Variants in many colors; rarely opaque white.

Type and Dimensions
Blown in full-size multipiece mold for pattern and shape. Neck and lip finished. Height: 2¹⁄₁₆″.

Locality and Period
The East. c. 1865–1900. Variants c. 1840–1900.

Comment
Patented in 1865 by Isaac N. Pierce of Philadelphia, this barrel design came in 2 sizes, the small size shown here and one about twice as large. Most barrel-shaped inks were made after about 1865, but some date from as early as Harrison's presidential campaign of 1840.

Hints for Collectors
The most common barrel ink is the upright bottle used by W.E. Bonney of South Hanover, Massachusetts.

Description
Square form with rounded corners. Rounded collar around cylindrical well. Cut diamond pattern on square base. Colorless.

Variations
Cut patterns on this shape may be more complex and cover sides. Form sometimes rectangular or circular. Top may have slot for pen. May have glass lid; may have metal collar rim and lid; may have silver cap with monogram or date.

Type and Dimensions
Free-blown, then tooled into shape. Collar applied. Base cut and collar ground after annealing. Height: 2¹⁄₁₆".

Locality and Period
Throughout the United States. c. 1880–1920.

Comment
Cut-glass desk accessories were popular around the turn of the century, when elegant appointments for ladies' and gentlemen's writing desks were in vogue. They came in a great variety of colors and ranged from a relatively simple inkwell like the one shown here to those with brilliant-cut patterns on all sides and heavy silver or glass stoppers. Sophisticated society of the late 19th century produced voluminous diaries and letters, and the increased availability of schooling for both boys and girls promoted greater literacy among the middle class.

Hints for Collectors
A simple desk accessory like the one pictured is usually inexpensive, but all Victorian antiques are gaining in popularity, and prices are rising. A cut-glass desk set is apt to cost more than the sum of its pieces, which may include a letter rack, tray, boxes for pen points or sand, and even a glass-handled paper cutter or ruler.

Mold-blown inkwells

Description
Conical or cylindrical form with flat collar around cylindrical well.
Closely spaced swirled ribs around body (left) or diamond
pattern above band of vertical ribs (right). Pontil mark on each
circular base. Colors: transparent dark brown, dark green, and
dark amber (these dark shades may appear black); rarely light
green and aquamarine.

Variations
Pattern may be diamonds in square alternating with ribs; body
may be plain.

Type and Dimensions
Left: blown in vertically ribbed dip mold, then expanded,
swirled, and tooled into shape after removal from mold; collar
applied. Height: 2¼″. Right: blown in full-size multipiece mold
for pattern and shape; collar applied. Height: 1⅞″.

Locality and Period
New England; probably Stoddard and Keene, New Hampshire,
and Willington, Pitkin, and Coventry, Connecticut. c. 1815–50.

Comment
The cylindrical inkwell shown on the right is a type of glass
collectors call blown 3-mold, although the molds used may have
had 3, 4, or 5 parts. Most of the blown 3-mold patterns imitate
the more expensive cut glass with geometric arrangements of
squares, vertical lines, and diamonds. The inkwell on the left is a
shape commonly found in ceramic and pewter inkwells of the
early 19th century.

Hints for Collectors
These early inkwells are among the most sought after and
expensive. Look for them in New England; only rarely will you
find them anywhere else.

Jars

The earliest method for preserving food in a glass container was developed in 1809 by the Frenchman Nicholas Appert in answer to a plea from the Emperor Napoleon. In 1795 Napoleon had offered 12,000 francs for an effective means of preserving food for the army to eat while on campaign. Appert suggested sealing the food in an airtight glass container and then boiling the container to keep the food inside from rotting. In 1812 Appert's prizewinning method was published in English in New York, and soon American glass companies began to produce glass preserving jars.

The Development of Airtight Lids

Free-blown cylindrical containers with wide, flanged mouths were the earliest jars made in America. Most often they were sealed with a cork covered with wax, or with wax covered by a piece of cloth. Because early jars varied greatly in size and their mouths were hand finished, it was impossible to produce a standardized lid.

In 1858 John Landis Mason, a tinsmith, patented both a mold for a jar with a threaded mouth and a zinc screw-on lid. All jars blown in the mold were of uniform size and, more important, all could use the same type of lid. Cheap to produce, the standard jars and lids became immediately popular and were copied by many firms. Soon the name Mason jar became identified with all preserving jars regardless of brand. Yet the Mason-type lid had a major drawback: The zinc imparted its taste to the food. In 1868 and 1869 Salmon B. Rowley of the Hero Glass Works tried to eliminate the zinc taste by covering the jar mouth with a flat glass insert kept in place by a zinc Mason-type lid. In 1869 Lewis Boyd of the New York Metals Company invented a white glass liner for the zinc lid that solved the problem. His lid, adopted by numerous companies, became a best-seller.

During the second half of the 19th century, a variety of other types of closures were developed and widely used. Many jars had pressed-glass lids that were fastened with metal clamps or wire bails. Some closures required a groove in the neck of the jar, which was fitted with a rubber ring; the lid pressed against the ring for a tight seal.

Until the 1890s, jars and lids were usually manufactured and sold separately, but toward the turn of the century, when fruit jars began to be blown in automatic machines, some lids and jars were sold as a unit. By the end of World War I, most jars were machine-blown. Regardless of brand, all early mold-blown Mason-type jars using zinc screw-on lids have ground mouths. Later machine-blown jars lack ground mouths.

Jar Colors

Most preserving jars are colorless, green, or aquamarine, but some were made in amber and, very rarely, bright green, dark blue, purple, or opaque white. Manufacturers claimed that the amber hue would protect the food inside the jar from sunlight, and these jars were marketed fairly successfully. But the rare colors were experimental and only made in limited quantities. The more common colors are widely available throughout the United States, making jars one of the easiest areas of bottle collecting for beginners, as well as one of the least expensive.

Mason's improved jar

Description
Cylindrical jar with sloping shoulders has small mouth with
screw threads. 1 side has inscription "MASON'S/IMPROVED" with
formée cross above. Circular base has "PAT NOV 26 67" and no
pontil mark. Colors: transparent aquamarine and light green.

Variations
Each arm of cross may have 1 letter of "H F J C"; cross may be in
middle of inscription; inscription may be "HERO." May have zinc
screw-on cap. Pint, quart, and 2 quarts.

Type and Dimensions
Blown in full-size multipiece mold for pattern and shape. Mouth
ground. Quart.

Locality and Period
Hero Glass Works, Philadelphia. 1882–84. Variants 1884–
c. 1900.

Comment
Salmon B. Rowley, who founded Hero Glass Works in 1856, was
granted more than 20 patents for jar designs between then and
1895. The HGW monogram was the firm's trademark until 1882,
when the Hero-cross logo was adopted. Because of the
tremendous success of its preserving jars, the glassworks
changed its name to Hero Fruit Jar Company in 1884, and after
that the cross had the company initials in its arms.

Hints for Collectors
The numerous types of Hero jars used both zinc caps and glass
lids, and it is not always possible to tell which type of lid was
original to which jar. Look for the Hero cross and "NOV 26 67"
separately or together; these marks belong to Hero or one of its
licensees.

Description
Cylindrical jar with rounded shoulders has small, plain mouth.
1 side has inscription "THE/VAN VLIET/JAR/OF 1881." Circular base
cut by groove; no pontil mark. Color: transparent light
aquamarine.

Variations
May have glass lid with metal yoke and thumbscrew anchored by
wire encircling jar vertically and fitting into groove on base.
Base of jar and lid may have "PAT. MAY 3d 1881."

Type and Dimensions
Blown in full-size multipiece mold for pattern and shape. Mouth
ground. Quart.

Locality and Period
Possibly East Stroudsburg Glass Company, East Stroudsburg,
Pennsylvania. c. 1881.

Comment
In 1881 Warren Van Vliet of East Stroudsburg was issued a
patent for the wire-and-groove closure. Although it is likely that
his jar was made in the East Stroudsburg glass factory, there is
no proof. Certainly the wire-and-groove closure was less
convenient than the clamp or bail method used on other jars.
Fewer jars are found with the Van Vliet closure than clamps or
bails, so it is entirely possible that the Van Vliet jar was not as
popular or used for as long a period.

Hints for Collectors
Van Vliet jars are much rarer than other jars with similar
closures and more highly prized. One without its lid is worth
much less than a complete example.

Hahne Mason jar

Description
Cylindrical jar has wide mouth with screw threads. 1 side has
5-pointed star with inscription "HAHNE & CO." above and "NEWARK
N.J." below; 1 side has "MASON'S/PATENT/NOV 30TH/1858." Circular
base; no pontil mark. Colors: transparent aquamarine and light
green.

Variations
Instead of star, may have keystone, circled keystone, sunburst,
or crescent moon and star. "MASON'S" may lack "S" or crossbar in
"A"; "30TH" may lack "TH" or have "HT"; "N" may be backward; "NOV"
may be "NOA." May have zinc screw-on cap.

Type and Dimensions
Blown in full-size multipiece mold for pattern and shape. Mouth
ground. Pint.

Locality and Period
New Jersey. c. 1880–1900. Variants from throughout the United
States.

Comment
One reason many jars of this period are so similar is that most
preserving jar factories ordered their molds from a few large
New York, Philadelphia, and Pittsburgh firms. The Hahne jar
illustrated here is probably a rare variant of the common Mason
preserving jar. Because of its shape, this jar type can be dated to
the last 2 decades of the 19th century.

Hints for Collectors
Jars with errors are generally rarer than perfect examples
because the faulty molds were usually eliminated as soon as they
were noticed.

Ball Mason jar

Description
Cylindrical jar has wide mouth with screw threads. 1 side has
inscription "Ball" in script with "MASON" below. Circular base; no
pontil mark. Colors: transparent bluish-aquamarine and green.
Zinc screw-on cap.

Variations
May have inscriptions "Ball/MASON'S/PATENT/NOV 30TH/1858"; "THE/
BALL/MASON"; "Ball/PERFECT/MASON"; "Ball/SANITARY/SURE SEAL";
"Ball/SPECIAL"; "Ball/STANDARD"; or others. Pint, quart, and
2 quarts.

Type and Dimensions
Blown in full-size multipiece mold for pattern and shape. Mouth
ground. Pint.

Locality and Period
Ball Brothers Glass Company, Muncie, Indiana. 1895–c. 1910.
Variants 1888–1935.

Comment
Frank Ball and his 4 brothers started manufacturing metal cans
in Buffalo, New York, in the early 1880s. They set up a glass
furnace there in 1885, but a fire in 1886 forced them to relocate.
By 1888 Ball Brothers Glass Company was producing jars in
Muncie. The firm, still in business today as Ball Brothers
Company, was the first to use semiautomatic glass-blowing
machinery, which enabled jars to be made more cheaply, more
quickly, and in standard sizes.

Hints for Collectors
The majority of Ball jars were made with automatic machinery
after 1900 and lack the ground mouth. Earlier examples with the
mouth ground are slightly more valuable.

Atlas Mason jar

Description
Cylindrical jar has wide mouth with screw threads. 1 side has inscription "ATLAS/STRONG SHOULDER/MASON." Circular base. Colors: transparent aquamarine, light green, and colorless. Zinc screw-on cap and rubber ring.

Variations
Rounded square jar with "ATLAS/GOOD LUCK." Cylindrical jar with "ATLAS/E–Z/SEAL/TRADEMARK REG"; "ATLAS/IMPROVED/MASON"; "ATLAS/SPECIAL/MASON"; "ATLAS/WHOLE FRUIT/JAR"; "ATLAS/MASON'S/PATENT/NOV 30TH/1858"; or shortened versions. Also transparent amber, blue-green, and dark green. Pint, quart, and 2 quarts.

Type and Dimensions
Blown in automatic bottle-blowing machine for pattern and shape. Pint.

Locality and Period
Hazel-Atlas Glass Company, Wheeling, West Virginia. c. 1915–30. Variants 1896–c. 1940.

Comment
The Hazel Glass Company was founded in Wellsburg, West Virginia, by C.N. Brady in 1886. The next year Brady moved his factory to Washington, Pennsylvania, and in 1896 he built the Atlas Glass Company for the new glass-blowing machinery developed by Charles Blue. It was the first factory in the country to rely solely on automatic equipment. In 1902 the firms became the Hazel-Atlas Glass Company, one of the largest glass factories in the United States.

Hints for Collectors
Atlas and Hazel-Atlas jars are all machine-made, very common, and a good starting point for a collection.

Mason's patent jar

Description
Cylindrical jar has wide mouth with screw threads. 1 side has inscription "MASON'S/PATENT/NOV 30TH/1858." Circular base has "25" and no pontil mark. Colors: transparent bluish-aquamarine and light green; very rarely transparent amber, dark blue, purple, and opaque white. Zinc screw-on cap.

Variations
Shape varies greatly; may be barrel-shaped or round-shouldered. There are at least 20 inscriptions, some with errors; design may include keystone, sunburst, formée cross, or other symbol. Pint, quart, and 2 quarts.

Type and Dimensions
Blown in full-size multipiece mold for pattern and shape. Mouth ground. Pint.

Locality and Period
Throughout the United States. c. 1880–1900. Variants 1858– c. 1920.

Comment
In 1858 John Mason patented a zinc cap for sealing preserve jars that fitted the shoulder rather than the mouth. After the patent expired, other companies used his name and patent date on their own jars, even though these jars used a variety of closures.

Hints for Collectors
Because of the great number of jars with similar wording, dating a Mason-type jar can be a challenge. Jars ground around the mouth date to the 19th century. Later machine-blown jars have smooth, rounded mouths. To date a jar, check reference books that list the variations with their dates.

Description
Cylindrical jar has wide mouth with screw threads. 1 side has inscription "14 OZ NET/FRENCH'S/MEDFORD/BRAND/PREPARED/ MUSTARD." Circular base. Colorless; sometimes with purple tint. Zinc screw-on cap.

Variations
May have "FRENCH'S/PERFECT/MUSTARD."

Type and Dimensions
Blown in automatic bottle-blowing machine for pattern and shape. 14 ounces.

Locality and Period
The East. 1904–c. 1910.

Comment
A family business, R.T. French was founded in New York City in 1876 and specialized in coffee, tea, and spices. In the 1880s French moved to Rochester, New York, where the company purchased a flour mill and manufactured its own spices. In 1904 it began to market the creamy mustard that has since become the company's mainstay. French acquired the Medford brand through a merger.

Hints for Collectors
French purchased some, but not all, of its jars from the Hazel-Atlas Glass Company of Wheeling, West Virginia, so it is hard to pin down the factory where a particular jar was made. Collecting food jars, except for the early pepper-sauce and early cathedral-type pickle bottles, is comparatively new, and rarity or commonness has yet to be established.

Magic fruit jar

Description
Cylindrical jar has wide mouth. 1 side has 5-pointed star with inscription "THE MAGIC" above and "FRUIT JAR" below. Circular base. Glass lid has "CLAMP PAT. MARCH 30TH 1886." Colors: aquamarine; rarely transparent amber. Cast-iron and iron wire closure.

Variations
Inscription on lid may be "KANT KRACK/TRADE MARK/PAT FEB 23, 1909." Another jar has "MAGIC/FRUIT JAR/WM MCCULLY & CO PITTSBURGH PA/SOLE PROPRIETORS" on front; reverse with "PATENTED/BY/R.M.DALBEY/JUNE 6TH 1886."

Type and Dimensions
Jar blown in automatic bottle-blowing machine for pattern and shape. Lid pressed. Pint.

Locality and Period
New England and New Jersey. c. 1900–15. Kant Krack 1909. McCully variant from Pittsburgh. 1866–c. 1880.

Comment
The 2 kinds of jars marked "MAGIC FRUIT JAR" cannot easily be confused since McCully's name is on the earlier jar only. In contrast to the jar illustrated here, the McCully jar is mold-blown and has a ground mouth. It is also found in aquamarine and amber. The jar shown was made by an unknown manufacturer for Smalley, Kivlan & Onthank, a Boston glass jobber.

Hints for Collectors
Because of its rare amber color, this jar would be a find for a collector. Do not be misled by the 1886 date on the lid; it refers to one of the patent dates and not the date of manufacture.

Description
Cylindrical jar with rounded shoulders has short neck with plain mouth. 1 side has inscription "TRADE MARK/LIGHTNING." Circular base; no pontil mark. Glass lid fits on top of mouth. Colors: transparent amber, green, and aquamarine. Wire ring and bail closure.

Variations
May have "LIGHTNING" on 1 side and "PUTNAM" on base; or "LIGHTNING" with "REGISTERED" above and "U.S.PATENT OFFICE" below. Pint, quart, and 2 quarts.

Type and Dimensions
Jar blown in full-size multipiece mold for pattern and shape. Lid pressed. Lid and mouth ground. Quart.

Locality and Period
Possibly Lyndeboro Glass Company, Lyndeboro, New Hampshire, 1882–86; Hazel Glass Company, Wellsburg, West Virginia, and Washington, Pennsylvania, 1886–1902; or machine-made by Atlas Glass Company, Washington, Pennsylvania, 1896–1901.

Comment
In 1875 Charles de Quillfeldt of New York City patented a toggle-type seal for beverage bottles called the Lightning closure. By 1882 Henry W. Putnam had patented a wire-bail adaptation for fruit jars. Putnam, who lived in Bennington, Vermont, may have had the first jars made in New England and distributed in nearby Canada and upstate New York, because most Lightning jars are found today in these 3 areas.

Hints for Collectors
The Lightning closure was used by jar factories besides the 3 mentioned, but their jars do not bear the "LIGHTNING" inscription.

Millville jar

Description
Cylindrical jar with rounded shoulders has short neck with plain mouth. 1 side has inscription "MILLVILLE/ATMOSPHERIC/FRUIT JAR"; 1 side has "WHITALL'S PATENT/JUNE 18TH 1861." Circular base; no pontil mark. Glass lid has "WHITALL'S PATENT/JUNE 18TH 1861" and fits on top of mouth. Colors: transparent very light green and aquamarine; extremely rarely dark blue. Metal screw-clamp closure.

Variations
May have "MILLVILLE/PAT JUNE 18 1861" or "MILLVILLE/W T CO/ IMPROVED." Pint, quart, and 2 quarts.

Type and Dimensions
Jar blown in full-size multipiece mold for pattern and shape. Neck and mouth finished. Lid pressed. Quart.

Locality and Period
Whitall, Tatum & Company, Millville, New Jersey. 1862–c. 1880. Variants 1861 and c. 1880–1900.

Comment
The patent date on the jar illustrated here is the earliest patent for jars made by Whitall, Tatum & Company. A second patent was issued to the owner, John Whitall, on November 4, 1862, but for some reason he put the year-old date on the second jar, too. The inside of the mouth has a groove for a rubber ring, which when clamped down provided an effective seal. In most cases the ring is no longer attached.

Hints for Collectors
A jar that was originally sold with a glass lid and metal clamp is considered incomplete without them. In contrast, a jar made to be closed with a zinc cap is collectible without the cap.

Ribbed jar

Description
Cylindrical jar with angled shoulders has short neck with plain mouth. Vertical ribs around body from base to neck. Circular base slightly pushed into body; no pontil mark. Glass lid fits on top of mouth. Color: transparent green.

Variations
May have square panel on side showing swan; inscription "BROUGH & Cº." above and "LIVERPOOL" below, with "TRADE" to left and "MARK" to right of swan. Quart.

Type and Dimensions
Jar blown in full-size multipiece mold for pattern and shape. Neck and mouth finished. Lid pressed. Quart.

Locality and Period
Probably New England. c. 1860–80. Swan variant from England.

Comment
This unusual jar lacks a name or date but was probably made in New England, where a few similarly ribbed pieces are known to have been made. Two unribbed jars in this shape have inscriptions, naming W. McCully of Pittsburgh, who was primarily a flask and bottle maker, and A.R. Kline, who patented a glass lid in Philadelphia. The manufacturer of the jar shown could have been a window glass factory. Sometimes when business was slack, the glassmakers would blow jars from the topmost layer in the pot. The bubbles and unmelted batch that could ruin windows did no harm in jars.

Hints for Collectors
Ribbed and unribbed jars in this shape were blown before the days of mass production and are quite scarce. The jar illustrated may have originally held salt.

Early free-blown jar

Description
Cylindrical jar with rounded shoulders has short neck with wide, flanged mouth. Pontil mark on circular base slightly pushed into body. Colors: transparent green, brown, amber, aquamarine, and rarely colorless.

Variations
May be barrel-shaped; mouth may lack flange. About 1 quart to 1 gallon.

Type and Dimensions
Free-blown, then tooled into shape. Height: 7¾". About 1½ quarts.

Locality and Period
New England, New York, New Jersey, and Pennsylvania. c. 1790–1850.

Comment
Early free-blown glass jars like the one pictured here may have held salted or brined food, such as pickles and other condiments. Until the widespread use of sealed preserving jars in the mid-19th century, jars were closed with improvised lids, such as a cork, a cork covered with pitch, or perhaps a cloth tied on with string and coated with wax. The addition of either pitch or wax was an attempt to keep air from the contents. Probably these jars were made in bottle glasshouses and some tableware factories of the late 18th and early 19th centuries.

Hints for Collectors
Although early free-blown jars are much rarer than the late 19th-century Mason-type jars, they are not as well known.

Description
Cylindrical jar has wide, flanged mouth. 2 rings around body. Pontil mark on circular base. Dome-shaped glass lid with wide flange rests on mouth; mushroom-shaped hollow knob. Colorless.

Variations
Rings sometimes transparent blue, red, or green glass. Base may lack pontil mark.

Type and Dimensions
Jar blown in dip mold, then expanded and tooled into shape after removal from mold. Rings applied. Lid free-blown and tooled; knob applied. Height: 9″. About 1½ quarts.

Locality and Period
The East and Midwest. c. 1850–70. Variants without pontil mark c. 1870–1900.

Comment
Common ring jars, as they were called in 19th-century glass catalogues, were intended primarily for use in apothecary shops. Unlike fruit jars, they were not designed to be sealed and were therefore never used for canning. This type of jar seems to have been a staple of many New England glasshouses as well as several midwestern firms. Since none were signed and their shape did not change, it is impossible to date them accurately or identify a manufacturer.

Hints for Collectors
For a collector interested in handmade objects, ring jars are a good point of departure.

Grocery storage jar

Description
Cylindrical jar has wide, flanged mouth. Raised design of 4 large peanut shells with inscription "PLANTERS" vertically in between. Circular base. Glass lid fits on top of mouth; knob in form of peanut. Colorless.

Variations
Sides may be plain or show name of another product. May have metal cap.

Type and Dimensions
Jar blown in automatic bottle-blowing machine for pattern and shape. Lid pressed. Height: 13½". Gallon.

Locality and Period
Throughout the United States. c. 1932–35.

Comment
Grocery storage jars were displayed on store counters. The example illustrated here was probably supplied by the Planters Company to store owners as an advertisement. Peanuts were not popular outside the South until the 20th century, when they were grown in large quantities and promoted as snacks nationwide.

Hints for Collectors
Collectors of such advertising memorabilia as trays, product trade cards, and boxes might be interested in jars like this. Because food containers in general are new collectors' items, many lack established market values, although the popular Planters Peanut jar commands a relatively high price.

Drug, Perfume, and Other Fancy Bottles

The diverse bottles in this section are generally elaborate, having glass stoppers, pewter caps, or fancy decoration around the sides. They include apothecary and poison bottles, perfume and barber bottles, and food containers.

Drug, Specimen, and Poison Bottles

Bottles for druggists have been manufactured in America since the opening of the first glasshouses. The role of the druggist, or apothecary, as a healer was a well-established European tradition that continued in this country through much of the 19th century. Like a family doctor, the druggist prescribed cures, either his own mixtures or a ready-made medicine, and many of the bottles he used for storage bore permanent enameled or painted labels. These elaborately decorated drug bottles, as well as simpler specimen bottles, had ground glass stoppers for an airtight fit.

Some drug bottles contained poison. In accordance with the 1872 recommendation of the American Medical Association, most poison bottles from the 1872–1930 period are rough textured for immediate recognition by touch, and many have unusual shapes. The most impressive druggists' containers are the tall, multitiered bottles popularly called show globes. Most were made by tableware firms, whereas drug bottles were usually manufactured in specialized bottle factories, at first primarily in New Jersey and New England and later in the Pittsburgh-Ohio area.

Perfume, Cologne, Scent, and Barber Bottles

Like drug bottles, perfume bottles were among the earliest products of American glasshouses. From Colonial days until almost the end of the 19th century, perfumes and scents were commonly used to mask unpleasant odors. Scent, or smelling salts, contained perfume mixed with ammonia, and was used to prevent fainting or for what 19th-century society called "social smelling." Cologne, perfume diluted with alcohol, was introduced around 1830.

By the end of the 19th century, barbers kept their shops' hair tonics, shaving lotions, and other preparations, such as the scent called bay rum, in handsomely decorated bottles. These sometimes bore the proprietor's label or the name of the customer.

Toilet water, smelling salts, and similar products were often sold in labeled bottles, but since few paper labels have survived, it is often difficult to identify what toiletry a bottle contained. Many of these commercial bottles are brightly colored or fancifully shaped.

More ornamental purse-size or dresser perfume and cologne bottles were sold empty. Like the show globes, which often required extensive hand finishing, they were made in tableware factories. Some of the most elegant perfumes reflect the height of the glassmaker's artistry, including cameo carving, shaded glass, and the latest innovations from Lalique, Tiffany, and Steuben.

Food Bottles and Other Containers

Many condiments and other foods were marketed in distinctive bottles. Pepper sauce, for example, was sold in bottles with long necks and ridged bodies. Other ornamental bottles, such as the cut or engraved oil-and-vinegar cruets and the double, or gemel, bottles, were filled by the purchaser. These as well as one-of-a-kind objects like bellows bottles were made in both bottle glasshouses and tableware factories.

Specimen bottle

Description
Cylindrical bottle with wide, short neck. Flanged lip. Polished pontil mark on circular base. Flat-topped, cylindrical lid with square knob fits into neck. Colorless.

Variations
Height and width vary. 3–24″.

Type and Dimensions
Bottle blown in full-size 1-piece mold for shape. Neck and lip finished. Lid pressed. Neck and lid ground. Height: 22″.

Locality and Period
New England Glass Company, Cambridge, Massachusetts; possibly other eastern glasshouses. 1859–88. Variants c. 1850–1900.

Comment
In 1859 the great naturalist Louis Agassiz founded the Museum of Comparative Zoology at Harvard University as a teaching museum for display of scientific specimens. To exhibit the specimens, Agassiz ordered a large quantity of scientific glassware from the New England Glass Company, then one of the largest general glass companies in the country. The museum records show that he spent more than $10,000 in one year for bottles and jars. After the company closed in 1888, replacements were obtained from other firms.

Hints for Collectors
In order to raise money for research projects, the museum Agassiz founded sold its collection of early 19th-century hand-blown specimen bottles at nominal prices, complete with certificates of authenticity, in 1975. By now many of these bottles with their certificates are in antiques shops.

Chemical and medicine bottles

Description
Cylindrical bottle with wide, short neck. Left: pinched-in neck and plain lip. Polished pontil mark on circular base and on top of hollow, cylindrical cap that fits over neck. Right: straight neck and flanged lip. Circular base without pontil mark. Solid stopper with flat disk. Colors: (left) transparent dark blue; (right) transparent dark blue and colorless.

Variations
Bottle at the right may be 5–10″ tall.

Type and Dimensions
Bottle blown in full-size multipiece mold for shape. Neck and lip finished. Left: cap free-blown and tooled. Height: 11″. Right: stopper pressed; neck and stopper ground. Height: 5″.

Locality and Period
Left: Boston & Sandwich Glass Company, Sandwich, Massachusetts. c. 1870–88. Right: also other glasshouses in the East. c. 1870–1900.

Comment
Large bottles like the one pictured on the left are found in an 1876 stereoscopic slide of a Boston & Sandwich exhibit. It is unusual for a bottle as late as this to have a pontil mark. The small one is a more standard type. In both cases, the dark color protected the contents from the harmful effects of light.

Hints for Collectors
Although plain bottles are not as popular as those with fancy shapes or designs, such as figurals, bitters, and figured flasks, even a simple blue bottle may interest a collector who specializes in this color.

Apothecary bottles

Description
Cylindrical bottle with short neck. Flanged lip. Name of drug painted in black on gilt panel. Left: label covered with thin layer of colorless glass. Pontil mark on circular base. Hollow stopper with flat disk. Right: gilt scrollwork and panel with name of drug; no glass cover. Pontil mark on circular base slightly pushed into body. Solid stopper with square knob. Colors: transparent blue, opaque white, and colorless.

Variations
Name of drug and style of lettering vary. Base may lack pontil mark; a few have polished pontil marks. About 4–10″

Type and Dimensions
Left: bottle blown in full-size 1-piece mold for shape. Neck and lip finished. Layer of glass glued over label after annealing. Height: 9¾″. Right: bottle free-blown, then tooled into shape. Height: 8″. Both: gilt fixed by firing; paint applied. Stoppers pressed; necks and stoppers ground.

Locality and Period
The East and Midwest. Left: c. 1850–90. Right: c. 1790–1855.

Comment
Fancy bottles like those shown here were usually sold to an apothecary in sets of 4 or more, each labeled with the name of a standard medicine. They were made of a better quality glass than the green glass used for ordinary bottles.

Hints for Collectors
Early bottles without the glass cover and those in transparent blue and opaque white are much scarcer than colorless examples with glass over the label. A set of early bottles is a real find.

Engraved cologne bottle

Description
Cylindrical bottle, narrower toward base. Medium-length neck. Wide, flanged lip. Cut panels on neck; engraved, polished flowers and leaves around body. Polished pontil mark and acid-stamped "S" in a wreath on circular base. Mushroom-shaped stopper with engraved leaf design. Colorless.

Variations
Bottle may be globe-shaped or oval. Engraved motifs occasionally include birds, insects, or other designs.

Type and Dimensions
Bottle and stopper free-blown separately and tooled into shape. Copper-wheel engraved, cut, and polished after annealing. Neck and stopper ground. Height: 6¼".

Locality and Period
H.P. Sinclaire & Company, Corning, New York. c. 1920–29. Variants from throughout the United States. c. 1900–35.

Comment
Although engraved dresser sets are less common than cut-glass sets, they were popular slightly longer. Cut-glass sets often included components such as the puff box and hair receiver box, which went out of vogue after World War I when bobbed hair and different makeup came into fashion. Since engraved sets did not usually feature these accessories, they remained stylish longer.

Hints for Collectors
Engraved colognes with trademarks are often more valuable than those without, but do not overlook unmarked pieces with high-quality engraving. Excellence of execution is even more important than a trademark.

Brilliant-cut cologne bottle

Description
Bell-shaped bottle with long neck. Wide, flanged lip. Cut panels on neck; cut geometric pattern around body. Cut multipointed star on circular base and on top of flat mushroom-shaped stopper with air bubble inside. Colorless.

Variations
Bottle may be globe-shaped or cylindrical. Cut motifs vary widely, including strawberry diamonds, fans, hobnails, hobstars, cane pattern, or any combination of these designs. Rarely cased with transparent red, blue, green, or yellow glass, with designs cut through colored layer. Stopper may be silver.

Type and Dimensions
Bottle and stopper free-blown separately and tooled into shape. Cut after annealing. Neck and stopper ground. Height: 6¾".

Locality and Period
Throughout the United States. c. 1890–1910.

Comment
While cut-glass dressing table accessories were often made in matched sets of 3 to 7 pieces, cologne bottles were also sold singly or in pairs. A piece like the one shown here with elaborate cut motifs over nearly the entire surface is typical of the period and in a style called brilliant-cut glass.

Hints for Collectors
Many cut-glass colognes bear acid-etched trademarks on their bases. Look also for a trademark on the shank of the stopper and be sure that the stopper fits the bottle.

French dressing bottle

Description
Corset-shaped bottle with short neck. Wide, flanged lip formed into pouring spout. Faint vertical ribs around body. 1 side has engraving of flower and leaf sprays with "Oil" above and "Vinegar" below. Polished pontil mark on circular base. Flat mushroom-shaped stopper. Colorless.

Variations
Engraved floral decoration varies greatly. May have cut, gilt, or colored enameled decoration. May have acid-etched signature "Hawkes" on base.

Type and Dimensions
Bottle blown in vertically ribbed dip mold, then expanded and tooled into shape after removal from mold. Stone-wheel engraved after annealing. Stopper pressed. Neck and stopper ground. Height: 7½".

Locality and Period
T.G. Hawkes & Company, Corning, New York. 1914–c. 1945. Variants from Fostoria Glass Company, Moundsville, West Virginia. 1916–c. 1935.

Comment
Townsend deMoleyns Hawkes, a first cousin of T.G. Hawkes, patented this French dressing bottle in 1914. As fashions changed so did the engraved decorations; only the corset shape and the words "Oil" and "Vinegar" were constant. In 1916 Hawkes sold Fostoria a license enabling it to make the same shape with gilt or enameled decoration, but did not permit cut or engraved embellishment.

Hints for Collectors
With or without a trademark, Hawkes colognes are much more valuable than those by Fostoria.

Dresser perfume bottle

Description
Hexagonal bottle with short neck. Flanged lip. Each side has raised hexagonal panel patterned with diamonds. Slight indentation on hexagonal base. Pointed, pineapple-patterned stopper. Colors: opaque white, blue, and green.

Type and Dimensions
Bottle pressed in mold from bottom for pattern and shape. Base tooled closed after removal from mold. Stopper pressed separately. Neck and stopper ground. Height: 4¾".

Locality and Period
New England Glass Company, Cambridge, Massachusetts. c. 1869. New England and the Midwest. c. 1860–80.

Comment
Several major tableware factories, such as the Boston & Sandwich Glass Company and New England Glass Company in Massachusetts and others in Pittsburgh, made ornamental perfume bottles for the dressing table as well as bottles to be sold to cosmetics manufacturers through china and glass retailers. Most of the ornamental bottles were free-blown or mold-blown, then decorated with cutting, engraving, or gilding. A few were pressed in simple molds with no further decoration, like the example illustrated, which appears in an 1869 New England Glass Company catalogue. The technique of pressing a bottle from the bottom and then tooling the base closed was developed in the second half of the 19th century, and was more common in the Midwest.

Hints for Collectors
Since the bottle shown is seldom recognized as a New England Glass Company product, it may be sold for less than its true value.

Description
Rectangular or cylindrical bottle with medium-length neck. Narrow, flat collar. Left: bumps around body; 1 side has panel with inscription "VAPO-CRESOLENE/PATD US JULY 17 85." Square base without pontil mark. Colors: transparent aquamarine and colorless. Right: 1 side has recessed panel with plain surface for label. Circular base without pontil mark. Stopper with pointed bumps has "POISON" on 1 side. Color: transparent dark blue.

Variations
Height and width vary slightly. Bumps and inscriptions vary.

Type and Dimensions
Bottle blown in full-size multipiece mold for pattern and shape. Stopper pressed. Neck and stopper ground. Height: 4″.

Locality and Period
Left: throughout the United States. c. 1885–1910. Right: Whitall, Tatum & Company, Millville, New Jersey. 1872–c. 1910.

Comment
In 1872 the American Medical Association suggested that drug companies use rough-textured colored bottles for poison so that they could be recognized by touch. The bottle on the left contained Vapo-Cresolene, a poisonous substance that when burned was supposed to give off healthful fumes. It probably had a cork stopper. The bottle on the right came in 9 sizes from one-half to 16 ounces.

Hints for Collectors
Collecting poison bottles is a comparatively new field, and many bottles are still available at moderate prices.

150 Hexagonal smelling salts bottle

Description
Hexagonal bottle with short neck. Plain lip. Horizontal rib on 4
sides; other 2 flat. Hexagonal base without pontil mark. Colors:
transparent light and dark purple, light and dark green, blue-
green, and colorless; opaque white and blue; 2 or more opaque
colors of any hue may be marbled. White metal push-on cap.

Variations
Bottle may be more violin- or pear-shaped; both with flat panels
around sides. Rarely with engraved initials, a short name, or
dates. May have paper label.

Type and Dimensions
Blown in full-size multipiece mold for shape. Neck and lip
finished. Height: 2½".

Locality and Period
Boston & Sandwich Glass Company, Sandwich, Massachusetts;
New England Glass Company, Cambridge, Massachusetts; and
probably firms in Pittsburgh area. c. 1850–80.

Comment
The bottle pictured here was presented to a relative by the
family of a worker at Boston & Sandwich. Bottles of this type are
occasionally found with paper labels identifying the contents as
smelling salts. Judging from their small size, they were probably
carried in a lady's purse or reticule. Since tight corsets were
popular at the time, women occasionally took a whiff of smelling
salts to keep from fainting.

Hints for Collectors
Blue and purple are the colors most eagerly sought today. Dated
or monogrammed bottles in any color are rare.

Turlington's Balsam bottle

Description
Flattened, angular, pear-shaped bottle with short neck. Flanged lip. Front has inscription "BY/THE/KINGS/ROYALL/PATENT/GRANTED/ TO"; reverse side has "ROB^T/TURLI/NGTON/FOR/HIS/INVENTED/ BALSOM/OF LIFE." 1 edge has "LONDON," and other has "JAN 26 1754." Pontil mark on oblong base. Colors: transparent light green, light aquamarine, and colorless.

Variations
Bottle may have "THE/KINGS/PATENT" on front and "TUR/LING/TONS/ BALSAM" on reverse. "ROYALL" may have only 1 "L." Edges may be smooth, or have "JAN 28 1770." Lip may be plain.

Type and Dimensions
Blown in full-size multipiece mold for pattern and shape. Neck and lip finished. Height: 2⅜".

Locality and Period
England; widely exported to the United States. 1754–c. 1850. Some variants from New England and New Jersey. c. 1800–80.

Comment
Robert Turlington, a London apothecary, started using bottles in this unusual shape in 1754 to prevent "the villainy of some persons who buying up my empty bottles have basely and wickedly put therein a vile spurious counterfeit." The oldest patent medicine, his balsam seems to have been the first remedy to be sold in a distinctive bottle. By the 19th century American apothecaries were compounding their own Turlington Balsam, and American glasshouses copied the angular bottles.

Hints for Collectors
It is impossible to distinguish English and American Turlington bottles. Condition is more important.

Lalique perfume bottle

Description
Circular bottle with short neck. Plain lip. 1 side has bird and foliage, with inscription "LE JADE" near base; other has foliage and "ROGER ET GALLET PARIS" near base. Acid-stamped "R.LALIQUE FRANCE" on narrow, oblong base; no pontil mark. Matching mushroom-shaped stopper. Color: opaque green.

Variations
Many shapes, designs, and colors; usually transparent blue, amber, or grayish colorless glass. Many have large, elaborate stoppers. Base may have "LALIQUE," "R.LALIQUE," or lack mark.

Type and Dimensions
Bottle blown in full-size multipiece mold for pattern and shape. Stopper pressed. Neck and stopper ground, then polished. Height: 3¼".

Locality and Period
René Lalique et Cie, Wingen-sur-Moder, France; widely exported to the United States. c. 1920–30. Variants 1907–40.

Comment
The work of René Lalique, jewelry and glass designer and manufacturer, spans both the Art Nouveau and Art Deco styles. In 1907 François Coty commissioned him to design perfume bottles, first made by the LeGras factory in St. Denis, but after 1908 by Lalique's own company. Some Lalique designs have been produced since the 1930s, but many new ones were introduced in the 1960s.

Hints for Collectors
When Lalique glass became extremely popular in the 1970s, prices soared; they are somewhat more reasonable today.

Lion-design smelling salts or cologne bottle

Description
Flattened rectangular bottle with recessed shoulders and base. Short neck. Flanged lip. 1 side has rectangular panel with lion facing left with its left paw on a ball; scrolls above and below. Other side has scrolls but rectangle is blank. Plain edges. Pontil mark on rectangular base. Colors: opaque white and light blue, and transparent dark blue, aquamarine, and colorless.

Variations
Sizes of lion and scrolls vary. Neck length varies. Lip may be plain.

Type and Dimensions
Blown in full-size multipiece mold for pattern and shape. Neck and lip finished. Height: 4½″.

Locality and Period
Williamstown Glass Works, Williamstown, 1840–54; Stanger Glass Works, Glassboro, 1848–52; and other New Jersey glasshouses, c. 1840–60. Possibly France and Bohemia. c. 1840–60.

Comment
According to factory records, both the Williamstown and Stanger glasshouses made cologne bottles with a lion design on 1 side. At least 4 different molds were made for these bottles, but there is no way to tell which factory used which molds. Williamstown sold their bottles to perfumers for 62½ cents per dozen. The lion pictured on these bottles resembles the Lion of Lucerne, a bas-relief monument in Lucerne, Switzerland.

Hints for Collectors
Because the opaque white and dark blue versions of this bottle are more popular with collectors, they are considerably more expensive.

154 Philadelphia Memorial Hall cologne bottle

Description
Flattened rectangular bottle on oblong base has long, ornate neck. Narrow, flat collar. 1 side has oval frame with design of Philadelphia Memorial Hall and inscription "MEMORIAL HALL 1876"; diamond pattern above and floral design below. Other side has same designs but oval is blank. Oblong base without pontil mark. Colorless.

Type and Dimensions
Blown in full-size multipiece mold for pattern and shape. Neck and collar fire-polished before annealing. Height: 6½".

Locality and Period
Probably the East; possibly Gillinder & Sons, Philadelphia. 1876.

Comment
This bottle was made later than most similar mold-blown cologne bottles and does not have the earlier, simple flanged lip. Both the molded collar and the absence of a pontil mark date the bottle to the 1870s or 1880s. Hundreds of glass souvenirs, most in pressed glass, were manufactured for the Centennial, and Gillinder & Sons even built a glasshouse on the Centennial grounds. This cologne bottle may have been blown there, but it was more likely made elsewhere, filled at a perfume distillery, and then sold at the Centennial.

Hints for Collectors
Since the Bicentennial, Centennial souvenirs have been avidly collected. Although some of the pressed-glass souvenirs were reproduced in 1976, this one was not.

Hall's Hair Renewer bottle

Description
Rectangular bottle with medium-length neck. Flanged lip. 1 side
has inscription "HALL'S"; 1 side has "HAIR RENEWER." Paper label
around neck printed with same words. Square base has "RPH &
CO" and no pontil mark. Stopper with small knobs. Color:
transparent dark blue-green.

Variations
Similar bottles for other hair preparations, such as "MRS. A.
ALLEN'S WORLD HAIR RESTORER," "AYER'S HAIR VIGOR," and "DR.
TEBBETT'S PHYSIOLOGICAL HAIR REGENERATOR." Variants purple,
blue, and reddish-purple, respectively.

Type and Dimensions
Bottle blown in full-size multipiece mold for pattern and shape.
Neck and lip finished. Stopper pressed. Height: 7¼".

Locality and Period
Probably New Jersey. 1866–c. 1890. Variants also from Ohio.

Comment
Reuben P. Hall of Nashua, New Hampshire, first marketed his
Purely Vegetable Sicilian Hair Renewer in 1866, but soon
shortened the name. It became so popular that Hall bought
another formula, Buckingham's Whisker Dye. He eventually sold
his hair renewer to James C. Ayer, who manufactured Ayer's
Hair Vigor in Lowell, Massachusetts. Hall's and Ayer's bottles
are very much alike and have the same kind of stopper. Because
these bottles were meant to be kept on a dressing table, they
were usually made in bright colors.

Hints for Collectors
Colored hair grower bottles are quite rare. An example in good
shape, in an unusual color, and with its matching stopper will be
expensive.

Pepper sauce bottle

Description
Rectangular bottle with steeply sloping shoulders and short neck
bent to 1 side. Double rounded collar. Protruding horizontal ribs
around body; inscription "E.R./DURKEE/1874" near base. Hexagonal
base with "E.R.DURKEE/E C./N.Y." and no pontil mark. Colors:
transparent aquamarine, green, and colorless.

Variations
Spacing between ribs varies; ribs may be vertical or slightly
spiraled. Sides may have pointed arched panels. Bottle usually
lacks inscriptions. Neck usually straight. 6–12″.

Type and Dimensions
Blown in full-size multipiece mold for pattern and shape. Neck
finished; collar applied. Height: 8¼″.

Locality and Period
The East. c. 1850–70.

Comment
In the 19th century, pepper sauce was a popular seasoning,
which consisted primarily of vinegar, peppers, and spices. In the
days before electric refrigeration, pepper sauce, catsup, and
other condiments helped disguise the taste of meat or vegetables
that were beginning to turn. Today's Tabasco sauce is a modern
survivor of this product. The pepper sauce once contained in the
bottle shown here was distributed by the Durkee company, still
in business today.

Hints for Collectors
Pepper sauce bottles were made in many factories for a long
time, but not one bears a glass manufacturer's mark. They vary
so greatly in decoration and size that a large collection could be
assembled without repeating the same bottle.

Description
Rectangular bottle with steeply sloping shoulders and medium-length neck. Flanged lip. Each side has broad vertical rib. Paper label has pink roses, green leaves, gilt scrolls, and portrait of Jenny Lind in a military costume with "JENNY LIND" above and "COLOGNE" below. Square base without pontil mark. Colors: transparent blue, opaque white, and colorless.

Variations
Bottle may be cylindrical; may have 8–12 vertical panels around sides. Label may name another brand; may lack label.

Type and Dimensions
Blown in full-size multipiece mold for pattern and shape. Neck and lip finished. Height: 8¾".

Locality and Period
Probably New England or New Jersey. 1850–51.

Comment
Cologne bottles from the mid-19th century came in a wide variety of shapes, and the one illustrated here is among the simplest. These graceful bottles were a staple of most bottle glasshouses, but because so few were marked, it is rarely possible to know the manufacturer or date. Jenny Lind, a Swedish singer, toured the United States in 1850–51. She was an immediate success, and her likeness appeared on a variety of bottles. On this one, she is dressed for her role in *Daughter of the Regiment*.

Hints for Collectors
Sometimes it is possible to date an unknown bottle by comparing it with a similarly shaped datable example, such as the Lind cologne.

Description
Cylindrical bottle with long neck. Plain lip. Narrow neck ring.
Swirled ribs around body; blank oval for label on 1 side. Paper
label printed with woman's head and "BAY RUM" below with
"A.W.HOLSAPPLE." (left) or "GEORGE CLARK." (right), and covered
with thin layer of colorless glass. Circular base without pontil
mark. Colors: opaque blue and white. Metal sprinkler cap.

Variations
Lip may be flanged. Body may lack swirled ribs; may have
enameled floral decoration or cut decoration. Label may be
printed "TOILET WATER." May lack thin layer of glass over label.

Type and Dimensions
Blown in full-size multipiece mold for pattern and shape. Neck
and lip finished. Layer of glass glued over label after annealing.
Height: 11½".

Locality and Period
Throughout the United States. Europe; widely exported to the
United States. c. 1870–1910.

Comment
Bay rum was a popular men's scent used after shaving in the late
19th century. It is likely that both bottles shown here contained
the same brand of bay rum, and that Clark and Holsapple were
the owners of 2 barbershops, since it was common for the
proprietor to have his own printed label.

Hints for Collectors
There are many reproductions of barber and bay rum bottles,
but none were made using 19th-century methods. Although some
authentic bottles lack the glass-covered label, no reproduction
has it.

Barber bottles

Description
Globe-shaped bottle with long neck. Flanged lip (left, center) or plain lip (right). Enameled and gilt decoration of a little girl blowing bubbles, a woman's head with "VEGEDERMA" below, or flowers. Polished pontil mark on circular base. Colors: transparent purple, blue, red, and amber; opaque white and blue; and colorless. Metal sprinkler cap.

Variations
May have engraved floral or leaf designs, or molded ribs or diamonds. May have "WITCH HAZEL," "HAIR TONIC" or "TONIC" enameled, engraved, or on paper label.

Type and Dimensions
Blown in dip mold, then expanded and tooled into shape after removal from mold. Neck and lip finished. Enamel and gilt fixed by firing after annealing. Left height: 9″. Center height: 9¼″. Right height: 8¾″.

Locality and Period
Throughout the United States. Bohemia; widely exported to the United States. c. 1870–1910.

Comment
Toward the end of the 19th century, the barber's role changed from barber-surgeon to haircutter, and he often stocked his hair preparations in fancy bottles. The type of white enameling on the bottle at the left is called Mary Gregory decoration because early collectors believed it was all done by Mary Gregory of the well-known Boston & Sandwich Glass Company. However, 90 percent of this glass is Bohemian.

Hints for Collectors
Beware of the many reproductions on the market; most look quite new.

Show globes

Description
Tier of 3 globe-shaped bottles, each with cut circles around sides, short neck, and flanged lip. Top 2 globes have shank that fits into neck of globe below; lowest globe has circular foot, with polished pontil mark and paper label underneath. Faceted ball stopper. Colorless.

Variations
May have 2–4 globes, other cut patterns, or plain sides.

Type and Dimensions
Globes and stopper free-blown separately and tooled into shape. Shanks and foot applied. Globes and stopper cut after annealing. Necks, shanks, and stopper ground. Height: 33″.

Locality and Period
C. Dorflinger & Sons, White Mills, Pennsylvania. c. 1880–1900. Variants from the East and Midwest. c. 1820–1900.

Comment
During the 19th century, fancy show globes like those shown here were set in windows or on counters of apothecary shops to attract clients. Each globe was filled with a colored liquid, usually water. The example illustrated bears the paper label of C. Dorflinger & Sons, a well-known tableware manufacturer, which used this name after 1881. Plain show globes appear in several glass-company catalogues from the 1850s to the 1880s. Nineteenth-century travel accounts describe similar bottles displayed in Philadelphia as early as the 1820s.

Hints for Collectors
Be careful when handling these globes; the sections come apart easily.

Bellows bottle

Description
Pear-shaped bottle with long neck. Plain lip. Incomplete colored stripes around sides. Raised decoration of leaf shapes and ribbonlike threading on body; 3 rings around neck. Straight stem with circular foot and pontil mark underneath. Long-shanked stopper with bird-shaped finial. Colors: transparent blue, green, purple, yellow, opaque white, and colorless with contrasting stripes.

Variations
Wide variety of body proportions, decoration, coloring, and finials. Bottle may be single color and lack contrasting stripes. May lack stopper.

Type and Dimensions
Bottle free-blown, then tooled into shape. Stripes applied and marvered into surface before annealing. Collar, leaf shapes, threading, rings, stem, and foot applied. Stopper free-blown and tooled. Finial applied. Height: 14″.

Locality and Period
The East. England; widely exported to the United States. c. 1850–80.

Comment
Bottles of this type were designed primarily for display. In the example illustrated, the neck and stopper are not ground, an indication of the bottle's purely decorative purpose. The name comes from the bellowslike shape. Although most bellows bottles were found in New England, probably every tableware glasshouse in the East made them. Each is a one-of-a-kind object and reflects the personality and skill of its maker.

Hints for Collectors
If any decoration is missing or chipped, value decreases.

Amberina perfume bottle

Description
Slender, oval bottle with short neck. Flaring, scalloped, flanged
lip. Faint vertical ribs around body. Circular foot with polished
pontil mark underneath; acid-stamped "Libbey" in a circle and
"Amberina" in script. Ball stopper with knop and long shank.
Colors: transparent amber at base shading to deep red at top.

Variations
Same shape in colorless or transparent colored glass with or
without engraving, or in iridescent blue or gold (Aurene by
Steuben), but *these are not Amberina*.

Type and Dimensions
Bottle blown in vertically ribbed dip mold, then expanded and
tooled into shape after removal from mold. Partially reheated to
develop shading before annealing. Stopper pressed. Neck and
stopper ground. Height: 6⅝".

Locality and Period
Libbey Glass Company, Toledo, Ohio. 1917.

Comment
The New England Glass Works produced the shaded amber and
red Amberina glass from 1883 to 1888. After the company
became the Libbey Glass Company, Amberina was revived in
1917 for only a year. The 20th-century pieces bear the acid-
stamped trademark "Libbey" on the base and come in more
modern shapes, such as the one illustrated.

Hints for Collectors
Look for the trademark on all Amberina glass. If there is no
trademark, the piece could be from the 1880s or it could be a
reproduction made in the past 10 years. Reproductions are
usually of thicker, heavier glass and have harsher or paler colors.

Whimsy bottle

Description
Wide, pear-shaped bottle with wide, short neck. Flanged lip.
Flower and scroll design around body. 2 elaborate handles with
crested bird perched on each. Pontil mark on irregular, circular
base. Colors: transparent aquamarine and colorless; light purple
bird.

Variations
Scroll design and neck width vary according to bottle mold.
Handles and other decoration vary greatly.

Type and Dimensions
Blown in full-size multipiece mold for pattern and shape. Neck
and lip finished. Handles and birds applied. Height: 4½″.

Locality and Period
Probably New Jersey; possibly Massachusetts. c. 1840–60.
Variants from the East.

Comment
Whimsies like the one illustrated here were made in many
glasshouses. Each is unique, depending on the whim and skill of
the maker. This one may have been used as a vase.

Hints for Collectors
An individualized bottle is much harder to find than a bottle that
remains true to the mold. This one was blown in a standard
cologne bottle mold, but widened at the neck and embellished
with handles and birds. Whimsical pieces tend to be popular
with collectors and much more expensive than the unadorned
equivalent. Because they were probably made as gifts and were
highly prized by their original owners, most have been carefully
kept. Thus they may turn up at house sales, but are seldom
found at dump sites or during impromptu digs.

Standing gemel bottle

Description
Body consists of 2 flattened oval bottles joined at base. 2 curved necks point in opposite directions. Plain lips. Alternating loops of white and colored glass around body. Raised branchlike decoration on sides. Circular foot with pontil mark underneath. Colors: 1 color or any 2 or 3 combined; opaque or transparent red, green, and blue; opaque white; transparent amber, aquamarine, and purple; colorless.

Variations
Looped decoration varies. May have engraved flowers, leaves, or initials instead of loops.

Type and Dimensions
Each bottle free-blown separately and tooled into shape. Loops applied and marvered into surface, and bottles joined before annealing. Branchlike decoration and base applied. Height: 11⅛″.

Locality and Period
New England, southern New Jersey, and western Pennsylvania. England and continental Europe; widely exported to the United States. c. 1850–70. Variants c. 1830–70.

Comment
Vessels made to hold 2 or more liquids have been known since Roman times. The form was revived in the 19th century, with double bottles for oil and vinegar, and 2-, 3-, and 4-bottle decanters for liqueurs. This one has a capacity of about 8 ounces in each section. It is attributed to the Pittsburgh area, where opaque white glass with colored loops was particularly popular around mid-century.

Hints for Collectors
Brightly colored glass has always been prized by collectors.

Horizontal gemel bottle

Description
Body consists of 2 flattened oval bottles joined at base. 2 curved necks point in opposite directions. Plain lips. Crimped, ribbonlike decoration on edges; leaf shape on 2 sides. Pontil mark on narrow end. Colors: 1 color or any 2 or 3 combined; opaque or transparent red, green, and blue; opaque white; transparent amber, aquamarine, purple, and dark brown; colorless.

Variations
May have engraved flowers, leaves, or initials. May have colored loops within glass. Ribbonlike decoration varies.

Type and Dimensions
Each bottle free-blown separately and tooled into shape, then joined before annealing. Ribbonlike decoration and leaf shapes applied. Length: 7⅞".

Locality and Period
New England, southern New Jersey, and western Pennsylvania. England and continental Europe; widely exported to the United States. c. 1820–60.

Comment
Bottles with 2 joined parts like the examples shown here and on the opposite page are called gemel bottles. This horizontal bottle was possibly a perfume container for the dressing table: One part held perfume and the other was probably filled with an ammonia-based scent. It was blown in a glasshouse in Tansboro, New Jersey; the leaf decoration is found on only a few pieces from southern New Jersey.

Hints for Collectors
Horizontal gemel bottles like this one are much less common than the standing type.

Seahorse scent bottle

Description
Bottle in form of spiral with neck as vertical extension of coil.
Plain lip. White parallel stripes run lengthwise through spiral.
Crimped decoration on sides. Pontil mark on bottom of coil.
Colors: 2 or 3 colors combined; transparent blue, green, amber,
and purple, opaque white, and colorless.

Variations
Shape and applied decoration vary. Stripes may be latticelike or
twisted; may lack stripes. May have ribs.

Type and Dimensions
Free-blown, then tooled into shape. Stripes applied and
marvered into surface before annealing. Crimped decoration
applied. Height: 2½″.

Locality and Period
Probably Boston & Sandwich Glass Company, Sandwich,
Massachusetts; New England Glass Company, Cambridge,
Massachusetts; and other New England factories. Possibly
southern New Jersey or England. c. 1820–50.

Comment
Collectors call spiral bottles like the one illustrated here seahorse
scent bottles. Closed with small cork stoppers, they were carried
in a pocketbook or used on a dressing table. Most have been
found in New England, suggesting that the majority were made
there.

Hints for Collectors
Seahorse scent bottles have been collected longer than most
other perfume bottles and they are often expensive today.

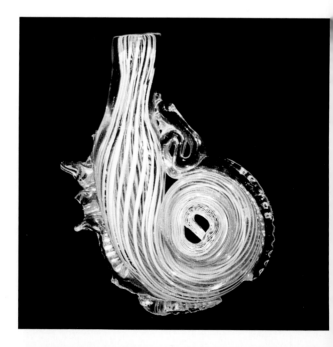

Verre de Soie perfume bottle

Description
Bulb-shaped bottle with 8 lobes at base and short neck. Flanged lip. Horizontal green threads around body. Polished pontil mark on base. Matching pointed oval stopper with 6 vertical ribs and long, pointed shank. Colors: iridescent colorless with transparent yellow, green, or blue threads.

Variations
Shape may be oval. May lack threading and have engraved initial or monogram. Bottle may be iridescent dark blue or iridescent gold and lack threading; *these are Aurene.*

Type and Dimensions
Bottle and stopper free-blown separately and tooled into shape. Neck and lip finished; threading applied. Sprayed with chemical for iridescent finish before annealing. Neck and stopper ground. Height: 4¾".

Locality and Period
Steuben Glass Works, Corning, New York. 1903–32.

Comment
Iridescent colorless glass of the type illustrated is called Verre de Soie, and the iridescent blue or gold finish was named Aurene. Most Steuben pieces are marked, usually "Steuben Aurene" in script with a stock number or "Steuben" and the fleur-de-lis trademark. The bottle shown is unmarked, but its shape and decoration are unquestionably Steuben.

Hints for Collectors
Perfume bottles like this were made singly and in sets for dressing tables. Tiffany iridescent blue and gold Favrile glass is identical to Aurene, but all pieces are marked.

Art-glass perfume bottle

Description
Long, conical bottle with short neck. Plain lip. Gilt flower-and-leaf decoration around body. Polished pontil mark on narrow end. Colors: transparent dark red, pink, purple, and blue, all lined with opaque white. Silver collar with screw threads; silver screw-on cap with flowers engraved on top.

Variations
Bottle may be globe-shaped. May have diamond quilting or herringbone air-trap design and matt finish. Cap may be monogrammed. Bottle may have glass stopper.

Type and Dimensions
Opaque white glass free-blown and cased with colored glass, then tooled into shape. Gilt fixed by firing. Height: 11¼″.

Locality and Period
England; probably Thomas Webb & Sons or Stevens & Williams Glass Company, Staffordshire; widely exported to the United States. c. 1880–1910. Possibly Massachusetts and Phoenix Glass Company, Monaca, Pennsylvania. c. 1880–90.

Comment
Art-glass perfume bottles in this shape were designed for a purse if they were 4″ or shorter. Longer bottles were usually placed on the dressing table. Although American firms that specialized in art glass, such as Mt. Washington Glass Company and New England Glass Works, may have produced similar perfume bottles, the great majority were imported.

Hints for Collectors
Only some English bottles bear the glassmaker's name, but all silver fittings are marked. If the symbols can be read clearly, consult a book on English silver trademarks.

Cameo perfume bottle

Description
Flattened, egg-shaped bottle with short neck. Plain lip. Raised
design of white leaves and flowers. Polished pontil mark on
narrow end. Colors: opaque purple, pink, red, blue, yellow, and
green, all cased with opaque white.

Variations
Shape may be much longer and more pointed, globe-shaped, or in
form of bird's head with beak. Cameo design may include birds
or insects. Bottle may have glass or silver stopper or silver collar
with hinged lid and glass stopper inside.

Type and Dimensions
Colored glass free-blown and cased with white glass, then tooled
into shape. Partly acid-etched, partly hand-carved after
annealing. Lip ground. Height: 4⅛″.

Locality and Period
England; probably Thomas Webb & Sons or Stevens & Williams
Glass Company, Staffordshire; widely exported to the United
States. c. 1880–1910. Similar bottles by Gillinder & Sons,
Philadelphia. c. 1890–1900.

Comment
Cameo glass gets its name from the type of carving done on
ancient Roman gems: The design is of one color and the
background another. As far as is known, only a few pieces of
cameo glass were ever made in the United States, all at the
factory of Gillinder & Sons.

Hints for Collectors
Purchase expensive cameo glass only from a reputable dealer.
The more delicate the shading, the better the cameo carving and
the more desirable the piece.

Miscellaneous Glass

Not only did American glassmakers produce a wide variety of bottles, jars, lamps, and candlesticks, but they also created numerous miscellaneous objects. Some, such as furniture knobs, dresser sets, and pressed miniatures, were manufactured as part of a tableware company's inventory; others, such as banks and bells, were made by individual glassblowers working on their own time between shifts; still others, such as paperweights and lampworked souvenirs, were fashioned by specialized craftsmen. Windows were generally the products of window glasshouses and, in the late 19th and early 20th centuries, of design studios.

Products of Tableware Companies

During the early years of the American glass industry, production was devoted to such necessities as bottles, windows, and drinking glasses. By the 1800s, the expanding population as well as an increased demand for fine stemware and bowls encouraged several enterprising companies to concentrate on tableware.

In the 1830s and 1840s, shortly after the introduction of the pressing machine, tableware firms began to offer miniature cups, saucers, pitchers, and bowls along with their full-size products. As pressed glass became easier and cheaper to make, the inventory continued to diversify, and by the end of the 19th century, included doorknobs, eyecups, figural inkstands, match strikers, and souvenir slippers.

If pressed glass appealed to the pocketbooks of most of the population, cut and engraved glass attracted primarily the wealthy. As early as the 1820s, tableware firms employed specially trained cutters and engravers. Some of the fanciest cut or engraved glassware was cased with one or sometimes two colors. In the 1880s, when brilliant-cut patterns became fashionable, cut glass companies advertised elaborate dresser sets, letter racks, card trays, humidors, and many other

Detail of a cut-glass jar.

frivolities. This lavish style was replaced after World War I by simpler designs.

Lampworked Novelties

The technique of lampworking was brought to this country by European glassblowers in the 19th century. Instead of blowing molten glass, the lampworker remelted bits of manufactured glass over a flame. Since at first a lamp flame was often used, these craftsmen came to be called lampworkers. Throughout most of the 19th century, itinerant lampworkers traveled to fairs and carnivals in rural areas, where they staged demonstrations of their art in the hopes of selling souvenirs. The pens, miniature ships, and small animals they created are prized today.

Paperweights

Perhaps some of the most elaborate 19th-century glass designs are paperweights, in which a pattern, often of colored glass, is enclosed in a colorless dome or globe. Beginning in the 1840s, paperweights experienced a sudden vogue in Europe, and many weights of the highest quality were made in French factories at Baccarat, St. Louis, Clichy, and Pantin. They set a standard copied by paperweight manufacturers in England, Bohemia, and the United States. No one knows exactly what caused their popularity, although it has been suggested that the creation of regular postal service and a sharp drop in the price of paper contributed to a surge in letter writing and the desire for desk accessories.

The millefiori and flower weights created by workers at Sandwich, New England Glass, Gillinder, and Dorflinger are among the most distinctive 19th-century American designs. By 1900, artists at Whitall Tatum and Mt. Washington were fashioning large, single-flower weights, sometimes known as Millville and Mt. Washington roses. Paperweight making

Detail of a target ball.

continued in the 20th century at firms such as Pairpoint, Steuben, and several small midwestern factories. Today, paperweight artists employ the same techniques and often similar patterns to those developed in the 19th century.

Window Glass

The first colonists either brought their windowpanes with them from Europe or simply made do with oiled paper or wooden shutters and went without daylight in cold weather. Although some of the short-lived 17th-century glasshouses probably made small panes, most window glass had to be imported from England.

By the end of the 18th century, a few American glasshouses were producing windowpanes, using either the crown or the cylinder method of glassblowing. From 1790 to 1830 the crown method, which produced a smooth, clear surface, was preferred. But because cylinder glass could be blown less expensively and cut into larger panes, it gradually became the standard, and following the Civil War the manufacture of crown glass essentially ceased.

The production of cast plate in the United States began in 1854 with the founding of the Lenox Glass Works in Massachusetts. Since the equipment for both casting and polishing was extremely costly and the process time-consuming, plate glass proved unprofitable. The company closed in 1872, and American manufacture of cast plate did not resume for several years. The casting of plate glass was eventually replaced in the 1950s by the cheaper float method, developed by Pilkington Brothers, Ltd., in England. Today this technique is used to make most plate window glass.

Beginning in the 1880s, decorative windows became enormously popular in American homes. Acid-etched or, rarely, engraved

Detail of a millefiori paperweight.

flowers and monograms decorated both expensive cased windows and moderately priced frosted panes. Even more affordable pressed-glass panes featured floral patterns or crinkled surfaces. Most elaborate were the stained-glass windows, ranging from simple flower-and-leaf designs to complex scenic or figural tableaux. Beveled colorless glass, used for door panels, interior windows, and cabinet panes, had finely polished edges. The panes could be assembled in a variety of geometric patterns, with lead or wood between the panes. Toward the end of World War I, however, all of these fancy panes went out of style in favor of simpler sash windows.

Detail of a stained-glass window from Ballantine House. Collection of the Newark Museum.

Dresser Sets, Bells, and Other Ornamental Glassware

Many of the decorative pieces illustrated in this section were designed to enhance a dressing table, desk, or parlor shelf. Fancy containers such as letter holders and humidors are typical examples of the Victorian love for detail and elegance. Fishbowls, banks, and garden and smoke bells were first popular much earlier, but the demand for them continued into the 19th century.

Dresser Sets

Fashionable in Europe for centuries, many silver, gold, porcelain, and glass containers for a lady's or gentleman's dressing table were exported to the United States during the 19th century. Although wealthy Americans were able to buy American-made bottles and jars of fine cut or engraved glass by mid-century, it was not until about 1870 that porcelain and glass sets, often with silver or silver-plate fittings, were within the financial reach of the middle class.

The smallest dresser set for a lady consisted of two cologne or perfume bottles and a powder jar, cut or engraved and sometimes cased in colored glass. By the 1890s, the number of pieces in a set had increased to include matching powder shakers, small perfume bottles, boxes for jewelry and gloves, pin trays, and other toiletry containers. Accessories for a gentleman, while less extensive, included equally lavish boxes for collars, cuffs, and jewelry, and bottles for bay rum and other toilet lotions.

Although most late 19th-century dresser sets had intricate brilliant-cut patterns, some were also made in the porcelain-like enameled glass that collectors now call art glass. To compete with this more expensive blown ware, companies that made pressed glass promoted fancy sets in iridescent colors, collected today as Carnival glass. After World War I, changes in styles of makeup, hair, and clothing made several types of containers unnecessary, and the multipiece dresser set gradually went out of fashion.

Desk Accessories and Other Ornamental Glassware

For the lady's desk, Victorian manufacturers advertised fancy letter boxes and racks, and small card trays for visiting cards. A humidor for cigars was deemed essential in the gentleman's study. Elsewhere in the Victorian home, glass bells, ornate banks, and string holders decorated the parlor shelf, while simpler fishbowls sat on a side table.

Dresser and desk accessories were produced as part of tableware companies' inventories. Although some of the glass was made here, usually it was imported from England and continental Europe. Imported plain blanks were enameled or otherwise embellished in American shops, or, more often, finished pieces were shipped to the United States and sold with American-made metal stands or fittings. One-of-a-kind banks and bells were also made in tableware factories, but, unlike the dresser accessories, these pieces were usually fashioned by workers on their own time. In contrast, simple garden bells were made in window or bottle glasshouses, while the smoke bells were produced by manufacturers of tableware and lamps.

170 Dresser set in frame

Description
3-piece set with 2 cologne bottles and powder jar in silver-plated frame with handle and 4 feet. Bottles: each globe-shaped with long neck and plain lip; stoppers with flaring, scalloped rims. Jar: globe-shaped; lid with finial that matches stoppers. Gilt trim on cut grooves around necks, stoppers, and finial; birds and branches around globes. Polished pontil mark on each circular base. Colors: opaque white enameled pink shading to light blue; details in brown, yellow, green, and white. Frame marked "Meriden Britannia Co."

Variations
Bottles and jar may be more rectangular. Decoration often flowers.

Type and Dimensions
Bottles and jar blown in separate full-size multipiece molds for shape. Necks and jar mouth finished. Stoppers and lid pressed. Necks and stoppers ground, and scalloped rims and grooves cut. Enamel and gilt fixed by firing. Bottle height: 6″. Jar height: 4½″. Frame height: 10″.

Locality and Period
Glass: probably Bohemia. Frame: Meriden Britannia Company, Meriden, Connecticut. c. 1870–90.

Comment
During the late 19th century, American metalworking firms often imported European glass. A few, such as the Pairpoint Corporation, made both the glass and the silver frames and also supplied glass inserts to other frame manufacturers.

Hints for Collectors
A complete set with bottles, stoppers, jar, and lid is rare.

Dresser set

Description
3-piece set with 2 cologne bottles and powder jar. Bottles: each pear-shaped with long neck and flanged lip; pointed oval stoppers. Jar: squat globe shape; lid with solid knob. Gilt decoration and cut pattern of diamonds and ellipses on bottles, jar, stoppers, and lid. Polished pontil mark on each hexagonal base. Colors: colorless cased with transparent red, green, blue, or yellow; single transparent color, opaque white, and colorless.

Variations
Many cut patterns; may have enameled designs. Set may include small hairpin box, small pin tray, and large set tray.

Type and Dimensions
Bottles, jar, stoppers, and lid free-blown separately and cased with colored glass, then tooled into shape. Pattern cut through and gilt fixed by firing after annealing. Necks and stoppers ground. Bottle height: 9½″. Jar height: 3¾″.

Locality and Period
New England Glass Company, Cambridge, Massachusetts. c. 1860–70. Variants from the East and Midwest. England and continental Europe; widely exported to the United States. c. 1860–1900.

Comment
The set illustrated was made for the daughter of a New England Glass Company superintendent. A similar set in green was commissioned for her sister.

Hints for Collectors
Many dresser sets were made in Europe, and it is difficult to distinguish imported sets from American ones. The quality of the decoration is more important than origin.

Description
Trumpet with 1 ring below mouthpiece and 2 sets of double rings around shaft. Shaft has engraved leaf designs and engraved inscription "Presented/to/David M. Lyle/of/Philadelphia/By/Harry Tatnall/of/Pittsburgh"; bell has "John Steen/Maker/Pittsburgh, Pa." within wreath. Colorless.

Variations
Trumpet may have other inscriptions, be plain, or have ribs. Shape may be bugle or French horn. Variants colorless and frequently transparent dark blue.

Type and Dimensions
Free-blown, then tooled into shape. Rings applied. Mouthpiece cut into shape and body copper-wheel engraved after annealing. Height: 19¾".

Locality and Period
Pittsburgh. 1860–68. Variants from the East and Midwest. c. 1800–80. England; widely exported to the United States. c. 1700–1850.

Comment
The glass horn shown here is a fireman's presentation trumpet, used in parades of volunteer firemen in the 19th century. Most fireman's trumpets are brass, but a number of glass ones have been found, usually elaborately engraved. Other glass horns, such as the dark blue or colorless ribbed variations, are whimsies, created for fun. Some of them actually produce a sound when blown, but this trumpet does not.

Hints for Collectors
Collectors of firemen's memorabilia are always delighted to find presentation horns, and glass ones are especially desirable because they are so rare.

Description
Bell has solid handle with 3 knops. Loop decoration around body; glass loop inside with wired-on metal clapper. Colors: transparent red, blue, purple, green, and yellow; opaque white, red, blue, and green; colorless; and 2 opaque or transparent colors for body and loops, or for body and handle.

Variations
Decoration may be engraved, cut, or enameled; body may lack loop decoration; may have ribs. Rarely with metal handle. Sizes 3–15″; 3–8″ most common.

Type and Dimensions
Free-blown, then tooled into shape. Loop decoration applied and marvered into surface before annealing. Handle tooled into shape and applied; glass clapper loop applied. Height: 6″.

Locality and Period
Southern New Jersey and the Pittsburgh area. England; widely exported to the United States. c. 1850–80. Variants from the East and Midwest. c. 1800–1900. England and continental Europe. c. 1600–1900.

Comment
Most bells made in the 19th century were simply decorative. Bells with loop decoration are often attributed to Nailsea, England, but research has revealed that this kind of decoration was made in many areas of England, specifically near Stourbridge, and that the Nailsea factory produced ordinary bottles.

Hints for Collectors
No longer easy to find, bells are most likely to turn up in a general antiques shop.

Description
Conical body with slot for coins in flat top. 4 rods support 3 solid knops; twisted threading from rods to top knop. Loop decoration around body. Hollow stem with 3 rings. Flat circular foot with pontil mark underneath. Colors: transparent purple, blue, aquamarine, light green, opaque white, colorless, and colorless combined with any other color.

Variations
Many shapes and types of threaded decoration. Body may have ribs. Stem may have knops; may have coin in stem and/or in hollow knop. Top may be fancier, perhaps with a bird; may have more knops.

Type and Dimensions
Free-blown, then tooled into shape. Loop decoration applied and marvered into surface before annealing. Rods, knops, threading, stem, foot, and rings applied. Height: 11⅝". Foot diameter: 3¾".

Locality and Period
Boston & Sandwich Glass Company, Sandwich, Massachusetts; New England Glass Company, Cambridge, Massachusetts; and other factories in New England, New York, New Jersey, and possibly the Midwest. c. 1820–50.

Comment
During the mid-19th century, ornate glass banks were made in a wide variety of colors, shapes, and sizes. Applying the rods, knops, and threaded decoration on the example pictured required great care to prevent the entire structure from collapsing.

Hints for Collectors
Some banks had even fancier designs than the one illustrated. All are quite rare and expensive.

Bank

Description
Globe-shaped body with wide, short neck and concave top with slot for coins. Zigzag threading around rim and berrylike prunts on body and neck. Flat circular foot with pontil mark underneath. Colorless.

Variations
Body and neck may lack prunts and/or have applied threading.

Type and Dimensions
Free-blown, then tooled into shape. Zigzag threading, prunts, and foot applied. Height: 5½". Foot diameter: 3".

Locality and Period
The East and Midwest. c. 1860–80.

Comment
This bank was probably made 30 or 40 years later than the one with ornate applied decoration (opposite), judging from the presence and shape of the berry prunts. In the 1870s and 1880s prunts were frequently used on art glass to cover pontil marks, and the decoration was even more common in England than the United States. Many banks were broken because there was no way to remove the coins without chipping away the slot or smashing the bank. Since a number have survived, at least some were used only for display.

Hints for Collectors
Later banks, like the one pictured here, should cost less than the more elaborate examples with loops and threading. However, both types are rare and expensive. Look for them at estate sales or in shops specializing in American antiques.

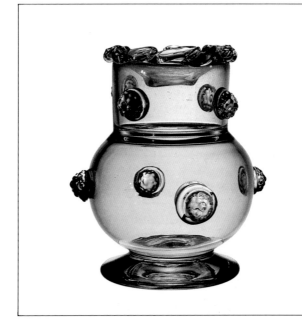

Description
Globe-shaped body has wide mouth with plain rim. Hollow,
funnel-shaped stem widens to circular foot with folded-out base
rim. Pontil mark on base of globe. Colors: colorless; rarely
transparent light aquamarine and light green.

Variations
Mouth size varies. Foot often taller.

Type and Dimensions
Free-blown, then tooled into shape. Stem with foot applied. Base
rim folded for extra strength before annealing. Height: 9¼″.
Bowl diameter: 7⅜″.

Locality and Period
The East and Midwest. c. 1845–80.

Comment
Fishbowls like the example illustrated were made in many
glasshouses in the 19th century. Since they are almost always
colorless, they were probably produced by manufacturers of
tableware rather than makers of windows or bottles. Maintaining
a fishbowl in the 19th century was considered a frivolity and
probably confined only to wealthy city dwellers. Their use is
documented in several paintings of the 1840s and 1850s.
Fishbowls are also found in several glass-company catalogues
from the 1860–90 period. During the 1870s, the catalogues
showed both this type of fishbowl and the round, flat-bottomed
type common today. By the turn of the century, however, the
footed fishbowl had disappeared from catalogues almost entirely.

Hints for Collectors
Fishbowls appeal primarily to collectors of blown glass. Like
string holders, they are rare but not in great demand.

Description
Cylindrical dome with flat collar around small opening at top.
Left: decorated with cut circles. Right: engraved stems and
leaves, with collar and base rim in contrasting color. No pontil
mark. Colors: transparent red, blue, green, yellow, purple,
opaque white, and colorless; single color or 2 or 3 combined;
colorless cased with any of these transparent hues except purple.

Variations
Body may lack decoration and have rim and collar in contrasting
color. May have other simple geometric cut design or floral
engraving. Pressed variants may have ribs, dots, or panels.

Type and Dimensions
Left: colorless glass free-blown and cased with colored glass,
then tooled into shape. Collar applied. Circles cut through after
annealing. Height: 4¾″. Rim diameter: 4⅜″. Right: free-blown,
then tooled into shape; rim and collar applied. Copper-wheel
engraved after annealing. Height and rim diameter: 4⅝″.

Locality and Period
The East. c. 1850–70. Pressed variants from the East and
Midwest. c. 1870–1900.

Comment
Glass string holders were made at many factories in both blown
glass and pressed glass during the second half of the 19th
century. Some match tableware patterns, but many are unique.
The plainer pressed-glass examples were probably meant for use
in the kitchen, while the engraved or cut string holders were
intended for display in a more prominent place.

Hints for Collectors
Pressed string holders are easier to find than blown examples.

Description
High dome with folded-out base rim. Solid round knob. Pontil mark inside dome below knob. Colors: transparent light aquamarine and light green; rarely colorless.

Variations
Dome may be slightly higher or wider.

Type and Dimensions
Free-blown, then tooled into shape. Knob applied and rim folded before annealing. Height: 9½″. Rim diameter: 8⅞″.

Locality and Period
New England, New York, and southern New Jersey. c. 1840–80.

Comment
Garden bells were used to protect delicate plants outdoors and for forcing flowers to bloom early. This function is documented in a few paintings and advertisements, but there is no mention of the bells in any glass-company catalogue. Most garden bells were made in bottle and window glasshouses and are found primarily in what collectors call green glass. It was less costly to produce than colorless glass because no special decolorizers were required.

Hints for Collectors
Because garden bells are not common household objects, few people recognize them, but now and then they turn up at country auctions and barn sales. Along with fishbowls and string holders, garden bells are considered part of a group of early blown-glass oddities.

Smoke bell

Description
Low dome has wide flange with folded-out base rim. Round loop handle. Pontil mark inside dome below handle. Colors: transparent amber and blue, opaque white, opalescent white, and colorless.

Variations
Dome may be slightly higher, larger, or smaller; rarely engraved. Rim may be fluted or applied red or blue glass.

Type and Dimensions
Free-blown, then tooled into shape. Handle applied and rim folded before annealing. Height: 4⅜″. Rim diameter: 16¾″.

Locality and Period
The East and Midwest. England; widely exported to the United States. c. 1800–40. Variants c. 1840–80.

Comment
During the 19th century a smoke bell was used to protect the ceiling of a room or hall from the smoke of a hanging light, usually a candle fixture, but occasionally a whale-oil lamp, and later a gas lamp. Most were undecorated, although a few were engraved to match the fixture. The bell was hung just far enough above the suspended lamp to allow a draft to reach the flame. Since the bell was attached to the lamp by a metal frame, the whole unit could be taken down for cleaning and refueling. The use of smoke bells declined around the turn of the century. Later bells for gas fixtures are taller and narrower than the one illustrated.

Hints for Collectors
Anyone who wants to restore a 19th-century hanging fixture should try to find a smoke bell for complete authenticity.

Letter holder

Description
Rectangular box. Plain rim. Raised scroll design on 3 sides; front has enameled floral design. Rectangular base with ink-stamped inscription "NAKARA/C.F.M.CO." and no pontil mark. Colors: opaque white enameled gray-blue, with design in pink, white, and green. Metal rim at top.

Variations
Box shape and floral designs vary. Enameled background always pastel color, including pink, beige, or green. Base may have enameled trademark or lack trademark.

Type and Dimensions
Blown in full-size multipiece mold for pattern and shape. Enamel fixed by firing after annealing. Height: 2⅝". Length: 4¼".

Locality and Period
Blank: probably Europe; possibly the Northeast. Enameling: C.F. Monroe Company, Meriden, Connecticut. c. 1892–1915.

Comment
The C.F. Monroe Company was strictly a decorating firm, doing enamel work on glass blanks imported from Europe or purchased from nearby manufacturers such as the Mt. Washington Glass Company and later the Pairpoint Corporation. Much of the enameled decoration resembles that on Mt. Washington's Crown Milano ware. Monroe registered the names Wave Crest and Kelva in 1898 and 1904, but Nakara, the line pictured here, was never registered.

Hints for Collectors
C.F. Monroe glassware is not as well known as the products of the Mt. Washington firm and is consequently much less expensive.

Ointment box

Description
Circular box. Plain rim. Row of large raised diamonds between rows of beading around sides. Circular base with concentric circles. Color: opaque white. Push-on metal cap, also with concentric circles.

Variations
May have flat panels on sides and a glass lid.

Type and Dimensions
Pressed in mold for pattern and shape. Height: 1″. Diameter: 2½″.

Locality and Period
New England Glass Company, Cambridge, Massachusetts. c. 1865–88. Variants also from other firms in the East and Midwest. c. 1865–1900.

Comment
The box illustrated appears in a New England Glass Company catalogue of about 1869. It is a simple utilitarian piece, however, and may have been in production for longer than 10 years, probably wholesaled to a compounder of creams and ointments rather than sold empty for an unspecified use. Similar pressed ointment boxes were probably made by all glasshouses that manufactured druggists' supplies.

Hints for Collectors
This sort of box is not a popular collector's item, and if you run across one it will probably be quite inexpensive. Because the box illustrated can be reliably attributed to a specific, and very well-known, glasshouse, it is probably the most desirable box of this type. An assortment of small everyday dresser accessories makes an excellent, inexpensive, specialized collection.

Dresser box

Description
Circular box with slightly domed lid, both with overall cut geometric designs. Cut sunburst on circular base. Colors: colorless; rarely cased with transparent blue, green, red, or yellow. Metal rim on box hinged to metal rim on lid.

Variations
Many elaborate cut patterns, usually with hobstars, fans, and other brilliant-cut motifs. May have glass lid without metal rim and hinge; some lids have hole about 1½″ in diameter. May have acid-etched trademark on inside of bottom. Box may be part of dresser set.

Type and Dimensions
Box and lid free-blown separately and tooled into shape. Cut after annealing. Height: 3½″. Diameter: 5¾″.

Locality and Period
J. Hoare & Company, Corning, New York. c. 1890–1910. Variants from throughout the United States. c. 1885–1915.

Comment
Dresser boxes were occasionally lined and used as jewelry boxes, but most often they held loose face powder or large powder puffs. Similar boxes with holes in the lid are hair receivers. Ladies collected hair from their brushes to be made into "rats" to puff out the pompadours then in vogue. Large cut-glass dresser sets came with matching powder jar, puff box, hair receiver, and 1 or 2 cologne bottles.

Hints for Collectors
The trademark of a cut glass company may be acid-etched inside the box on the bottom. If you find one, this mark will raise the value of the box.

Powder jars

Description
Left: cylindrical jar has wide mouth with screw threads. 9 cut vertical panels around sides with acid-etched flower and leaf design over panels. Cut sunburst on 9-sided base. Flat silver shaker top screws onto mouth; silver push-on cap with raised floral design on top. Right: globe-shaped jar has wide mouth with plain rim. Cut overall geometric design around sides. Acid-etched maple-leaf trademark inside jar on bottom. Cut sunburst on circular base. Silver push-on cap with raised floral design. Colors: both colorless; rarely cased with red, blue, green, or yellow.

Variations
Many cut patterns. Jar on right may have cut-glass lid.

Type and Dimensions
Left: pressed in mold for shape; panels and sunburst cut, and flower and leaf acid-etched, both after annealing. Height: 4¼". Diameter: 1¾". Right: free-blown, then tooled into shape; cut and acid-etched after annealing. Height: 3". Diameter: 4¼".

Locality and Period
Throughout the United States. c. 1888–1920.

Comment
The globe-shaped jar on the right is a typical turn-of-the-century shape for puff jars and powder boxes. The pressed cylindrical jar with the shaker top was used for bath powder and is a less common type. It was cut to make it look like the more expensive free-blown pieces.

Hints for Collectors
Look for cut-glass dresser accessories at house sales and flea markets. They are seldom as expensive as cut-glass tableware.

Description
Cylindrical jar with angled or rounded shoulders and short neck. Wide, flanged lip. Left: engraved initials "W.S.B." and flower sprays on 1 side. Cut sunburst on circular base and hollow stopper. Right: cut design of hobstars and strawberry-diamonds around sides. Cut sunburst on circular base acid-stamped "Libbey." Cut hobstar on hollow stopper. Colors: colorless; rarely cased with transparent red, green, yellow, or blue.

Variations
Many engraved and cut designs.

Type and Dimensions
Jar and stopper free-blown separately and tooled into shape. Copper-wheel engraved and cut after annealing. Neck and stopper ground. Left height: 9½". Base diameter: 5⅞". Right height: 9¼". Base diameter: 4½".

Locality and Period
Left: Union Glass Company, Somerville, Massachusetts. c. 1890–1900. Right: Libbey Glass Company, Toledo, Ohio. c. 1900–10. Variants from throughout the United States. c. 1890–1915.

Comment
Humidors were popular around the turn of the century, when cigar smoking was especially fashionable among the very rich. The jar on the left bears the initials of W.S. Blake, a Union Glass Company superintendent. The one on the right belonged to a descendant of John Jacob Astor, the founder of the millionaire family.

Hints for Collectors
Jars like those shown here are rarely recognized as humidors and often can be purchased relatively inexpensively.

Humidor

Description
Barrel-shaped jar with wide mouth. Plain lip. 1 side has enameled floral design and the word "Cigars" in script. Circular base with enameled inscription "WAVE CREST/TRADE/MARK/The C.F.M.Co." and no pontil mark. Glass lid has raised sunburst and enameled floral design. Colors: opaque white enameled light gray-blue, with design in pink, red, white, yellow, and green. Brass rim on jar hinged to brass rim on lid.

Variations
Shape of jar and floral designs vary. Enameled background always pastel color, including pink, beige, or green. Base may have ink-stamped trademark or lack trademark.

Type and Dimensions
Jar and lid blown in separate full-size multipiece molds for pattern and shape. Enamel fixed by firing after annealing. Height: 6⅛". Base diameter: 4¼".

Locality and Period
Blank: probably Europe; possibly the Northeast. Enameling: C.F. Monroe Company, Meriden, Connecticut. c. 1892–1915.

Comment
In the 1880s many glass companies began experimenting with different colors, including graduated shades and the porcelain-like enamel seen here. C.F. Monroe, a small decorating shop, specialized in art-glass accessories for the desk—letter boxes and racks, inkwells, and humidors—or the dresser—powder boxes, puff jars, and jewelry boxes.

Hints for Collectors
When buying art glass, expect to pay high prices.

Toy Glassware

Small glass replicas of full-size objects have been made in America since at least the end of the 18th century, but it was not until the introduction of the pressing machine in the 1820s that they became widely produced as children's toys. Today, miniatures appeal to those who specialize in glass toys as well as to collectors of full-size tableware because many of the toys were made in tableware shapes.

Early Miniatures

The first American glass toys were probably blown by workers for their children. Later, in the 1820s and 1830s, when glass companies began to use pattern molds for full-size tableware, they also added a few toy decanters and pitchers. Some miniatures of the same period have been found with blown 3-mold patterns combining squares, diamonds, ribs, waffles, and sunbursts.

The pressing machine made production of glass toys substantially cheaper. Toy tureens, pitchers, salt dishes, bowls, cups, and saucers with stippled lacy patterns date from the 1830s and 1840s. Some plainer designs, such as panels and ellipses, may be from the 1840s and 1850s. For a long time, collectors thought that early pressed miniatures were salesmen's samples made in small sizes that were easy to carry. But because none of the patterns and few of the shapes match full-size tableware, this seems unlikely.

In the early days of pressed glass, glassmakers seem to have selected the forms for miniatures almost at random rather than trying to assemble a set. For example, there are toy creamers but no matching sugar bowls. Since miniatures were produced before the days of printed glass-company catalogues, it is difficult to attribute pre-1850 toy glassware to specific factories.

Tableware Sets

Toy glassware appeared in many sales catalogues of the 1860s, and production records of some Pittsburgh factories show that thousands of miniatures were made in a single year. By the 1890s, tableware sets were advertised for children in patterns sometimes matching the full-size sets. Manufacturers offered glasses, cups, saucers, bowls, and plates, as well as water sets (pitcher and tumblers), berry sets (large bowl and smaller bowls), table sets (sugar bowl, creamer, spoon holder, and butter dish), wine sets (decanter and wineglasses), punch sets (punch bowl and cups), castor sets (four or five condiment bottles), and a few odd shapes. Tableware factories in Ohio, West Virginia, and western Pennsylvania produced many of these toys.

Like full-size tableware, miniature glassware began to be mass-produced using automatic machines in the 1920s. Pressed toy baking sets and tea sets with little plates, cups, and saucers were sold as boxed sets. Production of miniature glassware in a tremendous variety of shapes, colors, and patterns continued until the end of World War II, when metal and plastic became the preferred materials for mass-produced children's tableware.

Description
Left: hexagonal baluster-shaped stem has cylindrical socket with flange and domed circular foot. Center and right: hexagonal baluster-shaped or knopped stem has hexagonal socket and flat hexagonal foot. Colors: (left) colorless; (center) colorless and transparent yellow; (right) colorless, transparent purple and blue, and opalescent white.

Variations
Candlestick may lack stem and have circular handle.

Type and Dimensions
Pressed in mold for shape. Left height: 2½″. Center height: 2⅛″. Right height: 1¾″.

Locality and Period
Left: the East and Midwest or possibly Europe. c. 1860–80. Center: probably New England. c. 1840–70. Right: M'Kee & Brothers, Pittsburgh. c. 1855–75. Possibly Cape Cod Glass Company, Sandwich, Massachusetts. 1858–69.

Comment
The miniature candlestick shown on the left was probably made later than the others, and not many in that shape are known. The short type on the right appeared in M'Kee catalogues between 1859 and 1871. Cape Cod Glass also advertised short and tall toy candlesticks, but they are not illustrated in any catalogue.

Hints for Collectors
Of the candlesticks pictured, the one on the right is the most popular, probably because it was made in several colors. A much greater variety of shapes was produced from about 1890 to 1920, when toy candlesticks with 1, 2, or 3 branches were designed for children.

Toy castor set

Description
Set with 4 hexagonal bottles in metal frame. 2 bottles with stoppers have narrow necks and flanged lips. 2 have wide necks and plain lips; 1 with lid. Panels around wider upper sides alternate pattern of United States shield with stars and stripes and floral pattern; narrow lower parts have plain panels. Colorless. Metal frame has 4 slots for bottles and finial handle in center.

Variations
Pattern may be diamonds or vertical ribs. Bottles may be shorter and have metal shaker caps. Stand may have large loop handle.

Type and Dimensions
Each bottle pressed in mold for pattern and shape. Neck and lip finished. Stopper and lid pressed. Bottle height: 2–2½". Stand height: 3".

Locality and Period
Possibly Gillinder & Sons, Philadelphia, or midwestern firm. 1876. Variants c. 1875–1900.

Comment
Because of the patriotic motif, most collectors believe that the castor set shown here was made by Gillinder & Sons as a Centennial souvenir. Gillinder made a number of Centennial pieces, including a children's tableware set in its Liberty Bell pattern. However, since Gillinder marked most of its pieces, it is more likely that the unmarked set illustrated was made by a rival firm.

Hints for Collectors
Since 1976 the demand for Centennial souvenirs has greatly increased. This trend and a new interest in children's toys has made miniature castor sets in the pattern pictured hard to find.

Toy blown 3-mold decanter

Description
Barrel-shaped decanter with long neck and flanged lip; double ring around neck and shoulder. Pattern of diamonds around middle with vertical ribs above and below. Pontil mark on circular base. Wheel-shaped stopper. Colors: colorless; very rarely transparent purple and blue.

Variations
Decanters made in a few geometric patterns, combining diamonds, ribs, and sunbursts.

Type and Dimensions
Decanter blown in full-size multipiece mold for pattern and shape. Neck and lip finished; rings applied. Stopper pressed and ground. Height: 5".

Locality and Period
New England; probably Boston & Sandwich Glass Company, Sandwich, Massachusetts. c. 1825–35.

Comment
Tableware with a pattern like the one on this example was named blown 3-mold glass in the 1920s by collectors who believed that all the molds used to produce these patterns had 3 parts. Although many did, some had 2, 4, or even 5 parts. Miniature blown 3-mold glass is very rare, and only a few decanters, pitchers, and small cordial glasses have been found. All are too big for dollhouses but could have been used for children's tea parties and games.

Hints for Collectors
Blown 3-mold glass is expensive, so beware of reproductions. Most are in bright greens and blues, which were not used in the 19th century, but colorless copies are harder to recognize.

Toy decanter and pitcher

Description
Left: barrel-shaped decanter with long neck and flanged lip; spiral threading around neck. Pontil mark on circular base. Solid ball stopper. Right: cylindrical pitcher with pinched pouring lip, solid ear-shaped handle, and circular foot with pontil mark underneath. Colors: transparent purple, blue, aquamarine, green, yellow, colorless, and opalescent white; rarely colorless with opalescent white.

Variations
Decanter may be more cylindrical. Pitcher often has waist.

Type and Dimensions
Each form free-blown and tooled into shape. Threading, handle, and foot applied. Decanter height: 4½″. Pitcher height: 2″.

Locality and Period
Decanter: New England Glass Company, Cambridge, Massachusetts. c. 1830–50. Pitcher: the East and Midwest. c. 1800–50.

Comment
Although many free-blown toys are made of bottle glass, the 2 shown here are of such fine quality glass that they were obviously produced in a tableware factory. The decanter is attributed to a blower at the New England Glass Company who is said to have made it for his daughter around 1840.

Hints for Collectors
Do not confuse the early free-blown toys with similar-looking lampworked miniatures, which never have a pontil mark and are often of thinner glass. Many toys were lampworked in the second half of the 19th century, and others are still made as souvenirs sold at fairs and carnivals.

Toy creamer with cup and saucer

Description
Left: cylindrical creamer with wide pouring lip and solid ear-shaped handle; diamond and scroll design on stippled background; plain base rim. Right: cylindrical cup with flanged rim and solid ear-shaped handle; tulip and scroll design on stippled background. Circular saucer with rose and scroll design and stippling. Colors: creamer transparent light and dark purple, blue, yellow, colorless, and opalescent white; cup and saucer transparent blue, colorless, and opalescent white.

Variations
Design on creamer may be larger and more irregular; creamer may have scalloped base rim. Extremely rare cup in diamond and scroll pattern has flat handle without central hole. Cup (without handle) and saucer may have shell pattern. Another cup (with or without handle) and saucer may have panel pattern.

Type and Dimensions
Each form pressed in mold for pattern and shape. Creamer height: 1¾". Cup height: 1¼". Saucer diameter: 1⅞".

Locality and Period
New England; probably Boston & Sandwich Glass Company, Sandwich, Massachusetts. c. 1835–55. Variants from the East and Midwest.

Comment
Collectors call intricate stippled designs lacy patterns. This ware is one of the earliest types of American pressed glass.

Hints for Collectors
Some 19th-century French miniature cups and saucers have stippled acanthus-leaf designs, and the cups have peaked handles. French glass should cost less than American.

Toy mug

Description
Cylindrical mug with plain rim and solid D-shaped handle.
Pattern of grape bunches and vines. Circular base. Colors:
transparent purple, green, yellow, colorless, and opaque white.

Variations
Pattern may be ABCs, animals, or figures from nursery rhymes.

Type and Dimensions
Pressed in mold for pattern and shape. Height: 2″.

Locality and Period
King, Son & Company, Pittsburgh. c. 1870–80. Variants from
western Pennsylvania, West Virginia, and Ohio.

Comment
The Vine pattern illustrated appeared in a King, Son & Company
catalogue of about 1874. The mug came in 3 sizes: The smallest
was a toy mug with matching creamer and sugar bowl; the
medium size is shown here; and the large mug probably served
as a child's cup. Children's glassware was immensely popular in
the last quarter of the 19th century. Most of it was made in
tableware factories, such as Doyle & Company and King, Son &
Company, both of Pittsburgh. In 1875 in Vermont, Doyle sold
20,000 toy table sets (sugar bowl, creamer, butter dish, and
spoon holder), a staggering figure considering the rural
population. In some villages this meant about a set per family.

Hints for Collectors
The value of miniature toys has escalated rapidly in the past few
years. Since the mug pictured is not very rare, it is less
expensive than many toy tableware examples of the same period.

Toy table set

Description
4-piece set with (left to right) covered sugar bowl, covered butter dish, spoon holder, and creamer, all with vertical panels. Sugar bowl, spoon holder, and creamer cylindrical; each has foot with sunburst underneath and scalloped rim. Circular plate of butter dish has scalloped rim. Domed covers of sugar bowl and butter dish have plain rim and solid finial. Colors: transparent blue, green, yellow-green, and colorless.

Variations
Colorless examples may have enameled flowers.

Type and Dimensions
Each form pressed in mold for pattern and shape. Sugar bowl height: 3″. Butter dish height: 2⅝″. Spoon holder height: 2¼″. Creamer height: 2½″.

Locality and Period
Cambridge Glass Company, Cambridge, Ohio. c. 1900–20. Variants from western Pennsylvania, West Virginia, and Ohio.

Comment
The 4 pieces pictured here constitute what was listed as a table set in glass catalogues of the 1860–1920 period. Capitalizing on the popularity of full-size tableware, many manufacturers produced toys for children. Cambridge Glass advertised the set illustrated as part of its Newcut line, No. 2630. Since the pattern is similar to the full-size Colonial pattern, collectors call the toy set Cambridge Colonial.

Hints for Collectors
Toy Colonial sets are easy to find today in all colors. Check condition: Chipped examples have little value.

Toy tumblers and sugar bowl

Description
Left: cylindrical tumbler with ellipses around body; circular foot. Center: cylindrical tumbler with panels around body; thick base. Right: round sugar bowl with panels around body; small domed foot; paneled, peaked cover with solid finial. All with plain rims. Colors: (left) transparent blue, purple, yellow, colorless, opalescent white, and opaque white; (center) transparent blue, yellow, colorless, and opalescent white; (right) transparent turquoise and colorless.

Variations
Tumbler at left may have enameled or gilt decoration.

Type and Dimensions
Each form pressed in mold for pattern and shape. Left tumbler height: 1¾". Right tumbler height: 1⅝". Sugar bowl height: 2⅛".

Locality and Period
Left tumbler: probably Boston & Sandwich Glass Company, Sandwich, Massachusetts. Right tumbler and sugar bowl: New England and probably Pittsburgh area. c. 1840–70.

Comment
Collectors call toy tumblers whiskey tasters; they are somewhat larger than dollhouse-size toys, yet their capacity is less than a jigger. The covered sugar bowl is the earliest patterned miniature in this shape.

Hints for Collectors
The tumbler with ellipses is more popular than the one with panels, possibly because of the variety of colors, but both patterns cost about the same.

Toy tureen with tray

Description
Oval bowl with curved handle at each end. Slightly domed cover with solid finial. Separate oval tray with scalloped rim. Bowl, tray, and inside of cover have pattern of fans and scrolls on stippled background. Colors: transparent yellow, blue, purple, and colorless; opalescent white; and opaque light blue and blue-green.

Variations
Tureen may be 3″ high. Tray may have plain rim and panels instead of stippling.

Type and Dimensions
Each form pressed in mold for pattern and shape. Height: 2¼″.

Locality and Period
New England; probably Boston & Sandwich Glass Company, Sandwich, Massachusetts. c. 1835–50.

Comment
Early collectors thought that miniature tableware and washstand sets were not toys but samples carried by traveling salesmen, called drummers. No full-size pressed-glass tureens in the shape or lacy pattern illustrated have ever been discovered, and it is much more logical to assume that this tureen as well as most other pieces were designed as toys.

Hints for Collectors
Colored lacy-pattern miniatures have been eagerly collected for 50 years and are quite expensive. Be careful when selecting miniature lacy-pattern cups, saucers, bowls, compotes, and plates. If the design is very ornate, the piece may be a 19th-century European example and should cost less.

Toy butter dish

Description
Domed cover with solid finial; circular plate with scalloped rim.
Both with pattern of hobstars, fans, and diamonds within
diamonds. Colors: opaque and opalescent white and colorless.

Variations
Patterns vary; most have hobstars, fans, and diamonds. May
have gilt trim.

Type and Dimensions
Each form pressed in mold for pattern and shape. Height: 2⅜″.

Locality and Period
Westmoreland Glass Company, Grapeville, Pennsylvania.
c. 1890–1910. Variants from western Pennsylvania, West
Virginia, and Ohio. c. 1890–1920.

Comment
Opaque white glass, which collectors call milk glass, was
extremely popular from the 1870s until after 1900. It was used
for a wide variety of full-size tableware and eventually for
children's toys. The pattern illustrated here was part of a full
table set with matching sugar bowl, creamer, and spoon holder,
as well as a cake stand and a punch set with rare matching tray.

Hints for Collectors
Most pieces in this pattern are colorless, making opaque and
opalescent white examples especially valuable. In the 1950s
Westmoreland Glass Company reproduced the table set in this
pattern in transparent amber, blue, green, and opaque white.
Because Westmoreland used old molds, the opaque white
reproductions are nearly impossible to spot, and many collectors
have stopped buying the milk-glass miniatures.

Description
Left: oval serving dish with beaded, small-scalloped rim; tulip
and scroll design on stippled background around sides; plain
base. Right: oval salt dish with large-scalloped edge; scroll
design on stippled background around sides; base has stippling
with scrolls and diamonds. Colors: (left) transparent light yellow,
colorless, opalescent white, and opaque blue; (right) same colors
and transparent green and purple.

Variations
Rim of serving dish may have larger scallops or alternating
scallops and points. Salt dish may have rope pattern near base.
Both dishes may be colorless with scallop-shell and scroll design.

Type and Dimensions
Each form pressed in mold for pattern and shape. Left length: 3″.
Right length: 1¾″.

Locality and Period
New England; probably Boston & Sandwich Glass Company,
Sandwich, Massachusetts. c. 1835–50. Shell-pattern variants
possibly from the Midwest.

Comment
These shallow dishes are among the earliest tableware
miniatures and are much less common than later examples that
came in large sets.

Hints for Collectors
Early lacy-pattern toys are considered especially desirable and
are more expensive than most children's dishes. Unlike later toy
dishes, those with lacy patterns have not been reproduced.

Toy Pyrex loaf pan and pie plate

Description
Left: rectangular loaf pan with plain rim, sloping ends, and inscription "2½" just below rim; circle in center of base has "PATENTED/PYREX/May 27 1919." Right: circular pie plate with plain rim, sloping sides, and "25AA" on rim; circle in center of base has "PATENTED/PYREX/May 27 1919." Colorless.

Variations
Similar shapes may have slight blue tint, scroll pattern lightly etched on sides, and "FIRE-KING" in a circle on base.

Type and Dimensions
Each form machine-pressed in mold for pattern and shape. Loaf pan length: 4¹¹⁄₁₆". Pie plate diameter: 4¾".

Locality and Period
Corning Glass Works, Corning, New York. c. 1920–35. Variants from Anchor-Hocking Glass Corporation, Lancaster, Ohio.

Comment
In the 1920s and 1930s, many glass manufacturers experimented with heat-resistant cooking ware. Pyrex was the registered trademark of Corning Glass Works; Fire-King was made by Anchor-Hocking; and "RADNT" was manufactured briefly by H.P. Sinclaire & Company, also of Corning. Sinclaire produced only full-size cookware, but both Corning and Anchor-Hocking made similar children's sets with an assortment of baking dishes. Corning Glass called its line the Pyrexette set, and Anchor-Hocking's was named Sunny Suzy.

Hints for Collectors
Single small ovenware dishes are easy to find at flea markets and house sales, but a complete set in the original box is rare and prized.

Description
2-piece set with bowl and pitcher. Conical bowl has wide rim at top, panels around sides, and narrow base rim. Matching pear-shaped pitcher has wide pouring lip, circular foot, and solid ear-shaped handle higher than lip. Colors: transparent blue, blue-green, yellow, colorless, opalescent white, and opaque light blue.

Variations
May have scroll design on stippled background. Pitcher may be more cylindrical.

Type and Dimensions
Each form pressed in mold for pattern and shape. Bowl diameter: 3". Pitcher height: 2½".

Locality and Period
New England; probably Boston & Sandwich Glass Company, Sandwich, Massachusetts. c. 1840–60.

Comment
The miniature set in the paneled design illustrated may have been made a few years later than the stippled variant, but it comes in many of the same colors and shapes and probably was produced in the same factory. The paneled set included cups, saucers, sugar bowl, creamer, circular plate, oval tray, oval bowl, circular footed bowl, and tumblers.

Hints for Collectors
Brightly colored miniatures are much more popular with collectors than colorless examples. As a result, the colored toys are harder to find and more expensive. Note that paneled objects are not as likely to chip as stippled ones with their tiny, fragile projections.

Toy water set

Description
7-piece set with pitcher and 6 tumblers. Cylindrical pitcher, narrower toward base, has high pouring lip, scalloped rim, and solid ear-shaped handle. Pattern of large cross-hatched diamonds and ellipses around body. Short stem with knop and hexagonal foot. Matching cylindrical tumblers have plain rims. Colors: colorless, colorless with gilt trim, and colorless with gilt and purple trim.

Variations
Many patterns include panels, imitation cut-glass designs, and flowers.

Type and Dimensions
Each form pressed in mold for pattern and shape. Gilt fixed by firing after annealing. Pitcher height: 4⅝". Tumbler height: 1¾".

Locality and Period
United States Glass Company, Pittsburgh. c. 1900–20. Variants from western Pennsylvania, West Virginia, and Ohio.

Comment
Collectors call the pattern illustrated Pattee Cross. It appeared in a catalogue of the United States Glass Company, a consortium of 18 factories in the western Pennsylvania, West Virginia, and Ohio area that joined together in 1891 and opened a factory in Gas City, Indiana, in 1905. The set also appears in the catalogues of Butler Brothers and Sears & Roebuck. Both companies bought the glass from the consortium.

Hints for Collectors
In this set, examples with gilt trim are more desirable than plain ones, but they are usually not more expensive.

Toy punch set

Description
7-piece set with punch bowl and 6 cups. Circular bowl has scalloped rim and hollow conical foot; pattern around body shows Little Red Riding Hood, small house, and wolf in bed wearing nightgown. Matching cylindrical cups, each with plain rim, solid ear-shaped handle, and less detailed design. Colors: transparent dark blue, colorless, and opaque white and light blue.

Variations
Many patterns include panels, imitation cut-glass designs, and flowers.

Type and Dimensions
Each form pressed in mold for pattern and shape. Bowl diameter: 4⅝″. Cup diameter: 1⅜″.

Locality and Period
United States Glass Company, Gas City, Indiana. c. 1905–20. Variants from western Pennsylvania, West Virginia, and Ohio.

Comment
Advertised in a mail-order circular published by Butler Brothers in 1910, the set shown here was part of a large children's collection with fairy-tale patterns. For example, a berry set showed children holding hands, a pitcher had Jill carrying a pail of water, and the spoon holder in a table set featured Puss-in-Boots. However, not all pieces were available in all colors. A dozen punch sets sold for 92 cents.

Hints for Collectors
A toy set in opaque white is much more popular and expensive than the same pattern in colorless glass. For this type of set, check dealer listings and advertisements in collectors' magazines.

Toy berry set

Description
7-piece set with large serving bowl and 6 small bowls. Serving
bowl has alternating scallops and points on rim; overall pattern of
octagonal daisylike flowers intersected by crisscrossing lines that
form overlapping squares and diamonds. Matching small bowls
have first row of octagons forming scallops on rim. Colors:
colorless; rarely transparent light green.

Variations
Bowls with other imitation cut-glass designs, panels,
strawberries, and children and grape leaves.

Type and Dimensions
Each form pressed in mold for pattern and shape. Serving bowl
diameter: 4″. Small bowl diameter: 2¼″.

Locality and Period
Probably western Pennsylvania, West Virginia, and Ohio.
c. 1910–25.

Comment
Called Lacy Daisy by collectors, the pattern illustrated is one of
the easiest berry sets to collect. But unlike most pressed
patterns, it does not have any other matching pieces.

Hints for Collectors
Beware of bowls in both opaque dark green and opaque white in
this pattern; neither color is authentic. Westmoreland Glass
Company of Grapeville, Pennsylvania, is currently marketing the
opaque white bowls as salt dishes, but the maker of the green
reproductions is unknown. The set shown is the only miniature
berry set that has been reproduced.

Description
5-piece set with teapot, cup, saucer, sugar bowl, and creamer. All except saucer have solid triangular handle, plain circular base, and widely spaced horizontal rings around body; 2 have triangular spouts. Saucer has ray design. Pitcher, sugar bowl, and creamer have additional icicle-like design below rim. Colors: opaque light and dark blue, turquoise, green, yellow, orange, and white.

Variations
Tea sets made in several patterns, usually with different spacing of horizontal rings, vertical panels, or ribs. Some pieces have panels on inside and outside.

Type and Dimensions
Each form machine-pressed in mold for pattern and shape. Teapot height: 2⅜″. Cup height: 1¼″. Saucer diameter: 2¾″. Sugar bowl height: 1¼″. Creamer height: 1¼″.

Locality and Period
Akro Agate Company, Clarksburg, West Virginia. c. 1935–45.

Comment
The Akro Agate Company, founded in 1911, originally manufactured marbles and games. By the 1920s it had captured three-fourths of the American marble market (previously most marbles were imported from Germany). In 1935, when other American firms began producing marbles, Akro Agate started experimenting with other products, including colorful children's ware in half a dozen patterns. The set illustrated also has orange plates.

Hints for Collectors
Many but not all Akro Agate products bear its trademark: a large "A" with a crow flying through it.

Toy flatirons

Description
Triangular form with solid D-shaped handle. Colors: transparent green, purple, blue, yellow, colorless, and opalescent white.

Type and Dimensions
Pressed in mold for shape. Length: 1⅜″.

Locality and Period
M'Kee & Brothers, Pittsburgh. c. 1855–75. Cape Cod Glass Company, Sandwich, Massachusetts. 1858–69. Possibly Doyle & Company and King, Son & Company, Pittsburgh. c. 1865–85.

Comment
Toy flatirons are illustrated in catalogues of the M'Kee firm from 1859 to 1871; in 1860 they sold for $2.70 a gross. But by 1880 these items had disappeared, replaced by toy mugs and table sets. Flatirons are included in a printed price list of the Cape Cod Glass Company. Certainly several firms manufactured these popular toys, nicely scaled for use in dollhouses. In the days before electric irons, housewives kept several cast-iron flatirons, or sadirons, on the back of the kitchen stove to heat. When the iron in use grew too cold, it was returned to the stove and replaced by a hot one. Most dollhouses probably had several flatirons, too.

Hints for Collectors
Among the most appealing miniatures, toy flatirons are considerably less expensive than many elaborate tableware toys. An attractive collection can be made of the various colors.

Miscellaneous Objects

The unusual glass objects described in the entries that follow represent a wide variety of functional and nonfunctional forms. They range from curtain-rod finials, spectacles, and eyecups to toys and cigarette holders. One-of-a-kind powder horns and funnels were created as early as the 1830s, although less practical objects, such as canes and pipes, date from after 1850. Many factory items, including automobile vases and fruit knives, were produced from the late 19th to the mid-20th centuries. While a few of the more unusual items illustrated in this group appeal only to specialized collectors, most are readily available today at low prices and are ideal starting points for a new collection.

Whimsies
Purely decorative glass objects are by and large a post-1850 phenomenon, since before then most of the population had little time to indulge in frivolities. Pressed novelties in the forms of slippers, hats, or animal-shaped containers are typically late Victorian, dating to the 1870s and 1880s. Animal figurines, fashionable in the 1930s and 1940s, are 20th-century additions to the knickknack shelf. Unlike these factory items, the canes, stocking darners, gavels, rolling pins, and ornamental chains designed by individual glassmakers were made during the 19th century as presents for friends and family. Since each piece had to be totally handmade, few were created.

Souvenirs
Although glass rolling pins were sold at English country fairs and carnivals as early as 1830, tourist souvenirs did not begin to be common in America until the second half of the 19th century. Traveling lampworkers who roamed the country demonstrating their craft often sold the miniature ships, animals, cigarette holders, and pens they fashioned to their audiences. Pens proved such popular souvenirs that Corning Glass Works sold a pen with its own case at the 1939 New York World's Fair. Another souvenir, the fiberglass necktie, was manufactured by the Libbey Glass Company for the 1893 Chicago World's Fair.

Production Items
During the last decades of the 19th century, stiff competition among glass companies as well as the public's fascination with gadgets created an atmosphere in which experimentation flourished. Among the more bizarre household inventions were glass mousetraps and flytraps, which, like most such inventions, were produced for a relatively short period. By the 20th century, inexpensive pressed or machine-blown glass was used by industry, and some of these purely functional objects are collected now. Telephone and telegraph insulators, for example, can be found with hundreds of slight variations in at least six different colors, including iridescent hues.

Curtain-rod or newel-post finials

Description
Hollow oval knobs with pattern of bumps. Smooth circle at top; smooth neck below. Brass fittings in opening at bottom. Colors: opaque light green, blue, and white.

Variations
Knob may be globe-shaped with vertical ribs.

Type and Dimensions
Blown in full-size multipiece mold for pattern and shape. Brass fitting affixed after annealing. Length: 7¾".

Locality and Period
New England; probably Boston & Sandwich Glass Company, Sandwich, Massachusetts, or New England Glass Company, Cambridge, Massachusetts. Possibly France. c. 1840–60.

Comment
Glass finials like those shown here were made in pairs for each end of a long brass curtain rod. The same knob with a different brass fitting served as the finial for a newel post at the foot or top of a flight of stairs. Mold-blown curtain-rod or newel-post finials are usually from the mid-19th century, while most cut-glass examples date from the end of the century. Some of the more elaborate cut-glass newel-post finials were cased with red, blue, or white glass and a pattern of circles or hexagons was cut through.

Hints for Collectors
Until quite recently, curtain-rod and newel-post finials were often overlooked by collectors, since few people recognized their function. Today such ornaments are again valued and are consequently becoming harder to find.

Stocking darners

Description
Hollow globes attached to hollow handles. Left: collar at joint. Pontil mark on end of each handle. Colors: opaque green, blue, red, purple, and white; stripes in 2 or more of these colors; and iridescent gold and blue.

Variations
Collar may be applied and more prominent. Stripes may be swirled.

Type and Dimensions
Free-blown, then tooled into shape. Left: collar finished. Right: stripes applied and marvered into surface before annealing. Left length: 6¼". Right length: 5¾".

Locality and Period
Throughout the United States. c. 1880–1920.

Comment
The rattlelike objects pictured are stocking darners, which were inserted in the toe or heel of a sock while mending a hole. They were produced in glass, wood, and china. Not part of the factory inventory, both the glass darners with handles and the egg-shaped examples were made as presents by glassblowers working on their own time. Most darners are from the last 2 decades of the 19th century. Those in the iridescent art glass known as Aurene were blown at Steuben Glass Works in Corning, New York, until about World War I.

Hints for Collectors
Iridescent darners made at Steuben are among the most expensive. But because Steuben non-iridescent darners resemble those made at other factories, they are difficult to distinguish and are usually moderately priced. Steuben darners always have an applied collar, but so do some of the others.

Automobile flower vase

Description
Conical vase rounded at top, with incurved rim. Solid lower part has 8 vertical panels and ends in acornlike knob. Colors: transparent blue, purple, amber, colorless, and colorless with iridescent orange lining.

Variations
Vase may have realistic or abstract pressed pattern or cut geometric design.

Type and Dimensions
Pressed in mold for pattern and shape. Rim finished. Interior sprayed with chemical for iridescent finish before annealing. Height: 7¼".

Locality and Period
Glasshouse unknown; western Pennsylvania, West Virginia, Ohio, or Indiana. c. 1905–15.

Comment
Early automobiles were modeled after turn-of-the-century horsedrawn vehicles. Like the coaches, they had dashboards, whip sockets, and glove compartments (gloves and whips being indispensable to the buggy driver). Some also had small flower vases held upright with brackets. Automobile vases are found in pressed glass, cut glass, and more rarely in the Carnival glass illustrated. This vase is unusual because it was sprayed on the interior instead of the exterior, producing a particolored effect.

Hints for Collectors
Automobile vases are of interest chiefly to car buffs who lovingly restore early 20th-century autos down to the last detail. The vases occasionally turn up at flea markets or garage sales, and are usually quite inexpensive.

Powder horn

Description
Hollow conical horn, slightly curved, with solid knob at wide end; cone tapers to necklike end with plain lip. Pontil mark on knob. Colors: transparent aquamarine, green, amber, brown, and colorless; rarely, any of these with opaque white stripes or loops.

Variations
Horn may have applied lily-pad decoration, threads, or chains. Shape may be wider or more curved.

Type and Dimensions
Free-blown, then tooled into shape. Knob applied. Length: 9¼″.

Locality and Period
The East. Possibly western Pennsylvania and Ohio. c. 1830–60.

Comment
Although glass seems an unlikely container for as volatile a substance as powder or shot, the use of glass powder horns is well documented in several paintings of the 1840–50 period from New York. They show hunters with glass powder horns hung over their shoulders on leather straps. It seems likely that glass horns were also used in New England, Pennsylvania, and on the western frontier. In some cases a leather covering may have protected the glass, but no examples of this kind survive today. The gunpowder was sealed inside the powder horns with cork stoppers.

Hints for Collectors
All glass powder horns are rare and expensive. Those with applied decoration are the most costly.

Apothecary glass

Description
Below: funnel-shaped eyecup with folded-out rim; hollow shaft closed at end. Opposite left: trumpet-shaped breast pump with folded-out rim; long, hollow shaft with globe-shaped chamber at 1 side; rubber bulb at end. Opposite right: hollow bowl-like nipple shield with opening at center and spout at 1 side. All colorless. Rectangular cardboard box has paper label on lid printed "No. 309/ENGLISH BREAST PUMP./DAVOL RUBBER CO. PROVIDENCE, R.I."

Variations
All 3 shapes vary slightly. Eyecup may lack shaft and be rounded or oval with a foot.

Type and Dimensions
Each form free-blown separately and tooled into shape. Pump chamber and shield spout applied. Eyecup length: 2″. Breast pump length: 6″. Nipple shield diameter: 4⅜″.

Locality and Period
The East, western Pennsylvania, West Virginia, and Ohio. c. 1870–1900.

Comment
Late 19th-century apothecary glass includes a wide assortment of unusual containers and medical apparatuses ranging from the forms illustrated here to syringes, tubes, and apothecary bottles. These objects appeal primarily to collectors of drugstore items, although nursing bottle collectors are often interested in breast pumps, nipple shields, and other nursing paraphernalia.
Some collectors specialize in eyecups, which come in a surprising variety of shapes. Early examples were free-blown and usually irregular, while later types were pressed or machine-blown in more uniform shapes.

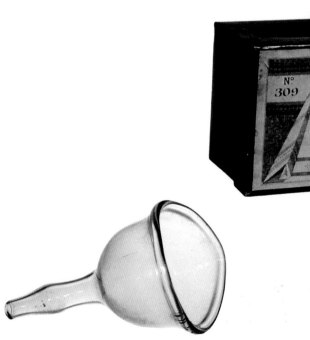

It is rare to find apothecary items in their original packages. The box pictured here contained an English-style breast pump distributed by the Davol Rubber Company. Davol probably bought the glass, added the rubber bulbs, and sold the product. The design of nursing pumps has hardly changed, except that the most recent examples are made of plastic. Nipple shields, rarely found today, were used by nursing mothers to protect sore nipples. Both the breast pump and the nipple shield were widely advertised in 19th-century catalogues of druggists' wares. Whitall, Tatum & Company of Millville, New Jersey, for example, specialized in apothecary glass, listing all 3 types shown here. Although some druggists' ware may have been imported from Europe, probably most used in the United States was made here, primarily at New Jersey pharmaceutical supply factories.

Hints for Collectors
Apothecary items are hard to find; many are already part of museum collections. Occasionally examples are found in the basement or attic of an old drugstore. Because these unusual devices and containers are not much in demand, they are quite inexpensive. Note the broken spout on the nipple shield illustrated. This defect lessens the value only slightly since nipple shields are relatively scarce.

Description
Flaring bell-shaped funnel has hollow bulbous shaft with opening at end. Colors: transparent aquamarine, light green, amber, and colorless.

Variations
Width and length of funnel vary slightly.

Type and Dimensions
Free-blown, then tooled into shape. Length: 4⅞″. Rim diameter: 3⅞″.

Locality and Period
New England, New York, New Jersey, western Pennsylvania, West Virginia, and Ohio. c. 1840–70.

Comment
During the 19th century, funnels were often made of metal. Glass examples like the one pictured were blown by workers in window or bottle glasshouses, usually for their wives. Some may also have been made on company time and sold in the company store. The funnels come in the typical bottle-glass shades of green, aquamarine, and amber, all a result of iron ore impurities. No 2 glass funnels are exactly alike. A common design, the funnel illustrated was found in northern New York and is said to have been made at the window glass factory in Redford.

Hints for Collectors
Any free-blown piece that can definitely be attributed to a factory will cost more than an unidentified example. Before you pay a high price for an attribution, however, be sure to learn all the details and then judge the facts. Unfortunately, attributions are often merely hearsay.

Flip-flop

Description
Hollow bulb of membrane-thin glass, flat at end. Hollow twisted stem. Colors: transparent aquamarine and colorless.

Variations
Length and shape of stem vary; stem may not be twisted.

Type and Dimensions
Free-blown, then tooled into shape. Length: 7″. Rim diameter: 3½″.

Locality and Period
New England, New York, New Jersey, and possibly the Midwest. c. 1840–80.

Comment
This out-of-the-ordinary object, called a flip-flop, is a noisemaker. Similar noisemakers, called *pokon-pokon*, were known in Japan in the 19th century, and possibly the design was brought to the States from the Orient. Blowing into the hollow stem caused the flat paper-thin glass to vibrate, producing a popping sound. Toys like this were usually made for glassmakers' children. They were quite fragile, and it is unlikely that the general populace ever had access to them. Another favorite 19th-century glass toy was the Jacob's ladder. The lower end of this thin ladder was fastened to a glass or wooden base, while the upper end could sway freely.

Hints for Collectors
Except for lampworked animals and ships, 19th-century glass toys are usually impossible to find today outside of heirloom collections or museums.

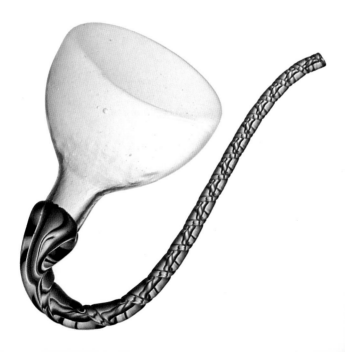

Pipe and cigarette holder

Description
Left: pipe with cylindrical bowl and hollow curved stem. Colors: opaque white with transparent red, blue, and turquoise splashes and stripes. Right: hollow cylindrical cigarette holder with scalloped rim, ridge at center, and folded-out lip. Colors: opaque white with transparent blue, yellow, and red dots.

Variations
Stem curve varies. Very large pipes have detachable stems and usually more regular decoration. Cigarette holder may lack scalloped rim and dots; may have applied threads. Pipe and holder in practically any color combination.

Type and Dimensions
Pipe bowl free-blown; splashes and stripes applied and marvered into surface, then cased with colorless glass and stem drawn out before annealing. Length: 9¾″. Cigarette holder lampworked from colored rods; dots applied before cooling. Length: 3″.

Locality and Period
The East and Midwest. England; widely exported to the United States. c. 1850–1900.

Comment
Glass pipes were only made for show. Many English pipes were sold here along with other whimsical pieces, such as glass canes and miniature ships, collectively called friggers in England. Cigarette holders are rarer than pipes, since cigarette smoking was not really considered respectable until the 20th century.

Hints for Collectors
Collecting glass pipes is far more popular in England than here; consequently the same pipe costs much less in the United States. English examples are usually more elaborate.

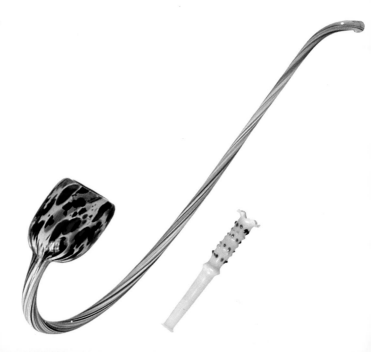

Gavel

Description
Solid cylindrical head with solid handle rounded at end. Colors:
1 color or any 2 or 3 combined; transparent amber, aquamarine,
purple, dark brown, and colorless; opaque and transparent red,
green, and blue; and opaque white.

Variations
Length of handle varies slightly. Head may be round or barrel-
shaped.

Type and Dimensions
Gather tooled into shape. Colored stripes applied and marvered
into white glass, which is cased with colorless glass before
annealing. Length: 10½″.

Locality and Period
Throughout the United States. c. 1880–1920.

Comment
Made for family members and friends or as a special order for
clubs, each glass gavel is unique and virtually impossible to
identify and date. Throughout the 19th century, workers'
organizations and later labor unions held parades in which the
men displayed the products they had made. The gavel shown
here may have been a parade souvenir. Newspaper accounts
from England are particularly detailed in listing unusual glass
objects, but accounts of parades in this country, mostly from the
1890s, are sketchier.

Hints for Collectors
Gavels are rare. Although you might spot one at a flea market,
they are more likely to be found for a high price in a specialized
glass dealer's shop.

Description
Solid, flat, oval blade, rough on both sides. Smooth solid handle, rounded at end. 1 side of blade has inscription "PATENTED" near tip and "AUG 18 85" near handle. Color: transparent blue.

Type and Dimensions
Pressed in mold for pattern and shape. Length: 4″.

Locality and Period
The Pittsburgh area. 1885.

Comment
The patent date on the match striker illustrated helped date and identify it. This device was carried in the pocket and used with wooden matches. Judging from the fact that not many have been found, the match striker was not a commercial success. During the 1880s and 1890s, several hundred glass objects and decorating processes were patented. Many of these novelty items were not produced in great number nor sold especially well. They include pressed-glass shingles, sash blocks for windows, and a combination saltcellar and knife.

Hints for Collectors
Very often the only means of identifying an unfamiliar object is to write to the U.S. Patent Office; you must include the patent number or date. Ask for a copy of the original patent, which will describe the article, its use, and give the name of the inventor and sometimes the manufacturer. A small fee is charged for this service. Because there is virtually no demand for these curious articles, they are usually quite inexpensive.

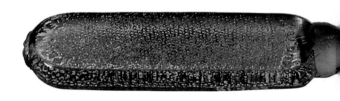

Fruit knife

Description
Solid knife blade, curved and beveled at 1 edge. Solid handle
with design of stars and diamonds. At joint of handle and blade,
1 side has inscription "MADE IN/U.S.A."; 1 side has "PAT. PEND/1F S2."
Colors: transparent pink, blue, amber, and colorless.

Variations
Handle may have pressed floral or scroll pattern, enameled
flowers, or be plain. Other pressed patterns also in transparent
green and opaque white. Sizes 7½–9½".

Type and Dimensions
Machine-pressed in mold for pattern and shape. Edge ground.
Length: 9⅜".

Locality and Period
Throughout the United States. c. 1920–40.

Comment
Introduced in the 1920s, glass fruit knives are now collected as
Depression glass. Westmoreland Glass Company of Grapeville,
Pennsylvania, made some, but most fruit knives are
unattributable. Glass knives were less expensive than metal
ones, but their chief virtue was their sparkling cleanliness;
carbon steel knife blades tended to leave rust spots. "The acids of
fruit will not stain this knife. It will always be clean," proudly
proclaimed the words on a 1930s knife box. The manufacturer of
the Dur-x knife assured buyers that a chipped or dull blade could
be returned and reground.

Hints for Collectors
Colorless knives are the most plentiful, although pink, amber,
and green are fairly easy to find. Blue and opaque white are the
most expensive.

215 Rolling pin

Description
Hollow cylindrical rolling pin with knob at each end. Printed black and gilt inscription "Love the Giver" between pictures of sailing ships, with "THE GREAT EASTERN" below ship at right. Colors: transparent dark brown, green, aquamarine, colorless, and opaque white.

Variations
Pictures and inscriptions vary, including "REMEMBER ME," "Be Always True," or other sentimental message. May have enameled flowers, marvered, twisted threads, or may be plain.

Type and Dimensions
Free-blown, then tooled into shape. Decoration transfer-printed and gilded after annealing. Length: 11″.

Locality and Period
England. 1851–55. Variants from the East and England.
c. 1830–80. Antiques widely exported to the United States.
c. 1920–present.

Comment
The rolling pin pictured here with its printed decoration is typical of the inexpensive factory-made souvenirs sold at English country fairs during the mid-19th century. These antiques have been popular with American collectors since the 1920s. Rolling pins attributed to American glasshouses are of brown or green bottle glass and lack decoration; these were made by glassmakers for their wives, mothers, and sweethearts. The ship depicted on the example illustrated was a steamship with auxiliary sails built in 1851 for trade between England and India.

Hints for Collectors
Prices for English and American rolling pins depend on decoration and condition, not the country of origin.

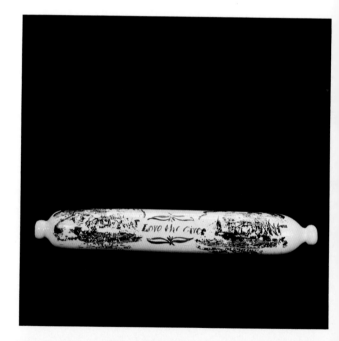

Fiberglass necktie

Description
Rectangular necktie of braided threads. Rectangular cardboard box with printed inscription "LIBBEY GLASS CO/WORLD'S COLUMBIAN EXPOSITION/CHICAGO 1893/PRINCIPAL FACTORY/TOLEDO/OHIO." Color: silvery white.

Variations
Fiberglass doll in identical box. Fiberglass bookmarks without box.

Type and Dimensions
Glass fibers handwoven. Length: 45″. Width: 2″.

Locality and Period
Libbey Glass Company, Toledo, Ohio. 1893.

Comment
In 1893 the Libbey Glass Company, one of the largest and most successful glass manufacturers in the country, built a factory at the Chicago World's Fair. Like the Gillinder glasshouse at the Centennial celebration in Philadelphia in 1876, Libbey's Chicago exhibit proved enormously popular. Its fiberglass items attracted national attention. Several formal fiberglass gowns were presented to notable women, among them a daughter of Queen Victoria. Princess Eulalie of Spain also ordered a dress. Despite its popularity, fiberglass was not initially profitable because each item was woven by hand. It was not until the late 1930s, with the advent of machine-made fiberglass, that large-scale production became financially advantageous.

Hints for Collectors
For collectors of world's fair memorabilia, the package is often as valuable as the object inside since it is an historical document.

Description
Left: oval lenses with thin, gold-colored metal frame; temple pieces wider at ends. Center: oval lenses with thick brass frame; folding brass temple pieces with loops at ends. Right: octagonal lenses with thin brass frame; folding brass temple pieces with small loops at ends and sliding device to adjust length.

Variations
Frames may be gold, silver, steel, or other metal. Lenses may be round or rectangular.

Type and Dimensions
Cast optical glass, ground by lensmaker, then fitted to frames. Left frame width: 4¼". Center and right frame width: 4½".

Locality and Period
Left: the East, western Pennsylvania, West Virginia, and Ohio. c. 1850–1900. Center: England; widely exported to the United States. c. 1770–1800. Right: the East and England. c. 1820–50.

Comment
By the early 19th century, spectacles were made in a few major American cities. The frames, usually gold or silver, were often crafted in jewelry shops. In 1883 this country's first lens grinding plant was established, and lenses no longer had to be imported.

Hints for Collectors
Collecting early American eyepieces is a growing field, and prices have increased substantially. Many collectors are more interested in decorative lorgnettes and monocles than the homely eyeglasses illustrated here.

Chain

Description
Chain of joined round and oval links; ends of first and last links
bent straight. 3 short chain sections meant to hang down at
evenly spaced intervals. Colors: transparent amber, aquamarine,
blue, green, and colorless; opaque white; and combination of 2 or
more colors.

Variations
Links vary in size and shape, including fanciful shapes such as
hearts. Short chains may be arranged as swags.

Type and Dimensions
Each link lampworked from a colored rod and looped through
another link; ends joined before cooling. Chain length: 3'.
Link length: 1¼".

Locality and Period
Throughout the United States. c. 1860–1900.

Comment
Glass chains were made by specialized glass craftsmen called
lampworkers, who formed objects from glass rods, which they
heated until pliable. These traveling artists often sold their
creations at fairs and exhibitions; they made such pieces as
miniature toys and ships with elaborate sails and rigging. At first
most lampworkers were European, but by the late 19th century,
many Americans had learned the craft. Chains like the one seen
here were hung in windows over the curtains and in doorways.

Hints for Collectors
Chains are fragile, hard to display, and difficult to date.
Nevertheless they are quite popular with collectors of folk art.

Description
Far left: cylindrical pen case with printed decoration and inscription "SOUVENIR/NEW YORK WORLD'S FAIR 1939/CORNING GLASS WORKS." Center: 3 elongated pens with body of twisted colored threads, 2 with decorative tops. Far right: cylindrical pen holder, with cut pattern, for push-on steel nib. Colors: transparent red, blue, pink, green, yellow, purple, colorless, and opaque white; threading or added decoration in any color.

Variations
Decoration varies.

Type and Dimensions
Far left: machine-blown in mold for shape. Center: each form lampworked from colored rods. Far right: yellow rod cut. Length: 5–6″.

Locality and Period
Far left and left: Corning Glass Works, Corning, New York. 1939. Center, right, and far right: throughout the United States. England and Bohemia; widely exported to the United States. c. 1850–1900.

Comment
Many glass pens are ornamental, although it is possible to write with them by constantly dipping them in ink. The yellow example is probably factory-made and less common than the 2 with ornate handles. The New York World's Fair pen case and the pen next to it were sold at the Corning pavilion.

Hints for Collectors
Collecting odd items like the ones illustrated can be a challenge to the beginner. Of the pens shown, the world's fair set with the original marked case has the greatest value.

Description
Long, solid, cylindrical canes with round head at 1 end and point at other end (not shown). Decorated with colored stripes. Colors: transparent blue, red, yellow, green, colorless, and opaque white; stripes of 1 or more colors.

Variations
Head may be curved to form ring or shepherd's crook. Cane may be twisted and lack stripes.

Type and Dimensions
Gather tooled into shape. Stripes applied and marvered into surface before annealing. Length: 40–65″.

Locality and Period
The East and Midwest. c. 1840–90. Throughout the United States. c. 1890–1910.

Comment
During the 19th century, glass canes were probably made in every glasshouse in the United States, England, and on the Continent. Although a few American canes are listed in glasshouse inventories before 1860, the majority were created between 1880 and 1910 as showpieces, whose intricacies displayed the glassblower's skill. According to newspapers from the 1890s, the canes were carried in Labor Day parades.

Hints for Collectors
Look for glass canes in country shops near the former locations of 19th-century glass factories. Unless purchased from a descendant of the maker, it is virtually impossible to identify or date a cane.

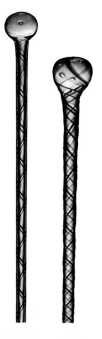

Description
Slippers with pointed toes, high insteps, and square heels.
Enameled flowers (left), plain (center), or with hobnail and star
design and inscriptions on sole "PATD/OCT 19/86" and "CRYSTAL
SLIPPER/BOSTON THEATRE" (right). Colors: (left) opaque white
enameled pink; (center) opaque blue; (right) transparent blue,
purple, green, amber, and colorless.

Variations
Left and center may have other enameled or gilt designs. Right
may name another theater, lack words, or have other patterns;
may have bow at instep, plain surface, and "GILLINDER & SONS/
CENTENNIAL EXHIBITION" inside.

Type and Dimensions
Left and center: blown in full-size multipiece mold for shape; toe
finished. Left: enamel fixed by firing after annealing. Right:
pressed in mold for pattern and shape. Length: 5–6¼".

Locality and Period
Left and center: the East and Midwest. c. 1870–90. Right:
George Duncan & Sons or Bryce Brothers, both of Pittsburgh.
c. 1886–95. Variants c. 1870–1900.

Comment
The pressed slipper in the Daisy and Button pattern was
patented in 1886 by John Miller, who sold the patent to both
Duncan and Bryce. This one was a souvenir for a Boston
performance by the Chicago Opera House Company in 1888.

Hints for Collectors
Beware of 20th-century copies of the Daisy and Button slipper.
Reproductions lack the inscriptions and come in many sizes and
colors, including transparent blue and amber.

Brilliant-cut whimsies

Description
Solid forms with brilliant-cut patterns on front; flat on back. Book-shaped (left, right) or heart-shaped (center). Colors: colorless; rarely cased with transparent red, blue, green, or yellow.

Variations
Shapes include cradle, boat, diamond, club, and spade. Many cut patterns. Back may have names or initials and date.

Type and Dimensions
Gather tooled into shape. Cut into final form and designs cut after annealing. Left height: 4⅛". Center height: 2⅞". Right height: 1¼".

Locality and Period
Throughout the United States. c. 1880–1920.

Comment
Ornamental whimsical forms like this were almost always made as presents. The book shape is probably the most common. It can be found with simple diamond and cross designs that date to the early 1880s, as well as with the more complex patterns, like those illustrated, that date from the 1880s to the early 20th century. The small book at the right, a souvenir from a cutting shop, was made around 1900. The heart was an engagement present made in 1903, and the back is inscribed "Agnes."

Hints for Collectors
Cut-glass oddities like this have not particularly interested most collectors and are often much less expensive than cut-glass bowls and decanters. The whimsies rarely bear trademarks, although they may have been made in well-known glasshouses. They are the type of curio that you might find in a relative's attic or possibly in a general antiques shop.

Description
Hats, each with flaring brim. Body plain (left), with diamonds and squares (center), or panels (right). Pontil mark on each flat base. Colors: transparent brown, amber, yellow, green, aquamarine, blue, purple, milky colorless, and colorless; opaque and opalescent white.

Variations
Pattern may be vertical or swirled ribs or hobnail and star design; may have threading. Brims vary from flared to curled.

Type and Dimensions
Left: free-blown, then tooled into shape. Height: 3½″. Center: blown in full-size multipiece mold for pattern and shape; brim finished. Height: 2¼″. Right: pressed in mold for pattern and shape; brim finished. Height: 1½″.

Locality and Period
The East and Midwest. c. 1825–75.

Comment
Blown hats were created in many 19th-century bottle and window glasshouses in New England, New York, and New Jersey. The hat in the center is an early type that collectors call blown 3-mold; these were made at Boston & Sandwich and probably elsewhere in the East. Both the blown 3-mold and pressed hats shown here were first shaped in miniature tumbler molds, then tooled into hats. After 1875 pressed examples were formed entirely in the mold without any hand finishing.

Hints for Collectors
The blown 3-mold pattern shown at the center has been copied in colorless glass and has no distinguishing marks. Reproduction hats in the Daisy and Button pattern (hobnail and star variant not shown) were made in amber, purple, and blue.

Christmas-tree lights

Description
Cylindrical forms rounded near base, with ring below plain rim
and diamond patterned body. Small buttonlike circular base.
Colors: transparent amber, blue, purple, red, and green.

Variations
Light may have folded rim, lack buttonlike base, and have pontil
mark. Pattern may be vertical or swirled ribs or irregular
diamonds.

Type and Dimensions
Blown in full-size multipiece mold for pattern and shape.
Height: 3¾".

Locality and Period
Probably West Virginia and Ohio. c. 1850–80. Variants with
pontil marks c. 1800–20.

Comment
Although collectors call these small candleholders Christmas-tree
lights, their use on trees is not documented. They may have held
votive candles, and at least one account from the West Indies
suggests that they were used in theaters as footlights. Another
source posits that the vessels contained water with a layer of oil
on the surface. A wick inserted through a cork floated on top of
the oil. Smaller baglike candleholders have pontil marks,
irregular diamonds or occasionally ribs, and were blown in part-
size pattern molds. They were formerly attributed to
H.W. Stiegel, but are probably English.

Hints for Collectors
Holders without pontil marks should be less expensive than
those with them. Do not pay more for the Stiegel name.

Description
Domed forms with flange and hollow skirt; screw threads on interior of dome. Skirt has inscription "HEMINGRAY—20" (left) or "WHITALL TATUM CO." (right). Colors: transparent light and dark aquamarine, green, and colorless; colorless with iridescent orange or purple.

Variations
Designs vary slightly. May be marked "CORNING PYREX," "STERLING," "W.BROOKFIELD NY," "BROOKFIELD NY," or name of another manufacturer. Sizes up to 7″ high.

Type and Dimensions
Machine-pressed in mold for pattern and shape. Height: 4″.

Locality and Period
Left: Hemingray Glass Company, Covington, Kentucky. c. 1900–20. Right: Whitall Tatum Company, Millville, New Jersey. c. 1920–30. Variants also from Brookfield Glass Company, Brooklyn, New York, 1897–1920; Corning Glass Works, Corning, New York, 1923–40; and other smaller firms, c. 1900–40.

Comment
Glass insulators for electrical wires were first patented in the mid-19th century. Their form remained virtually unchanged from the 1870s until they went out of use in the 1940s. Although several hundred variations have been identified, insulators were made by only a few companies. Hemingray and Brookfield were probably the largest.

Hints for Collectors
Look for glass insulators on the ground near telephone poles, where they may have been left when modern devices were installed.

Flower frog

Description
Cylindrical form with domed top. 7 holes around central hole; all
extend through frog. Colors: transparent aquamarine, green,
amber, colorless, and colorless with iridescent orange.

Variations
Shape may be square, hexagonal, or octagonal. Any shape may
have human figure (by Steuben and others) or animal figure (by
Heisey) on top. Holes may form different pattern.

Type and Dimensions
Pressed in mold for pattern and shape. Sprayed with chemical
for iridescent finish before annealing. Height: 1¼". Diameter:
2¼".

Locality and Period
Throughout the United States. c. 1905–20. Variants c. 1880–
1950.

Comment
Although flower frogs were made in ceramic in the 18th and 19th
centuries, most glass examples date from the late 19th and early
20th centuries, when a number of flower-holder designs were
patented. In 1905 Edwin Garnsey of La Grange, Illinois, was
granted a patent for a cylindrical holder with holes for the flower
stems, and this design became the classic flower frog shape.
Machine-made Depression-glass flower frogs tend to be simple.
The example shown here with its iridescent finish is typical of
Carnival glass.

Hints for Collectors
Glass flower frogs may be found in a great variety of shapes,
styles, and prices. Depression and Carnival glass are the
cheapest.

Description
Hollow conical form with screw threads around rim and perforated tin screw-on cap. Doughnut-shaped lower part with 3 ball feet. Opening in center of bottom covered with metal screen cone. Inscription on 1 side "UNIQUE/PAT'D 1-27-14/FLY TRAP." Colorless.

Variations
Trap may have stopper and lack inscription; may have long neck.

Type and Dimensions
Blown in full-size multipiece mold for pattern and shape. Height: 8".

Locality and Period
Throughout the United States. c. 1880–1930.

Comment
This unusual-looking object is a flytrap, patented in 1914. A solution of sugar and water was placed in the doughnut-shaped part; flies attracted to the liquid would enter the trap through the base and be unable to fly out again. The trap was emptied by removing the cap. Flies were common indoor pests before the era of screened windows, but it was not until the late 19th century that their role as disease carriers was widely publicized.

Hints for Collectors
All glass flytraps resemble each other. Early free-blown examples, dating from the 1880s, have long decanterlike necks. Later mold-blown examples like the one illustrated are easier to find.

Mousetrap

Description
Hollow cylindrical form with notch on side opposite bulge. Closed at 1 end and open at other. Inscription on 1 side "MOUSE EXTERMINATOR/MFG. AND SOLD BY/N.J.WIGGENTON/WINCHESTER, VA./PAT JULY 30, 1918." Colorless.

Type and Dimensions
Blown in full-size multipiece mold for pattern and shape. Length: 6¾".

Locality and Period
Glasshouse unknown; western Pennsylvania, West Virginia, Ohio, or Indiana. 1918–20.

Comment
The mousetrap shown here was invented and sold by the retailer N.J. Wiggenton. It was meant to operate like a seesaw; the notch was supposed to rest on a stick or rod so that the open end lay on the ground while the closed end with the bait was raised. A mouse that entered the trap would creep along the passage, but once over the bump above the notch, the mouse's weight would tip the trap, sending the unfortunate victim head-first to the closed end. The fact that these glass traps are rare would seem to indicate that they were not a commercial success, and today they have been completely replaced by the wood and steel-spring design.

Hints for Collectors
Oddities like mousetraps and flytraps occasionally turn up at house sales and flea markets. Despite their rarity, these items are generally low priced.

Description
Left: rooster with comb and long tail stands on flat circular base. Center: ring-necked pheasant with long tail stands on base in form of clump of grass. Right: crouching rabbit with ears back; flat stomach for base. Colors: rooster transparent red, red-orange, and colorless; pheasant and rabbit colorless.

Variations
Rooster may have rectangular base and spread tail feathers; may lean forward with tail straight up. Pheasant may have domelike base. Rabbit may be sitting and have ears up or head bent toward paws.

Type and Dimensions
Pressed in mold for pattern and shape. Rooster height: 8″. Pheasant height: 4¾″. Rabbit height: 2½″.

Locality and Period
Rooster and rabbit: New Martinsville Glass Manufacturing Company, New Martinsville, West Virginia. c. 1945–60. Pheasant: A.H. Heisey & Company, Newark, Ohio. 1942–53. Variants from K.R. Haley, Greensburg, and Duncan & Miller Glass Company, Washington, Pennsylvania; Cambridge Glass Company, Cambridge, Ohio; and other firms in same area. c. 1930–60.

Comment
Glass animal figurines, especially roosters, hens, swans, and horses, were extremely popular in the late 1930s and 1940s.

Hints for Collectors
The Imperial Glass Company of Bellaire, Ohio, reproduced several animals, including the Heisey pheasant illustrated, and used a removable sticker to identify the copies.

Wall pocket for matches

Description
Flat-backed wall pocket with front in form of woman's head
wearing classical headdress and drapery under chin. Inscription
on back "PAT⁴ JUNE 13, 1876" and hole near top. Colorless.

Variations
Pocket may be in form of jester's head with cap and bells. Shape
may be flat-backed cone with floral design on front.

Type and Dimensions
Pressed in mold for pattern and shape. Height: 4½".

Locality and Period
Pittsburgh area. 1876–c. 1880. Conical variant from England;
widely exported to the United States. c. 1880–1900.

Comment
This curious object is a wall match safe patented in 1876 by
Washington Beck. It was designed to hang near the stove, safely
out of the reach of children. Beck was associated with several
Pittsburgh-area glasshouses and patented a number of pressed
novelties, including the jester's head variant. The wall pocket
shown is probably in the form of Columbia, a common 19th-
century personification of the United States.

Hints for Collectors
There are several English designs for wall match safes dating to
the same period. Most have a Design Registry mark—a diamond
with letters and numbers—impressed on the back, and it can
help date the design. American collectors usually consider
American examples more valuable.

Knobs, Balls, and Paperweights

Dating from the mid-1820s to the present, most of the glass objects in this section are unusually decorative in view of their function. Mantel ornaments, lightning-rod balls, and witch balls may have been used only for display, and Christmas balls continue to be popular. In contrast, glass furniture knobs, picture hangers, and buttons were designed to be both functional and elegant. Although paperweights certainly serve a practical purpose, collectors often treasure them solely for their beauty.

Doorknobs, Furniture Knobs, and Curtain Tiebacks

Glass doorknobs and furniture knobs are among the first articles made with the pressing machine. Some examples date from as early as 1825. Throughout the 19th century and well into the next, pressed-glass knobs provided an attractive substitute for metal or wood. When in the 1880–1915 period cut glass became a sign of prestige, makers of pressed glass marketed imitations at prices most households could afford. Curtain tiebacks, often with patterns similar to those on doorknobs, were also made in the early days of the pressing machine. Some were produced in such quantity that many are still available today.

Witch Balls, Target Balls, and Lightning-rod Balls

Since the hollow globe is perhaps one of the easiest shapes to blow, it is not surprising to find a wide variety of both free-blown and mold-blown balls. One of the oldest examples pictured is the witch ball, dating to 1840 and supposedly used to ward off evil spirits. Unlike these usually plain balls, the late 19th-century target balls were often made in bright colors that were easy to spot from a distance. Lightning-rod balls, used in rural areas from 1880 to 1930, can be found in such a variety of colors and shapes that they are the focus of specialized collections.

Paperweights

In the 17th century, glass paperweight-like objects may have been used as hand coolers, intended to keep a lady's hands from getting warm and moist. Glass paperweights of the types collected today were first made in Europe during the 19th century and became especially popular in France and England from 1845 to 1860. By the 1850s, they were being made in the United States, perhaps by glassblowers who had seen paperweights at the 1851 Crystal Palace Exhibition in London. Most mid-19th-century American examples were copies of European designs.

By the 1880s, individual artists in a number of American factories began to create their own patterns. Some paperweights are so distinctive that they can be traced by their designs to specific factories, such as New England Glass, Gillinder & Sons, Mt. Washington, and Whitall Tatum.

During the last decades of the 19th century, glass manufacturers advertised a variety of pressed-glass paperweights, including those with historical portraits. Less expensive weights bearing advertising slogans and mottoes were produced expressly for businesses to distribute as gifts to customers. While the commercial weights are no longer made today, many of the more decorative paperweights continue to be designed by contemporary artists in studios and factories devoted exclusively to paperweight making.

Unlike most antique American weights, modern American examples are usually signed and often dated on the base, using canes in the form of letters or dates. Some antique French and English paperweights are also signed with initial or date canes.

Description
Solid octagonal knobs. Top rounded (left) or flat (right). Both have panels around sides and taper to base with star design underneath. Metal shank at back ends in brass cap. Colors: transparent purple, blue, light and dark amber, and colorless.

Variations
Top may have pressed pattern of facets or panels. Rarely, knob may be cased with colored glass, with circles, diamonds, or squares cut through.

Type and Dimensions
Pressed in mold for pattern and shape. Top ground flat and polished after annealing (right). Shank and cap added. Diameter: 2¼″.

Locality and Period
Throughout the United States. c. 1870–1920.

Comment
Pressed-glass knobs were patented in the 1830s, but did not become common until the late 19th century. Made in many colors, they offered an alternative to metal knobs or to the elaborate but very expensive cut-glass knobs. While the cased knobs, which were of blown glass, were probably produced in the East, pressed examples both plain and patterned were manufactured throughout the country.

Hints for Collectors
To tell if a knob is cut or pressed, feel the edges. Cut edges are sharp and somewhat uncomfortable to hold. The best public collection of American doorknobs is at the Margaret Woodbury Strong Museum in Rochester, New York.

Furniture knobs

Description
Solid knobs with ray pattern on top; pinched in between top and
base. Left: octagonal with raised top and panels around sides;
hole through center with metal screw. Right: round with
recessed top; glass screw shank with inscription "PATENT" on
base. Colors: transparent light and dark amber, light and dark
blue, and colorless; opaque white and blue; and opalescent white.

Variations
Pattern on top varies; may be diamond, rosette, or dots and
stippling. Shank may have "BAKEWELL'S PATENT" on base.
Diameter varies from less than 1″ to 2½″.

Type and Dimensions
Pressed in mold for pattern and shape. Left: metal screw added.
Left diameter: 2″. Right diameter: 1¾″.

Locality and Period
Left: the East or Midwest. c. 1850–60. Right: Boston &
Sandwich Glass Company, Sandwich, Massachusetts. 1829–
c. 1840. Bakewell variants from Pittsburgh. c. 1825–35.

Comment
Glass furniture knobs were among the first objects to be made
with the mechanical press. Most knobs were attached by metal
screws, but in 1829 Deming Jarves of Boston & Sandwich
patented a knob with a glass screw shank. However, the shank
required such a large hole in the wood that it was not very
successful.

Hints for Collectors
Many glass knobs are still found on furniture from the mid-19th
century. Knobs by themselves usually turn up singly or in pairs
and are about the least expensive means of acquiring genuine
Sandwich or Bakewell glass.

Description
Solid flower-form disks with petals radiating from center.
Cylindrical ribbed shaft, with metal screw embedded in center.
Colors: transparent green, blue, purple, amber, and opalescent
white.

Type and Dimensions
Pressed in mold for pattern and shape around metal screw.
Diameter: 2¾″.

Locality and Period
Glasshouse unknown; the United States. c. 1930–50.

Comment
These picture hangers are adaptations of a curtain tieback design
that dates from the 1840s and 1850s. Technically they are not
reproductions, since no genuine 19th-century picture hangers
like these exist. However, reproductions of the original tiebacks
were made in the 1920s and 1930s. They came in 2 sizes, both
larger than the picture hangers shown here, and in a variety of
colors, including colorless with amber stain. Picture hangers with
metal screws embedded in the back are unlike anything made in
the 19th century. Nor are the colors the same as those used
before the turn of the century, as a comparison with old pressed
glass will show. No other patterns are known.

Hints for Collectors
You may want to buy modern picture hangers of the type
illustrated for their decorative appeal. But be aware that they
are not antiques.

Curtain tiebacks

Description
Solid circular or flower-form disks with flower-and-scroll or petal
design. Smooth back. Metal screw at center extends several
inches behind. Colors: transparent yellow, amber, purple, and
blue; opaque and opalescent white; and opalescent white with
amber trim and gilt decoration.

Variations
Floral patterns vary slightly. May be mercury glass.

Type and Dimensions
Pressed in mold for pattern and shape. Silver stain for amber
trim and gilt fixed by firing after annealing. Metal screw added.
Left diameter: 5½". Center diameter: 2½". Right diameter: 3¼".

Locality and Period
New England; probably New England Glass Company,
Cambridge, Massachusetts, or Boston & Sandwich Glass
Company or Cape Cod Glass Company, both of Sandwich,
Massachusetts. c. 1840–60.

Comment
Elaborate curtain tiebacks like the ones shown here were
probably pressed at any one of several New England
glassmaking establishments, since they turn up frequently in old
houses in New England and rarely in other areas. They would
have fit in well with Victorian draperies, especially the popular
swag curtains. Although produced in great numbers, the
tiebacks are found in surprisingly few patterns.

Hints for Collectors
Curtain tiebacks shaped like the 2 small examples pictured were
reproduced in yellow, blue, and purple. The copies come in 3½",
4¼", and other sizes, and have a recessed hexagon on the back.

Paperweight buttons

Description
Solid regular or faceted globe-shaped buttons with metal loop shank embedded in back. Left: enclosed design of white, red, and yellow flower with green leaves, surrounded by coppery glitter on blue ground; colorless dome. Right: millefiori mushroom design on white ground; colorless dome cased with red-orange, through which 5 circles are cut.

Variations
Floral patterns vary greatly; occasionally abstract millefiori designs.

Type and Dimensions
Center design formed of colored rods; design arranged in mold and picked up with prepared ground, then enclosed in colorless glass with metal shank and tooled into dome shape. Right: dome cased with colored glass; circles cut after annealing. Left diameter: ⅝″. Right diameter: ¹¹/₁₆″.

Locality and Period
Left: Thura Ericson, Millville, New Jersey. c. 1945–63. Right: Charles Kaziun, Brockton, Massachusetts. 1940–64.

Comment
Paperweight buttons are made very much like paperweights. Kaziun, probably the best-known paperweight-button maker, also makes paperweights and similar objects, such as stickpins and cordial glasses with flower designs in the bases. Ericson's work is less known, but also of excellent quality.

Hints for Collectors
Buttons like these command a high price, so it is advisable to buy from a knowledgeable dealer or collector.

Marbles

Description
Solid colorless spheres with enclosed design either of white eagle (left), or swirled opaque red, white, blue, and yellow threads (center, right).

Variations
Enclosed shape may be in form of lion, dog, or other animal; or, rarely, head of a person. Swirls vary in width and spacing; may include opaque and transparent colors.

Type and Dimensions
Left: ceramic eagle enclosed in colorless glass that is then tooled into shape. Diameter: 1½". Center and right: colorless and colored rods twisted and cut into small segments that are then tooled into shape. Diameter: 1½".

Locality and Period
Germany; widely exported to the United States. The United States east of Chicago. c. 1850–1914.

Comment
During the 19th century most marbles were imported from Germany; only occasionally were marbles handmade in the United States. It was not until after World War I that American companies mass-produced marbles using automated machinery. Collectors often attribute examples like those shown here to Nicholas Lutz, a foreman of the Boston & Sandwich Glass Company. But while Lutz did create paperweights, there is no evidence that anyone at Sandwich made marbles.

Hints for Collectors
Marbles like the one on the left with the ceramic enclosure are known as sulphide marbles, although no sulphide was used to make them. Minor scratches rarely affect value.

Description
Hollow globes with plain lip at top and bottom. Left: patterned globe with moon and stars. Center: rounded upper part with sunbursts; conical paneled lower part with 1 letter of inscription "HAWKEYE" per panel. Right: plain globe with "K" near top. Colors: transparent purple, red, green, and amber; opaque blue and white.

Variations
Pattern may be ribs or diamonds. May be silvery or silvery-gold. Shape may be polygonal.

Type and Dimensions
Blown in full-size multipiece mold for pattern and shape. Lips finished. Diameter: 4″.

Locality and Period
Probably western Pennsylvania, West Virginia, Ohio, and Indiana. c. 1880–1930.

Comment
Colorful glass balls like the ones shown here can still be seen on lightning rods throughout the East and Midwest, usually on barns but sometimes atop houses. These globes are purely decorative and appear in a variety of patterns, shapes, and colors. Although collectors of lightning-rod balls have been researching the history of these objects, the glass factories that made most of them are still unknown.

Hints for Collectors
Lightning-rod balls tend to turn up at country sales and auctions, and some bottle dealers handle them.

Christmas-tree ornaments

Description
Hollow silvery globes of thin glass, with metal hanger at top.
Colors: transparent blue, red, green, and colorless, all with
mercury lining.

Variations
Figural ornaments include Santa Claus, angel, horns, fruit,
reindeer, and other animals. Globe may have gilt, enameled, or
painted decoration.

Type and Dimensions
Blown in full-size multipiece mold for shape, lined with mercury,
then excess mercury poured out and opening sealed with hanger.
Left diameter: 3½″. Right diameter: 2¾″.

Locality and Period
Probably Lauscha, Germany; widely exported to the United
States. c. 1890–1915.

Comment
Decorating a Christmas tree with lights and ornaments was
originally a German custom, popularized in England by Queen
Victoria in the 1840s and 1850s. Most early tree ornaments were
made in southern Germany. During World War I, when export
ceased, Corning Glass Works converted its light-bulb plant in
Wellsboro, Pennsylvania, into a factory for the manufacture of
machine-blown Christmas decorations.

Hints for Collectors
Plain hand-blown Christmas balls in good condition are highly
prized, and figural ornaments are considered desirable even if
they have lost their silvering or gilt decoration. Machine-made
ornaments from the 1920s and 1930s are more common and
should be substantially less expensive.

Target balls

Description
Hollow globes, diamond patterned or plain, with short neck and plain lip. Below left: inscription around center "BOGARDUS GLASS BALL PATD APR 10 1877." Below right: paper inside. Opposite left: design of man firing gun on flat side. Opposite center: "N.B.GLASS WORKS PERTH" twice around center. Opposite right: "IRA PAINE'S FILLED BALL/PAT. OCT 23 1877." Colors: transparent light and dark blue, aquamarine, green, amber, purple, and colorless.

Variations
Pattern may be ribs or pictures of dogs and hunters. Other inscriptions include "FROM J H JOHNSTON/GREAT WESTERN GUN WORKS/164 SMITHFIELD STREET/PITTSBURGH PA/RIFLES, SHOT GUNS/ REVOLVERS, AMMUNITION/FISHING TACKLE/CHOKE BORING REPAIRING/& WRITE FOR PRICE LIST" and "MANUFACTURED BY THE/ KENTUCKY GLASS WORKS COMPANY/JOSEPH GRIFFITH & SONS SOLE AGENTS/ALSO DEALERS IN GUNS, PISTOLS AND FISHING TACKLE, LOUISVILLE/KENTUCKY."

Type and Dimensions
Blown in full-size multipiece mold for pattern and shape. Neck and lip finished. Below left diameter: 2⅝". Below right diameter: 2¼". Opposite diameter: 3".

Locality and Period
Western Pennsylvania, West Virginia, Ohio, and Indiana. c. 1860–1900. Variants also from Kentucky.

Comment
Shooting and marksmanship have always been popular in this country, and to this day it is common to have a turkey or pigeon shoot around the holidays. Originally the targets were live birds, but public resentment as well as problems in transportation led to the introduction of inanimate targets. Around the 1840s an

English marksman came up with the idea of glass balls, which were filled with paper, confetti, or feathers so they could be seen more easily when broken. Charles Portlock of Boston introduced the balls to this country in the 1850s, but it was not until the Wild West shows of the late 19th century that target balls were widely popularized and adopted by the general public. One of the tricks Buffalo Bill and Annie Oakley performed was to shoot several balls out of the air at one time.

In the 1880s Adam Bogardus invented a mechanical throwing device to toss the target balls into the air, and this greatly increased interest in the sport. He and several other target ball manufacturers made them with ribbed or diamond patterns. This feature increased the probability of a shot's breaking the ball instead of merely bouncing off it.

Without an inscription it is very difficult to pin down the factory in which a target ball was made. Since the balls were especially popular in frontier areas of the period, it is likely that many were produced in western Pennsylvania, West Virginia, Ohio, and Indiana. After the invention of the clay pigeon (a flat clay disk), the glass target ball gradually went out of favor, and by the turn of the century, was no longer used.

Hints for Collectors

Target balls turn up from time to time at bottle auctions and specialized bottle shops. Their historical value is often unrecognized, and, like lightning-rod balls, these curios can be purchased at moderate prices.

Witch ball

Description
Hollow, slightly flattened globe with small opening on 1 side.
Colors: transparent aquamarine, blue, green, amber, and
colorless; often colorless with stripes of 2 colors, including
opaque white and red stripes or opaque white and blue stripes.

Variations
Size varies; may have pontil mark and lack opening. Rarely with
applied lily-pad decoration.

Type and Dimensions
Free-blown, then tooled into shape. Diameter: 8⅝″.

Locality and Period
New England, New York, New Jersey, and the Midwest.
England; widely exported to the United States. c. 1840–1900.

Comment
The origin of the term "witch ball" and its use are somewhat
obscure. An English theory suggests that superstitious people
filled the balls with string and then hung them by their doors.
The visiting spirit was supposed to get so involved in pulling out
the string that the people inside the house would be safe. But
this story sounds unlikely. Many witch balls matched vases and
pitchers; by placing the balls on top of these vessels, they were
transformed into parlor ornaments.

Hints for Collectors
Many small glass balls found in antiques shops are not witch balls
but machine-made Japanese fishing floats. The floats have thick
walls and mold marks around the middle, while witch balls have
thinner walls and lack mold marks.

Darning egg

Description
Hollow egg with pontil mark on narrow end. Colors: opaque white with transparent red and blue spots.

Variations
Egg may lack spots and be white or off-white; may have molded design of chicken, flowers, or cross; may have inscription "HAPPY EASTER."

Type and Dimensions
Free-blown, then tooled into shape. Red and blue spots applied and marvered into surface before annealing. Length: 3″.

Locality and Period
The East, western Pennsylvania, West Virginia, and Ohio. c. 1870–1910.

Comment
Probably a darning egg, this decorative object was used inside the toe or heel of a knitted sock to hold the torn edges in place while the sock was mended. Eggs without spots may have been placed in nests to encourage hens to lay eggs. Common in the late 19th century, nest eggs were also made of white ceramic and occasionally of wood painted white. Turn-of-the-century trade papers, such as the *Crockery and Glass Journal*, are full of advertisements for blown-glass eggs and pressed-glass plates with designs of flowers, chickens, or rabbits and Easter inscriptions.

Hints for Collectors
Novelties made as factory items are much easier to identify than free-blown darning or nest eggs. Some Easter egg designs have been attributed to specific factories, mostly in western Pennsylvania and Ohio.

Fruit paperweights

Description
Hollow paperweights in form of apple and pear, each with stem and circular base. Colors: fruit red shading to yellow; base colorless.

Variations
Color of fruit varies slightly. Fruit may be quince. Base may be square.

Type and Dimensions
Each fruit lampworked opaque white glass cased with colored glass, then tooled into shape. Stem and base applied. Left base diameter: 3⅝″. Right base diameter: 2⅞″.

Locality and Period
New England Glass Company, Cambridge, Massachusetts.
c. 1860–75.

Comment
During the 18th century, realistic-looking fruit paperweights were blown in glasshouses in Venice. This type of paperweight was made for a limited time in the United States by the New England Glass Company. Since all examples are basically uniform, they are clearly production items and were probably created by only a few workmen.

Hints for Collectors
The shaded red and yellow color of the fruit paperweights resembles some art-glass hues, such as Peachblow and Amberina, which were made in the 1880s at the New England Glass factory. Possibly the earlier formulas developed to imitate the natural colors of fruit inspired the later art glass.

Flower paperweight

Description
Solid sphere enclosing design of rose with large green leaves.
Rounded collar at base of sphere and flat circular foot. Colors:
colorless with opaque pink, red, yellow, green, and white.

Variations
Flower may be lily. Sphere may have stem with circular foot;
sphere may have collar as base; or base of sphere may be ground
flat.

Type and Dimensions
Lampworked flat flower and leaf design formed of colored rods.
Using crimp, design is shaped by pushing it inside colorless ball.
Ball tooled into shape. Collar and foot applied. Height: 4″. Base
diameter: 3⅝″.

Locality and Period
Whitall Tatum Company, Millville, New Jersey. Possibly Victor
Durand's Vineland Flint Glass Works, Vineland, New Jersey.
c. 1890–1912.

Comment
The paperweight illustrated is usually called the Millville Rose
because it was thought that Ralph Barber, an employee at the
Whitall Tatum factory made all of the rose and lily paperweights.
However, they were also formed by 3 or 4 other glassblowers at
Millville working on their own time. Several of these men
continued to make rose paperweights when employed by the
nearby Vineland glasshouse.

Hints for Collectors
Flower paperweights resembling the one shown here have been
made recently in China and the United States. Because these
new weights are difficult to spot, it is important to buy antique
examples only from a knowledgeable dealer.

Mantel ornament

Description
Solid sphere with flat top and enclosed fountain design of air bubbles and glass splatter decoration. 2-knopped stem with circular foot and pontil mark underneath. Colors: colorless with multicolored splatters.

Variations
Sphere may have pattern of evenly spaced bubbles or enclosed flower; pattern of multicolored glass may resemble flames. May lack stem.

Type and Dimensions
Splatters formed from bits of glass. Using crimp, bits pushed inside colorless ball; air bubbles created in this process. Ball tooled into shape. Stem and foot applied. Height: 5⅜".

Locality and Period
The East, western Pennsylvania, West Virginia, Ohio, and Indiana. c. 1880–present. Variants may be earlier.

Comment
Ornaments with tall stems are much less common than ordinary low paperweights with the same designs. They were usually made in pairs for either side of the mantel. Paperweight manufacturers often produced other forms, including perfume bottles, inkwells, compotes, candlesticks with paperweight bases, and, rarely, decanters with paperweight stoppers.

Hints for Collectors
Because splatter paperweights are among the easiest types to make, they can be some of the least expensive. The example illustrated is flat on top, indicating a repair, which lessens value. A chip or bruise was probably ground down and polished away.

Pylon paperweight

Description
Solid pentagonal form with broad front facet, 2 narrow sides, and 2 narrow back facets that come together in sharp edge. Cut vase design along narrow back facets and edge decorated with enameled flowers and leaves; design seen through front as vase with flowers. Flat square base. Colors: colorless with red, yellow, white, and green enamel.

Variations
Designs cut on back vary slightly; may lack enameled decoration.

Type and Dimensions
Gather tooled into shape. Cut into final form, facets and design cut, and enamel fixed by firing, all after annealing.
Height: 6¾″.

Locality and Period
France and Bohemia; widely exported to the United States. Possibly the East. c. 1850–70.

Comment
Pylon paperweights were usually sold in pairs as part of a desk set that also included a metal or glass tray with spaces for pens and 1 or 2 cut-glass inkwells with silver or brass caps. This type of desk set was popular in Europe. Although similar sets are not found in American glass-company catalogues of the period, some may have been made in this country. The paperweight form shown here is not as practical as the lower, more stable dome weights.

Hints for Collectors
The intricacy of the cut and enameled design makes these paperweights unusually attractive display pieces.

Philadelphia Memorial Hall inkstand

Description
Inkstand in form of rectangular building with central dome and spire; rectangular tower in each corner. Front with inscription "MEMORIAL HALL"; top with "PATENT APPLD. FOR"; and 4 sides of rectangular bottom with "ESTAB. CHARLES YOCKEL 1855/PHILAD. PA. USA" and "GLASS MOULD MAKER/1876 235 BREAD ST." Dome lifts off; hollow well for ink below. Steps at front form pen rest. Colorless.

Variations
Inkstand may be in form of another building.

Type and Dimensions
Inkstand and lid pressed in separate molds for pattern and shape. Height: 4". Length: 6½". Width: 4".

Locality and Period
Probably Philadelphia; possibly New York, New Jersey, and western Pennsylvania. 1876.

Comment
Memorial Hall was the main building erected for the Philadelphia Centennial Exposition of 1876; it is still standing in Fairmount Park. The mold for the inkstand illustrated was commissioned from Charles Yockel, who operated one of the largest moldmaking establishments of the late 19th century. This piece was probably an advertising souvenir for one of the glass firms that used Yockel molds. It is interesting that as late as 1876 Yockel was still using the English spelling "mould."

Hints for Collectors
Building-shaped inkstands are relatively rare. Because of the inscribed date and the advertising message, this one is especially valuable.

Philadelphia Memorial Hall paperweight

Description
Solid paperweight in form of rectangular building with central dome without spire; rectangular tower in each corner. Engraved inscription "1776 Memorial Hall 1876" on front of flat oval base. Colors: building colorless with frosted surface; base transparent dark purple, which may appear black.

Type and Dimensions
Building and base pressed in separate molds for pattern and shape; joined after annealing. Building acid-treated for frosted finish and base copper-wheel engraved after annealing. Height: 2½″. Length: 6¼″. Width: 4½″.

Locality and Period
Possibly Gillinder & Sons, Philadelphia, or firm in Pittsburgh area. 1876.

Comment
This paperweight is one of many pressed-glass souvenirs produced for sale at the Philadelphia Centennial Exhibition. Most souvenirs were made by Gillinder & Sons, which built a factory on the fairgrounds. Widely publicized in newspapers, Gillinder's factory became one of the most popular attractions.

Hints for Collectors
Gillinder souvenirs are usually marked "GILLINDER & SONS/ CENTENNIAL EXHIBITION" on the back or base. Although the Memorial Hall paperweight is not marked by Gillinder, it is a prized and rare Centennial souvenir.

Lion paperweight

Description
Solid paperweight in form of reclining lion with raised head. Oval plinthlike base with scalloped edge; inscription "GILLINDER & SONS/CENTENNIAL EXHIBITION" underneath. Colorless with frosted surface.

Variations
Base may be more rectangular and lack scallops and inscription. A larger lion has "JD" and anchor on base; paperweight may be in form of dog or bird. Variants colorless, transparent blue, green, and amber.

Type and Dimensions
Pressed in mold for pattern and shape. Acid-treated for frosted finish after annealing. Height: 2⅝". Length: 5¾". Width: 2½".

Locality and Period
Gillinder & Sons, Philadelphia. 1876. Variants from Adams & Company and other firms in Pittsburgh area. England and Bohemia; widely exported to the United States. c. 1850–80.

Comment
Pressed-glass paperweights in animal shapes were popular in the last half of the 19th century. The lion paperweight illustrated could have been made by Gillinder on the Philadelphia Centennial Exhibition grounds, or it may have been produced at Gillinder's permanent factory. Adams & Company marketed the unmarked variant without scallops, and John Derbyshire of Manchester, England, made the larger lion marked "JD." An 1870s catalogue of the Bohemian firm Meyr's Neffe pictures similar lion paperweights.

Hints for Collectors
Since the Bicentennial of 1976, Centennial souvenirs have been popular, especially Gillinder glass with the word "CENTENNIAL."

Turtle doorstop

Description
Solid doorstop in form of turtle, with rounded top surface and wrinkled bottom surface. Colors: transparent light and dark brown, amber, green, and aquamarine.

Variations
Shape, size, and degree of verisimilitude vary.

Type and Dimensions
Gather tooled into shape. Diameter: 6¾″.

Locality and Period
New Jersey. c. 1910–20. Variants also from New England, New York, and probably the Midwest. c. 1840–90. Throughout the United States. c. 1890–1920.

Comment
Glass doorstops are occasionally confused with paperweights, although doorstops are almost always larger, clumsier shapes, and the colors are typical of bottle and window glass. Unlike the more common factory-produced metal doorstops, glass examples were usually fashioned as gifts by individual workers rather than as part of the planned production. While workmen at bottle factories in England also made them, it is unlikely that many English doorstops were imported here.

Hints for Collectors
Although the turtle doorstop illustrated was made in about 1915, it is virtually identical to examples from the mid-19th century. Some doorstops of this type can be traced to particular mid-19th-century glasshouses; however, be wary of attributions, which raise the price substantially and can seldom be proved.

Portrait paperweight

Description
Solid rectangle with rounded corners. Portrait of Abraham
Lincoln impressed underneath base; "Saratoga" engraved on top.
Colorless.

Variations
Portrait varies, including different likeness of Lincoln or portrait
of Christopher Columbus, Ulysses S. Grant, George Washington,
Benjamin Franklin, or Queen Victoria and Prince Albert. May
lack "Saratoga." Shape usually circular.

Type and Dimensions
Pressed in mold for pattern and shape. Copper-wheel engraved
after annealing. Length: 4½". Width: 3⅜".

Locality and Period
Throughout the United States. c. 1880–1900.

Comment
Some portrait paperweights can be easily dated because of the
person shown. For example, the Columbus weight was probably
made for the Columbian Exposition of 1893 in Chicago, and a
paperweight showing Grant was probably produced at the time
of his death in the 1880s. However, Lincoln and Washington
paperweights could have been made at almost any time and by
almost any manufacturer. It is likely that weights bearing the
inscription "Saratoga" were made for the spa at Saratoga
Springs, New York, around 1900, when the area's springs were
at the height of their popularity.

Hints for Collectors
Pressed paperweights with historical portraits have always been
admired by collectors. Compared to the millefiori and flower
weights, most are moderate in price.

Photographic paperweight

Description
Solid circular dome paperweight with photograph of young man in turn-of-the-century clothing printed on circular disk. Colors: colorless dome with opaque white base.

Variations
Portrait varies; may be man, woman, or child. Shape may be square or rectangular. Disk may have signature.

Type and Dimensions
Portrait printed with metallic oxides on white glass disk, then enclosed in colorless glass and tooled into shape. Diameter: 3″.

Locality and Period
Throughout the United States. c. 1880–1900.

Comment
To make this type of paperweight, the photographic image was printed on glass instead of paper, a process very similar to that used for advertising paperweights of the late 19th century, on which words, trademarks, or photographs were combined with advertising messages. It is a misconception that a photograph on paper was enclosed within the weight; this would be impossible since the extreme heat needed to shape the glass would destroy the photograph.

Hints for Collectors
Photographic paperweights were never really common. They usually appeal to people interested in the history of photography or to collectors who like curiosities. Try dating an example by identifying the clothing shown. If photographic paperweights were made as political souvenirs, they can often be traced to specific campaigns.

Description
Solid circular dome paperweight with printed inscription "GEO. A
MACBETH COMPANY,/Pearl Glass/and/Pearl Top/Lamp Chimneys./
PITTSBURG, PA., U.S.A." on circular disk. Colors: colorless dome
with opaque white base.

Variations
Advertising messages vary. Color of disk varies; may include
picture of building or equipment. Shape may be oblong.

Type and Dimensions
Inscription printed on white glass disk, then enclosed in colorles
glass. Dome tooled into shape. Diameter: 3″.

Locality and Period
Pittsburgh. c. 1885–89. Variants from throughout the United
States. c. 1880–1900.

Comment
Advertising paperweights became popular in the last part of
the 19th century, when all forms of advertising proliferated.
They were probably given away to favored customers and not
produced for sale. Most of these paperweight designs are simply
lettering; some incorporate a picture of a factory or one of the
products the company sold.

Hints for Collectors
The George A. Macbeth Company manufactured lamp chimneys
and later, as the Macbeth-Evans Company, made Depression
glass, so the advertising paperweight illustrated might appeal t
collectors of Macbeth lamps or Depression tableware. Look for
advertising paperweights at secondhand shops, flea markets, an
junk shops, as well as through paperweight dealers.

Motto paperweight

Description
Solid circular dome paperweight with design of house encircled by motto "HOME SWEET HOME" on base. Circular facet on top. Colors: colorless dome with transparent amber, green, blue, or purple background and white design and letters.

Variations
Design may be clasped hands with "FRIENDSHIP"; sailing ship with "ROCKED IN THE CRADLE OF THE DEEP"; anchor and wreath with "HOPE"; house or no design with "REMEMBER MOTHER"; house or log cabin with "NO PLACE LIKE HOME"; battleship with "REMEMBER THE MAINE"; or wreath, flower, or fruit with "REMEMBER ME."

Type and Dimensions
Powdered glass arranged in mold to form pattern that is picked up with prepared amber ground and then enclosed in colorless glass. Dome tooled into shape. Facet ground and polished after annealing. Diameter: 3¼".

Locality and Period
The East, western Pennsylvania, West Virginia, Ohio, and Indiana. c. 1890–1910.

Comment
A motto paperweight took much less skill to make than the lampworked flowers and millefiori designs. In a sense, it was a mass-produced factory product: One paperweight made from the same mold looked much like the next. Around the turn of the century, many firms produced motto paperweights, especially large eastern bottle glasshouses and small midwestern paperweight factories.

Hints for Collectors
Motto paperweights are one of the least expensive types.

Fruit paperweight

Description
Solid circular dome paperweight enclosing design of apples, pears, cherries, and leaves in center against filigree ground. Polished pontil mark on base. Colors: colorless dome with opaque and transparent multicolored glass.

Variations
Design may be other fruit, arrangement of 3 small flowers, or 1 flat flower, such as clematis or poinsettia.

Type and Dimensions
Lampworked center design formed of colored rods. Design arranged in mold and picked up with gather containing the filigree, then enclosed in colorless glass and tooled into shape. Diameter: 3″.

Locality and Period
New England Glass Company, Cambridge, Massachusetts, or Boston & Sandwich Glass Company, Sandwich, Massachusetts. 1852–c. 1870.

Comment
The crisscross background of the paperweight design pictured is known as filigree work, but collectors also call it a latticinio ground. Some fruit paperweights with a filigree background can definitely be attributed to the New England Glass Company, since a few have survived among the descendants of the workers who made them. Paperweights of this type were also made in France, but American examples are generally simpler.

Hints for Collectors
Prices for fruit paperweights like this can be quite high. For intricate, classic patterns, consult specialized dealers, who will know the history of their objects as well as attributions.

Millefiori paperweight

Description
Solid circular dome paperweight with millefiori designs against filigree ground. Cut facets on top and sides. Polished pontil mark on base. Colors: colorless dome with opaque and transparent multicolored glass.

Variations
Millefiori patterns may include concentric rings, mushroom shapes, floral bouquet, or densely packed circle.

Type and Dimensions
Millefiori designs made by slicing groups of colored rods that are first fused together then elongated. Slices arranged in pattern in mold and picked up with gather containing the filigree, then enclosed in colorless glass and tooled into shape. Facets cut after annealing. Diameter: 2¾".

Locality and Period
New England Glass Company, Cambridge, Massachusetts, and Boston & Sandwich Glass Company, Sandwich, Massachusetts. 1852–c. 1870. Variants possibly from other factories in the East.

Comment
Millefiori paperweights are named for the numerous rods used to make them (*millefiori* means "a thousand flowers" in Italian). The example illustrated is especially beautiful because of the cut facets that highlight the enclosed design.

Hints for Collectors
All antique millefiori paperweights are expensive. Chinese and Venetian copies made in the 1930s and 1940s should be only a tenth or less the price of a good American weight.

Windows

A surprising number of antique windows can be found today, ranging from rare early 19th-century panes to the more common turn-of-the-century stained-glass windows. Until recently most of the late 19th- and early 20th-century windows were considered old-fashioned and discarded during renovations. With the current interest in old houses, especially those of the Victorian era and the 1920–40 period, windows and panes of all types are now the focus of collector attention.

Early Blown and Pressed Panes

The first windowpanes made in America were small, irregular squares of glass. The free-blown bull's-eye windowpane, with its bubbles and imperfections, is typical of these early products. By the late 1820s and 1830s, some tableware companies were manufacturing pressed windowpanes with raised patterns that resembled designs on tableware. Most of these were colorless and fairly small, but a few colored panes have also been found. The Bakewell company and the Curling & Robertson firm, both of Pittsburgh, as well as John & Craig Ritchie of Wheeling, West Virginia, produced panes marked with the company names. Bakewell also advertised glass for steamboats, but no 19th-century steamboat has survived with these windows in place.

Colored and Stained-glass Windows

Most of the antique panes and windows now available were made after 1880, when people decorated their homes with colored, patterned glass and stained-glass windows, formerly seen only in churches. Depending upon how much they could spend, the public could choose from all kinds of decorative panes: frosted etched glass, colored pressed glass, cased and engraved glass, and stained glass.

Late 19th-century pressed panes featured floral and abstract designs and often bore a mixture of patterns and textures, perhaps in imitation of stained glass. They could be used by themselves or in combination with colorless glass. In contrast, stained-glass windows consisted of many small pieces of glass fastened together with soft lead channels, or strips, inspiring collectors to call them leaded-glass windows. The term "stained glass" is actually a misnomer. Although colorless portions were sometimes stained with minerals and fired to produce a particular effect, usually the glass was cast or blown in the color desired.

Designers of Stained-glass Windows

The best-known manufacturer of stained-glass windows is Louis C. Tiffany of Tiffany Studios in Corona, New York, but many other studios also operated at the same time. For example, Chicago became the center of an active stained-glass window industry from the 1870s until World War I. Most large cities had at least one company that supplied church windows and did home commissions on the side. Small windows were also designed by local craftsmen.

The great majority of stained-glass windows are not signed, making identification difficult. Only now are the names of some artists beginning to be known, as, for example, the Boston painter John La Farge, who designed stained-glass windows for buildings throughout the country. Another overlooked stained-glass artist is the architect Frank Lloyd Wright, whose severe geometric windows can be seen in many of his houses.

Bull's-eye windowpane

Description
Square pane with rough circular knob in center. Sharp edges. Colors: transparent light aquamarine and colorless; rarely light amber and light green.

Variations
Pane may be circular sheet 36″ or more in diameter.

Type and Dimensions
Free-blown, then formed into large sheet. Cut into individual panes after annealing. Height: 6″. Width: 6″.

Locality and Period
The East and Midwest. c. 1760–1850.

Comment
The bull's-eye windowpane gets its name from the central knob, which looks like a bull's-eye in a target and which is actually leftover glass. During the 17th and 18th centuries, most windows were made by first blowing molten glass into a bubble several feet in diameter and next attaching a pontil rod to the bubble opposite the blowpipe. The glassmaker then removed the blowpipe, leaving a large hole in the bubble, and rotated the pontil rod rapidly. The resulting centrifugal force enlarged the hole until the whole bubble opened into a large circular sheet, attached to the pontil rod by a knob at the center. After annealing, the sheet was cut into panes, and only the center pane had the bull's-eye.

Hints for Collectors
Bull's-eye panes are quite hard to find, but antiques dealers, especially in New England, sometimes have a small stock tucked away. Reproductions look new, while old ones will usually be worn where they were puttied into place.

Description
Square pane with raised pattern on 1 side: 4 pairs of leaflike
scrolls surrounding floral cross with bull's-eye in center; 1 fleur-
de-lis in each corner. Smooth edges. Color: transparent amber.

Variations
Several similar patterns, mostly flowers or leaves, in opalescent
white, transparent purple, and colorless.

Type and Dimensions
Pressed in mold for pattern and shape. Height: 5⅞″. Width: 5⅞″.

Locality and Period
Boston & Sandwich Glass Company, Sandwich, Massachusetts;
New England Glass Company, Cambridge, Massachusetts; and
factories in the Pittsburgh area. c. 1850–70.

Comment
Although pressed-glass panes from the 1820–40 period are rare,
those from the 1850s and 1860s are even rarer. By the last
quarter of the 19th century, panes for front, parlor, and dining
room doors had become extremely fashionable, but in mid-
century they were not much in demand. The example illustrated
lacks the stippled background of the earlier panes, and its
pattern is not as naturalistic as those produced around 1900.
None of the mid-century panes are marked, but since their
patterns are similar to designs on the pressed-glass tableware
popular during this period, it is likely that both were made in the
same factories.

Hints for Collectors
Most mid-century examples are moderately priced. The earliest
pressed panes are rare and expensive, whether or not they are
signed, but those from the late 19th century are quite
reasonable.

Rectangular windowpane

Description
Rectangular pane with raised pattern on 1 side: large, multipetaled flower at center with rays in each corner; acanthus leaves at short sides, each leaf with pair of bull's-eyes. Smooth edges. Colors: transparent purple and colorless.

Variations
Patterns include Gothic arches, ship, flowers, and geometric designs; background may be stippled or plain. Back may have faint mark "BAKEWELL"; front may have "J. & C. RITCHIE" or "CURLING & ROBERTSON" in design. May be opalescent white. Width 6–12".

Type and Dimensions
Pressed in mold for pattern and shape. Height: 5". Width: 7".

Locality and Period
Probably Boston & Sandwich Glass Company, Sandwich, and New England Glass Company, Cambridge, Massachusetts. c. 1830–40. Variants from Benjamin Bakewell & Company and Curling & Robertson, Pittsburgh, and J. & C. Ritchie, Wheeling, West Virginia.

Comment
Windowpanes similar to the one pictured here are among the first pressed-glass products. Two panes, one with a Gothic design and one with a geometric pattern, are marked "BAKEWELL." So far Bakewell panes have been found in and around the doors of houses, in the door of a desk, and even in a hall lantern. No marked panes can be traced to New England, but some collectors connect examples like those shown with the Sandwich and New England Glass companies.

Hints for Collectors
Early pressed panes are extremely rare.

Assorted windowpanes

Description
Rectangular or square panes with raised pattern on 1 side: twining vine or mixed geometric and floral designs; with or without crinkled background. Smooth edges. Colors: transparent blue, blue-green, aquamarine, purple, pink, amber, and colorless.

Variations
Designs include ivy spray, swan and ferns, 3-leaf spray, quatrefoil and diamond, grape bunches, grape leaves and dots, ivy on trellis, dogwood, daisies, fan and diamond, and leaf and square. Surface may be crinkled and lack design.

Type and Dimensions
Pressed in mold for pattern and shape. Left height: 10¼"; width: 5". Upper right height: 4"; width: 4". Lower right height: 5"; width: 4".

Locality and Period
Addison Glass Factory, Addison, New York. 1894–1908. Crinkled panes from firms throughout the United States. c. 1880–1910.

Comment
The elaborately patterned windowpanes made by Addison are representative of the moderately priced panes popular around 1900. They were usually displayed where the pattern could be readily seen, whereas the crinkled panes without designs were often relegated to attics and stairways. Many pressed panes of both types can still be seen in late 19th-century Queen Anne homes.

Hints for Collectors
Addison panes are scarce; crinkled examples are common and may be found in stores that carry accessories for old houses.

Glass screen

Description
Wooden frame with 11 square or rectangular panes. Each has raised floral and/or geometric pattern on 1 side. Smooth edges. Colors: shades of transparent purple, blue, blue-green, green, amber, and colorless.

Variations
Screen may have more or fewer panes. Other designs include vines, scrolls, swans, and fish.

Type and Dimensions
Each pane pressed in mold for pattern and shape. Screen height: 22″; width: 21½″. Individual pane height: 5–10¼″; width: 4–8″.

Locality and Period
Addison Glass Factory, Addison, New York. 1894–1908.

Comment
The Addison Glass Factory was never very large, although in its heyday it had at least 2 furnaces. The firm's only known products were colored pressed-glass windowpanes. Found all over the East and Midwest, these panes were probably meant to be installed individually in interior doorways or as inexpensive substitutes for stained glass. A screen made of assembled panels is unusual; the one shown here was probably made and sold by a carpenter.

Hints for Collectors
The 3 hooks at the top of this screen were added recently so that it could be hung for display. Pressed panes are usually much less expensive than stained glass.

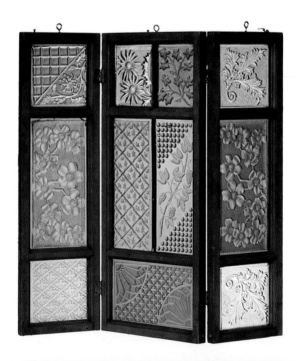

Stained-glass window

Description
Rectangular window with flower-and-leaf swag design, festoon of bellflowers, and scroll panel. Painted poem: "Whilst the cuckoo-buds and broom/Race the furze which next shall bloom/Merrily, merrily let us sing,/This is the daybreak of the spring." Colors: transparent marbled yellow-green, aquamarine, light purple, and opalescent white. Each glass piece outlined in lead. Outer edges covered with lead.

Variations
Designs may be floral and geometric; some windows combine small colorless and colored geometric shapes. Sizes range from 6″ × 12″ pane to picture window size.

Type and Dimensions
Combined free-blown and cast pieces. Cut into shapes after annealing. Pieces fastened with soft lead channels. Inscription painted. Height: 19¾″. Width: 33½″.

Locality and Period
Probably Boston, New York City, Philadelphia, and Chicago. c. 1890–1915.

Comment
Around the turn of the century, when the wealthy were ordering stained-glass windows from Tiffany and other well-established studios, less affluent individuals purchased simpler designs, like the one pictured here, from less known firms.

Hints for Collectors
Simple windows by unidentified firms are often moderately priced. Although few stained-glass windows are signed, always look for a signature, usually found on the lower edge.

Description
Rectangular window divided into 12 panels by oak bars. Overall design of tree, flowers, and sun with rays, framed by mosaic arch. Smooth edges. Colors: predominantly shades of transparent yellow, red, blue, green, and brown. Each glass piece outlined in lead. Oak frame (not shown).

Variations
Windows made in many abstract patterns and landscapes combining colorless and colored glass. Edges may be beveled. Shape may be square or round.

Type and Dimensions
Combined free-blown and cast pieces. Cut into shapes after annealing. Pieces fastened with soft lead channels. Height: about 13′. Width: about 11′.

Locality and Period
D.S. Hess & Company, New York City. 1885. Variants from firms throughout the United States. c. 1880–1910.

Comment
The window shown here was made for the beer baron Peter Ballantine to decorate a stair landing in his Newark, New Jersey, home. It cost $768, a price calculated per square foot, and represented a considerable sum at the time. The window is still in its original location, now part of the Newark Museum.

Hints for Collectors
While Tiffany stained glass is by far the best known today, several other companies also designed windows for churches and homes around the turn of the century. Other names to look for are John La Farge, a Boston painter and stained-glass designer; D.S. Hess & Company, the New York firm that made the example illustrated; and Redding, Baird & Company of Boston.

Tiffany stained-glass window

Description
Rectangular window in 3 panels separated by metal bars.
Realistic landscape with sky, hills, trees, lake, and rocks.
Smooth edges. Colors: predominantly shades of transparent blue,
yellow, green, brown, purple, and red. Each glass piece outlined
in lead. Wooden frame (not shown).

Variations
Windows may have religious motifs or floral designs. May have
enameled or acid-etched Tiffany signature on small panel in
lower right corner. May be up to 4 times size shown.

Type and Dimensions
Combined free-blown and cast pieces. Cut into shapes after
annealing. Pieces fastened with soft lead channels. Height: 82″.
Width: 29¼″.

Locality and Period
Tiffany Studios, Corona, New York. c. 1900. Variants 1893–
1924.

Comment
Although Tiffany windows for churches and chapels were mass-
produced, windows like the one pictured were commissioned for
homes and are unique designs. The glass is often rippled, folded,
or layered to create special lighting effects.

Hints for Collectors
To authenticate an unsigned Tiffany window, consult one of the
numerous books with illustrations of his works. In the 1920s the
Tiffany firm published a list of churches with Tiffany windows.
Tracking down the one-of-a-kind commissions is more difficult,
but color combinations and decorative motifs used in other
windows can provide clues.

Candlesticks and Lamps

Imagine a room brightened only by candles or kerosene lamps to see what dramatic changes lighting has undergone since the first settlers established their homes here in the 17th century. While few of the earliest candlesticks and lamps survive today, many middle to late 19th-century examples are still available at surprisingly moderate prices.

Early Candlesticks and Lamps
The most important source of light during the Colonial period was the candle, usually homemade of either beeswax or bayberry wax or of tallow rendered from animal fat. Few of the early candleholders were glass, and of these almost all were imported. However, several blown candlesticks are attributed to Caspar Wistar's factory, which operated in southern New Jersey from 1739 to 1780; both H.W. Stiegel's glasshouse and the Kensington Philadelphia Glass Works advertised glass candlesticks in the 1770s.

For lamps, most colonists used shallow, open, metal or pottery containers filled with oil or grease. A wick of twisted or woven fibers floated or rested on the fuel.

Production in the 19th Century
By the beginning of the 19th century, candlesticks and lamps were produced in limited quantities by most American glasshouses. The advent of the pressing machine in the 1820s brought a boom to the industry, enabling glassware to be made more cheaply and in greater numbers than ever before. The same stems and bases could be used for both candlesticks and lamps: The addition of a socket produced a candlestick, while an added font formed a lamp. Pressed or even blown lamp fonts and candle sockets appeared with a variety of pressed bases and stems, the two parts joined by a glass disk.

Many candlesticks with only pressed parts were made from the

Detail of a candleholder.

1830s through the 1850s. Boston & Sandwich and New England Glass were among the foremost producers, turning out lacy patterns in the 1830s, and both the popular dolphin candlesticks and Petal and Loop candlesticks by the 1850s. As the century progressed, the lamp gradually became the preferred lighting device, and by the 1870s only a limited number of candlesticks were manufactured. During the 1900s, the soft glow of candles found new favor in American homes. More candlesticks were probably made between 1900 and 1930 than during the previous thirty years.

Lamp Fuels and Burners

From 1789 until 1865, whaling was a thriving industry in New England, and glass manufacture flourished along with it. Whale-oil lamps with blown fonts were used in every room of the house. Most had simple drop burners, consisting of metal plates with either one or two upright metal wick tubes. These burners were often held in place by a thin layer of cork.

Since whale oil was expensive, numerous other fuels were tried until the discovery of kerosene, refined from petroleum. The first burning fluid, a mixture of alcohol and turpentine, was patented in 1830 by Isaiah Jennings. Among the widely used burning fluids were pine oil and camphene. Although these fuels had a less objectionable odor and were cheaper than whale oil, all were highly flammable. For this reason, the burners had tall, diverging wick tubes that did not extend into the font, and each tube had a cap to prevent evaporation.

At the same time that alternative fuels were being explored (each requiring its own special burner), manufacturers began to fit lamp fonts with threaded metal collars. Because the burners also had screw threads, one burner could easily be replaced with another. All but the early whale-oil lamps with drop burners used metal collars and screw-in burners.

Detail of a cranberry-glass miniature lamp.

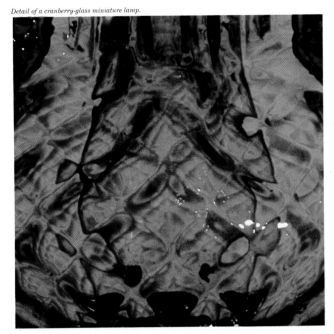

The Kerosene Era

During the second half of the 19th century, lamp production was a major part of the American glass industry. Even metal and ceramic lamps needed glass chimneys or shades, opening up a whole new branch of manufacture, especially in western Pennsylvania, near the source of the new fuel. Suited to most pocketbooks, kerosene was available throughout the country and burned with a safe, clean, bright light.

The earliest glass kerosene lamps were shaped somewhat like whale-oil lamps, with a font resting on a stem and usually a square base. Many had frosted chimneylike shades; by the 1880s fonts with matching colored shades were common. The typical flat-wick kerosene burner came with a built-in holder for a shade or chimney.

From the 1880s into the early 20th century, kerosene lamps were made in every conceivable art-glass style as well as in brilliant-cut glass. Simplicity was not considered a virtue, and elaborately decorated lamps became status symbols. Although much glassware of the period was pressed, most kerosene lamps continued to be mold-blown and hand decorated at such well-known shops as Fostoria, Pairpoint, T.G. Hawkes, and Dalzell, Gilmore & Leighton.

The same decades saw the peak in popularity of the miniature kerosene lamp, which was usually no more than eight inches tall. Used as night-lights, they were also placed on desks and dressing tables. Since most sold for ten to twenty-five cents apiece, and hardly ever for more than a dollar, nearly every household could afford these enchanting lamps.

Gas and Electric Lighting

Although gaslight illuminated the streets of Baltimore in 1814, and most American cities by 1850, other kinds of lighting prevailed in the home. The indoor use of gas became more

Detail of a hurricane shade.

widespread with the development of the incandescent Welsbach mantle in 1885. Those who could afford gas bought cut-glass gasoliers or metal gaslights with glass domes. Nevertheless, most people still used kerosene because it was cheap and available.

On January 1, 1880, Thomas Edison offered his first public demonstration of electric light, and by the 1920s electricity illuminated homes and offices. Like gas, electricity required a central source and was confined at first to cities that could afford to build power plants. Kerosene lamps continued to light rural households until the 1930s.

Detail of a lamp font.

Candlesticks

Ever since candlesticks were first blown in America, the predominant candlestick form has been a tall, usually six- to twelve-inch, single candleholder, customarily used with a matching partner. There are, of course, exceptions. In the late 17th and 18th centuries, multibranched sconces, candelabra, and chandeliers illuminated the largest homes and public buildings. Fancy lamplike candlesticks became popular in the late 19th century, and low candleholders were fashionable from the Depression until after World War II.

Candlesticks in Early America
Nearly all glass candlesticks used by 17th- and early 18th-century Americans had to be imported from England, and these often had enameled or cut designs. Metal candleholders were far more common. The first glass candlesticks made here were free-blown in bottle and window glasshouses, usually in transparent aquamarine, amber, green, and colorless. Making candlesticks tall began as a practicality: The candles needed to be high enough to spread the light, but not so high as to be unstable. Shorter candlesticks with handles, referred to as chambersticks, were used in and on the way to the bedroom.

Designs in the 19th Century
Excited by the possibilities inaugurated by the pressing machine in the 1820s, glassmakers experimented with new patterns, shapes, and colors. Some candlesticks had blown sockets and pressed bases, but more were pressed in one piece or two parts joined with a disk. In mid-century, candlesticks were among the many forms made in the lacy patterns and opaque color combinations popular at the time. Candlesticks also took on architectural or naturalistic forms, and, in the several decades following, appeared in such shapes as dolphins, female figures, and crosses.

During the last three decades of the 19th century, the production of candlesticks dwindled. Kerosene had become the rage, electricity was in its infancy, and candlesticks were considered primarily decorative. Still, candles illuminated some bedrooms, kitchens, and servants' quarters. In the 1880s and 1890s, the appeal of English art-glass fairy lamps proved so great that many were imported to this country.

New Forms in the 20th Century
American glassmakers produced a variety of distinctly 20th-century candlestick shapes and styles, including freestanding candleholders with two or more branches. Between 1905 and 1920, Carnival-glass candlesticks were displayed alongside matching iridescent vases and compotes, while in the 1920s and 1930s, console sets, comprised of a bowl and matching candlesticks, ranged from Carnival glass to Venetian-style designs.

When pressing became fully automated, manufacturers offered numerous inexpensive mass-produced forms, such as simple tall candlesticks in bright red, green, and purple. Low candleholders, immensely popular from the 1930s to the mid-1950s, often matched pressed tableware, and many a Depression-glass set included at least one pair.

Reproductions of mid-19th-century pressed candlesticks became fashionable in the 1920s and 1930s, when "early American" home decorating first came into vogue. These as well as recent copies of both blown and pressed candlesticks could fool an uninformed collector.

Linen smoother

Description
Solid spindle-shaped stem with 4 knops and upcurved slot at top. Heavy, flat, circular foot, smooth underneath. Colors: transparent dark green, dark brown, amber, aquamarine, and colorless.

Variations
Shape and length of stem vary.

Type and Dimensions
Gather tooled into stem shape. Foot and crimped disk for slot applied. Height: 5¼".

Locality and Period
The East and Midwest. England and continental Europe; widely exported to the United States. c. 1800–50.

Comment
This object looks like a candlestick but is completely solid, without the socket for a candle. Called a linen smoother, it is an early version of the flatiron. The heavy foot served as the iron, while the spindle-shaped stem provided the handle. To use it, the person ironing grasped the handle, placing the thumb in the slot at the top, and pressed the foot against the linens. It was probably used at room temperature. Although early colonists brought European-made linen smoothers to this country, examples were also made here in bottle and window glasshouses.

Hints for Collectors
Linen smoothers are rare, but not much in demand. They were impractical because if heated too much, the glass could crack.

Early blown candlesticks

Description
Hollow spindle-shaped stem with 2 knops. Cylindrical socket. Solid conical foot with pontil mark underneath. Colors: transparent aquamarine, green, light amber, and dark amber, which may appear black.

Variations
Stem may have 1, 3, or 4 knops. May have threaded decoration over entire candlestick.

Type and Dimensions
Free-blown, then tooled into shape. Height: 7½".

Locality and Period
New Hampshire, Connecticut, New York, and southern New Jersey. c. 1800–50.

Comment
Candlesticks like those shown here were created by bottle glasshouse workers, who were not always particularly skilled. The feet are clumsy and the candlesticks heavier than necessary. The pair illustrated is said to have been made in Westford, Connecticut, but similar shapes were formed in several other northeastern glasshouses. For example, dark amber is associated with factories in Stoddard, New Hampshire; Westford and Willington, Connecticut; Saratoga, Ellenville, and Lockport, New York; and southern New Jersey.

Hints for Collectors
Despite their heaviness, candlesticks like these are valued by collectors of early glass. They are considered folk art and are hard to find today.

Hexagonal candlestick

Description
Solid hexagonal stem with swelling in middle. Hexagonal urn-shaped socket with flange; pinched-in section between socket and stem. 6-paneled foot with circular rim. Colors: opaque green and purple, transparent green, and colorless.

Variations
May lack pinched-in section between socket and stem. May have silver or black enameled decoration.

Type and Dimensions
Machine-pressed in mold for shape. Height: 7⅜".

Locality and Period
Cambridge Glass Company, Cambridge, Ohio. c. 1920–40. Variants from Duncan & Miller Glass Company, Washington, Pennsylvania, and New Martinsville Glass Company, New Martinsville, West Virginia.

Comment
This candlestick is representative of the plain, inexpensive pressed-glass candleholders of the 1920s and 1930s. Nearly identical versions of this popular type were produced by 3 major tableware factories, and like most 20th-century patterns, the candlestick design illustrated is identified by a number. Cambridge called it Nearcut No. 2862; Duncan & Miller listed it as No. 66; and New Martinsville dubbed it No. 19.

Hints for Collectors
Although the shape of this candlestick is relatively common, the decidedly unusual color increases its appeal. Examples with silver or black enameled decoration are also considered very desirable.

Console candlestick

Description
Hollow baluster-shaped stem. Cylindrical socket with wide
flanged lip. Cut circles on socket; cut prisms and panels on stem.
Circular foot with cut sunburst underneath and acid-etched
"Hunt" in script. Colors: transparent blue, purple, green, yellow,
colorless, and 2 or 3 of these colors combined; also colorless cased
with transparent blue, green, red, yellow, or purple.

Variations
Cut decoration varies. Shape and length of stem vary, but socket
always same shape.

Type and Dimensions
Socket free-blown; stem and foot applied; all tooled into shape.
Cut after annealing. Height: 11⅞".

Locality and Period
Hunt Glass Company, Corning, New York. c. 1925–40. Similar
candlesticks from throughout the United States.

Comment
During the 1920s and 1930s, tall and short candlesticks were
made in pairs or sets of 4 to match a shallow, wide bowl.
Together they constituted a console set, to be displayed on a
sideboard or side table in the living room. Frequently the
candlesticks were made of one color and trimmed in another in
a style influenced by 17th- and 18th-century Venetian glass.

Hints for Collectors
Look underneath cut glass for an acid-etched trademark or
signature. Like the candlestick shown here, many pieces made
after 1895 bear a manufacturer's mark.

Venetian-style candlesticks

Description
Hollow baluster-shaped stem with 2 knops. Urn-shaped socket with wide flanged lip. Circular foot with knoplike top and folded-up edge; polished pontil mark underneath. 1 colorless disk between socket and knops; 1 colorless disk between stem and foot. Vertical ribs on socket, knops, stem, and foot. Colors: transparent purple, amber, green, and blue; rarely iridescent blue or gold, opaque white, and colorless.

Variations
Body may lack ribs. Ribbed or plain stem may have more knops and disks; part of stem may be twisted.

Type and Dimensions
Socket, stem, and foot blown one after another in same vertically ribbed dip mold; all expanded and tooled into shape after removal from mold. Parts joined with disks before annealing. Left height: 10″. Right height: 8″.

Locality and Period
Steuben Glass Works, Corning, New York. 1918–32. Variants from Pairpoint Corporation, New Bedford, Massachusetts; H.C. Fry, Rochester, Pennsylvania; Libbey Glass Company, Toledo, Ohio; and a few other tableware companies. c. 1918–35.

Comment
Candlesticks of colorful transparent glass were particularly popular in the 1920s. They are often referred to as Venetian-style glass because they are similar to pieces first made in Venice in the 17th century.

Hints for Collectors
Although these Steuben candlesticks are not marked, they are characteristic of Steuben work during the 1918–32 period.

Blown candlestick reproductions

Description
Left: stem has 2 solid baluster-shaped sections with disk in between. Tall cylindrical socket with wide flanged lip; gadrooning below socket. Flat circular foot with pontil mark and "MMA" scratched underneath. Right: hollow spindle-shaped stem, solid near base. Tall cylindrical socket with narrow flanged lip. Domed circular foot with pontil mark and "CMG" scratched underneath. Authentic colors: (left) transparent aquamarine; (right) transparent greenish-aquamarine. Reproduction colors: (left) colorless; (right) transparent greenish-aquamarine.

Type and Dimensions
Left: socket free-blown; stem and foot applied; all tooled into shape. Extra gather applied for gadrooning; stem sections joined with disk before annealing. Height: 9″. Right: socket and stem free-blown; foot applied; all tooled into shape. Height: 8¼″.

Locality and Period
Left: Pairpoint Glass Company, Sagamore, Massachusetts, for The Metropolitan Museum of Art, New York City. c. 1970–80. Right: Erickson Glass Company, Bremen, Ohio, for The Corning Museum of Glass, Corning, New York. 1963.

Comment
Museum reproductions are usually clearly marked. The candlesticks shown here are copies of well-known designs that have been illustrated in several books on American glass but cannot be attributed to a factory.

Hints for Collectors
The candlestick on the right was made by Carl Erickson, a former employee of the Pairpoint, Libbey, and Blenko glass companies. Today all of his pieces are popular with collectors.

Early blown candlesticks

Description
Hollow baluster-shaped stem with 2 disklike sections. Tall
cylindrical socket with small drip pan. Short solid section above
flat circular foot. Pontil mark underneath. Colors: transparent
aquamarine and colorless.

Variations
Stem may have coin inside. Base of socket may have gadrooning
or threaded decoration. Foot may be tooled into 4 petals.

Type and Dimensions
Socket and stem free-blown separately; foot applied; all tooled
into shape and joined before annealing. Height: 9″.

Locality and Period
New England, upstate New York, and New Jersey. c. 1820–50.

Comment
The fine candlesticks shown here were probably blown at the
window glasshouse of Redford, New York, which operated from
1831 until 1850, but they could have been made earlier at any of
the window glasshouses in New England, New York, and New
Jersey. Glass candlesticks of this type are not generally
associated with the Midwest; metal candlesticks and grease
lamps were more common on the western frontier, at least in the
first part of the 19th century. The well-designed candlesticks
illustrated display much more skill than many examples from
window and bottle factories.

Hints for Collectors
Be sure to buy candlesticks like these from an experienced
dealer. They are quite rare as well as high priced.

Blown candlestick with pressed base

Description
Hollow baluster-shaped stem with 2 horizontally ribbed knops.
Cylindrical socket with wide drip pan. 8-lobed, 4-step base with
ribs underneath. Colorless.

Variations
Knops may be plain.

Type and Dimensions
Socket and stem free-blown separately, then tooled into shape.
Base pressed in mold for pattern and shape. Parts joined before
annealing. Height: 9¼".

Locality and Period
New England and the Midwest. c. 1830–40.

Comment
Candlesticks that combine free-blown and pressed parts were
made during the infancy of the American pressed glass industry,
when glassmakers were experimenting with new techniques and
combining designs in different ways. This long candle socket
with a drip pan is typical of blown candlesticks of the period. The
8-lobed, 4-step pressed base is also found with blown compote
tops, blown lamp fonts, and candlesticks with a pressed socket.
Because they have this base in common, it is likely that all were
made in the same tableware factory.

Hints for Collectors
Early candlesticks of colorless glass with combined pressed and
blown parts are easier to find and less expensive than the rare
free-blown candlesticks from window and bottle factories. They
are also more common and usually cost less than the lacy-pattern
pressed candlesticks.

Candlestick with air-twist stem

Description
Solid baluster-shaped stem with double-spiral air twist inside.
Cylindrical socket with wide flanged lip. Horizontal ribs between
socket and stem; 2 disks between stem and flat circular foot.
Pontil mark underneath. Colorless.

Variations
May lack ribs between socket and stem.

Type and Dimensions
Socket free-blown; stem and foot applied; all tooled into shape
and joined before annealing. Height: 9⅝″.

Locality and Period
Probably Pittsburgh area. c. 1820–40.

Comment
Free-blown candlesticks as elegant as the example shown here
are rare in American glass. They could have been made as an
extra item for a window-glasshouse inventory or possibly by a
glassblower working on his own time. Too few examples exist to
assume that the spiral air-twist design was commercially
produced. Air twists are much more common in English glass,
but this candlestick, although finely crafted, is not sophisticated
enough to be English. In rare instances, English candlesticks are
found with twisted glass threads in the stem; this design was
called enamel glass. H.W. Stiegel, one of America's earliest
glassmakers, listed enamel glass in his account books, but his is
the only existing record in this country.

Hints for Collectors
The few known American candlesticks with air-twist stems are in
museum collections.

Pillar-molded candlestick

Description
Hollow baluster-shaped stem. Flower-form socket with wide
flanged lip. 2 disks between vertically ribbed socket and stem;
1 disk between stem and solid section above flat circular foot.
Pontil mark underneath. Colors: transparent amber, blue,
purple, and colorless.

Variations
Number and spacing of ribs vary. Number of disks varies.

Type and Dimensions
Socket and stem blown in separate vertically ribbed dip molds,
each part expanded and tooled into shape after removal from
mold. Foot applied and parts joined with disks before annealing.
Height: 12⅜".

Locality and Period
Western Pennsylvania. c. 1830–50.

Comment
Glassware like the piece illustrated is called pillar-molded glass.
Candlesticks are much less common than pitchers, celery vases,
decanters, compotes, and footed bowls with this type of vertical
ribs. This example is one of a pair discovered in western
Pennsylvania, where most pillar-molded glass made in the mid-
19th century seems to have originated. Extremely heavy and
sturdy, this type of glass is said to have been used on Ohio and
Mississippi River steamboats.

Hints for Collectors
Pillar-molded candlesticks are much easier to find in the Midwest
than New England or the South. Because of the high prices, it is
best to buy from a reputable dealer.

Petal and Loop candlesticks

Description
Solid stem with 1 baluster-shaped and 1 knopped section, with disk in between. Flower-form socket. Hollow skirtlike foot with 6 loop-shaped panels. Colors: transparent yellow, light and dark blue, purple, and colorless; translucent light blue; opaque white, turquoise, light green, blue-gray, and 2 opaque colors combined.

Variations
Stem may be different shape, such as dolphin-form or columnar.

Type and Dimensions
Socket with baluster stem section and foot with knopped section pressed in 2 separate molds for pattern and shape; joined with disk before annealing. Height: 7⅛″.

Locality and Period
New England; probably Boston & Sandwich Glass Company, Sandwich, Massachusetts, or New England Glass Company, Cambridge, Massachusetts. c. 1850–70.

Comment
Early collectors called this candlestick design Petal and Loop. It is probably the most familiar pattern in pressed-glass candlesticks and comes in the greatest variety of colors. Around mid-century some enterprising workmen at one or both of the big Massachusetts factories noticed that by combining mold parts it was possible to make many different candlestick, vase, and lamp designs.

Hints for Collectors
Candlesticks like these have been copied since the 1920s, in colorless, yellow, amber, and blue glass. If a continuous mold seam runs through the disk, then the candlestick is a reproduction.

Columnar candlestick

Description
Hollow columnar candlestick in 4 paneled tiers, top tier forming socket. Solid section below socket; scalloped base rim. Small diamonds formed where panels join. Colorless. Metal candle cup inside socket.

Variations
Stem may be baluster-shaped, with urn-shaped socket and hexagonal base. Variant transparent dark green, blue, purple, yellow, and colorless.

Type and Dimensions
Pressed in mold for pattern and shape. Height: 8¼".

Locality and Period
M'Kee & Brothers, Pittsburgh. c. 1860–80. Variant also from other firms in the Pittsburgh area.

Comment
In the mid-19th century comparatively few candlesticks matched sets of tableware. The candlestick shown here, however, belongs with a large set in the Excelsior pattern that includes ale, champagne, and wine glasses, bitters bottles, bowls, and decanters. Oddly, it does not appear in any of the printed M'Kee catalogues or price lists that show Excelsior tableware. The variant is illustrated in 2 M'Kee catalogues, first in 1860 in the pattern Six Flute and then in 1880 as French Candlestick.

Hints for Collectors
Excelsior candlesticks are hard to find, and it is best to seek them in shops specializing in 19th-century glass. The Six Flute candlesticks are more common and must have been made in greater quantities.

Lacy-pattern candlestick

Description
Hollow columnar stem with 1 ringed and 1 tiered section, with disk in between. Urn-shaped socket with flange. Hollow plinth base. Vertical ribs on exterior of socket and tiered stem section, and on interior of base. Colorless.

Variations
Socket, stem, and base shapes and patterns vary: Socket may have peacock-feather pattern; base may be circular, cruciform, or quatrefoil. Various combinations of different stems and sockets.

Type and Dimensions
Socket with ringed stem section and base with tiered section pressed in 2 separate molds for pattern and shape; joined with disk before annealing. Height: 7″.

Locality and Period
Probably New England; possibly Boston & Sandwich Glass Company, Sandwich, Massachusetts, and New England Glass Company, Cambridge, Massachusetts. c. 1830–40.

Comment
The candlestick illustrated dates from the earliest period of pressed glass, shortly after the mechanical press was invented. At that time, glassmakers were experimenting with new molds and introduced fancy overall patterns to camouflage mold marks and chill wrinkles. Collectors call these early designs lacy patterns.

Hints for Collectors
Be prepared to pay a substantial price for lacy-pattern glass. Do not pay more for Sandwich glass, since there is no way to prove this attribution.

Description
Solid columnar or baluster-shaped stem with vertical ribs (left) or acanthus-leaf pattern (right). Flower-form or urn-shaped socket. Solid plinth or hexagonal base. Disk between socket and stem. Colors: opaque white, green, blue, and 2 opaque colors combined; transparent light and bright yellow (left only) and colorless.

Variations
Socket and stem shapes and patterns vary. Various combinations of different stems and sockets.

Type and Dimensions
Socket and stem with base pressed in 2 separate molds for pattern and shape; joined with disk before annealing. Left height: 8¾". Right height: 8⅞".

Locality and Period
New England; probably Boston & Sandwich Glass Company, Sandwich, Massachusetts, and New England Glass Company, Cambridge, Massachusetts. c. 1850–70.

Comment
The opaque white, green, and blue glass of these candlesticks, the dolphin candlesticks, and some similar-looking lamp fonts often has a peculiarly rough texture, instead of the usual glossy surface. Exposure to different temperatures and humidities over the years probably caused the unstable mix of ingredients to crackle.

Hints for Collectors
It is unlikely that the glass will continue to deteriorate today, but it is wise to protect crackled examples from extremes in humidity and temperature. These candlesticks are harder to find than Petal and Loop candlesticks with similar sockets.

Crucifix candlestick

Description
Hollow cruciform stem with figure of Christ below inscription "INRI." Urn-shaped hexagonal socket and hollow hexagonal base. Colors: transparent light and dark blue, dark green, and colorless; opaque white; and probably other opaque and transparent colors.

Variations
Base may be taller or square. Socket may have flared rim.

Type and Dimensions
Pressed in mold for pattern and shape. Height: 9¾".

Locality and Period
New England Glass Company, Cambridge, Massachusetts; possibly Boston & Sandwich Glass Company, Sandwich, Massachusetts, and firms in Pittsburgh area. c. 1860–1900.

Comment
Crucifix candlesticks may have been inspired by one of the religious movements that periodically swept the East in the 19th century. It is surprising that glass companies produced so many of these candlesticks during a period when kerosene lamps were the preferred lighting source in most homes and candles were used primarily as decoration.

Hints for Collectors
In the early 20th century, crucifix candlesticks were reproduced in several bright colors, such as transparent turquoise and light purple. These hues are not characteristic of authentic 19th-century glass.

Caryatid candlesticks

Description
Solid stem in form of lady in classical dress. Urn-shaped octagonal socket and hollow hexagonal plinth base. Colors: transparent blue-green, green, light yellow, and colorless; translucent white; opaque green; and probably other transparent, translucent, and opaque colors.

Type and Dimensions
Pressed in mold for pattern and shape. Height: 10¼″.

Locality and Period
Boston & Sandwich Glass Company, Sandwich, and New England Glass Company, Cambridge, Massachusetts. c. 1870–80.

Comment
A revival of interest in Greek architecture in the mid-19th century may have prompted this caryatid candlestick design. On classical buildings a caryatid is a column in the form of a draped female figure, and the most famous caryatids are on the Acropolis in Athens. The patent for the candlesticks shown was registered to Henry Whitney of New England Glass on May 10, 1870. However, the caryatid is illustrated in an 1870s Boston & Sandwich catalogue. Several compote bowls and vases have an identical stem, and some bear the initials of the Sandwich firm. Possibly Boston & Sandwich was licensed by New England Glass to use the pattern, and probably it paid a small royalty for the privilege. Examples of cooperation between competing glass firms are quite common.

Hints for Collectors
Caryatid candlesticks are hard to find, but unlike some of the other popular patterns, these have not been reproduced.

Description
Solid stem in form of dolphin. Flower-form socket above tail.
Disk between socket and stem. Solid square or scalloped circular
base. Authentic colors: (left) opaque white, blue, green, and
2 opaque colors; transparent yellow, blue, and colorless; (right)
opaque white, colorless, and rarely opaque dark blue.

Variations
May have gilt trim. Dolphin stem may have square 2-step base or
hollow, scalloped, skirtlike base. Either type may have socket
with raised design of dolphins on panels.

Type and Dimensions
Socket and stem with base pressed in 2 separate molds for
pattern and shape; joined with disk before annealing. Left
height: 10⅜". Right height: 6½".

Locality and Period
Left: Boston & Sandwich Glass Company, Sandwich, or New
England Glass Company, Cambridge, Massachusetts. Right: Mt.
Washington Glass Company, New Bedford, Massachusetts. Both
c. 1850–70. Variants by other New England firms and Bakewell,
Pears & Company and M'Kee & Brothers, Pittsburgh. England
and Bohemia; widely exported to the United States.

Comment
For many years dolphin candlesticks have been associated with
Boston & Sandwich. However, Mt. Washington made the type
with the scalloped base; Bakewell produced the ones with
skirtlike bases, called petticoat dolphins; and other kinds are
found in English and Bohemian catalogues of the same period.
European dolphins are often colorless or blue, with elaborate gilt
decoration, and were also used for compotes and epergnes.

Authentic candlesticks

Hints for Collectors

Because dolphin candlesticks were made in many colors by many companies in the mid-19th century, it is hard to make definite attributions. In addition, Westmoreland Glass Company has sold reproductions since the 1930s, mostly in opaque white glass, including the 9½″ and 10½″ candlesticks illustrated. The one with the square base was manufactured in the 1930s and is not marked, but since the mold seams run continuously from top to bottom, the candlestick was obviously pressed in 1 piece. The socket and base of authentic examples were pressed separately and joined with a glass disk while hot; thus the mold seam does not go through the disk, and often the seams do not match. The candlestick with the hexagonal base was made in the 1960s, when Westmoreland started marking its glass with a "W" superimposed on a "G". Although the company has used paper stickers since the 1950s, they come off readily, so it is wise to examine the glass carefully.

Other dolphin reproductions include one with a hexagonal base and one with a circular base, both by the Cambridge Glass Company in Ohio. These are 8½″ and 9½″ tall and come in a great variety of colors unique to the firm, such as an opaque pale blue and an unusual red. Colorless and opaque white copies with a square 2-step base and urn-shaped socket were produced for the wholesaler K.R. Haley of Greensburg, Pennsylvania, from about 1945 to about 1960. A.H. Heisey & Company of Newark, Ohio, marketed petticoat dolphin candlesticks with a matching compote. Most bear the pressed "H" in a diamond, but even without the mark their opalescent white and pink colors should alert the collector that they are not antiques. Unlike figural bottles where some late examples are collected, most reproduction candlesticks are not considered valuable.

Reproductions

Burmese candlestick

Description
Hollow baluster-shaped stem. Globe-shaped socket with flanged lip and wide, upcurved, scalloped flange below. Disk between wide flange and stem. Vertical ribs on socket, flange, and domed circular foot; diamond pattern on stem. Polished pontil mark underneath foot. Matt finish. Colors: opaque pale salmon-pink shading to pale lemon-yellow.

Variations
Stem may be S-shaped, shorter, or have a small ring handle at 1 side, or combination of these.

Type and Dimensions
Socket, flange, and foot blown one after another in same vertically ribbed dip mold; stem blown in diamond-patterned dip mold; all expanded and tooled into shape after removal from mold. Partially reheated to develop pink shading and parts joined with disks before annealing. Acid-treated for matt finish after annealing. Height: 7½″.

Locality and Period
Mt. Washington Glass Company, New Bedford, Massachusetts. c. 1885–95.

Comment
In 1880 Frederick Shirley of the Mt. Washington Glass Company patented Burmese glass, an opaque salmon-pink shading to yellow. Burmese was made in a wide range of shapes, some free-blown and some mold-blown, with either a glossy or matt finish.

Hints for Collectors
Burmese glassware has been reproduced since 1938. Copies have subtle color differences, and most are in modern shapes. Since Burmese glass is expensive, buy only from a knowledgeable dealer.

Fairy lamp

Description
Cylindrical shade rests in circular bowl, both with incurved crimped rim. Solid stem joins small bowl to larger, nearly identical bowl. Cuplike candleholder marked "CLARKE'S PATENT" rests inside small bowl. Swirled air-trap ribs on bowls and shade. Matt finish. Colors: opaque green, blue, white, and many others, with swirls of any transparent color.

Variations
Colors and decoration vary greatly. Shapes range from simple shade in bowl-shaped base to lamps with 2–4 branches and shades with hanging baskets or trumpet vases in epergnes.

Type and Dimensions
Shade and bowls blown in separate vertically ribbed dip molds; each part cased with colored and colorless glass, then expanded and tooled into shape. Stem applied. Acid-treated for matt finish after annealing. Candleholder pressed. Height: 8½".

Locality and Period
Stevens & Williams Glass Company and Thomas Webb & Sons, Staffordshire, England; widely exported to the United States. 1886–c. 1900. Variants from other English firms.

Comment
Samuel Clarke, an English candle manufacturer, patented the design of a cylindrical shade around a short, fat candle in 1886. Called fairy lamps, these popular candleholders were soon made in a tremendous variety of styles.

Hints for Collectors
Antique fairy lamps are extremely expensive. Fenton Glass of Williamstown, West Virginia, makes new opaque pink and yellow fairy lamps that are marked with the company name.

Low hobnail candleholders

Description
Cylindrical socket with vertical ribs. Hollow domed base with scalloped edge. Horizontal rows of hobnails around sides. Colors: colorless with opalescent white trim.

Variations
May have geometric patterns. Hobnails may be pointed. May lack opalescent white trim.

Type and Dimensions
Machine-pressed in mold for pattern and shape. Height: 2⅛".

Locality and Period
Anchor-Hocking Glass Corporation, Lancaster, Ohio. 1941–46. Variants from Macbeth-Evans Glass Company, Charleroi, Pennsylvania, and Fenton Glass Company, Williamstown, West Virginia. c. 1935–45.

Comment
The first pressed hobnail pattern was patented by Hobbs, Brockunier & Company of Wheeling, West Virginia, in the 1880s, and hobnails have been a favorite motif ever since. Patterns like the one illustrated were produced by 3 companies in the 1930s and 1940s, with only slight differences. Anchor-Hocking's hobnail pattern shown is called Moonstone by collectors. Strictly speaking it is not Depression glass, since it was made in the 1940s, but it is the same kind of mass-produced glassware as most Depression glass.

Hints for Collectors
The Moonstone pattern has grown rapidly in popularity over the past few years. It is one of the least expensive patterns in this type of opalescent glass.

Low finned candleholders

Description
Cylindrical socket on hollow conical base, with 3 fins from socket to base. Flower and scroll pattern around sides. Colors: transparent yellow, green, and colorless.

Variations
May have geometric or other floral patterns.

Type and Dimensions
Machine-pressed in mold for pattern and shape. Height: 2¾".

Locality and Period
Hazel-Atlas Glass Company, Wheeling, West Virginia. 1934–37. Variants from Jeannette Glass Company, Jeannette, Pennsylvania; Westmoreland Glass Company, Grapeville, Pennsylvania; and other firms in same area. c. 1930–40.

Comment
Collectors call the machine-pressed glassware produced in large matching sets in the 1920s and 1930s Depression glass. Of the 31 Depression-glass tableware sets with candlesticks, 25 have low, single candleholders, which were usually used in pairs. The pattern on the finned holders shown here is Florentine No. 2. One of the largest made, a set in this pattern included coasters, ashtrays, cups, saucers, bowls, plates, pitchers, tumblers, and a tray with 4 compartments for sugar bowl, creamer, and salt and pepper shakers.

Hints for Collectors
Although the candleholders in this pattern were made in only a few colors, many of the other pieces also came in transparent pink and light and dark blue. All are easy to find today.

Low candleholders

Description
Solid, crownlike, 8-lobed form, with cylindrical hole for candle in center. Flat polished base. Colorless.

Variations
Lobes may be swirled. Candleholder may be raised on 8-lobed foot. May be cube-shaped.

Type and Dimensions
Machine-pressed in mold for pattern and shape. Base ground and polished after annealing. Height: 2″.

Locality and Period
A.H. Heisey & Company, Newark, Ohio. c. 1935–56. Variants from Duncan & Miller Glass Company, Washington, Pennsylvania; Fostoria Glass Company, Moundsville, West Virginia; Cambridge Glass Company, Cambridge, Ohio; and other firms in same area.

Comment
These low crownlike candleholders were part of the Heisey Crystolite line of the mid-1930s, which featured a wide range of pieces in several patterns. This glassware was designed as a pressed imitation of the more expensive Steuben and Libbey cut glass. Many but not all Heisey objects have its "H" in a diamond trademark, which was adopted around 1900. If an example is not marked, use books on Heisey glassware featuring reprints of catalogue pages to help you date it.

Hints for Collectors
Heisey glassware has become one of the most popular kinds of pressed glass. Because quite a lot is still on the market, only consider examples in good condition.

Triple candleholder

Description
3 cylindrical sockets, pointed at bottom, and with vertical ribs at top; each socket set in loop of glass. Ball knop below central loop forms stem. Flat circular base. Colorless.

Variations
Sockets may have cut flutes instead of molded ribs. May be double candleholder. Many double and triple candleholders incorporate swirls, scrolls, or leaflike and geometric designs instead of loops. Variants in transparent pink, green, yellow, blue, and red; opaque white; and colorless.

Type and Dimensions
Machine-pressed in mold for pattern and shape. Height: 7″.

Locality and Period
A.H. Heisey & Company, Newark, Ohio. c. 1948–56. Variants from Duncan & Miller Glass Company, Washington, Pennsylvania; Cambridge Glass Company, Cambridge, Ohio; Fostoria Glass Company, Moundsville, West Virginia; New Martinsville Glass Company, New Martinsville, West Virginia; and other firms in same area. c. 1930–55.

Comment
This candleholder is an example of the Heisey Lariat pattern, a full line of tableware first produced in 1948. The variant with cut flutes was exhibited in New York City in 1950 at the Metropolitan Museum of Art as one of the best American postwar designs.

Hints for Collectors
Since 1956, when Heisey went out of business, Heisey glass has been eagerly collected, and there is even a Heisey collectors' club. The Heisey Glass Museum in Cambridge, Ohio, includes extensive factory archives and is well worth a visit.

Hand Lamps, Miniature Night Lamps, and Lanterns

Nearly all of the lamps in this section could have served as night lamps, used in the bedroom or carried in the hall. The several exceptions include an electric light-bulb cover, two outdoor lanterns, and a lamp filler. All but the lanterns are quite small, ranging from two to ten inches high.

Peg Lamps

Named for the peg at the bottom of their globe-shaped font, peg lamps are one of the earliest glass lights, dating from about 1810. The peg fit into a candlestick, converting it into a lamp at little expense. Peg lamps typically used whale-oil burners, although some had burning-fluid burners. By the time kerosene was widely available, peg lamps were outmoded.

Hand Lamps

Most hand lamps are short, portable lamp fonts with handles. They were used from about 1810 until the early 1900s. During the Colonial period, it was usual to light the way to bed with a candle, but by the 1820s, whale-oil lamps, which gave a brighter light, were also common. These simple, functional vessels held only a small amount of fuel, and most ranged from two to four inches high.

Sales catalogues of the 1860s and 1870s advertised some four- to six-inch hand lamps as kitchen lamps. Like the earlier hand lamps, most kitchen lamps were of transparent glass and lacked shades and ornate designs.

Miniature Night Lamps

Small, elaborate replicas of late 19th-century parlor lamps were popular from 1880 until 1920. Used as night lights, these miniatures were rarely over twelve inches high and consisted of a matching font and shade, chimney, and kerosene burner. A few miniature night lamps with matching font and shade were made for electricity in the 1900s, although the font, or fuel reservoir, was no longer necessary.

Many miniature lamps are of opaque colored glass. Some have a porcelain-like finish decorated with gilt or enamel, while others bear raised patterns or a combination of effects. Although these lamps were certainly functional, the dazzling array of styles indicates that the lamps must have been highly prized for their appearance. As their popularity grew, so did the competition, and many tableware houses brought out novel shapes, colors, and patterns, including time lamps, which soundlessly measured the hours, and a wide assortment of floral and geometric designs.

Lanterns

Intended for outdoor use, lanterns have a housing, usually metal, to shield the light source from wind and rain. All lanterns from the 17th and 18th centuries burned candles. Many of these early lanterns were made of tin, which was pierced to let the light through; others had wooden frames and horn panes. Whale-oil lanterns with glass globes and oil burners were introduced early in the 19th century. By the 1860s, most lanterns came with kerosene burners and wire cages to protect the glass globes, although catalogues of the period also featured lanterns with candle sockets or oil burners.

Shoe lamp

Description
Font in form of shoe with flat heel and sole and solid C-shaped handle. Brass collar around opening at top for kerosene burner. Colors: transparent amber, blue, and colorless.

Type and Dimensions
Pressed and blown simultaneously in same mold for pattern and shape. Top finished. Height: 3″.

Locality and Period
Atterbury & Company, Pittsburgh. 1868–75.

Comment
Atterbury manufactured this unusual lamp using a process patented in 1868 that allowed for simultaneous pressing and blowing. First, glass was dropped into the handle part of the mold; next, more glass was inserted into the main part; and then the mold was closed. The glass in the hollow shoe was blown using compressed air, while the solid handle was pressed rather than applied by hand. This technique saved time and labor, and the lamp could be sold relatively cheaply, probably fitted with a kerosene burner and colorless chimney. Atterbury was known for its glass novelties, including other unusual lamp forms as well as a series of covered dishes and bottles in the forms of various animals.

Hints for Collectors
Colored shoe lamps are more popular than colorless examples. Many shoe lamps complete with burner and chimney are still available.

88 Log cabin lamp

Description
Font in form of log cabin with horizontal ribs resembling logs around all 4 sides, vertical ribs on gable roof, and door and windows on 1 side. Solid C-shaped handle and flat base. Brass collar around opening at top for kerosene burner. Colors: transparent amber, blue, colorless, and opaque white.

Type and Dimensions
Pressed and blown simultaneously in same mold for pattern and shape. Top finished. Height: 3⅜″.

Locality and Period
Atterbury & Company, Pittsburgh. 1868–75.

Comment
Like the shoe lamp, the log cabin lamp was manufactured using Atterbury's patented simultaneous pressing and blowing process. The popularity of the log cabin shape began in 1840, when William Henry Harrison adopted the log cabin and cider barrel as campaign symbols in his successful bid for the presidency. The Harrison campaign also inspired a flask in the form of a cabin, and flasks and pressed plates with the picture of a log cabin. In the 1860s and 1870s, E.G. Booz, the Philadelphia distiller, sold his whiskey in a house-shaped bottle, as did the manufacturer of Jacob's Cabin Tonic Bitters.

Hints for Collectors
Of all the glass in the shape of a log cabin, this lamp is probably the least known and the most available. It is one of the earliest colored glass night lamps.

Lamp filler

Description
Globe-shaped vessel with solid ear-shaped handle, crimped at bottom, opposite long narrow spout. Mouth has circular lid with solid knob. Flat circular foot with pontil mark underneath. Colors: transparent aquamarine and colorless.

Variations
Shape may be more cylindrical. Length, angle, and position of spout vary.

Type and Dimensions
Vessel and lid free-blown separately and tooled into shape. Handle, spout, foot, and knob applied. Height: 4½″.

Locality and Period
Probably New England; possibly southern New Jersey. c. 1815–30.

Comment
Lamp fillers were used once a day to fill whale-oil lamps. Because the burner openings at the tops of these early lamps were small, it was necessary to use a lamp filler with a long spout to transfer the oil from the large container in which it came into the font. Each filler had such a limited capacity that every home had at least 1 or 2; therefore, it is surprising that so few examples have survived. Perhaps the fragile, narrow spouts broke easily and the damaged fillers were thrown away.

Hints for Collectors
In antiques shops, lamp fillers are sometimes mislabeled as glass teapots. However, glass teapots were not made in England or the United States before the invention of heat-resistant glass during the early 20th century. The few 18th-century German glass teapots are extremely rare.

Oil Guard lamp

Description
Globe-shaped font with solid D-shaped handle and upturned flange around shoulder. Opening at top for kerosene burner. Slightly domed circular foot with inscription "OIL GUARD LAMP PATᵈ SEP. 20, 1870." Colorless.

Variations
Font may have 1 handle on each side. Lamp may lack inscription; may have straight stem and flat foot with inscription.

Type and Dimensions
Pressed in mold for pattern and shape. Top finished. Height: 4".

Locality and Period
Union Glass Company, Somerville, Massachusetts. c. 1870–90.

Comment
The date on Oil Guard lamps like the one pictured refers to the patent granted to George Henry Lomax of Somerville, Massachusetts, in 1870. This patent was for the shoulder flange, which prevented oil from running down the side of the lamp and staining the table. Produced for 10 to 20 years, the Oil Guard lamp came in a variety of sizes and shapes. The version illustrated is called the Globe Lomax Hand Lamp in the Union Glass Company catalogue, and the variant with a stem and foot, the Plain Lomax Kitchen Lamp. Despite Lomax's patent, a few other firms made lamps with drip catchers and called these oil guard lamps, but only Lomax lamps have the inscription and patent date. All oil guard lamps burned kerosene.

Hints for Collectors
Because Lomax lamps are relatively late and not very fancy, most are inexpensive compared with other kerosene lamps.

Description
Squat globe-shaped font with solid ear-shaped handle crimped at bottom. Opening at top for burner. Left: single-wick, tin, whale-oil drop burner. Pattern of diagonal ribs around globe and rays on base. Right: plain surface. Pontil mark on each circular base. Colors: (left) colorless; (right) also transparent blue.

Variations
Plain lamp may be cylindrical.

Type and Dimensions
Left: blown in mold for pattern and shape; top finished and handle applied. Height: 1⅝". Right: free-blown, then tooled into shape; handle applied. Height: 1⅞".

Locality and Period
The East. c. 1810–30.

Comment
Hand lamps in the shape shown here and the wineglass shape are sometimes called sparking lamps by collectors. Used as bedside night-lights, they contained just enough oil to burn for the time it took to go from the parlor to the bedroom and undress quickly. The patterned lamp was blown in a mold normally used to make stoppers for blown 3-mold decanters. Since a number of lamps in the same pattern were made this way, they may have been sold commercially. Usually when a piece is made in a mold meant for another object, it is only made in very small quantities.

Hints for Collectors
Look for hand lamps in shops that specialize in early American antiques, particularly glass and lighting devices. Plain lamps are far more common than those with patterns.

Description
Conical font with solid ear-shaped handle crimped at bottom.
Brass collar around opening at top for burner. Left: pattern of
vertical ropes around body, each rope encircled by plain ring;
rope pattern around top and bottom rims. Right: pattern of
diamonds and swirled circles; plain rims. Both have circular
bases. Colors: colorless; rarely opaque white and green.

Variations
Patterns may be geometric or floral, such as Waffle and
Thumbprint and Bleeding Heart. Colorless lamps may lack
pattern.

Type and Dimensions
Blown in mold for pattern and shape. Top finished; handle
applied. Height: 4".

Locality and Period
The East and Midwest. c. 1850–80.

Comment
Glass-company catalogues of the 1860s and 1870s advertised
lamps similar to those shown here as kitchen lamps. Their
patterns usually matched large sets of pressed-glass tableware,
as do the 2 patterns illustrated, known as Cable and Ring (left)
and Bull's-eye with Diamond (right). Hand lamps and syrup jugs
were always mold-blown instead of pressed, probably because
the font opening or neck was then easier to finish. Kitchen lamps
were often made for burning fluid, although some burned
kerosene.

Hints for Collectors
Thick-walled and sturdy, many kitchen lamps are in good shape
today. Look for them in a general antiques shop.

Match-holder miniature lamp

Description
Conical shade with vertical ribs; plain chimney at top. Cylindrical font with matching ribs has sunburst design on base. Cylindrical container attached to font has basket-weave pattern on body, rope pattern around top and bottom rims, and circular handle. Brass kerosene burner and shade holder combination. Colors: transparent amber, blue, and colorless.

Type and Dimensions
Shade with chimney blown in mold for pattern and shape. Font with match holder pressed and blown simultaneously in separate mold for pattern and shape. Chimney and font top finished. Height: 7⅝".

Locality and Period
Probably United States Glass Company, Pittsburgh. c. 1891–1900. Possibly earlier at one of the United States Glass Company's formerly independent firms.

Comment
The novelty match-holder lamp illustrated was advertised as the Happy Thought Night Lamp in a United States Glass Company catalogue of the early 1890s. The same catalogue pictured a cigar-lighter lamp, featuring a font with 3 metal holders for wire brushes that could be held in the lamp flame until red hot and then used to light a cigar. The United States Glass Company, started in 1891, was a merger of 18 Pennsylvania, West Virginia, and Ohio firms.

Hints for Collectors
All colors of the lamp shown are available, but amber and blue are preferred. Colorless is often the easiest to find.

Ruffle-top miniature lamp

Description
Conical shade with ruffled top and ring below ruffle. Oval font with slightly domed circular foot. Shade and font have enameled flowers. Colorless baluster-shaped chimney. Brass kerosene burner and shade holder combination. Colors: opaque white, turquoise, blue, and pink, with enameled details in green, black, white, yellow, and pink.

Variations
Enameled flowers vary in color and design. Some shades have molded geometric or floral patterns.

Type and Dimensions
Shade and font blown in separate molds for shape; shade and font tops finished. Enamel fixed by firing after annealing. Mold-blown chimney. Height: 9¾″.

Locality and Period
Throughout the United States. Bohemia; widely exported to the United States. c. 1890–1910.

Comment
Lamps of this type, which combine opaque, porcelain-like colored glass with enameled decoration, closely resemble bowls, vases, and dresser sets that were very popular in the late 19th century both in this country and abroad.

Hints for Collectors
The name of an American manufacturer on the burner is not a guarantee that a lamp is of American origin; several New York City manufacturers of metal lamp parts imported the glass. The source of a lamp whose burner has the name of a European company is certain, since no American firms are known to have shipped glass to European lampmakers.

Diamond miniature lamp

Description
Bowl-shaped shade with crimped top. Globe-shaped font has colorless base with 4 pointed feet. Shade and font have diamond pattern. Colorless baluster-shaped chimney. Brass kerosene burner and shade holder combination. Colors: shade and font transparent red, blue, purple, and colorless; opaque white, blue, turquoise, and pink; base colorless or opaque white.

Variations
Shade and font may have smooth surface with enameled flowers or rib pattern and enameled decoration. Font may lack footed base and be flat on bottom.

Type and Dimensions
Shade and font blown in separate part-size molds for pattern, then expanded and tooled into shape after removal from mold. Base applied. Mold-blown chimney. Height: 9″.

Locality and Period
Throughout the United States. England; widely exported to the United States. c. 1890–1910.

Comment
Collectors call transparent red glass "cranberry glass." Lamps made of cranberry glass are rare; the more usual forms are epergnes and vases. Although some cranberry glass has molded patterns, most examples are plain with applied decoration of cranberry or colorless glass. Much cranberry glass is English, made in the Stourbridge area, but a good deal was also produced in this country.

Hints for Collectors
The origin of miniature lamps, unlike many other types of glass, does not affect value. Condition and appeal are more important.

Pinecone miniature lamp

Description
Umbrella-shaped shade with flanged top. Globe-shaped font with flat base. Shade and font have diamond pattern. Colorless baluster-shaped chimney. Brass kerosene burner and shade holder combination. Colors: opaque pink, yellow, blue, and green.

Variations
Shade and font may have other patterns. May be opaque white with smooth surface and enameled flowers.

Type and Dimensions
Shade and font blown in separate molds for pattern and shape; font top finished. Mold-blown chimney. Height: 8″.

Locality and Period
Fostoria Shade & Lamp Company, Fostoria, Ohio. 1892–93. Consolidated Lamp & Glass Company, Fostoria, 1893–96, and Coraopolis, Pennsylvania, 1896–1900. Variants from throughout the United States. c. 1885–1905.

Comment
The Fostoria Shade & Lamp Company, established in 1890, made a great variety of night lamps. Its manager Nicholas Kopp was highly praised in trade journals for his glassware designs. In 1901 he founded his own firm, the Kopp Lamp & Glass Company, which made several of the same designs, but not the lamp shown here.

Hints for Collectors
This lamp and its variants are among the most available late 19th-century miniature lamps. Collectors call the diamond pattern seen on this lamp Pinecone.

Quilted Phlox miniature lamp

Description
Globe-shaped shade and font with flat base. Shade and font have diamond-quilted design with phloxlike blossoms at intersections of diamonds. Colorless baluster-shaped chimney. Brass kerosene burner and shade holder combination. Colors: opaque light green, pink, and blue.

Variations
Shade and font may be opaque white with plain surface and enameled flowers.

Type and Dimensions
Shade and font blown in separate molds for pattern and shape; font top finished. Mold-blown chimney. Height: 7½″.

Locality and Period
Probably Northwood Glass Company and Dugan Glass Company, both of Indiana, Pennsylvania. c. 1894–1905. Variants from throughout the United States. c. 1885–1905.

Comment
Harry Northwood, an English glassmaker, came to the West Virginia-Pennsylvania area in 1885 and worked for a number of companies before founding his own in the 1890s. Northwood never advertised lamps, but night lamps are found in several patterns associated with his factories. In 1904, after Northwood relocated in Wheeling, West Virginia, the Dugan Glass Company, run by Northwood's uncle, took over the plant in Pennsylvania. It probably continued to produce the same lines.

Hints for Collectors
Because many collectors specialize in Northwood glass, it is somewhat difficult to find. The floral-quilted patterns, such as Quilted Phlox, are especially popular.

Coin Spot miniature lamp

Description
Globe-shaped shade and font, which swells slightly at flat base. Shade and font have transparent circles on opalescent surface. Colorless baluster-shaped chimney. Brass kerosene burner and shade holder combination. Colors: colorless with opalescent red, pink, or blue-green.

Variations
Pattern may be swirls or stripes. Font may have handles or colorless pressed stem and foot.

Type and Dimensions
Shade and font blown in separate molds for pattern and shape; font top finished. Partially reheated to develop opalescent color before annealing. Mold-blown chimney. Height: 7¾″.

Locality and Period
Probably Hobbs, Brockunier & Company, Wheeling, West Virginia; possibly another firm in same area. c. 1886–1900.

Comment
Hobbs, Brockunier & Company produced several lamps in what collectors call Coin Spot or Coin Dot. In 1886 the Hobbs firm was granted a patent for opalescent glass, and some of its products bear the paper label "PATENTED 1886."

Hints for Collectors
Beware of reproductions in transparent red cranberry glass, made for L.G. Wright Company. Wright lamps have globe- or umbrella-shaped shades and globe-shaped fonts, and come in several circle patterns, including Opal Dot, Honeycomb, and Thumbprint. Some of the older copies command a surprisingly high price.

Description
Globe-shaped shade and font, which swells slightly at flat base. Raised design of owl's eyes, beak, and feathers on shade, and wings, feathers, and feet on font. Colorless baluster-shaped chimney. Brass kerosene burner and shade holder combination. Colors: opaque white with enameled details in green, pink, and brown.

Variations
Lamp may be electric, in form of slightly different owl or parrot.

Type and Dimensions
Shade and font blown in separate molds for pattern and shape; font top finished. Enamel fixed by firing after annealing. Mold-blown chimney. Height: 8″.

Locality and Period
Glasshouse unknown; the United States. c. 1890–1910. Variants from United States Glass Company, Pittsburgh. 1923–30.

Comment
One of the most interesting and unusual night lamps, the owl design pictured has never been linked with a manufacturer. Many miniature lamps were heavily advertised in trade publications like the *Crockery and Glass Journal* and in the *Ladies' Home Journal* and other women's magazines. From these advertisements, along with glass-company catalogues, we know that the small lamps were intended for use on nightstands.

Hints for Collectors
Perfect examples of the owl lamp are extremely expensive. Rarely will you find both the shade and the font intact.

Pan-American Exposition miniature lamp

Description
Globe-shaped shade and font, rounded at flat base. Each globe has enameled design showing maps of North and South America with superimposed figures and printed inscription "PAN-AMERICAN EXPOSITION 1901. BUFFALO, N.Y. USA." Brass kerosene burner and shade holder combination. Colors: opaque white with enameled pink background; enameled details in pink, yellow, and black.

Variations
Other lamps may have enameled flowers on plain or enameled background.

Type and Dimensions
Shade and font blown in separate molds for shape; font top finished. Enamel fixed by firing and inscription printed after annealing. Height: 8½".

Locality and Period
William Hengerer Company, Buffalo, New York. 1901. Variants from throughout the United States. c. 1890–1910.

Comment
The lamp illustrated was sold as an official souvenir of the 1901 Pan-American Exposition in Buffalo, a trade fair somewhat smaller than the better-known expositions in Chicago and St. Louis. The exposition featured a wide variety of manufactured products, including glass, pottery, aluminum, furniture, and hardware. It is probably best remembered, however, because President William McKinley was assassinated there.

Hints for Collectors
The Pan-American Exposition lamp is one of the most prized night lamps partly because a limited number were made. Like the owl, it is extremely hard to find and always expensive.

Description
Globe-shaped font with opening at top for burner and solid glass peg at bottom. Left: cut fans and ovals around globe and pewter collar with flat-wick, tin, whale-oil drop burner. Right: plain globe. Colorless.

Variations
Font pattern may be simple cut design, usually including fans or diamonds; may be cased with colored glass and design cut through; may have applied, usually colorless, rigaree or threaded decoration. Shape may be cylindrical.

Type and Dimensions
Free-blown, then tooled into shape. Cut after annealing (left). Height: 3⅝".

Locality and Period
The East and Midwest. c. 1810–70.

Comment
Made in many American lamp factories, peg lamps were used to convert a candlestick into a lamp by those who preferred lamplight to an open flame. Peg lamps remained in glass-company catalogues until as late as the 1860s, although they were probably most common in the first half of the 19th century. The burner on the cut peg lamp is marked "S. Rust Patent New York"; Samuel Rust patented the design in 1825. Its most unusual feature is the wheel that raises the wick as it burns. A standard element on later kerosene lamps, the movable wick is seldom found on whale-oil or burning-fluid lamps.

Hints for Collectors
Examine a peg lamp carefully. If the peg part has a rough surface and one or more notches in it, it is a lamp font meant to be fastened by a brass connector to a base.

Electrical fixture

Description
Bulb-shaped light cover consisting of 4 glass sections, each
outlined in metal; 2 filigree metal strips fastened to metal collar
crisscross bulb, holding sections in place. Colors: opaque green
shading to yellow.

Type and Dimensions
4 sections cut from sheet of flat glass, heated, and shaped in
mold. Sections fastened with metal strips after annealing.
Height: 6¼".

Locality and Period
Probably the East. c. 1890–1900.

Comment
The light fixture illustrated is said to have been made for a
building designed by Louis Sullivan, the famous turn-of-the-
century architect. Sullivan helped establish a modern, functional
architectural style, in opposition to the extravagant Beaux Arts
designs then in vogue. His first important success was the
transportation building designed for the 1893 World's Fair
Exposition in Chicago. Like Frank Lloyd Wright, Sullivan often
designed many of the interior furnishings for his buildings, and
the fixture shown is a fine example of his practical yet decorative
style. A similarly shaped 2-piece bulb cover with elaborate cut
designs was advertised by J. Hoare & Company of Corning, New
York, in a catalogue of about 1887, but few of these are found
today.

Hints for Collectors
Early electrical fixtures like the one pictured have only recently
attracted collectors, and many examples are still available.

303 Whale-oil lantern

Description
Oval globe open at top and bottom. Tin lantern has peaked cylindrical cover with immovable ring handle; cylindrical base has wide, flat bottom. Double-wick whale-oil burner in lantern base. Colors: colorless, with upper part cased with blue-green; usually completely colorless; sometimes transparent red or green.

Variations
Globe rarely with engraved inscriptions and dates. Glass manufacturer's name may be inscribed on metal lantern base.

Type and Dimensions
Globe free-blown, then tooled into shape. Lantern height: 16½″.

Locality and Period
The East. c. 1840–60.

Comment
All of the whale-oil lanterns discovered so far that bear the name of a glass company on the metal base date from about 1850. Among the best known are those by the New England Glass Company, the Brooklyn Flint Glass Company, and several Pittsburgh firms. The lanterns with inscriptions and dates engraved on the glass globes were not meant for use, but were presentation pieces given to mark a special occasion. Since most globes with inscriptions have whale-oil burners, it seems likely that the practice of giving presentation pieces went out of fashion after the Civil War, by which time kerosene had largely replaced whale oil.

Hints for Collectors
Lanterns with 2-color globes are rare and, along with the inscribed and dated examples, always command a high price.

Kerosene lantern

Description
Oval globe open at top and bottom; pebbly surface and raised cleat design around body. Tin lantern has flat-topped cylindrical cover with movable loop handle; cylindrical base has wide, flat bottom. Wire cage around globe. Kerosene burner in lantern base. Colors: transparent green, red, and colorless.

Variations
Globe may have cleats, but with smooth surface in between. Glass manufacturer's name may be inscribed on lantern base.

Type and Dimensions
Globe blown in mold for pattern and shape. Top and bottom finished. Lantern height: 10½".

Locality and Period
Probably the Midwest. c. 1860–90.

Comment
Lanterns did not have wire cages or movable handles until the latter part of the 19th century. The handle made the lantern safe to swing about for maximum light. The equivalent of the modern flashlight, lanterns were used by brakemen on the railroad, watchmen on their rounds, and even homeowners on the way from the house to the barn or the carriage house.

Hints for Collectors
Because kerosene lanterns were made in such great quantities and the design hardly changed, it is difficult to date a lantern precisely and virtually impossible to identify the manufacturer if the metal parts are not marked. On many old lanterns, the globe has been replaced with a new machine-made globe, which can be extremely hard to distinguish from the old.

Table Lamps

Most of the lamps in this group were probably placed in the formal rooms of the house. The modern term "table lamp" encompasses both the plain examples that our ancestors called stand lamps and the taller, more decorative parlor and banquet lamps. The fascinating diversity of types ranges from all-glass whale-oil lamps to kerosene lamps that combine glass, metal, and stone.

Stand Lamps
The first glass stand lamps, made from 1810 to 1860, consisted of free-blown fonts and tooled bases. During the 1830–50 period, lamps with pressed bases became common, and soon fonts were also being pressed in many shapes and patterns. By mid-century, however, metal stems became highly fashionable. On lamps with stone bases, the metal stem had screw threads that fit into the stone, making the lamp more stable. These metal joints proved so popular that in 1868 Atterbury & Company patented a brass connector to fasten glass fonts and glass bases. Despite the patent, the idea was copied later by many other companies. In the mid-1870s, Atterbury advertised pressed one-piece lamps as even stronger than those with connectors.

Innovative Lamps and Burners
Several antique oil lamps have unusual burning mechanisms. Although these lamps were made in a variety of materials, including brass, silver, and porcelain, all used glass chimneys and the more elaborate types also had glass shades.
The earliest innovation was the Argand burner, invented in 1782. Its tubular wick increased the amount of oxygen feeding the flame and thereby produced a brighter light. Astral and sinumbra lamps, first used in this country in the 1820s, had novel circular fuel reservoirs, in which hollow tubes arranged like the rim and spokes of a wheel conveyed oil to the burner. This wheel shape nearly eliminated the shadow cast by the font. The solar lamp, perfected in the early 1840s, burned lard oil. Its long wick tubes kept the lard from congealing when cold, and the lamps often had metal fonts to conduct the heat. Finally, the Welsbach mantle, devised in the late 1800s, employed a cotton hood or bag impregnated with chemicals. Mounted over a Bunsen-type gas burner, it produced an incandescent light. In the early 20th century, a similar mantle was adapted for kerosene Aladdin lamps and Coleman lanterns.

Electrical Fixtures
When electricity replaced liquid fuel, the lamp shade rather than the font became the basic glass element. Glass stems and bases, once fashionable for stand oil lamps, were succeeded in many cases by metal or stone bases that camouflaged wiring. Hanging fixtures ranged from hall lanterns to bent-glass shades and elaborate Tiffany-type leaded-glass examples.

Dating Antique Lamps
In dating an antique lamp, generally the more elaborately decorated, the later it was made. Although Argand, astral, sinumbra, and solar lamps dating from the 1810–50 period are ornate and have unique burning mechanisms, the glass components are usually colorless and the decoration restricted to traditional cutting, frosting, and engraving. In contrast, late 19th-century glass lamps come in a variety of shapes and colors and bear unusual finishes and designs.

305 Whale-oil hand lamp

Description
Globe-shaped font with rigaree decoration and solid ear-shaped handle, crimped at base. Opening at top for whale-oil drop burner. Solid stem with disk in center. Domed saucer-shaped base with folded-out rim. Pontil mark underneath. Colors: transparent blue and purple; colorless, sometimes with gray or purple tint.

Variations
Rigaree decoration may be crossed. Font may have prunts.

Type and Dimensions
Font free-blown, then tooled into shape. Rigaree decoration, handle, stem, and base applied. Height: 7⅝".

Locality and Period
The East. Possibly western Europe. c. 1820–40.

Comment
The lamp illustrated is known as a hand lamp because it was designed to be carried from room to room. Lamps that did not have handles were often referred to in manufacturers' catalogues as stand lamps. Hand lamps are generally shorter. The font shown here has elaborate crimped stripes, called rigaree decoration. This traditional European style is unusual on American lamps. Since the quality of the glass is good, this lamp was probably made in a tableware house rather than a bottle or window glasshouse.

Hints for Collectors
Lamps with rigaree decoration are rare. Yet because they are unfamiliar, a lamp's true value may go unrecognized and it may be bought at a bargain price.

Whale-oil stand lamp

Description
Globe-shaped font with opening at top for whale-oil drop burner.
Solid stem with disk in center. Conical saucer-shaped base with
folded-out rim. Pontil mark underneath. Colors: transparent
dark blue and colorless, singly and combined.

Variations
Font may be more conical or baluster-shaped.

Type and Dimensions
Font free-blown, then tooled into shape. Stem and base applied.
Height: 7″.

Locality and Period
New England; probably Thomas Cains's South Boston Flint
Glass Works or Cains's Phoenix Glass Works, Boston. 1813–
c. 1830. Possibly Boston & Sandwich Glass Company, Sandwich,
or New England Glass Company, Cambridge, Massachusetts.
1818–c. 1830.

Comment
The saucer-shaped base on the lamp shown here was considered
a desirable feature: It kept oil spilled during filling from running
onto the table. The wide base also prevented the lamp from
tipping over. Lamps of this type were clearly staple products of
several of the major New England tableware glasshouses, and all
are in the same colors. It is doubtful that any were made in the
Midwest, since whale oil was not used much there.

Hints for Collectors
This lamp is most common in New England. Blue examples
command much greater prices than colorless ones.

Whale-oil wineglass lamps

Description
Globe-shaped font (left) or diamond-shaped font with sloping
shoulders (right). Opening at top with single-wick, tin, whale-oil
drop burner. Solid spindle-shaped stem with 4 knops (left) or
straight stem with disk in center (right). Flat circular foot with
pontil mark underneath. Colors: transparent dark blue and
colorless.

Variations
Font shape varies slightly. Number and placement of knops
vary. Rarely, saucer-shaped base instead of circular foot.

Type and Dimensions
Font free-blown, then tooled into shape. Left: stem with tooled
knops and foot applied. Height: 3⅞″. Right: stem, disk, and foot
applied. Height: 3⅛″.

Locality and Period
The East. c. 1810–30.

Comment
Collectors have named these lamps wineglass lamps because
their profiles resemble simple wineglasses of the same period.
According to often repeated stories, they were also called
sparking lamps since they were supposedly lit during courting,
known as sparking in the late 19th century. In reality, during the
early 19th century, these small lamps served as bed lamps and
were used primarily at inns. Each guest was allowed only enough
whale oil to last 15 minutes, time to undress and get into bed.

Hints for Collectors
Colorless lamps are still available in antiques shops; blue
examples are considerably rarer and more costly.

Whale-oil hand lamp

Description
Conical font with sloping shoulders and solid ear-shaped handle, crimped at base. Opening at top with incomplete, double-wick, tin, whale-oil drop burner. Solid spindle-shaped stem with 4 knops. Flat circular foot with pontil mark underneath. Colors: transparent light green and aquamarine.

Variations
Font may be globe- or barrel-shaped; may lack handle.

Type and Dimensions
Font free-blown, then tooled into shape. Handle, stem with tooled knops, and foot applied. Height: 7⅛".

Locality and Period
New England, New York, and southern New Jersey. c. 1830–60.

Comment
The lamp illustrated is said to have been made at the Isabella Glass Works in southern New Jersey around 1848–50, but ones like it were probably blown in other window and bottle glasshouses in the Northeast. The burner used for the early whale-oil lamps is called a drop burner because it was simply dropped into an opening at the top of the lamp and could easily be removed. Some but not all drop burners had cork inserts to make a tight fit between the metal and the glass.

Hints for Collectors
Although the tin plate and wick tubes in the center of the burner shown are original, the outer metal part is a later addition, which is closed at the bottom, and serves no function. Since lamps of this type are rare, this alteration does not affect value.

309 Lamp with engraved font

Description
Conical font with sloping shoulders and engraved with grapevine and leaves. Brass collar around opening at top for burner. Solid stem encloses double-spiral air twist and single red thread. Flat circular foot with polished pontil mark underneath. Colors: colorless; thread opaque red, blue, or white.

Variations
Engraved patterns vary, often floral. Stem usually plain. Stem and foot may be pressed.

Type and Dimensions
Font free-blown, then tooled into shape. Air twist formed and colored thread enclosed in colorless glass, then stem cut to length. Stem and foot applied. Font copper-wheel engraved after annealing. Height: 8⅜".

Locality and Period
Probably the Midwest; possibly the East. c. 1845–65.

Comment
Lamps with spiral-twist stems, like the one shown here, are quite rare. Since the grapevine pattern would have required a trained engraver, it is likely that this lamp was made in a tableware factory with an engraving shop. Grape and grape-leaf motifs were exceptionally popular in the 19th century and used on all kinds of glassware, from punch bowls to platters.

Hints for Collectors
Engraved fonts are less common than plain ones or those with mold-blown or pressed patterns and are valued highly by collectors of lighting devices. This type of lamp could have been fitted with either a screw-in whale-oil or burning-fluid burner.

Mercury-glass lamp

Description
Cylindrical font narrower toward base and engraved with grapevine and leaves. Mouth has pewterlike collar with opening for burner; colorless glass font liner attached to collar. Hollow baluster-shaped stem with circular foot. Polished pontil mark underneath. Colors: colorless with silvery lining; rarely cased with transparent blue, green, or red.

Variations
Engraved patterns vary, sometimes floral.

Type and Dimensions
Lamp free-blown, then tooled into shape. Interior coated with mercury, and font copper-wheel engraved, both after annealing. Font liner free-blown and tooled, then fastened to metal collar. Height: 9¼".

Locality and Period
New England; possibly Boston Silver Glass Company and New England Glass Company, both of Cambridge, Massachusetts. c. 1855–70. Variants from England and Bohemia; widely exported to the United States.

Comment
Mercury glass, advertised as nontarnishing silver, was patented in London in 1853 and by Boston Silver Glass in 1855. Simpler objects, such as goblets, were created by pushing half of the blown bubble down into itself to form a double-walled vessel. The mercury coating was poured in through a hole in the bottom and sealed inside by a cork or glass disk.

Hints for Collectors
Lamps of mercury glass are quite rare. This one could have had a whale-oil, burning-fluid, or kerosene burner.

Description
Cylindrical font with rounded shoulders and pattern of large circles with swirled diamond-patterned tails. Brass collar around opening at top for burner. Disk between font and hollow baluster-shaped stem with hexagonal base. Colorless.

Variations
Base sometimes square.

Type and Dimensions
Font and stem with base pressed in 2 separate molds for pattern and shape; font top finished. Parts joined with disk before annealing. Height: 10¼″.

Locality and Period
M'Kee & Brothers, Pittsburgh. c. 1850–70. Possibly Boston & Sandwich Glass Company, Sandwich, Massachusetts, or New England Glass Company, Cambridge, Massachusetts. c. 1850–80.

Comment
Collectors call the pattern on the lamp illustrated Horn of Plenty, although the manufacturer named it Comet. The pattern appears in the sales catalogues of M'Kee & Brothers from 1860 until 1870, but was probably made before and after those dates. Found in a wide range of tableware shapes, the Comet pattern is one of the few 19th-century pressed designs with a matching lamp. Some of these lamps may have had burning-fluid burners, but most were probably fitted with kerosene burners when they were sold.

Hints for Collectors
Look for lamps in the Horn of Plenty pattern at antiques shops specializing in early American glass. Some of the tableware in this pattern was reproduced, but no lamp reproductions are known.

Waffle and Thumbprint lamp with tin liner

Description
Cylindrical font with rounded shoulders and narrower toward base; pattern of squares and circles around body. Brass collar around opening at top with double-wick, brass, burning-fluid burner with wick tube caps and chains. Font above shoulder lifts off and is attached to tin fuel liner. Disk between font and hollow baluster-shaped stem with hexagonal base. Colorless.

Variations
Font may have another pattern, usually hobnails.

Type and Dimensions
Lower font and stem with base pressed in 2 separate molds for pattern and shape; joined with disk before annealing. Font top pressed separately, then fastened to tin liner. Height: 10⅛".

Locality and Period
New England Glass Company, Cambridge, Massachusetts; Curling, Robertson & Company and James B. Lyon & Company, Pittsburgh. Without liner c. 1850–70. With liner c. 1855–60.

Comment
The pattern shown here, now called Waffle and Thumbprint by collectors, was listed as the Palace pattern in 19th-century tableware catalogues. The lamp illustrated has an unusual tin receptacle for fuel, patented by Elbridge Harns in 1855. It was supposed to keep the fluid from spilling.

Hints for Collectors
Exercise care when examining a lamp of this type. The separate glass shoulder section and the body should be cemented together, but often the cement has dried over the years so that the top and bottom come apart very easily.

Amberette lamp

Description
Thistle-shaped font with pattern of alternating plain panels and
panels with 3 vertical circles above diamond pattern. Brass collar
around opening at top for kerosene burner. Disk between font
and hollow baluster-shaped stem with hexagonal base. Colors:
colorless with amber stain on plain panels.

Variations
Font may have brass stem and square marble base.

Type and Dimensions
Font and stem with base pressed in 2 separate molds for pattern
and shape; font top finished. Parts joined with disk before
annealing. Silver stain for amber fixed by firing after annealing.
Height: 9⅞″.

Locality and Period
George Duncan & Sons, Pittsburgh; Dalzell Brothers & Gilmore,
Brilliant, Ohio; and Alexander J. Beatty & Sons, Steubenville,
Ohio. 1886–c. 1895. Variant also from West Virginia.

Comment
Although the burner is missing on this lamp, it was probably a
kerosene burner. By the mid-1860s kerosene had virtually
replaced both whale oil and volatile burning fluids in the average
American home. With this inexpensive fuel, the production of
glass lamps greatly increased. The amber stain on the example
shown was popular in the 1870s and 1880s, but it was not as
common as red stain. Duncan called the pattern with amber stain
Amberette.

Hints for Collectors
Amberette lamps with brass stems and marble bases are rare
and were made earlier than the all-glass examples.

Acanthus-leaf lamp

Description
Thistle-shaped font with rounded shoulders and pattern of
acanthus leaves below scalloped flange. Opening at top for
burning-fluid burner. Disk between font and hollow baluster-
shaped stem with acanthus-leaf pattern. Hollow, square, stepped
base. Colors: opaque white, green, blue, and combinations of
these; white with blue or green most common; rarely blue with
green.

Variations
Font may have vertical panels instead of acanthus leaves. Stem
may be columnar with square base. Base may have gilt
decoration, usually lines on edges.

Type and Dimensions
Font and stem with base pressed in 2 separate molds for pattern
and shape; font top finished. Parts joined with disk before
annealing. Height: 12⅞″.

Locality and Period
Boston & Sandwich Glass Company, Sandwich, and New
England Glass Company, Cambridge, Massachusetts. c. 1840–60.

Comment
Lamps of the type shown were made in the same colors as
candlesticks with columnar stems or with acanthus-leaf sockets
and stems. Both the candlesticks and lamps have an unusual
surface, which has roughened over the past century because the
ingredients of the glass mixture were probably incompatible.

Hints for Collectors
Many of these lamps were converted for use with electricity in
the 1920s and 1930s. Check the stem or base to see if holes were
drilled for a cord; these greatly lower the lamp's value.

Whale-oil or burning-fluid lamps

Description
Conical font with rounded shoulders and pattern of circles and ellipses. Pewter collar around opening at top with double-wick, pewter, burning-fluid burner. Disk between font and hollow columnar stem with square base. Colors: transparent purple, blue, and yellow; rarely blue-green and colorless.

Variations
Patterns on font and stem with base vary. Various combinations of different fonts and bases. Base may be hexagonal.

Type and Dimensions
Font and stem with base pressed in 2 separate molds for pattern and shape; font top finished. Parts joined with disk before annealing. Height: 10⅞".

Locality and Period
New England. Possibly Pittsburgh area. c. 1845–65.

Comment
Lamps like those shown here predate printed glass-company catalogues and are therefore difficult to attribute to any one company. Vases from this period were made in the same patterns with the same bases, suggesting that the lamps and vases might have been intended for use together in the parlor. Some lamps of this type have whale-oil burners.

Hints for Collectors
Many of these lamps were adapted for use with electricity in the 1920s and 1930s, and some were also reproduced. A reproduction has the mold seam running continuously from top to bottom through the disk, indicating that the lamp was pressed in a single piece.

Whale-oil lamp

Description
Broad conical font with sloping shoulders. Opening at top for
whale-oil drop burner. 3 disks between font and hollow stem with
interior vertical ribs; 3 scalloped circles above hollow square base
with vertical ribs on interior and exterior. Pontil mark
underneath. Colors: colorless; rarely transparent aquamarine or
light green; or a combination of 2 of these colors.

Variations
Base varies; may be circular or have another pattern.

Type and Dimensions
Font free-blown, then tooled into shape; stem with base pressed
in mold for pattern and shape. Parts joined with disks before
annealing. Height: 7⅛″.

Locality and Period
New England. c. 1830–40.

Comment
Despite the absence of a handle, a short lamp like this was
probably carried from room to room rather than kept on a mantel
or tabletop. Most lamps were made in tableware factories, but
aquamarine is generally associated with bottle and window
glasshouses: The color, which naturally results from impurities,
is one of the cheapest to produce. Since the pale aquamarine of
this lamp is bluer than bottle-glass aquamarine, it was probably
deliberately mixed in a tableware factory. For this period, the
combination of blown and pressed parts is not unusual.

Hints for Collectors
Small lamps like the one seen here cost much less than the more
imposing tall parlor lamps.

Whale-oil or burning-fluid lamp with shade

Description
Conical font with sloping shoulders and cut fans and diamonds above vertical panels. Disk between font and hollow globe-shaped stem; disk between stem and scalloped circular base. Tall vase-shaped shade with flaring rim and frosted globe. Double-wick, pewter, burning-fluid burner and shade holder combination; brass wick tubes. Colorless.

Variations
Font may be baluster-shaped or broad cone. Cut decoration varies, usually with fans and diamonds; stem may have cut pattern. Base may be square or circular.

Type and Dimensions
Font and stem free-blown separately and tooled into shape; base pressed in mold for pattern and shape. Parts joined with disks before annealing. Font cut after annealing. Shade free-blown and ground for frosted finish. Lamp height: 10⅜″. Shade height: 6⅝″.

Locality and Period
New England, Philadelphia, and Pittsburgh. c. 1825–40.

Comment
Most whale-oil and burning-fluid lamps have simple screw-in burners and lack shades. More expensive lamps of the period are sometimes found with a burner and shade holder unit. The type of shade seen here also functioned as a chimney.

Hints for Collectors
A lamp with the original shade intact is difficult to find. The burner on this example is probably a period replacement since it was easy to substitute a burning-fluid burner, designed for the cheaper fuel, for a whale-oil burner.

Whale-oil lamp

Description
Baluster-shaped font with painted green leaves on frosted surface. Opening at top for whale-oil drop burner. 3 disks between font and hollow triangular pedestal base with C-scrolls and paw feet. Pontil mark underneath. Colorless.

Variations
Font may be plain. Base may have another pattern; may be square and stepped.

Type and Dimensions
Font free-blown, then tooled into shape; base pressed in mold for pattern and shape. Parts joined with disks before annealing. Font ground for frosted finish and painted after annealing. Height: 10⅝″.

Locality and Period
New England. c. 1830–40.

Comment
A rough-ground font like the one illustrated is most often seen in combination with a similarly ground shade. Its unfired painted decoration is easily chipped and quite rare. Originally sold with a drop burner, this lamp was one of a pair, each probably placed at either end of the fireplace mantel, as documented in paintings and prints of the period. The triangular base, shown here with a font, was also used with at least 2 differently patterned candle sockets and a compote top.

Hints for Collectors
These lamps used to be common in New England antiques shops, but are found less often today.

319 Cut lamp with pressed base

Description
Baluster-shaped font with cut fans, cross-hatching, and diamonds above vertical panels. Brass collar around opening at top for burner. Disk between font and hollow baluster-shaped stem with cut ellipses; disk between stem and solid, straight section above square footed base with interior vertical ribs. Polished pontil mark underneath. Colorless.

Variations
Font may be conical or globe-shaped. Stem sections vary, usually including a globe shape. Cut decoration varies, usually with fans and diamonds. Base patterns vary.

Type and Dimensions
Font and stem free-blown separately and tooled into shape; base pressed in mold for pattern and shape. Parts joined with disks and solid section applied before annealing. Cut after annealing. Height: 13⅜".

Locality and Period
New England and Pennsylvania. c. 1830–45.

Comment
The earliest whale-oil lamps had burners that were dropped into an opening in the font. In the 1830s, when burning fluid was also used, manufacturers adopted metal collars so that customers could choose a screw-in burner for either fuel. Burning fluid burned brighter than whale oil but was extremely flammable and explosive.

Hints for Collectors
Elaborate lamps of this type were made with a wide variety of bases, fonts, and cut patterns. A collection of all possible variants could have as many as 20 lamps.

Lamp with hand-pressed base

Description
Globe-shaped font. Brass collar around opening at top for burner.
Disk between font and hollow 3-knopped stem; disk between
stem and solid, straight section above square base with ribs
underneath. Colors: colorless, or colorless with opaque white
font.

Variations
Font may be conical or cylindrical. Stem may be baluster-shaped;
stem may contain early 19th-century coin. Number and type of
base ribs vary.

Type and Dimensions
Font and stem free-blown separately and tooled into shape; base
hand-pressed. Parts joined with disks and solid section applied
before annealing. Height: 9¾".

Locality and Period
Probably New England Glass Company, Cambridge,
Massachusetts. 1818–c. 1830. Possibly Thomas Cains's South
Boston Flint Glass Works or Cains's Phoenix Glass Works,
Boston. 1813–c. 1830.

Comment
Square hand-pressed bases were made in only a few American
factories before the development of the pressing machine in the
1820s. In England and continental Europe they were commonly
used on compotes, salt dishes, and goblets, but usually not on
lamps. The handpress resembled an old-fashioned lemon
squeezer.

Hints for Collectors
The collar on the example shown is too big to be original; the
lamp probably burned whale oil. Many lamps of this type can still
be found in New England.

Description
Globe-shaped font narrower toward base; lower part in dark blue has recessed ovals with white stars. Brass collar around opening at top for burner. Brass connector between font and hollow columnar stem with square base. Colors: font opaque white and dark blue or colorless and dark blue; base opaque white, rarely opaque blue.

Variations
Patterns on stem with base vary slightly; may have gilt decoration. Stem may be brass; base may be marble. Connector may have inscription.

Type and Dimensions
Font blown and pressed in same mold for pattern and shape; blue and white glass poured in mold one right after the other. Font top finished. Stem with base pressed in mold for pattern and shape. Font and base joined with connector. Height: 10½″.

Locality and Period
Atterbury & Company, Pittsburgh. 1862–c. 1870.

Comment
The example illustrated, with its bicolor font, was manufactured under a patent granted to Atterbury & Company in 1862. Since this lamp and other objects made using the same unusual process are scarce, they were probably too difficult to produce on a commercial scale, or perhaps the 2 colors proved unstable when combined. This lamp probably burned kerosene.

Hints for Collectors
Bicolor lamps are quite rare. However, lamps with a single-color pressed font joined to a pressed base by a brass connector are fairly easy to find.

Atterbury lamp

Description
Globe-shaped font, narrower toward base, with pattern of diamonds above wide vertical panels. Brass collar around opening at top for kerosene burner. Brass connector with horizontal ribs between font and hollow columnar stem with square base. Colors: font transparent blue, yellow, green, and colorless; base opaque white, rarely opaque black.

Variations
Font patterns vary greatly; may be floral or geometric, including honeycomb and tulip. Base may be taller; rarely may have gilt decoration; may be cast metal.

Type and Dimensions
Font and stem with base pressed in 2 separate molds for pattern and shape; font top finished. Font and base joined with connector. Height: 12″.

Locality and Period
Atterbury & Company, Pittsburgh. 1868–c. 1880. Variants from the East and Midwest.

Comment
Because this lamp has a patented Atterbury connector, we can be certain of its maker. In the 1870s, when most lamp production was centered in Pittsburgh, Atterbury was probably the largest American manufacturer of lamps. Many similar lamps with plain, unribbed connectors were made by other firms.

Hints for Collectors
Collectors call the pattern on the font illustrated Sawtooth Band and Panel. Since this Atterbury font has been found with bases not made by the firm, it is probable that storeowners who bought the font added it to the best-selling base in their area.

Atterbury lamp

Description
Globe-shaped font with chainlike pattern above inscription "PATENTED SEPTEMBER 29, 1868." Brass collar around opening at top with kerosene burner and "PAT. FEB. 19, 1865/HOLMES, BOOTH & HAYDEN" on wick raiser. Brass connector, with horizontal ribs and same inscription as font, between font and hollow columnar stem with square base. Colors: font transparent blue, yellow, green, and colorless; base opaque white, rarely opaque black.

Variations
Font patterns vary greatly; may be geometric or floral. Base may be taller, rarely may have gilt decoration; may be cast metal.

Type and Dimensions
Font blown in mold for pattern and shape; font top finished. Stem with base pressed in mold for pattern and shape. Font and base joined with connector. Height: 11".

Locality and Period
Atterbury & Company, Pittsburgh. 1868–c. 1880.

Comment
The 1868 date on the font and brass connector refers to the patent for the connector. Atterbury used this brass connector on a great variety of lamps of the same general type. Holmes, Booth & Hayden of Waterbury, Connecticut, made the kerosene burner. The firm was one of the largest manufacturers of metal lamp parts.

Hints for Collectors
This lamp would be more desirable if it were complete with its chimney and chimney brackets.

Cased lamp

Description
Bulb-shaped font with cut oval pattern. Brass connector between
font and hollow columnar stem with square base. Tulip-shaped
shade with scalloped rim; engraved grapevine and leaves below
frosted upper part. Colorless baluster-shaped chimney. Brass
kerosene burner and shade holder combination. Colors: font any
combination of colorless, opaque white, and transparent red,
blue, green, and purple; base opaque white or black.

Variations
Cut patterns vary. Base may be circular or have gilt trim. Lamp
may have cased shade and/or stem, and stone base.

Type and Dimensions
Font free-blown and cased with white and red, then tooled into
shape; cut after annealing. Stem with base pressed in mold for
pattern and shape. Font and base joined with connector. Shade
and chimney free-blown and tooled; shade ground for frosted
finish, then copper-wheel engraved. Height with chimney: 24″.
Height to font top: 13″.

Locality and Period
New England or the Midwest. c. 1865–75.

Comment
The origin of the lamp shown here is puzzling, since pressed
white bases with connectors are usually attributed to the
Midwest, while cased fonts are associated with the Boston &
Sandwich and New England Glass companies.

325 Lamp with prisms

Description
Bulb-shaped font with engraved floral pattern; prisms hang from metal collar. Brass connector between font and hollow columnar stem with square base; gilt trim on base. Tulip-shaped shade with scalloped rim; engraved grapevine below frosted upper part. Brass shade and chimney holder combination. Colors: font colorless, opaque white, opaque and transparent blue and green, and any combination, including colorless cased with color; base opaque white, rarely opaque black.

Variations
Font may have variety of pressed or mold-blown patterns. Base shape varies slightly; may lack gilt trim.

Type and Dimensions
Font and stem with base pressed in 2 separate molds for pattern and shape; font top finished. Font copper-wheel engraved, and gilt on base fixed by firing, both after annealing. Font and base joined with connector. Shade mold-blown and rim finished; ground for frosted finish and engraved. Prisms pressed and polished. Height with shade: 23″. Height to font top: 13″.

Locality and Period
Lamp: probably the Midwest. Prisms: probably France and Bohemia. c. 1860–80. Replacement prisms possibly after 1900.

Comment
In the 19th century few if any American firms made prisms.

Hints for Collectors
Replacement prisms are acceptable if they match each other and are the right type for the lamp. The shade and holder on this lamp are 19th-century replacements, but there is no burner and the gadget in the middle is not original.

Argand lamp

Description
Cylindrical domed font has knob and brass ring with prisms.
Brass stem and arm unit between font and hollow baluster-
shaped stem with domed circular foot; collar and flange with
prisms above stem. Burner rings with prisms support frosted
vase-shaped shades with cut floral pattern and plain cylindrical
chimneys. Font, stem with foot, collar, flange, and burner rings
with elaborate cut patterns. Colorless. Tubular-wick, brass,
oil-burning burners. Brass plates on brass burners inscribed,
respectively, "BEMIS & VOSE/BOSTON" and "WILLIAM BROOKES/
MANUFACTURER/LONDON."

Variations
Cut patterns vary. Shades may be bulb-shaped with folded rims.
Font or base may be metal or ceramic. Lamp may have 1 arm;
these lamps are usually used in pairs.

Type and Dimensions
Font, stem with foot, collar, flange, burner rings, shades, and
chimneys free-blown and tooled into shape; cut after annealing;
shades ground for frosted finish, then cut. Prisms pressed and
polished. Lamp assembled. Height: 24¼". Width: 18".

Locality and Period
Lamp: the East. England; widely exported to the United States.
Prisms: probably France and Bohemia. c. 1790–1830.

Comment
The Argand lamp is named for the Swiss Ami Argand, who in
1782 invented the tubular-wick burner. Abigail Adams used one
of these lamps at the White House.

Hints for Collectors
Many Argand lamps have been damaged, and sometimes the
parts of 2 or more have been combined or married.

Hurricane shade

Description
Barrel-shaped shade, flared at top and bottom. Band of cut
flowers and leaves around center; band of cut fans and diamond-
patterned ellipses near top and bottom. Base rim folded under.
Colorless.

Variations
Cut designs are usually simple. May have engraved flowers or
initials.

Type and Dimensions
Free-blown, then tooled into shape. Cut after annealing.
Height: 23⅝".

Locality and Period
New England. Possibly England. c. 1820–50.

Comment
Hurricane shades of the type shown were designed to protect
candles from drafts. Exceptionally large, the shades had to
enclose the combined height of the candle and candlestick.
Illustrations from the 19th century show that hurricane shades
were used extensively in the West Indies and often in the South.
In both of these warm climates, windows were apt to be open,
creating troublesome drafts. Since there were no glass factories
in the South or West Indies during this period, the hurricane
shades were probably shipped from New England or imported
from England.

Hints for Collectors
There are many reproductions of blown hurricane shades,
including those made for Colonial Williamsburg. None are
marked. Original shades are rare, and most found today are
reproductions.

Aladdin lamp

Description
Cylindrical font with vertical ribs and swags; fuel hole with brass cap. Hollow columnar stem with circular base. Colorless cylindrical chimney acid-stamped "Aladdin//REG. U.S. PAT. OFF./ MADE IN U.S.A." Brass kerosene burner and chimney holder combination; cloth mantle. Colors: transparent red, green, blue, amber, and colorless; opaque white and green; translucent ivory and ivory with pink tint.

Variations
Font and base have many patterns and shapes. May have umbrella-shaped shade. Lamp may be brass with glass shade. Ivory and pink bases may have "Alacite by Aladdin" underneath; other colors have other names. Burner may have inscriptions; these vary greatly, usually "Aladdin" or "Mantle Lamp Company."

Type and Dimensions
Font machine-blown and stem with base machine-pressed in 2 separate molds for pattern and shape. Parts joined before annealing. Chimney mold-blown. Height: 23⅝".

Locality and Period
Mantle Lamp Company, Chicago. 1938–50. Variants c. 1909–50.

Comment
Victor Johnson, founder of the Mantle Lamp Company, introduced the Aladdin lamp in 1909, having patented a kerosene burner that gave a bright white light. It used a small cloth bag called a mantle rather than the conventional wick. The ivory lamp color shown here, called Alacite, was developed in 1938.

Hints for Collectors
Whatever the shape or color, you can recognize an Aladdin lamp by the characteristic burner mantle.

Swan stem lamp

Description
Globe-shaped font with chainlike pattern around body. Brass
connector with horizontal ribs between font and solid swan-form
stem with hollow hexagonal plinth base. Colorless baluster-
shaped chimney with ruffled rim. Brass kerosene burner and
chimney holder combination. Colors: font transparent blue,
yellow, green, and colorless; stem opaque blue, white, green,
and colorless.

Variations
Font patterns vary greatly; may be floral or geometric. Stem
figure may be woman. Base may be marked "Sept. 29, 1868" and
"Nov. 1869."

Type and Dimensions
Font blown in mold for pattern and shape; font top finished.
Stem with base pressed. Font and stem with base joined with
connector. Chimney mold-blown and rim finished. Height: 18″.

Locality and Period
Atterbury & Company, Pittsburgh. 1869–c. 1890. Variants from
the East and Midwest.

Comment
In 1868 Atterbury patented the 2-part ribbed brass connector
with screw threads. This device enabled the font and stem to be
joined by screwing together the top and bottom halves of the
connector, eliminating the need for cement or plaster.

Hints for Collectors
When the Atterbury patent expired in 1885, several other firms
made similar connectors, so do not assume that all lamps with
ribbed connectors are by Atterbury. Swan stem lamps are rare.

Double lamp

Description
2 globe-shaped fonts joined by diamond-shaped center section; cylindrical container with cover between fonts. Each font with brass kerosene burner and shade holder combination. Colorless, frosted, tulip-shaped shades with scalloped rims. Bronze stem with square footed base. Colors: translucent white, blue, green, and colorless.

Variations
Fonts and center section may be 2 contrasting colors. Bases vary greatly. Glass base may be square in opaque white, diamond-shaped in translucent white, or lyre-shaped in colorless. Lamps may have chimneys and/or shades.

Type and Dimensions
Center section pressed, then 2 fonts blown simultaneously while still in mold for pattern and shape; font tops finished. Cover pressed in separate mold. Shades mold-blown and rims finished; ground for frosted finish. Lamp assembled after annealing. Height: 20″. Width: 9½″.

Locality and Period
Ripley & Company, Pittsburgh. 1870–c. 1880.

Comment
Daniel C. Ripley registered a number of glass patents, but the combined pressing and blowing process he used to create his double lamps was one of the most innovative. Collectors call them marriage or wedding lamps. All double lamps, including the one seen here, have a matchbox in the center.

Hints for Collectors
Double lamps are scarce. The many font and base combinations and various colors make these lamps especially desirable.

Brilliant-cut banquet lamp

Description
Globe-shaped shade and font with cut hobstars, fans, and diamond-patterned arches. Ribbed glass collar below font with brass fitting inside. Hollow baluster-shaped stem with domed circular foot; stem has notched vertical ribs, and foot pattern matches globes. Polished pontil mark underneath. Colorless cylindrical chimney with cut flat hexagons. Double-wick brass kerosene burner and shade holder combination. Colors: colorless; rarely cased with transparent red, blue, or green.

Variations
Lamp may have larger globe- or vase-shaped font, no stem, and globe- or umbrella-shaped shade. Patterns vary widely.

Type and Dimensions
Shade, font, collar, stem with foot, and chimney free-blown separately and tooled into shape. Cut after annealing. Font and base joined with brass fitting. Height: 35¾". Shade diameter: 9¼".

Locality and Period
T.G. Hawkes & Company, Corning, New York. c. 1895–1905. Variants from throughout the United States. c. 1885–1905.

Comment
Lamps of the size and type shown, called banquet lamps, are quite rare. This example is cut in the Hawkes Venetian pattern, and the chimney is their simple version of the Russian pattern.

Hints for Collectors
Although the lamp pictured is unmarked, an identical example appeared in a Hawkes ad in a *Ladies' Home Journal* in 1905. The piece may predate use of the Hawkes trademark in 1895.

Cased lamp

Description
Globe-shaped shade, baluster-shaped font, and hollow baluster-shaped stem, all with cut keyhole design and gilt scrollwork. Brass fitting between font and stem. Square, stepped, marble-and-brass base. Colorless baluster-shaped chimney. Single-wick, brass, kerosene burner and shade holder combination. Colors: transparent green, blue, amber, red, and colorless, each cased with opaque white; or 3 layers, each in a different color.

Variations
Cut patterns vary, including circles or arches. Font may be globe-shaped or cylindrical. Stem may be cylindrical.

Type and Dimensions
Shade, font, and stem free-blown separately and cased with opaque white, then tooled into shape. Pattern cut and gilt fixed by firing, both after annealing. Font and stem joined with brass fitting. Chimney mold-blown. Height: 25½". Shade diameter: 7".

Locality and Period
New England; probably Boston & Sandwich Glass Company, Sandwich, Massachusetts, or New England Glass Company, Cambridge, Massachusetts. Possibly the Midwest. c. 1850–75.

Comment
Many fancy cased lamps, popular during the 1850–75 period, burned whale oil or burning fluid, both widely used before the discovery of kerosene in the 1860s. Since the lamp shown here appears to have an original kerosene burner, it probably dates after 1860.

Hints for Collectors
In the 1920s, cased replacement parts and entire lamps were imported from Czechoslovakia. Watch for patterns that do not match.

333 Solar lamp

Description
Globe-shaped shade with cut swirled bands and circles. Brass
font and shade holder combination. Hollow hexagonal stem has
pink and white panels with cut flower design. Square, stepped,
marble-and-ormolu base with "Thomas Leighton" engraved in
script. Colors: shade colorless; stem colorless and opaque white,
or either color cased with opaque pink, red, or blue.

Variations
Stem decoration may be twisted threads of colored glass. Stem
often metal. Base often all metal; rarely glass.

Type and Dimensions
Shade free-blown, then tooled into shape; cut after annealing.
Stem free-blown, cased with pink, and tooled into shape; flowers
cut. Shade and stem joined with brass fittings. Height: 26½".
Shade diameter: 9½".

Locality and Period
New England Glass Company, Cambridge, Massachusetts.
c. 1843–49. Variants from Cornelius & Company, Philadelphia.
1843–55. Boston & Sandwich Glass Company, Sandwich,
Massachusetts; Starr, Fellows & Company, New York City; and
possibly other firms in the East. c. 1845–55.

Comment
The solar lamp was patented in 1843 by Cornelius & Company to
burn lard oil, using a modified Argand-type burner. However,
the discovery of cheap kerosene soon made the burner obsolete.

Hints for Collectors
Few solar lamps, including the one shown here, are found with
their original burners intact. Such a discovery would be of great
interest to a collector.

Sinumbra lamp

Description
Frosted, colorless, umbrella-shaped shade with cut floral design.
Doughnut-shaped brass oil reservoir (elliptical in cross section)
with tubular-wick burner. Brass columnar stem with square
base.

Variations
Shade may lack design. Stem very rarely glass; may be cased.
Oil reservoir may be round in cross section (astral lamp). Same
shade used for hanging fixtures.

Type and Dimensions
Shade free-blown, then tooled into shape. Ground for frosted
finish and cut, both after annealing. Height: 31¾". Shade
diameter at widest: 14".

Locality and Period
Boston, Philadelphia, or New York. Possibly England.
c. 1840–50.

Comment
Both the sinumbra lamp shown and the similar astral lamp are
variations of the Argand lamp. The sinumbra's doughnut-shaped
oil reservoir functions as the font. Its open shape was designed
to let light down through the center, unlike the astral's
reservoir, round in cross section, which cast a shadow. The
earliest astral fixtures were made in France as hanging lamps
(*astrale* is "star" in French). In 1820 George Phillips developed a
tubular fuel receptacle, elliptical in cross section, which cast no
shadow, and called it the sinumbra, or shadowless, lamp.

Hints for Collectors
Astral and sinumbra lamps are equally valuable.

Figural stem lamp

Description
Flattened globe-shaped font with simple fleur-de-lis design.
Brass collar around opening at top for kerosene burner. Brass
fitting between font and cast britannia-metal figure of child
eating grapes and holding goat. Square black stone base with
inset brass ring. Colors: colorless with frosted surface; and
opaque white, blue, and green.

Variations
Font may be plain or have another simple pattern, such as ribs
or diamonds. Stem figure may be bust or full figure of man or
woman. Stone base may be white; may have patent date.

Type and Dimensions
Font blown in mold for pattern and shape; acid-treated for
frosted finish after annealing. Lamp assembled after annealing.
Height: 10".

Locality and Period
The East and Midwest. c. 1860–85.

Comment
With the widespread use of inexpensive kerosene fuel after 1860,
the production of glass lamps vastly increased. Those with cast-
metal stems, both figural and nonfigural, were among the most
popular. The stems were made of cast iron or the alloy britannia
metal and usually gilded or painted black. Most portrayed
allegorical or historical figures, including the French Empress
Eugenie.

Hints for Collectors
As long as the metal figure is undamaged, a surface worn with
age does not matter. Avoid buying a mix-and-match lamp; the
styles of all parts should be compatible.

Lamp with brass stem and marble base

Description
Conical font with rounded shoulders and swirled pattern of
stripes. Brass collar around opening at top for burner. Disk
between font and cylindrical brass stem with spiral design and
brass plate at bottom. Square marble base. Colors: colorless with
opaque white and dark blue stripes.

Variations
Plain font may have cut, engraved, or pressed design. Brass
stem may have vertical ribs. Marble base may have 2 steps and
be trimmed with brass or ormolu. Lamp may be much taller.
Variants opaque white, green, and blue; transparent blue,
purple, yellow, and colorless; single color or combinations,
including cased.

Type and Dimensions
Font free-blown, then tooled into shape. Stripes applied and
marvered into surface and disk applied to font before annealing.
Font and stem joined after annealing. Height: 9¼".

Locality and Period
The East; probably New England. c. 1840–60. Variants from the
Midwest. c. 1850–70.

Comment
Lamps with brass stems and marble bases were quite fashionable
in the mid-19th century. Brass-stemmed lamps with threaded
fonts like the one pictured were made in only a few eastern
factories and were probably fitted with kerosene burners.

Hints for Collectors
Many lamps with brass stems were converted for electricity in
the 1920s and 1930s. As long as a lamp lacks drill holes, its value
has not been lowered.

Brilliant-cut lamp

Description
Umbrella-shaped shade rests on collar of hollow baluster-shaped stem with circular domed foot. Design of cut hobstars, diamonds, and fans. Colorless. Electrical fittings under shade.

Variations
Shade may be more pointed. Stem may be cylindrical. Patterns vary greatly, combining hobstars, diamonds, fans, ellipses, and panels. Lamp may be smaller.

Type and Dimensions
Shade and stem with foot free-blown separately and tooled into shape. Cut after annealing. Height: 17⅝″. Shade diameter: 9¼″.

Locality and Period
Majestic Cut Glass Company, Elmira, New York. c. 1900–10. Variants from throughout the United States. c. 1900–20.

Comment
The elaborate cut patterns seen here are typical of the style called brilliant-cut glass, at its height of popularity from about 1890 to 1915. Lamps are among the largest and showiest examples of this style. Large lamps like the one shown were placed in the living or dining room; the smaller ones were advertised for the boudoir.

Hints for Collectors
Until the 1960s, brilliant-cut lamps were considered old-fashioned and uncollectible. Tastes have changed, but because of their size and high prices, the lamps can still be found relatively easily. The shade may be chipped or cracked, so examine it well.

Burmese lamp

Description
Umbrella-shaped shade with gilt trim around opening at top; flattened globe-shaped font. Shade and font with enameled and gilt fish-in-net design. Brass kerosene burner and shade holder combination; white metal collar around font top. Square, brass, footed base. Baluster-shaped chimney. Matt finish. Colors: opaque pale salmon-pink shading to pale lemon-yellow; details in brown enamel.

Variations
Shade may be globe-shaped. Decoration may be flowers or birds. Other opaque colors with enameled and gilt designs.

Type and Dimensions
Shade, font, and chimney blown in mold for shape. Partially reheated to develop pink shading before annealing. Acid-treated for matt finish, and enamel and gilt fixed by firing; both after annealing. Height: 19¼". Shade diameter: 10".

Locality and Period
Mt. Washington Glass Company, New Bedford, Massachusetts. 1885–95. Variants from western Pennsylvania and West Virginia. c. 1885–1905.

Comment
Many collectors call any similar lamp of opaque colored and enameled glass a Gone with the Wind lamp because one was used as a prop in the famous Civil War movie. However, these lamps definitely date from the 1880s and 1890s. This one is in the colors Mt. Washington called Burmese.

Hints for Collectors
Since the 1970s, many lamps of the type shown (but not the colors) have been made for sale in gift shops, and most have shiny metal fittings. Burmese lamps have not been reproduced.

Iridescent lamp

Description
Umbrella-shaped shade and hollow baluster-shaped stem with circular base; design of trailing leaves and stems. Signed on shade "TIFFANY FAVRILE 9546L"; on base "L.C.TIFFANY FAVRILE." Colors: iridescent gold or blue, with green, blue, red, white, and silver decoration. Electrical fittings.

Variations
Stem may be more bulbous or more cylindrical; base may be metal. Decoration may be stripes of silver glass or acid-etched floral designs; may lack decoration. May bear signatures of other manufacturers.

Type and Dimensions
Shade and stem with base blown in 2 separate molds for shape; top of shade and stem finished. Leaf decoration of green glass applied and marvered into surface. Sprayed with chemical for iridescent finish before annealing. Height: 16″. Shade diameter: 8″.

Locality and Period
Tiffany Studios, Corona, New York. c. 1900–10. Variants from A. Douglas Nash Associates, Corona, New York; Steuben Glass Works, Corning, New York; and Victor Durand's Vineland Flint Glass Works, Vineland, New Jersey. c. 1900–20.

Comment
Several glass studios of the period produced lamps with iridescent finishes, but Tiffany is the best known.

Hints for Collectors
Look for a signature or trademark, usually on the base. Nash glass has "A.D.N.A." or "NASH." Steuben pieces are nearly always signed "STEUBEN" or "steuben" on a ribbon across a fleur-de-lis. Vineland marked its works "V DURAND."

Lamp with painted shade

Description
Umbrella-shaped shade with painted background and scene of windmills and trees; metal frame. Metal baluster-shaped stem with circular base signed "M.L.CO." Colors: colorless with green, orange, blue, brown, and black paint. Electrical fittings.

Variations
Shade may have other landscapes or a floral design; may be signed. Stem may be cylindrical.

Type and Dimensions
Shade blown in mold for shape. Painted after annealing. Height: 19″. Shade diameter: 18½″.

Locality and Period
M.L. Company; location unknown. c. 1910–30. Variants from Pairpoint Corporation, New Bedford, Massachusetts; Edward Miller & Company and Handel & Company, both of Meriden, Connecticut; and H.J. Peters & Company, Chicago.

Comment
Electric lamps with painted shades were made by companies all over the United States during the early 20th century. M.L. Company, the signer of this lamp, has never been identified. In many cases, only the metal parts were made by the firm that sold the lamp. The glass was obtained elsewhere, possibly from Europe; many shades of variegated colored glass (here the background color is painted) came from Venice.

Hints for Collectors
Some of the most sought after shades of this type are Pairpoint designs, signed by one of its artists. On any painted lamp, examine the paint carefully. Paint is not fired on like enamel and may chip.

Tiffany lamp with leaded-glass shade

Description
Umbrella-shaped shade with rose-and-leaf pattern; each glass piece outlined in lead. Bronze stem and circular footed base with plantlike motifs. Colors: mixture of transparent and opaque red, pink, green, and amber. Electrical fittings.

Variations
Patterns represent many flowers, including wisteria, peony, and dogwood. Shades formed to fit flower depicted. Similar designs in floor-lamp size. Base may be marked "Tiffany Studios."

Type and Dimensions
Combined free-blown and cast pieces. Cut into shapes after annealing. Pieces fastened with soft lead channels. Height: 28″. Shade diameter: 24½″.

Locality and Period
Tiffany Studios, Corona, New York. c. 1895–1915.

Comment
Louis C. Tiffany was trained as an artist. In 1879, with Candace Wheeler and a few others, he founded Associated Artists, which designed and made decorative objects in glass, metals, ceramic, and textiles. After the firm was dissolved, Tiffany formed his own company in 1892, and in 1893 set up the Tiffany Furnaces. Best known for his Favrile glassware and stained-glass windows and glass lamp shades, Tiffany also designed and manufactured the metal parts for his shades, and most are marked with the company name.

Hints for Collectors
Although they are not rare, Tiffany lamps are extraordinarily expensive. There have been many imitations in the past 5 to 10 years, so buy only from a reputable dealer.

Tiffany pond-lily lamp

Description
12 pendant shades in form of lilies. Bronze base in form of water-lily pads, buds, and stems. Colors: shades of iridescent gold, white, and green. Electrical fittings.

Variations
Lamps may have flowers other than lilies, more or fewer shades (sometimes turned up), and slightly different bases. Base may be marked "Tiffany Studios." Shades may be marked "LCT," "Favrile," or combination of these words and a number. Simpler lamps with striated green and white shades in form of flower blossoms and buds were made by other manufacturers.

Type and Dimensions
Each shade blown in separate mold for shape. Sprayed with chemical for iridescent finish before annealing. Height: 21″.

Locality and Period
Tiffany Studios, Corona, New York. 1902–c. 1920. Variants from Handel & Company, Meriden, Connecticut, and other firms east of Chicago.

Comment
The pond-lily lamp illustrated is one of the most famous lamps produced by the Louis C. Tiffany company. It was designed in 1902 and exhibited that year in Turin, Italy. The lamp also appears in the 1904 and 1906 Tiffany catalogues, but was doubtless in production as long as it could be sold. In 1906 its price was $115. The simpler variant patented by Philip Handel's firm in 1902 was considerably less expensive.

Hints for Collectors
Always look for a trademark. Tiffany bronze bases are usually marked "Tiffany Furnaces." Handel lamps are marked "Handel" with or without a design number.

Description
Square shade with raised design of roses and butterflies on swirled background. Acid-stamped signature "THE PAIRPOINT CORP" inside shade on each corner. Square stem bulging in center. Square bronze base with "PAIRPOINT MFG CO/B3034" scratched underneath. Colors: colorless with predominantly pink, blue, green, and white paint. Electrical fittings.

Variations
Shade designs vary greatly, mostly floral. Shade may be circular.

Type and Dimensions
Shade blown in mold for pattern and shape. Interior painted after annealing. Lamp height: 25". Base of shade: 12" × 12".

Locality and Period
Pairpoint Corporation, New Bedford, Massachusetts. c. 1907–20.

Comment
The Pairpoint Corporation was not much influenced by the innovations of Louis C. Tiffany and Frederick Carder, first director of the Steuben Glass Works. Unlike the other firms, Pairpoint continued producing Victorian-inspired floral designs; the lamp shown here is in the Rose Albemarle pattern. This lamp is also an example of what collectors call "puffy Pairpoint" (puffy because of the high relief). The technique for making it was patented by Albert Steffin, the manager of Pairpoint in 1907.

Hints for Collectors
Pairpoint lamps of the type illustrated are easy to recognize, and most are signed. A signed lamp always brings a high price unless the lamp is in poor condition.

Emeralite desk lamp

Description
Rectangular shade. Square, columnar, pot-metal stem and rectangular base, both with bronze finish. Top of base has 2 square depressions, each with square colorless glass inkwell; front of base has brackets for pen. Base inscribed "EMERALITE"; plate attached to inside of shade has "PAT AUG 15 1916/EMERALITE DESK LAMP/H.G.MCFADDIN & CO. N.Y./U.S.A." Colors: transparent dark green with opaque white lining. Electrical fittings.

Variations
Base may have 1 inkwell or lack inkwells; inkwells may have glass or metal covers. Shade may have paper label printed "EMERALITE/MAY 11, 1909–AUG 15, 1916/MADE IN CZECHOSLOVAKIA."

Type and Dimensions
Shade mold-blown white glass cased with green. Inkwells blown in separate molds for shape. Shade edges and inkwell sides ground and polished. Height: 18″. Shade length: 7½″.

Locality and Period
Shade: Bohemia until 1918; Czechoslovakia after 1918; widely exported to the United States. Base: H.G. McFaddin & Company, New York City. Inkwells: throughout the United States. Entire lamp with inkwells 1909–c. 1930.

Comment
In the early 20th century, Emeralite desk lamps were popular in offices. The white inside the shade was supposed to intensify the light thrown onto the desk, while the green, hence the name Emeralite, was thought to soothe the eyes.

Hints for Collectors
A reproduction of the Emeralite lamp is currently for sale through mail-order advertisements in many magazines. These lamps are shiny, new looking, and not exact copies.

Hall lantern

Description
Hexagonal shade formed of 6 panes in cast-iron frame with 6 elaborate arches. Design of medieval tower alternates with landscape. Colors: frosted colorless panes with red stain and black paint.

Variations
Lantern may be rectangular or cylindrical. Panes may have other designs; these may be engraved through stain; rarely with pressed design.

Type and Dimensions
6 panes cut from sheet of flat glass. Panes acid-treated for frosted finish and red-stained on exterior, painted on interior, then fastened to frame, all after annealing. Height: 14″.

Locality and Period
The Northeast. c. 1850–75. Pressed variants c. 1830–50.

Comment
The hall lantern pictured was probably a hanging candle shade, although it has lost its candleholder. The candle had to be replaced fairly frequently, but if the lantern hung in a stairway, it could have been reached with a hook from the upstairs landing. The technique of painting and staining seen on these panes was popular throughout the second half of the 19th century, but the elaborate Gothic design of the arches dates the lantern to mid-century, when the Gothic Revival flourished in the United States.

Hints for Collectors
Fixtures like this are rare, since they were often thrown away. Even those in slightly damaged condition are worth collecting.

Lamp shade for hanging fixture

Description
Umbrella-shaped shade with flaring top. 8 curved panels of beige
striated glass above circular band of blue striated glass. Brass
bands around edges and seams of beige panels. Cutaway brass
band with design of windmills, houses, and trees over blue glass.
Brass ring for hanging at top. Colors: opaque beige, blue, green,
red, yellow, and purple, usually striated with opaque white.

Variations
Shade may be more square or domed. May be 1 piece of glass
supported by metal rim, or many small striated pieces connected
with metal. May have hanging border of glass beads.

Type and Dimensions
8 beige sections and blue strip cut from sheet of flat glass, then
heated and shaped in mold. Height: 17½″. Shade diameter: 20″.

Locality and Period
Throughout the United States. c. 1900–30.

Comment
Shades of striated glass and metal, known as bent-glass shades,
were made in numerous factories, sometimes as hanging fixtures
and sometimes as part of standing lamps. A scenic design cast in
metal is a cheaper variation of the elaborate leaded-glass or
hand-painted shades, both of which were more time-consuming
to produce. Hanging fixtures were designed for use with both
kerosene burners and electric light bulbs, although more were
produced after electricity became common.

Hints for Collectors
Since genuine Tiffany lamps are so expensive today, more
affordable fixtures like the one shown here have become popular.

Where to Look for Antique Glass

Bottles, lamps, and other glass objects are available at thousands of shops, shows, sales, flea markets, and auctions throughout the country. While adventurers may dig up bottles at dumps, around old houses, or at factory sites, it is unlikely that fancy perfumes, lamps, candlesticks, toys, or paperweights will be discovered in such places since they were seldom thrown away unless damaged. Many glass objects, including milk bottles, jars, lamps, and windows, can be found in almost any region; other types, such as certain flasks, are most common in the area where they were made.

Building Sites and Dumps
Because late 19th-century bottles were throwaways, often discarded while whole, perfect examples requiring only a thorough cleaning can still be uncovered at dumps as well as old house and factory sites. Fragments of even earlier bottles are not hard to find. Recent excavations in New York City unearthed thousands of fragments of bottles and other glass objects dating from the 18th century. Understandably, property owners dislike having strangers digging on their land, so it is wise to seek permission first. By law, if you remove your finds without the owner's consent, you are stealing and liable to prosecution. Public dumping grounds are exceptions to this rule, but local regulations may forbid excavation without permission.

Collectors' Shows and Sales
Major collecting organizations often sponsor annual shows and sales. Specialized bottle clubs, Depression glass clubs, and other associations exhibit collections, sell duplicates, and swap information. A wonderful source of knowledge for beginners, these shows are usually advertised locally and in club newsletters. If you are interested in any particular type of old glass, contact a collectors' society, and by all means join the group. Dues are rarely high, and you will meet other people who share your interest. Collectors' publications are also excellent resources.

Yard Sales and Flea Markets
Here the sellers are not professionals, but people trying to get rid of odds and ends, or those who deal in inexpensive household goods. Practically anything could turn up. You might spot a bargain the seller has overlooked, but by the same token you could be overcharged for a reproduction that went unrecognized. In this situation more than any other, you have to rely on your own knowledge of quality and the prevailing prices.

Antiques Shops
Many dealers specialize in bottles and flasks or lamps and candlesticks; others carry many different types of glass as part of their general stock. A dealer is usually glad to share his expertise with a beginning collector; after all you might turn out to be one of his best customers. In a shop you will have time to study the merchandise without being under the pressure you might feel at an auction. If you take up much of a dealer's time, it is polite to buy something, however small, but this is not absolutely necessary. A dealer who cannot give you firm provenance for every piece in his shop is not ignorant, but rather understands that unsigned pieces rarely can be attributed to a specific factory and has the integrity not to tell customers "Sandwich" or "Bakewell" (two well-known factories) just to make a sale.

Antiques Shows

These events are scheduled regularly, often as annual benefits for a church or charity. Antiques shows give collectors a chance to see the wares of many dealers at one time, and often dealers exhibit their finest pieces. (In fact, most of the largest shows exclude dealers who show substandard merchandise.) Although you may be able to view some excellent examples and gather valuable information from the participants, this is not the best market for a beginner who wants to build a collection. Most shows last only a day or two, and you may feel pressured to make a quick decision.

Auctions

Taking place anywhere from a large city auction house to a country barn, auctions offer a wide range of quality and especially unpredictable prices. At auction, buyers have only a few minutes to make up their minds and sometimes little chance to examine the goods beforehand or to return them afterward. The prices will be determined by the people who happen to be there that day. If the audience is sparse and uninterested, the prices might be quite low, but if two eager collectors start bidding against each other, an object might sell for several times the price it would fetch at an antiques shop. If you decide to buy at auction, arrive early enough to thoroughly examine the pieces that interest you.

Shopping Hints

No matter where you buy, be cautious, and do not be afraid to trust your own experience. Although few dealers and auctioneers are dishonest, any seller may be guilty of poor judgment or lack of knowledge. It is tempting to think a piece is genuine 18th-century when it is really a reproduction, and not everyone can tell the difference. If you question authenticity, condition, or price, you are always free not to buy.

How to Select Bottles, Lamps, and Other Glass Objects

Whether you have your eye on a small conical ink bottle or an elegant whale-oil lamp, there are certain accepted guidelines that collectors use when choosing antique glass. Several factors determine the desirability of a piece: age, color, condition, method of manufacture, shape, rarity of pattern, quality of decoration, maker, and origin. Not every criterion applies to every piece, and, while flask and lamp collecting are well-established fields, the standards for determining value in relatively new areas, like food bottles, have not been firmly set. The following tips will familiarize you with the qualities that are most important within each basic type.

Guidelines to Bottles

Many collectors believe that a pontil mark is proof that a bottle was made before 1850. While this is often true, collectors should be cautious. Factors such as the type of bottle and its place of origin must also be considered; moreover, the pontil rod is still employed today in factories where glass is hand blown. The snap case was introduced to replace the pontil rod starting in the mid-19th century but was not universally employed until 1900. Therefore, a bottle without a pontil mark can be the same age or even older than a pontiled example.

Examination of lips and collars can reveal whether a bottle was hand finished, but a flat versus a rounded collar is of no great significance in dating. However, mold lines extending all the way to the rim are usually, but not always, a sign of manufacture by automatic bottle-blowing machinery, which was introduced in the 1890s.

Most bottle collectors prefer a handmade look to machine-made perfection, so bubbles, unevenness in shape, or small stones do not usually decrease value and may even enhance appeal. But major flaws like cracks or large chips devalue all but the rarest examples. Be extremely careful that the rim of a bottle (or any other object) has not been ground down to eliminate a chip. Not only is value lowered, but the original proportions are irrevocably lost.

Minor scratches are acceptable, since it is expected that bottles and most other glassware were used and not put in a cabinet to be admired. Many reproductions, in addition to lacking signs of wear, are of better-quality glass with fewer bubbles than the authentic antiques. The difference is apparent after you have handled a few examples of both types. Finally, if a bottle has traces of original paint, do not try to repair it or scrape it off. In general, it is best to preserve the existing condition of old glass.

Apothecary and Druggists' Ware

Few people build collections of drug and chemical bottles; these are usually purchased to fill in existing collections of free-blown ware or early pontiled bottles. Age and method of manufacture are the primary factors here. Machine-made items from the early 20th century are not particularly desirable, and in most cases any hand-blown object is preferred to one blown in a mold.

Beer, Soda, Milk, and Other Beverage Bottles

Although many collectors choose to buy only those examples with pontil marks, most of these bottles do not have them. Soda and mineral water bottles with large collars, called blob tops, are quite popular. Rare designs and pictorials as well as unusual colors, such as greens and blues in beer and soda bottles and greens and ambers in milk containers, are especially sought after and usually more expensive.

Bitters and Patent and Proprietary Medicine Bottles

Because of the great number of different brands, designs, and colors available in this field, collectors of bitters and patent and proprietary medicine bottles tend to concentrate on gathering all possible variations of a single type. They also include what are popularly called "go withs," that is, the advertising material or packaging that accompanied the original bottles. The most common patterns and the many colorless and aquamarine bottles are a good place to start for a beginner. These bottle types were produced for a shorter time than flasks, so age is not as important, although early pontiled examples are treasured.

Figural Bottles

Above all, shape determines the appeal of a figural bottle. Collectors also like showy and rare colors. Age, origin, method of manufacture, and even whether the bottle is a reproduction or adaptation matter less here than in other fields.

Figured Flasks

The early flasks with detailed designs are the most highly prized, and many collectors feel that a common early flask is preferable to a scarce late one. After age, rarity of design and color are most important. Many flask collectors specialize in one type of design or, in the case of portraits, one hero or statesman; others collect different designs from a single factory or area. To help collectors who wish to consult the definitive McKearin flask charts for further technical information, the McKearin number is listed at the end of each description in the Figured Flasks section.

Free-blown Bottles

Early free-blown bottles are often irregularly shaped, with a pushed-in base and an obvious pontil mark. Most come in the ambers, greens, browns, and aquamarines collectively known as green glass. Free-blown types include early wine, household, and medicine bottles, as well as demijohns, carboys, and whiskey jugs. Few bear more elaborate decoration than an applied seal or handle.

Ink Bottles and Inkwells

While new collectors may seek readily available conical and umbrella ink bottles in a variety of colors, many advanced specialists concentrate on figural shapes, such as the teakettle, turtle, schoolhouse, and barrel inks. Pontiled examples and bright transparent colors or out-of-the-ordinary opaque hues are preferred to the prevailing clear greens, aquamarines, and ambers. With fancy inkwells, the condition and execution of the decoration are most important; many turn-of-the-century inkwells were part of ornate desk sets.

Jars

The earliest jars, with uneven shapes, pontil marks, and ground lips, and the mold-blown jars with rare inscriptions, designs, or colors are considered the most interesting. Depending on the chemical composition of the glass, sometimes a jar that was initially colorless will have developed a purple tint after long exposure to sunlight. Jars with unique matching closures are quite desirable, although a jar designed to be used with a standard zinc screw-on cap is certainly collectible without it.

Pattern-molded Bottles and Flasks

The majority of these bottles have an overall geometric design, often with ribs or diamonds. Since they were expanded to full size after removal from the pattern mold, their shapes are somewhat irregular. Some of the designs are rarer than others, as are some of the colors, especially purples and bright blues.

Perfume, Barber, and Dresser Bottles
With many eye-catching shapes, a wide range of colors, and all kinds of decoration, these bottles form some of the most ornate collections. In cut-glass examples, look for parallel straight lines and exact intersections. Most quality cut examples have a polished pontil mark or a cut sunburst underneath. Check to see if the bottle has an acid-stamped trademark, since this aids in identifying and dating the piece and frequently adds to its value. (You may have to use a raking light.) To tell if a bottle which appears to be cut is a pressed imitation, feel the design with your fingers: Real cut glass has sharp edges and lacks mold seams. With enameled and gilt decoration, the details should be complete, not sketchy, and cameo designs should be naturalistic, not stiff. Make sure that the colors of shaded glass blend into each other gradually without abrupt transitions.

Guidelines to Candlesticks and Lamps
Early candlesticks and lamps are mostly colorless, so an occasional rare color like purple, dark blue, or aquamarine will command a high price. Original colorless frosted shades are sought after, but few are in good condition. Given a lamp with cut or engraved decoration and a similar plain example, most collectors would choose the ornamented lamp.
The same criteria used to assess fancy perfume bottles and other items decorated in tableware factories and specialized shops apply to lamps with cut, engraved, gilt, and enameled designs. Lamps with mold-blown or pressed patterns were also produced by tableware firms, and some patterned lamps and candlesticks match tableware sets, even in 20th-century Carnival and Depression glass. With 19th-century pressed examples, opaque whites, blues, and greens are usually rarer and often more expensive than transparent yellows and purples.
Kerosene lamps should be as complete as possible, with font, shade, and chimney; an intact burner adds to the value of any oil lamp. While it is permissible to replace a missing 19th-century chimney with another, a lamp font and shade—whether cased, brilliant-cut, or art-glass—should always match. However, not all cut lamps originally had shades; glass-company catalogues show some with just chimneys. On lamps joined by metal connectors, it is appropriate to combine a font from one lamp with a base from another if the two are of the same period or style and the original combination was not.

Guidelines to Miscellaneous and One-of-a-kind Items
As with perfume bottles and desk and dresser sets, the quality of the decoration is most important. With plain and one-of-a-kind pieces, condition and appeal will be the determining factors. Banks, bells, pens, and other ornamental items should be skillfully formed, and the applied decoration should not be missing even a small section.

Guidelines to Paperweights
Quality, elegance of design, and age are key factors when selecting a paperweight. Learn to discriminate between highly skilled and sloppy assembly by studying classic mid-19th-century American and French paperweights. An intricate pattern or a

rare variation of a common design, such as an extra petal, flower, or an unusual color, adds greatly to a paperweight's value. For modern paperweights, it is desirable to have an example that is signed and dated; cheap gift and souvenir shop imitation weights from Europe and China usually have only a paper label. Some collectors seek 19th-century pressed weights and advertising and photographic examples which, although less glamorous, make a less expensive collection. Many paperweight collectors have the scratches ground off and the tops polished, but purists object to this because it alters both the weight's profile and the way the enclosed design was meant to be viewed.

Guidelines to Toy Glassware
Any colored miniature, including opaque white, is often more valuable than a colorless example. The market for early lacy-pattern pressed toys and free-blown and mold-blown toys is the most competitive in this field. Few of these early pieces were meant to be part of a set, but check to see that a cup has a matching saucer and a tureen its tray and cover. Turn-of-the-century pieces, which were often made in sets, are easier to collect. A complete set is usually more valuable than the same pieces bought individually. Although it will almost certainly be as well made and may have even more detailed ornamentation, a European toy is not as desirable to most American collectors as an American one of the same period.

Guidelines to Windows
There are few collectors of windows per se, since display, especially of large stained-glass windows, is difficult. However, people restoring old houses sometimes seek a period window replacement, and serious collectors of pressed lacy-pattern glass would be delighted to discover an early lacy pane. Collectors of Tiffany glass include windows within the scope of their collections. When considering a stained-glass window, check the quality of design, variety of color, type of glass, and skill of assembly. Few windows are signed, and fewer still have extant records that might indicate the manufacturer.

Care and Display

Glass is a fragile material and should be treated with care. Try to use both hands when examining a piece, and never carry antique glass by the handle. This puts the greatest strain on the weakest part of the object, and one day the handle may break off. When carrying lidded pieces, keep either one hand or both thumbs on the lid, but the best way is to carry the two parts separately. Be especially careful when examining show globes and lamps. Some of these elaborate composite structures have joints that may not be securely fastened.

Cleaning
It is best to avoid washing antique glass unless it is very dirty. Instead, use a soft, damp cloth, neither too hot nor too cold. Never use harsh abrasives, even on bottles that have just been unearthed. These and sooty lamp chimneys are hard to clean without washing, but risk is always involved.

To lessen the chance of breakage, line the sink with bath towels or some other soft material. Use only tepid water and mild hand soap, not detergent, and be careful when rinsing not to hit the glass against the faucet or to let it slip from your hands; when soapy, glass is very slippery. Never place glass you value in the dishwasher. The only old glass that can ever tolerate that is Depression glass. Even with these precautions, some glass may break spontaneously because it was improperly annealed. This is especially true of glass with air bubbles or air traps.

Packing and Transporting
Bubble pack is excellent material for protecting glass, but crumpled newspaper or disposable diapers will also do the job. Cushion the objects all around: They should not touch one another or the sides of the box, and, for greatest safety, double-box the glass, with a layer of packing material between the inner and outer boxes.

The worst thing for glass is to subject it to rapid change in temperature. If you receive a shipment on a cold day, do not open the box until it has come to room temperature. When traveling in winter, avoid storing glass in the trunk of your car or leaving it outside all night. Always allow glass to reach room temperature gradually before handling it.

Using Antique Glass
Most old glassware was meant to be used. While bottle collectors prefer to display their finds, many collectors of antique lighting like to try out their collections. When using an old candleholder, always snuff out the candle before it burns all the way down, since the direct heat could cause the glass to crack. When removing melted wax from a candlestick, be careful not to scratch the glass.

Old oil lamps are usually functional. It is a good idea not to let the fuel sit in them long enough to dry and harden because you might damage the glass when trying to remove it. If you wish to use a turn-of-the-century electric lamp, first check to see whether you will need to replace the wiring; it is often primitive or quite worn and could shock or start a fire. As long as this is done carefully, without damaging the lamp base, it will not lower the value of the lamp. Similarly, converting a turn-of-the-century art-glass fixture to electric use does not significantly lower its value as long as the piece is not damaged in the process. Never drill a lamp to insert an electric cord. This destroys the value of all but the rarest types, and the lamp might fracture while being drilled.

Display

Showing off a colorful collection in a sunny window may be attractive, but it is not particularly safe. In summer a southward-facing window will get very hot. In winter the glass is exposed to both extremes: Heat from the house warms one side while the other is cooled from outdoors. For similar reasons, try to keep any display away from heating units and air-conditioning ducts.

A cabinet with an interior light is probably the best place for glass; at most, the pieces will need an occasional dusting. Tablelike display cases with glass tops work well for such objects as miniatures, paperweights, and perfume bottles.

Many bottle collectors enjoy exhibiting their bottles on a shelf or sturdy table. Flasks and some other old bottles may have such irregular bases that they must be displayed on their sides. If an object is only slightly unstable, use one of several claylike products available in stationery stores: Apply a ball to the base, then press the bottle to the shelf. Do not use candlewax because it may form such a tight bond that later, when trying to remove the bottle, you may damage the glass. Since related advertising material adds to the educational value of any collection, be extremely careful in opening an original paper wrapper; it is old and may crack or tear.

Organizations for Collectors

Few clubs have permanent headquarters. In most cases, the addresses given are those of the current secretary or president. All of the organizations listed publish a newsletter or bulletin; titles are included below. To locate regional bottle clubs, write to the Federation of Historical Bottle Clubs. If you are interested in a subject other than bottles, many small associations advertise in collectors' periodicals, the names of which are listed at the end of the Bibliography.

Aladdin Knights of the Mystic Light
Route 1
Simpson, IL 62985
The Mystic Light of the Aladdin Knights

American Collectors of Infant Feeders
540 Croyden Road
Cheltenham, PA 19012
Keeping Abreast

Antique Bottle Collectors of Colorado
Box 63
Denver, CO 30201
Dump Diggers Gazette

Federation of Historical Bottle Clubs
10118 Schuessler Street
St. Louis, MO 63128
Federation of Historical Bottle Clubs Journal

Finger Lakes Bottle Collectors Association
Box 815
Ithaca, NY 14850
Applied Lip

Genesee Valley Bottle Collectors Association
P.O. Box 7528, West Ridge Station
Rochester, NY 14615
Applied Seals

Marble Collectors Society of America
P.O. Box 222
Trumbull, CT 06611
Marble-Mania

National Button Society
2733 Juno Place
Akron, OH 44313
National Button Bulletin

Paperweight Collectors Association
761 Chestnut Street
Santa Cruz, CA 95060
Paperweight Collectors Association Annual Bulletin

Rushlight Club
P.O. Box 3053
Talcottville, CT 06066
The Rushlight

Society of Inkwell Collectors
5136 Thomas Avenue South
Minneapolis, MN 55410
Stained Finger

Permanent Antique Glass Collections

Most large city art museums contain general collections of American glass. This list features specialized collections outside of local museums and historical societies.

Apothecary Glass
Louisiana. New Orleans: Historical Pharmacy Museum.
Missouri. St. Louis: St. Louis Medical Museum and National Collection of Quackery.
Pennsylvania. Bethlehem: Moravian Museum of Bethlehem. Philadelphia: Mütter Museum, College of Physicians.
Virginia. Alexandria: Stabler-Leadbeater Apothecary Shop Museum. Fredericksburg: Hugh Mercer Apothecary Shop.
Canada. Toronto: Museum of the History of Medicine.

Bottles, Flasks, and Other Containers
Florida. Pensacola: Pensacola Historical Museum.
Hawaii. Honolulu: The Hawaii Bottle Museum.
Indiana. Muncie: Ball Corporation Museum.
Kentucky. Bardstown: Barton Museum of Whiskey History.
Michigan. Dearborn: Henry Ford Museum and Greenfield Village.
New Jersey. Millville: Wheaton Museum of American Glass.
New York. Ballston Spa: National Bottle Museum, Verbeck House. Corning: The Corning Museum of Glass. Rochester: The Margaret Woodbury Strong Museum.
Washington, D.C.: National Museum of American History, Smithsonian Institution.

Candlesticks and Lamps
Delaware. Winterthur: Henry Francis du Pont Winterthur Museum.
Florida. Winter Park: The Morse Gallery of Art.
Massachusetts. New Bedford: New Bedford Glass Museum. Sandwich: Sandwich Glass Museum. Sturbridge: Old Sturbridge Village.
Michigan. Dearborn: Henry Ford Museum and Greenfield Village.
New York. Corning: The Corning Museum of Glass. Rochester: The Margaret Woodbury Strong Museum.
Washington, D.C.: National Museum of American History, Smithsonian Institution.

Miscellaneous Glass
Michigan. Detroit: Detroit Historical Museum.
New York. Corning: The Corning Museum of Glass. Rochester: The Margaret Woodbury Strong Museum.
North Carolina. Greensboro: Greensboro Historical Museum.
Pennsylvania. Philadelphia: Perelman Antique Toy Museum.
Vermont. Shelburne: Shelburne Museum.
Washington, D.C.: National Museum of American History, Smithsonian Institution.

Paperweights
California. Camarillo: Doheny Collection, St. John's Seminary.
Illinois. Chicago: The Art Institute of Chicago.
Louisiana. Shreveport: The R.W. Norton Art Gallery.
Missouri. Perryville: Doheny Museum, St. Mary's of the Barrens.
New Jersey. Millville: Wheaton Museum of American Glass.
New York. Corning: The Corning Museum of Glass.
Ohio. Cambridge: Degenhart Paperweight and Glass Museum.
Wisconsin. Neenah: Bergstrom-Mahler Museum.

Glossary

Acid-etching   A method of decorating glass after it is annealed, using hydrofluoric acid to eat away an exposed surface while the remainder of the surface is covered with a protective coating.

Acid-stamping   The process of etching a trademark or signature into glass after it is annealed, using a device resembling a rubber stamp; usually found on cut glass made after 1895.

Acid-treating   The process of exposing an annealed surface to acid fumes in order to produce an overall matt or frosted finish.

Air trap   A glass-enclosed air space, usually decorative, which may be a teardrop shape or spiral twist within a stem, or a herringbone or quilted design between 2 layers of cased glass.

Annealing   The controlled cooling of a glass object just after it has been formed to remove tensions that might lead to breakage.

Applied glass   A separate glob of glass attached to the main gather during blowing and shaping or just after pressing.

Art glass   Glassware, usually blown, with unusual opaque or shaded color effects and/or a matt finish, often further decorated by enameling; made from about 1875 to 1905.

Batch   A mixture of the unmelted raw materials used to make glass, such as sand, cullet, and other substances.

Blank   Any preliminary shape of glass that requires further decoration, such as cutting or enameling.

Blown glass   Glassware shaped by blowing air through a blowpipe into a glob of molten glass.

Blown 3-mold glass   A collectors' term used to describe glassware blown in full-size 2- to 5-piece molds and made from about 1815 to 1835. Most patterns are geometric, such as ribs, diamonds, sunbursts, and waffling, but may also include hearts, chains, and flowers.

Blowpipe   A hollow iron rod, 4 to 6 feet in length, used to make blown glass.

Bottle glass   Inexpensive glass made from sand with iron impurities that impart a green, aquamarine, amber, or brown color. Also called window or green glass.

Brilliant-cut glass   Blown glassware with elaborate cut patterns covering the entire surface; popular from about 1880 to 1915.

Britannia metal   A pewter-colored alloy that became popular in the mid-19th century as an inexpensive substitute for silver.

Broken-swirl ribbing   A double set of ribs on mold-blown glass. After a gather is blown in a vertically ribbed mold, it is twisted for a swirled effect, then redipped in the same or another ribbed mold to superimpose a second set of ribbing.

Burning fluid   A mixture of alcohol and turpentine, used as a lamp fuel in the 19th century.

Cane   A glass rod or a bundle of rods. In paperweights, glass rods of various sizes and colors are grouped into designs, such as flowers, dates, or initials; when the canes are sliced, each cross-section has the same pattern.

Carnival glass   Pressed glassware with a colorful iridescent finish; made from about 1905 to 1920.

Cased glass   Glassware made of 2 or more layers of glass, usually in contrasting colors. Each layer of glass is blown into another layer while both are still hot, or the initial glob of glass is dipped into molten glass of another color. Also called overlay glass.

Cast metal   Metal formed in a mold while molten instead of tooled into shape.

Chimney   A glass tube used to shield the flame of an oil lamp, trap soot, and increase draft; usually colorless and undecorated.

Collar   A band of applied glass around a rim; used on bottles to secure a cork. Also, a threaded metal ring around a lamp font opening; used to attach a screw-in burner.

Connector   A metal joint used to fasten a lamp font and base.

Cracking-off process   The severing of a glass object from the blowpipe or pontil rod.

Crimp   An iron tool used to form a flower or other design enclosed within a paperweight.

Crimped decoration   An applied gather pinched with a special tool; commonly seen as threading or on the bottom of a handle.

Cullet   Broken glass added to a batch to speed melting and to improve quality.

Cutting   A method of decorating glass after it is annealed, using a rapidly rotating stone or cast-iron wheel fed with an abrasive mixture such as sand; usually polished afterward with a fine abrasive or an acid bath.

Depression glass   Machine-pressed glassware of the 1920s, 1930s, and 1940s.

Dip mold   A cylindrical part-size mold that is open at the top.

Drip catcher   A flange on a lamp font or candle socket; designed to prevent spilled fuel or melted wax from running onto the table. Also called a drip pan.

Drop burner   A late 18th- and early 19th-century term for a whale-oil lamp burner that was dropped into the font and held above the fuel by a metal plate larger than the opening; often a cork ring was inserted for a tight fit.

Embossed design   A design formed in a mold.

Enameling   A method of decorating glass after it is annealed; a mixture of powdered glass and a fusing flux is painted and fired onto the glass.

Engraving   A method of decorating glass after it is annealed, using a rapidly rotating stone or copper wheel fed with an abrasive mixture such as sand. The process is similar to cutting, but the abrasions are shallower, allowing easier manipulation and thus greater detail.

Finishing   The process of tooling into final shape, or cracking-off, grinding, or polishing.

Fire-polishing   The finishing process of reheating an object before it is annealed in order to remove mold lines and produce a smooth glossy finish.

Font   The fuel reservoir of an oil lamp.

Free-blown glass   Glassware blown and shaped by hand without the use of a mold.

Frosted finish   A gray nonglossy finish created by exposing annealed colorless glass to acid fumes.

Full-size mold   A mold that forms final shape and pattern.

Gadrooning   Applied decoration that is tooled to form a ribbed or swirled band.

Gather   A glob of molten glass before it is tooled or fully shaped.

Gilding   A method of decorating glass in which a thin layer of gold is painted or fired on after the glass is annealed.

Green glass   Inexpensive glass made from sand with iron impurities that impart a green, aquamarine, amber, or brown color; characteristic of objects from bottle and window firms.

Hand press   A small hand-operated metal press shaped like an old-fashioned lemon squeezer; used to make lamp bases, bowls, goblets, decanter stoppers, and decorative prisms for light fixtures in the mid-18th and early 19th centuries.

Impressed design   A design formed in a mold.

Iridescent finish   A rainbowlike finish created by spraying a chemical onto glass before it is annealed; found on some Art Nouveau and Carnival glass.

Kick-up   The base of a free-blown or mold-blown bottle that has been pushed into the body to strengthen it or to prevent a rough pontil mark from scratching the table. Also called a push-up.

Knop   A decorative solid or hollow knob, often found on the stem of an object; may be applied or tooled.

Lacy-pattern glass   A collectors' term used to describe pressed glassware with a stippled background and usually a scroll-and-flower design; made from the mid-1820s to mid-1840s.

Lampworking   The process of heating pieces or rods of manufactured glass over an open flame, then shaping them by blowing and/or tooling.

Lead channel   A U-shaped lead strip used to connect the pieces of a stained-glass object. Also called a lead came.

Lily-pad decoration   Applied decoration consisting of broad flat swirls with knobs on their ends; found on glass made by eastern American firms during the second quarter of the 19th century.

Marked glass   A glass object signed with a glassmaker's name or initials.

Marver   To roll a glob of glass on a smooth stone or metal surface in order to make it symmetrical, to center it on the blowpipe, or to imbed applied threads into the surface as decoration. Also, the stone or metal surface used in this process.

Matt finish   A nonglossy finish created by exposing glass to acid fumes or by grinding it after annealing.

Mold-blown glass   Glassware made by blowing a partly expanded glob of molten glass into a mold.

446 **Mold mark**   A seam resulting from a joint of a multipiece mold.

Off-hand process   The blowing and shaping of glass without the use of a mold.

Ormolu   Gilded brass.

Part-size mold   A mold that forms preliminary pattern and shape; after removal from the mold, the gather is expanded and tooled into final shape.

Pattern mold   A mold with a decorative pattern; glass blown in this type of mold picks up the pattern on its exterior.

Pontil mark   The rough place on a blown object where the pontil rod was broken away; may be ground or polished to form a smooth circular depression. Also called a pontil scar.

Pontil rod   A solid iron rod that supports a glass object during the finishing process. After the object is blown, it is transferred from the blowpipe to the pontil rod for final shaping and decoration.

Pot metal   A cheap brittle alloy coated with another metal, often brass, to give the appearance of a better-quality metal.

Pressed glass   Glassware made by dropping molten glass into a mold and pressing it into shape with a plunger.

Prunt   A glob of glass applied to an object as decoration; often berry- or leaf-shaped.

Punty   A workman's term for a pontil rod. Also, a circular facet cut on the glass for decoration.

Raking light   A bright light directed at the side of a glass object to reveal faint surface details.

Rigaree decoration   Applied decoration consisting of a crimped ribbonlike band; found on American and European glass from the 18th and 19th centuries.

Seal   An applied or molded circle containing a name, initials, or a date; often found on the shoulder or side of wine bottles and whiskey jugs, usually made in Europe but occasionally in America, from the 18th and 19th centuries.

Snap case   A spring tool used instead of a pontil rod to hold a glass object during the finishing process. The snap had been introduced in America by the 1850s, but was not widely used until the 1860s. Also called a snap tool.

Stone   A piece of unmelted raw material accidentally left in the molten glass.

Swirled ribbing   A set of ribs on mold-blown glass; made by expanding and twisting a ribbed gather after it is removed from a vertically ribbed mold.

Thread   A strand of glass applied to an object as decoration.

Tooling   The process of shaping a solid or blown glob of glass, using pincers, paddle, shears, and other tools to finish the body and to form the handle, foot, stem, and other parts.

White metal   Any whitish alloy, including britannia metal, pewter, and various tin amalgams.

Wick raiser   A manual device on an oil-lamp burner, used to raise the unburned wick.

Picture Credits

Photographers
All photographs were taken by Raymond Errett with the exception of the following: Schecter Me Sun Lee photographed 77, 261, and 302; Nicholas Williams photographed 326, 331, 333, 338, and 341; the Newark Museum loaned 262.

Collections
The following individuals and institutions kindly allowed us to reproduce objects from their collections:

E.R. Brill Collection: 344.
The Corning Museum of Glass, Corning, New York: 1–49, 51, 52, 54–56, 59–61, 63–69, 71–76, 78, 80–89, 91–95, 101, 104–110, 112, 117, 118, 123, 126–133, 136–140, 142–154, 156, 157, 160–169, 171–182, 184–186, 188–201, 203, 207–225, 227–234, 236, 238, 239 left, 240–245, 247–260, 263–265, 267–282, 287–301, 303–321, 323, 324, 326–328, 330, 331, 333, 336–338, 341.
Osna Fenner: 206, 226, 266, 283, 285, 286.
Donald Hall: 284.
Huntington Galleries, Inc., Huntington, West Virginia: 202.
The Newark Museum, Newark, New Jersey: 262.
Private collections: 77, 122, 183, 261, 302.
Burton Spiller: 50, 53, 57, 58, 62, 70, 79, 90, 96–100, 102, 103, 111, 113–116, 119, 121, 134, 135, 141, 155, 158, 159, 237, 239 right, 246.
The Margaret Woodbury Strong Museum, Rochester, New York: 120, 124, 125, 170, 187, 204, 205, 235, 322, 325, 329, 332, 334, 335, 339, 340, 342, 343, 345, 346.

Price Guide

When buying antique bottles, lamps, and other glass objects, it is essential to become thoroughly acquainted with both the glass field and today's marketplace. Experienced collectors are much more likely to find bargains and avoid costly mistakes than novices are. It is also necessary to understand how collecting trends change—why certain types of glass suddenly become popular, causing their prices to double or triple within a few years, while others experience a sharp decline. To keep abreast of these trends, collectors should study auction reports and catalogues and talk with dealers about price variations.

Auction Prices versus Dealers' Prices

Dealers' prices are the most accurate guide to the market. Because dealers must remain competitive, their prices usually become fairly uniform over a period of time. Today many collectors look to auctions as the ultimate price determinant. Certainly, auctions do offer dramatic evidence of the market in action. A piece is presented, all bidders compete as equals, and the highest bidder gets the piece. However, anyone who has observed two avid bidders knows that such competition can drive prices well above a reasonable figure. And because some people seek out objects that were once owned by well-known collectors, prestige can also warp auction records. Conversely, auction prices can be unrealistically low if, for some reason, attendance at the sale is poor or if doubt is cast on the authenticity of a piece. Since dealers make many of the purchases, auction results are generally a good indication of wholesale values. And although auction prices can fluctuate wildly from one sale to the next, the overall averages do reflect long-term market trends.

This price guide is based on auction records and consultations with dealers and knowledgeable collectors. Remember that experienced collectors understand, and we agree, that a price guide is just that, a guide. No two buying situations are identical. The figures listed are national averages, although costs vary according to region and where you buy, be it an antiques shop, bottle sale, or auction. Except for Art Nouveau lamps and windows and some rare flasks, American glass is seldom as costly as major American paintings and furniture.

Condition, Scarcity, and Collectors' Tastes

Condition of a piece will obviously affect price. The prices given here assume that an object is in good condition, even if the example illustrated is flawed. Before you buy a repaired, altered, or damaged piece, be sure to adjust the prices given accordingly. On the other hand, if an example has outstanding decoration, an unusual inscription, or a well-known trademark, it will cost more than an average example.

Scarcity affects value, since other things being equal, rare and early pieces will command the highest prices. Moreover, unusual colors, such as dark blue, red, or purple, increase the value of all types of glass, particularly antique bottles and flasks.

Prices also rise and fall as particular types of glass increase or decrease in popularity. Twenty years ago only 18th-century and early 19th-century objects were favored by collectors and therefore valuable. However, now that glass from the Victorian era—which encompasses the last two-thirds of the 19th century and several artistic styles—is highly prized, items that were scorned only a few years ago are eagerly collected today. Changes in taste are hard to predict, so, to avoid making an unwise investment, buy what you like, and buy the best. That way you are less apt to be affected by fads.

Price Ranges
The price ranges given here are for the category of objects represented by the pieces illustrated, not just for the object shown. For bottles only, the prices refer to one example, even if two or more bottles are pictured. For all objects, if the price for any type within a category is quite different from the range for the average piece, more than one price is listed.

Figured Flasks

One of the most specialized bottle fields, figured flasks, particularly those in rare patterns and colors, have achieved the highest prices of any bottles. In the mid-1970s several sold for more than $15,000 each at auction. However, prices have not continued to rise, and, in the past two years, many figured flask prices have fallen below their 1970s peak. There are still many figured flasks available in the $75–100 range. The post-Civil War eagle and other late flasks are usually the least expensive. Pattern and color are the keys to value. A flask in a hard-to-find pattern may bring thousands of dollars, and an unusual color, such as dark blue or brownish-pink, is always costly. Other colors may be rare only for a particular flask type; for example, colorless glass is both desirable and expensive in oval sunburst flasks.

1 **American eagle/anchor flask**
   Ravenna $250–350
   New London $100–800
2 **Horseman/dog flask** $150–350
   With handle $1200–1800
3 **Pike's Peak/hunter flasks** $100–1200
4 **American eagle/Willington flasks** $75–175
   With "WESTFORD" on reverse $75–175
5 **American eagle/anchor flasks**
   New London $100–800
   Ravenna $250–350
6 **American eagle flask** $75–550
7 **Clasped hands/eagle flasks** $50–400
   With cannon or cannonball on reverse $70–350
8 **Duck flask**
   Lockport $150–700
   Unmarked $100–300
9 **Traveler's Companion flask**
   Marked with factory name $150–1500
   Unmarked $100–600
10 **Columbus pumpkinseed flask** $200–300
   Plain pumpkinseed flasks $10–65
11 **Pike's Peak/American eagle flasks** $55–500
12 **Sailor/banjo player and soldier/dancer flasks**
   Sailor/banjo player $100–400
   Soldier/dancer $100–1000
13 **Masonic/American eagle flask** $100–1500 (most $250–400)
   Marked "KEENE" $100–200
   Marked "1829" $6000–8500
14 **Masonic flask** $100–150
15 **Girl with bicycle flask**
   With plain reverse $150–650
   With American eagle and "A & DH.C." on reverse $150–500
16 **Lettered flask** $45–350

17 **Lafayette flasks**
With Clinton on reverse $250–400
With Masonic symbols on reverse $700–3000
With liberty cap on reverse $200–450
18 **Sunburst flask**
Marked "KEEN" $200–300
Unmarked $150–4000 (most $150–800)
19 **Sunburst flask** $150–1500 (most $150–900)
20 **Stag flasks**
Unmarked $100–175
Marked "COFFIN & HAY/HAMMONTON" $100–150
With hunter on reverse $200–800
21 **Railroad flask and reproduction**
Authentic Keene $100–175
Authentic with winged figure on reverse $2500–6000
Reproduction $3–7
22 **Sloop flask**
Marked "BRIDGETOWN" $150–1000
With Baltimore Washington Monument on reverse $100–3000
(most $100–1500)
With Kossuth on reverse $100–800
23 **Baltimore Battle Monument flask**
With "A/LITTLE/MORE/GRAPE/CAP^T BRAG" $100–2500
(most $100–1200)
With Washington on reverse $100–3500 (most $100–1500)
With cannon and "GEN^L TAYLOR NEVER SURRENDERS" on
reverse $100–2500 (most $100–1200)
24 **Cornucopia/urn flasks** $50–75
With eagle on reverse $300–600
25 **Baltimore Washington Monument/corn flask** $125–4500
(most $125–800)
26 **Tree flask**
Unmarked $100–2500 (most $100–1000)
With "SUMMER/WINTER" $100–3000 (most $100–1000)
27 **Washington/Farmers' Arms flask** $100–150
28 **Washington/Taylor flasks**
With Taylor, Washington, or Bragg inscriptions $75–3000
(most $75–1000)
Marked "DYOTTVILLE" $75–3000 (most $75–1000)
With Washington and blank reverse $75–800
29 **Taylor/corn flask** $150–2500
Purple up to $4000–5000
30 **Washington/classical bust flask** $350–2500
31 **Jackson/American eagle flasks** $800–4000
With Masonic symbols on reverse $2000–4500
32 **Franklin/Dyott flasks** $150–2500 (most $150–1200)
33 **Washington/American eagle flask** $100–2000 (most $100–1000)
34 **American eagle/cornucopia flasks**
With upright cornucopia $100–3000 (most $100–1500)
With upside-down cornucopia $250–3500 (most $250–2500)
35 **Taylor/Ringgold flask** $125–2500 (most $125–1200)
36 **Columbia/American eagle flask** $250–12,000 (most $250–4500)
Dark blue up to $20,000
37 **Kossuth cologne bottle** $100–150
Charley Ross cologne bottle $50–125
38 **Scroll flask and reproduction**
Authentic $50–1800 (most $150–1200)
Reproduction $3–7
39 **Bryan/coin flask** $150–375
40 **Bininger's regulator flask** $250–450

Round and Oval Bottles

Of the bottles in this group, the pattern-molded pocket flasks are the rarest and most expensive. Those with diamond-daisy and other molded patterns associated with the 18th-century glasshouses of Stiegel and Amelung command the highest prices, reaching up to $3500. Calabash bottles, made in some of the same factories as figured flasks, are also highly prized and sometimes costly. Of the handled whiskey bottles, examples with applied seals are the most desirable; jugs without seals are often inexpensive, usually ranging from $25 to $50. Carboys and demijohns are probably the least popular bottles in this section, partly because their large size makes them difficult to display; also, since they were made in many glasshouses over a long period, it is often impossible to date or attribute them to a glasshouse. Most range from $25 to $100.

41 **Louis Kossuth calabash** $150–850
   With "MISSISSIPPI" $175–2200 (most $175–1500)
42 **Jenny Lind calabashes** $125–2500 (most $125–1000)
   Violin-shaped flasks $700–1500
43 **Carboy** $45–300
44 **Demijohn**
   With basket $25–125
   Without basket $25–100
45 **Chestnut or Ludlow bottles** $45–500 (most $50–300)
46 **Pitkin-type flasks** $150–375
47 **Stiegel-type flasks** $1000–3500
48 **Midwestern pattern-molded flasks** $200–3500 (most $150–1500)
49 **Handled whiskey bottles** $25–850
50 **Handled whiskey bottles**
   With applied seal $300–400
   With molded seal $100–300
   Without seal $25–50

Cylindrical Bottles

Early 18th-century English wine bottles with dated seals have been collected for many years, and their prices can reach $1000 or more. However, antique American wine bottles with seals are considerably less expensive, usually ranging from $100 to $250, and those without seals may bring only $50 to $75. Most of the bottles included here were made for beverages. In general, the more handwork evident in the finishing of a bottle or the more unusual its form, color, or molded inscription or design, the higher its price will be. Beer, milk, and soft-drink bottles first produced in the late 19th and early 20th centuries tend to be the most available and least expensive.

51 **Early 18th-century wine bottles**
   Without seal $50–100
   With seal $300–1000
   Reproductions $50–60
52 **Late 18th-century wine bottles** $50–75
53 **Saratoga mineral water bottles** $35–800 (most $50–400)
   Other firms $50–500
54 **Oak Orchard Acid Springs bottle** $35–50
55 **19th-century wine bottles**
   Without seal but with base rim inscription $45–75
   With applied seal $100–250

56 **Porter bottle**
Ormsby $75–125
Other brands $75–200
57 **Mineral water bottles** $35–500 (most $50–300)
58 **Beer and ale bottles**
Without stopper $10–75
Bechtel bottle with Lightning stopper $10–40
59 **Coca-Cola bottles** $5–50
60 **Round-bottomed bottle**
Irish $2–4
American $50–400
61 **Huckleberry bottle** $50–150
62 **Milk bottles**
Without cap $15–500 (most $15–150)
With tin cap and bail $25–50
63 **Pickle bottle**
Bunker Hill $50–125
Other brands $25–75
64 **Glue bottle** $15–75
65 **Early medicine and essence bottles** $15–25

Rectangular Bottles

Snuff and gin bottles are some of the oldest American bottles, and their prices are relatively uniform; pontiled examples generally bring $100 to $200. In contrast, common patent and proprietary medicine bottles start at just a few dollars, although a rare example can be extremely costly. Since bitters collectors have been active for at least 20 years, many such bottles are scarce today; still, some widely available brands are priced well under $25. For most of these types, bottles with pontil marks or rare colors, such as dark blue or yellow, are the most expensive.

66 **Snuff jar** $100–250
67 **Snuff jar**
Unmarked with pontil $100–250
Marked "LORILLARD" or other inscription and no pontil $20–40
68 **Gin or case bottles**
c. 1760–1820 $75–200
c. 1820–50 $10–75
69 **Dr. Townsend's Sarsaparilla bottle** $50–100
Other brands $30–300
70 **Whiskey bottle**
Monk's $50–250
Other brands $5–400 (most $5–150)
71 **Dr. Hostetter's Bitters bottle** $5–15
72 **L.Q.C. Wishart's Pine Tree Cordial bottle** $75–200
73 **Early medicine bottles** $25–100
74 **Hood's Sarsaparilla bottle** $2–5
Other brands $2–50
75 **Dr. Kilmer's Swamp Root Cure bottle** $2–10
Other brands $1–150
76 **Medicine bottles**
With pontil $25–500
Without pontil $2–85
77 **G.W. Merchant bottles** $75–200
78 **Master ink bottle**
Carter $40–85
Other brands $15–2500 (most $15–300)
79 **Cathedral pickle bottles** $125–2000 (most $125–800)

80 **Doyle's Hop Bitters bottle** $15–25
Dr. Soule's Hop Bitters $50–100
81 **Shoe blacking bottle** $50–150
82 **Clemens Indian Tonic bottle**
In original wrapper $125–250
Without wrapper $100–200
Other brands $75–400
83 **J.B. Wheatley's Spanish Pain Destroyer bottle**
In original wrapper $200–350
Without wrapper $100–250
With "J.B.WHEATLEY'S COMPOUND" $50–125
84 **Lydia Pinkham's Vegetable Compound bottle** $2–20
85 **Warner's safe medicine bottle** $15–460
Warner's log-shaped bottle $35–400

Figural Bottles
The most popular figural bottles date from about 1840 to 1940.
Because of their unusual shapes, many sell for at least $100.
Several late 19th-century figurals and some early 20th-century
candy containers may be considerably less costly. Of the wide
variety illustrated, the Tippecanoe log cabin bottle is the rarest;
one recently sold for a record $10,000. Some figural bitters are
worth at least several hundred dollars. Cologne and smelling
salts bottles dating from the mid-19th century are good buys,
considering their age, and are often available for less than $50.
Adaptations and reproductions of antique bottles usually cost
between $3 and $25.

86 **Jacob's Cabin Tonic Bitters bottle** $3500–4000
87 **Log cabin bottle** $7500–10,000
88 **Booz's Old Cabin Whiskey bottle and adaptation**
Authentic $500–700
Adaptation $5–25
89 **Drake's Plantation Bitters bottle** $45–950 (most $45–350)
Other brands $150–3500
90 **McKeever's Army Bitters bottle** $1400–2100
91 **Cleveland and Stevenson/rooster flasks** $150–350
92 **Basket-weave and barrel-shaped smelling salts bottles** $15–45
93 **Bourbon whiskey bitters bottle** $140–160
Other brands $125–500 (most $125–700)
94 **Bourbon whiskey bottle** $125–175
95 **Hand fire grenade bottle** $100–200
Other shapes $40–100
96 **Hart's Hair Restorer bottle** $100–250
Other brands and shapes $5–80
97 **Cannon-shaped whiskey bottles** $1000–1500
Bitters variant $10,000–12,000
With "A.M.BININGER & CO" $250–350
98 **National Bitters bottles** $200–1500 (most $200–650)
Aquamarine up to $1500
99 **Indian Queen Bitters figural bottle** $250–375
Mohawk whiskey $900–1200
100 **Flaccus Brothers Catsup figural bottle** $75–175
Cylindrical variants with cow's or deer's head $40–125
101 **Poland Spring Water figural bottle** $75–125
Amber up to $325
Reproduction $4–10
102 **Little girl figural cologne bottle** $45–75
103 **Golfer figural bottle** $150–400

104 **Washington figural bottle reproduction** $3–7
    Authentic aquamarine $400–600
    Authentic amber $1000–1200
105 **Cleveland figural bottle** $85–150
106 **Crying baby figural bottle** $45–75
107 **Elephant figural cologne bottle** $45–85
108 **Fish figural bottle adaptation** $15–30
    Authentic amber $125–175
    Authentic colorless $700–950
    Authentic yellow-green $900–1200
    Cod-liver oil bottle $5–15
109 **Oyster figural bottle** $25–35
110 **Baby-in-a-basket figural bottle** $35–55
111 **Pig figural bottle**
    Suffolk Bitters $400–600
    Berkshire Bitters $800–1200
    With "SOMETHING GOOD/IN A HOG'S" $35–70
112 **Bear grease jars** $125–225
    Rare variants $150–900
    Man-shaped jar $75–600
113 **Rabbit candy container** $65–90
114 **Clock candy container** $100–175
115 **Train candy container** $50–75
116 **Amos 'n' Andy in a taxicab candy container** $350–450

Ink Bottles and Inkwells

The most expensive ink bottles, usually either figurals or old and rare examples of any type, are priced at several hundred dollars or more. A rare one-gallon Harrison's Columbian Ink bottle in dark blue recently fetched $4000 at auction. However, most ink bottles are more affordable; for instance, relatively common cylindrical, conical, and umbrella inks are usually $3 to $50, although unusual colors always exceed this range. All but the earliest and rarest nursing bottles remain relatively inexpensive.

117 **Nursing bottles** $15–150
118 **Snail inkwells in stand**
    Two or more bottles $35–125
    Single bottle $25–75
119 **Teakettle ink bottle** $125–250
120 **Turtle ink bottle** $15–150
    Harrison's Columbian Ink $50–450
121 **Harrison's Columbian Ink bottles** $50–450
    Dark blue gallon up to $4000
122 **Umbrella ink bottle reproduction** 50¢–$1.50
    Authentic bottle $40–175
123 **Conical ink bottle** $3–65
124 **Schoolhouse ink bottle** $100–850 (most $100–350)
125 **Barrel-shaped ink bottle**
    Horizontal $20–350
    Upright $15–150
126 **Victorian cut inkwell** $20–300
127 **Mold-blown inkwells** $100–3500 (most $100–1500)

Jars

Except for a few rare fruit jars in dark blue that fetch about $3000 or those with unusual closures worth $350 or more, preserving jars are within the reach of collectors with modest means. Jars produced in the 20th century by automatic bottle-blowing machinery sell for only a few dollars each, and many Mason-type jars from the 1880–1900 period are not much more expensive. Jar prices are not as well established as those for flasks and bitters bottles, but it is generally true that jars in unusual colors, such as dark blue, purple, and opaque white, are the most costly. An original, patented, metal-and-glass closure increases the value of early jars; later jars closed with standard screw-on zinc lids are valuable without the lid since most lids were interchangeable.

128 **Mason's improved jar** $2–8
129 **Van Vliet jar**
Without lid $200–250
With lid $300–350
130 **Hahne Mason jar** $35–45
131 **Ball Mason jar** $2–4
132 **Atlas Mason jar** $1–2
133 **Mason's patent jar** $2–3500 (most $2–35)
134 **French's mustard jar** $3–8
135 **Magic fruit jar**
Amber $650–850
Aquamarine $100–125
136 **Lightning jar** $15–125
137 **Millville jar** $25–95
Dark blue up to $3000 or more
138 **Ribbed jar** $125–175
Unribbed variants $75–125
139 **Early free-blown jar** $100–500
140 **Ring jar**
With pontil $25–100
Without pontil $15–75
141 **Grocery storage jar**
Planter's Peanuts $150–300
Plain $25–85

Drug, Perfume, and Other Fancy Bottles

Most of the bottles in this section held perfume, cologne, smelling salts, or other toiletries. Cut or engraved perfume bottles are prized by both collectors of perfume bottles and cut glassware. Depending on the quality of decoration and the presence of a trademark or signature, these prices range from $20 to $1000 or more. Some bottles that were originally relatively common and inexpensive have remained moderately priced. For example, many middle to late 19th-century cologne and perfume bottles are priced in the $50–150 range, and some smelling salts bottles sell for as little as $25. In contrast, unique art-glass, cameo, and Lalique perfume bottles are among the most expensive, costing several hundred or even several thousand dollars. Barber bottles, hair tonic bottles, poison bottles, and pepper sauce bottles are all sought by specialized collectors. Since many were mass-produced, they are usually less expensive than hand-fashioned perfume bottles. Figural poison bottles and quality art-glass barber bottles are exceptions, with prices starting at $100. Finally, early pharmaceutical and scientific bottles are generally reasonable, although elaborate examples can climb into the hundreds of dollars, such as fancy cut-glass druggists' show globes for up to $900.

Dresser Sets, Bells, and Other Ornamental Glassware

Like perfume and cologne bottles, the elaborate dresser sets, powder jars, and humidors span a wide price range depending on the type of decoration, quality of workmanship, and signature or trademark. Individual cut-glass accessories can sometimes be found at yard sales; except for rare patterns or types, these pieces are relatively inexpensive. Fancy cut or engraved sets, usually available through dealers, generally sell for over $500. Similarly, such one-of-a-kind objects as trumpets, ornate banks, and especially elaborate bells now cost several hundred dollars, since they are collected as a kind of folk art. Although string holders, fishbowls, garden bells, and smoke bells are not in great demand, they are fairly scarce, and unusual examples sometimes command more than $100.

170 **Dresser set in frame** $500–650
171 **Dresser set** $750–1000
172 **Trumpet** $500–750
173 **Bell** $150–200
    Variants $50–400
174 **Bank** $2000–3500
175 **Bank** $400–500
176 **Fishbowl** $200–300
177 **String holders** $300–425 (each)
    Pressed variants $50–100
178 **Garden bell** $75–150
179 **Smoke bell** $50–100
180 **Letter holder** $125–175
181 **Ointment box** $25–50
182 **Dresser box** $175–250
183 **Powder jars**
    Left $50–75
    Right $75–125
184 **Humidors**
    Left $175–250
    Right $300–450
185 **Humidor** $300–400

Toy Glassware

Interest in collecting toy glassware has greatly increased in the past 10 years, most of it focused on turn-of-the-century objects. The least costly miniatures are Depression-era tea sets at $15 and individual baking pans at $3. Although some Victorian pressed-glass sets still may be found for less than $50, most of these middle to late 19th-century miniatures range from $50 to $150. Early lacy-pattern toy tableware, which became popular and expensive in the 1950s, still commands prices in the hundreds. Since this area of collecting is likely to grow in popularity during the next decade, prices will undoubtedly rise.

186 **Toy candlesticks** $50–200 (each)
187 **Toy castor set** $60–120
188 **Toy blown 3-mold decanter** $150–350
189 **Toy decanter and pitcher**
    Decanter $80–150
    Pitcher $50–100
190 **Toy creamer with cup and saucer**
    Creamer $75–125
    Cup and saucer $100–150
191 **Toy mug** $40–55
    Other mugs $10–40
192 **Toy table set** $75–100
    Variant sets $50–300
193 **Toy tumblers and sugar bowl** $75–200 (each)
194 **Toy tureen with tray** $300–700
    Rare colors up to $800

195 **Toy butter dish** $25–40
   Variants $20–100
196 **Toy serving dish and salt dish** $150–250 (each)
197 **Toy Pyrex loaf pan and pie plate** $3–15 (each)
   Original boxed set $50–100
198 **Toy washstand set** $200–700
199 **Toy water set** $90–130
   Variant sets $50–150
200 **Toy punch set** $200–250
   Variant sets $60–300
201 **Toy berry set** $40–70
   Variant sets $30–150
202 **Toy tea set** $15–25
   Variant sets $12–50
203 **Toy flatirons** $75–200 (each)

Miscellaneous Objects
Most of the objects in this section have a very specialized appeal
and are not collected by large numbers of people. However,
there are some dedicated collectors of stocking darners, eyecups,
canes, pipes, telephone insulators, and even of the glass cups
placed under piano legs to protect the carpet. Because these
objects are so varied, it is difficult to generalize about their
prices. Many items included here cost less than $25, including
19th-century spectacles, apothecary glassware, and cigarette
holders. Depression-era fruit knives range from $5 to $10.

204 **Curtain-rod or newel-post finials** $125–250 (pair)
205 **Stocking darners** $35–200 (each)
206 **Automobile flower vase** $8–15
   Cut variants $35–70
207 **Powder horn** $150–300
208 **Apothecary glass** $10–40 (each)
209 **Funnel** $35–65
210 **Flip-flop** $95–150
211 **Pipe and cigarette holder**
   Pipe $125–200
   Cigarette holder $20–35
212 **Gavel** $200–350
213 **Match striker** $15–35
214 **Fruit knife** $5–10
215 **Rolling pin** $100–200
216 **Fiberglass necktie** $200–300
217 **Spectacles** $5–50 (each)
   Variants $25–200
218 **Chain** $75–175
219 **Pens** $10–35 (each)
220 **Canes** $50–100 (each)
221 **Slippers** $65–130 (each)
   Variants $15–200
222 **Brilliant-cut whimsies** $75–200 (each)
223 **Hats** $75–250 (each)
224 **Christmas-tree lights** $20–50 (each)
   Pontiled variant $75–100
225 **Telephone and telegraph insulators** $3–20 (each)
   Variants $1–300
226 **Flower frog** $5–8
   Variants $25–150
227 **Flytrap** $40–65

228 **Mousetrap** $20–35
229 **Animal figurines** $20–75 (each)
230 **Wall pocket for matches** $25–50

Knobs, Balls, and Paperweights
Glass knobs, curtain tiebacks, marbles, target balls, lightning-rod balls, and plain Christmas-tree ornaments are all relatively inexpensive. Most prices range from $10 to $75. However, witch balls may cost $100 or more if they have elaborate decoration or can be associated with a particular glasshouse. Paperweights and paperweight buttons are the most expensive items in this group. Even pressed paperweights usually command at least $100, and only simple photographic, advertising, and motto weights sell for less than $50. The best antique American paperweights may start at $2000, while prices for works by 20th-century glass artists range from several hundred to several thousand dollars, based on the intricacy of the designs and the reputations of the artists. Contemporary paperweights are well worth collecting, because in time they will increase in value, but mass-produced paperweights should be avoided.

231 **Doorknobs** $10–25 (each)
232 **Furniture knobs** $15–40 (each)
233 **Picture hangers** $3–10 (each)
234 **Curtain tiebacks** $35–70 (each)
235 **Paperweight buttons**
Left $50–250
Right $35–175
236 **Marbles** $15–75 (each)
237 **Lightning-rod balls** $20–75 (each)
238 **Christmas-tree ornaments** $10–20 (each)
Figural ornaments $15–300
239 **Target balls** $65–125 (each) (most $65–90)
240 **Witch ball** $50–150
241 **Darning egg** $15–65
242 **Fruit paperweights** $125–2500 (each)
243 **Flower paperweight** $200–2000
244 **Mantel ornament** $135–285
245 **Pylon paperweight** $350–700
246 **Philadelphia Memorial Hall inkstand** $400–500
247 **Philadelphia Memorial Hall paperweight** $225–300
248 **Lion paperweight** $100–150
249 **Turtle doorstop** $100–200
250 **Portrait paperweight** $150–475
251 **Photographic paperweight** $20–40
252 **Advertising paperweight** $20–150
253 **Motto paperweight** $20–60
254 **Fruit paperweight** $250–2000
255 **Millefiori paperweight** $275–2500

Windows
Antique windows range tremendously in value, from about $25 for colored pressed panes dating from the turn of the century to about $150,000 for stained-glass windows by such masters as Louis Comfort Tiffany or John La Farge. Price is not necessarily determined by size. Because large windows are difficult to display, they may cost less than smaller windows in perfect condition from the same studio.

256 **Bull's-eye windowpane** $25–50
Whole crown $500–600
257 **Square windowpane** $100–125
258 **Rectangular windowpane** $500–600
259 **Assorted windowpanes** $25–65 (each)
Crinkled variants $10–15
260 **Glass screen** $250–400
261 **Stained-glass window** $100–1000
262 **Ballantine House stained-glass window**
Windows of this quality $10,000–150,000
263 **Tiffany stained-glass window**
Signed Tiffany windows $20,000–150,000
Tiffany-type windows $1500–7000

Candlesticks

Color, rarity of pattern, and date are the determining factors
in pricing candlesticks. In general, an example that can be
positively attributed to a famous glasshouse will almost always
cost more than a similar candlestick by an unknown maker. The
least expensive examples are from the 1930s, 1940s, and 1950s.
Many of these were mass-produced and are readily available
starting at about $10 a pair. Harder to find and considerably
more expensive are the pressed candlesticks of the mid-19th
century. Especially popular patterns, such as the dolphin stem or
the Petal and Loop types, may cost up to $400 apiece. Although
early blown candlesticks from 19th-century window and bottle
glasshouses are even scarcer, these often command about the
same price. Art-glass candlesticks tend to be expensive; for
example, elaborate fairy lamps may bring up to $3000 at auction.

264 **Linen smoother** $300–450
265 **Early blown candlesticks** $350–600 (pair)
266 **Hexagonal candlestick** $7–15
267 **Console candlestick** $25–40
268 **Venetian-style candlesticks** $75–175 (pair)
269 **Blown candlestick reproductions** $25–35 (each)
270 **Early blown candlesticks** $500–750 (pair)
271 **Blown candlestick with pressed base** $150–275
272 **Candlestick with air-twist stem** $200–350
273 **Pillar-molded candlestick** $200–300
274 **Petal and Loop candlesticks** $75–400 (each)
275 **Columnar candlestick** $100–250
276 **Lacy-pattern candlestick** $225–375
277 **Columnar candlesticks**
Left $300–500
Right $250–400
278 **Crucifix candlestick** $300–600
279 **Caryatid candlesticks** $300–450 (each)
280 **Dolphin candlesticks and reproductions**
Authentic tall candlestick $300–400 (each)
Authentic short candlestick $200–275 (each)
Reproduction candlesticks $50–75 (pair)
281 **Burmese candlestick** $250–450
282 **Fairy lamp** $400–650
More elaborate variants up to $3000
283 **Low hobnail candleholders** $6–15 (pair)
284 **Low finned candleholders** $23–30 (pair)
285 **Low candleholders** $10–15 (pair)
286 **Triple candleholder** $25–40

Hand Lamps, Miniature Night Lamps, and Lanterns

Beginning in the 1970s, a growing interest in Victorian night lamps began to push up prices, and values continue to rise today. Many of the miniature lamps pictured in this section sell for $250 to $500. The older hand lamps, peg lamps, and lanterns are often much cheaper, although not more common.

287 **Shoe lamp** $225–300
288 **Log cabin lamp** $400–550
289 **Lamp filler** $225–400
290 **Oil Guard lamp** $85–110
291 **Hand lamps**
    Left $250–350
    Right $60–85
292 **Kitchen lamps** $75–150 (each)
293 **Match-holder miniature lamp** $275–350
294 **Ruffle-top miniature lamp** $200–340
295 **Diamond miniature lamp** $225–375
296 **Pinecone miniature lamp** $250–325
297 **Quilted Phlox miniature lamp** $300–375
298 **Coin Spot miniature lamp** $350–425
299 **Owl miniature lamp** $500–700
300 **Pan-American Exposition miniature lamp** $300–500
301 **Peg lamps**
    Left $150–200
    Right $85–120
302 **Electrical fixture** $65–120
303 **Whale-oil lantern** $125–200
304 **Kerosene lantern** $75–120

Table Lamps

With the possible exception of windows, lamps reflect the widest price range of all glass objects. In the case of both lamps and windows, this is because the works of Louis Comfort Tiffany are so expensive that they have substantially raised the upper end of the scale. Most 19th-century lamps cost from $150 to $300. The large solar and Argand lamps rarely sell for less than $1000, and are even more expensive if they have unusually elaborate decoration. Quality cut-glass and art-glass lamps range from one thousand to ten thousand dollars, depending on rarity and type. The top prices for genuine Tiffany fixtures (as distinct from Tiffany-type lamps) rose from $5000 to $10,000 in the 1960s, and doubled again in the 1970s. In 1980 one lamp was auctioned for a record-breaking $360,000. Although Tiffany lamps have been the darlings of antiques investors for the past 10 years as well as favorites with collectors of Art Nouveau, these lamps are not rare. Many examples of each design were made and are readily available for those with enough money to purchase them. In contrast to these extraordinarily expensive lamps, some Tiffany-type shades as well as many late 19th-century fixtures sell for $100 to $250.

305 **Whale-oil hand lamp** $150–275
306 **Whale-oil stand lamp** $450–750
307 **Whale-oil wineglass lamps**
    Left $225–300
    Right $75–200
308 **Whale-oil hand lamp** $150–220

309 **Lamp with engraved font** $150–200
310 **Mercury-glass lamp** $300–400
311 **Horn of Plenty lamp** $155–225
312 **Waffle and Thumbprint lamp with tin liner** $150–300
    Without liner $100–150
313 **Amberette lamp** $250–400
314 **Acanthus-leaf lamp** $400–500
315 **Whale-oil or burning-fluid lamps**
    Purple $750–1000 (pair)
    Other colors $250–750 (most $250–450 per pair)
316 **Whale-oil lamp** $250–350
317 **Whale-oil or burning-fluid lamp with shade** $300–425
318 **Whale-oil lamp** $175–250
319 **Cut lamp with pressed base** $275–350
320 **Lamp with hand-pressed base** $200–300
321 **Bicolor lamp** $250–350
322 **Atterbury lamp** $140–190
323 **Atterbury lamp** $130–175
324 **Cased lamp** $350–1000
325 **Lamp with prisms**
    Imperfect as shown $250–300
    Perfect $400–550
326 **Argand lamp** $1200–4500
327 **Hurricane shade** $225–300
328 **Aladdin lamp** $150–200
329 **Swan stem lamp** $275–350
330 **Double lamp**
    With non-glass stem and base $450–850
    With glass stem and glass base $650–1200
331 **Brilliant-cut banquet lamp** $2500–10,000
332 **Cased lamp** $900–1600
333 **Solar lamp** $1000–1800
334 **Sinumbra lamp** $500–750
    Astral lamp $500–750
335 **Figural stem lamp** $125–400
336 **Lamp with brass stem and marble base** $200–300
337 **Brilliant-cut lamp** $1500–2200
338 **Burmese lamp** $2000–5000
339 **Iridescent lamp**
    Signed $1000–4000
    Unsigned $600–850
340 **Lamp with painted shade** $350–1200
341 **Tiffany lamp with leaded-glass shade** $5000–165,000
342 **Tiffany pond-lily lamp** $6000–15,000
343 **Puffy Pairpoint lamp** $2000–4000
344 **Emeralite desk lamp** $350–450
    Variants $150–500
345 **Hall lantern** $175–250
346 **Lamp shade for hanging fixture** $75–250

The Price Guide was written by William C. Ketchum, Jr.

Bibliography

Bottles and Flasks
General
Ketchum, William C., Jr.
A Treasury of American Bottles
Indianapolis: Bobbs-Merrill, 1975.

Klamkin, Marian
The Collector's Book of Bottles
New York: Dodd, Mead & Co., 1971.

Klamkin, Marian, with Charles B. Gardner
American Blown Glass Bottles
Des Moines: Wallace-Homestead Book Co., 1977.

Kovel, Ralph and Terry
The Kovels' Bottle Price List
6th ed. New York: Crown Publishers, Inc., 1982.

Lohmann, Watson M., ed.
1904 Whitney Glass Works Illustrated Catalogue and Price List
Pitman, New Jersey: Review Printing Co., 1972.

McKearin, Helen
Bottles, Flasks and Dr. Dyott
New York: Crown Publishers, Inc., 1970.

McKearin, Helen, and Kenneth M. Wilson
American Bottles and Flasks and Their Ancestry
New York: Crown Publishers, Inc., 1978.

Morgan, Roy
Sealed Bottles: Their History and Evolution (1630–1930)
Burton-on-Trent, England: Midlands Antique Bottle Publishing Co., 1976.

Munsey, Cecil
The Illustrated Guide to Collecting Bottles
New York: Hawthorn Books, 1970.

Putnam, Hazel E.
Bottle Identification
Jamestown, California: published by author, 1965.

Stewart, Regina, and Geraldine Cosentina
Bottles: A Guide For the Beginning Collector
New York: Western Publishing Co., 1976.

Stockton, John
Victorian Bottles: A Collector's Guide to Yesterday's Empties
North Pomfret, Vermont: David & Charles, 1981.

Thomas, John L.
Picnics, Coffins, Shooflies
Weaverville, California: published by author, 1974.

Toulouse, Julian H.
Bottle Makers and Their Marks
Camden, New Jersey: Thomas Nelson & Sons, 1971.

Wilson, Bill and Betty
Spirits Bottles of the Old West
Wolfe City, Texas: Henington Publishing Co., 1968.

Wilson, Rex L.
Bottles on the Western Frontier
Tucson, Arizona: University of Arizona Press, in collaboration with
Southwest Parks and Monuments Association, 1981.

Beer, Soda, and Mineral Water Bottles
Anderson, Will
The Beer Book: An Illustrated Guide to American Breweriana
Princeton, New Jersey: The Pyne Press, 1973.

Dietz, Lawrence
*Soda Pop: The History, Advertising Art and Memorabilia of Soft Drinks
in America*
New York: Simon & Schuster, a Subsistence Press Book, 1973.

Jones, J.L.
Soda and Mineral Water Bottles
Greer, South Carolina: Palmetto Enterprises, 1972.

Candy Containers
Agadjanian, Serge, and George Eikelberner
American Glass Candy Containers
Belle Mead, New Jersey: published by authors, 1968.
More American Glass Candy Containers
Belle Mead, New Jersey: published by authors, 1970.

Drug, Perfume, and Barber Bottles
Crellin, J.K., and J.R. Scott
Glass and British Pharmacy, 1600–1900
London: Wellcome Institute of the History of Medicine, 1972.

Launert, Edmund
Scent Bottles
London: Barrie & Jenkins, 1974.

Matthews, Leslie
Antiques of the Pharmacy
London: G. Bell & Sons, 1971.

Namiat, Robert
Barber Bottles with Prices
Des Moines: Wallace-Homestead Book Co., 1977.

Percy, Christopher V.
The Glass of Lalique
New York: Charles Scribner's Sons, 1977.

Whitall, Tatum & Company
Whitall, Tatum & Co., 1880
Reprint of catalogue. Princeton, New Jersey: The Pyne Press, 1971.

Figural Bottles
Revi, Albert C.
American Pressed Glass and Figure Bottles
New York: Thomas Nelson & Sons, 1964.

Umberger, Art and Jewell
Collectible Character Bottles
Tyler, Texas: Corker Book Co., 1969.

Wearin, Otha D.
Statues That Pour: The Story of Character Bottles
Des Moines: Wallace-Homestead Book Co., 1965.

Ink Bottles and Inkwells
Covill, William E.
Ink Bottles and Inkwells
Taunton, Massachusetts: William S. Sullwold, 1971.

Rivera, Betty and Ted
Inkstands and Inkwells: A Collector's Guide
New York: Crown Publishers, Inc., 1973.

Jars
Brantley, William F.
A Collector's Guide to Ball Jars
Muncie, Indiana: published by author, 1975.

Creswick, Alice
Red Book of Fruit Jars, No. 3
Grand Rapids, Michigan: ABC Publishing, 1977.

Toulouse, Julian H.
Fruit Jars
New York: Thomas Nelson & Sons, 1969.

Milk and Food Bottles
Tutton, John
Udder Delight: A Guide to Collecting Milk Bottles and Related Items
Marshall, Virginia: published by author, 1980.

Zumwalt, Betty
Ketchup, Pickles, Sauces: 19th Century Food in Glass
Fulton, California: Mark West Publishers, 1980.

Nursing Bottles
Cone, Thomas E.
200 Years of Feeding Infants in America
Columbus, Ohio: Ross Laboratories, 1971.

Patent and Proprietary Medicine Bottles and Bitters Bottles
Baldwin, Joseph
A Collector's Guide to Patent and Proprietary Medicine Bottles of the Nineteenth Century
Nashville, Tennessee: Thomas Nelson & Sons, 1973.

Carson, Gerald
One For A Man, Two For A Horse
Garden City, New Jersey: Doubleday & Co., 1961.

DeGrafft, John
American Sarsaparilla Bottles
North Attleboro, Massachusetts: published by author, 1980.

Holbrook, Stewart
The Golden Age of Quackery
New York: The Macmillan Co., 1959.

Nielson, R. Frederick
Great American Pontiled Medicines
Medford, New Jersey: published by author, 1978.

Ring, Carlyn
For Bitters Only
Wellesley, Massachusetts: published by author, 1980.

Watson, Richard
Bitters Bottles
New York: Thomas Nelson & Sons, 1965.
Supplement to Bitters Bottles
Camden, New Jersey: Thomas Nelson & Sons, 1968.

Wilson, Bill and Betty
19th Century Medicine in Glass
Washington, D.C.: 19th Century Hobby and Publishing Co., 1971.

Miscellaneous Glass
General
Florence, Gene
Collectors Encyclopedia of Akro Agate Glassware
Paducah, Kentucky: Collector Books, 1975.

Frazier, Dale
Lightning Rod Ball Collectors' Guide
South Hutchinson, Kansas: published by author, 1973.

Lechler, Doris, and Virginia O'Neill
Childrens' Glass Dishes
Nashville, Tennessee: Thomas Nelson & Sons, 1976.

Milholland, Marian C. and Evelyn
Milholland's Final and Complete Glass Insulator Reference Book
Spanaway, Washington: published by authors, 1976.

Rehl, Norma and Dick
Depression Era Glass Knives
Milford, New Jersey: published by authors, 1981.

Zemel, Evelyn
American Glass Animals from A to Z
North Miami, Florida: published by author, 1978.

Eyeglasses
Bronson, L.D.
Early American Specs
Glendale, California: Occidental Publishing Co., 1974.

Corson, Richard
Fashions in Eyeglasses
London: Peter Owen, 1967.

Marbles
Baumann, Paul
Collecting Antique Marbles
Des Moines: Wallace-Homestead Book Co., 1970.

Randall, Mark E.
Marbles as Historical Artifacts
Trumbull, Connecticut: Marble Collectors Society of America, 1979.

Paperweights
Hollister, Paul
The Encyclopedia of Glass Paperweights
New York: Clarkson N. Potter, 1969.

Jokelson, Paul
Sulphides: The Art of Cameo Incrustation
New York: Thomas Nelson & Sons, 1968.

Melvin, Jean S.
American Glass Paperweights and Their Makers
Revised ed. New York: Thomas Nelson & Sons, 1970.

Windows
Duncan, Alastair
Tiffany Windows
New York: Simon & Schuster, 1980.

Duthie, Arthur
Decorative Glass Processes: Cutting, Etching, Staining and Other Traditional Techniques
Reprint of 1911 edition. New York: Dover Publications, 1982.

Harrison, Martin
Victorian Stained Glass
London: Barrie & Jenkins, 1980.

Candlesticks and Lamps
General
American Historical Catalog Collection
Lamps and Other Lighting Devices, 1850–1906
Princeton, New Jersey: The Pyne Press, 1972.

Burkhalter, Agnes S.
Historical Railroad Lanterns
Winchester, Pennsylvania: published by author, 1971.

Cooke, Lawrence S., ed.
Lighting in America: From Colonial Rushlights to Victorian Chandeliers
New York: Main Street-Universe Books, 1976.

Myers, Denys
Gaslighting in America: A Guide for Historic Preservation
Washington, D.C.: Office of Archaeology and Historic Preservation, U.S. Government Printing Office, 1978.

Russell, Loris S.
A Heritage of Light
Toronto: University of Toronto Press, 1968.

Art Glass, Art Nouveau, and Art Deco Lamps
Duncan, Alastair
Art Nouveau and Art Deco Lighting
New York: Simon & Schuster, 1978.

Grant, Joanne C.
The Painted Lamps of Handel
New Windsor, New York: published by author, 1978.

Handel Company
Handel Lamps and Fixtures
c. 1905 catalogue. Washington Mills, New York: Gilded Age Press, 1978.

Koch, Robert C.
Louis C. Tiffany's Glass, Bronzes and Lamps: A Complete Collector's Guide
New York: Crown Publishers, Inc., 1971.

Revi, Albert C.
American Art Nouveau Glass
Camden, New Jersey: Thomas Nelson & Sons, 1968.

Candlesticks
Butler, Joseph T.
Candleholders in America, 1650–1900
New York: Bonanza Books, 1967.

MacSwiggan, Amelia
Fairy Lamps, Evening's Glow of Yesteryear
New York: Fountainhead Publishers, 1962.

Lamps
Courter, J.W.
Aladdin, the Magic Name in Lamps
Simpson, Illinois: published by author, 1971.
Aladdin Collectors Manual and Price Guide
Simpson, Illinois: published by author, 1978.

Rochester Lamp Company
The Rochester Lamp Company Catalog
Reprint of 1891–92 catalogue. Washington Mills, New York: Gilded Age Press, 1978.

Thuro, Catherine M.V.
Oil Lamps: The Kerosene Era in North America
Des Moines: Wallace-Homestead Book Co., 1976.

Miniature Lamps
McDonald, Ann Gilbert
The Evolution of the Night Lamp
Des Moines: Wallace-Homestead Book Co., 1979.

Smith, Frank R. and Ruth E.
Miniature Lamps
Camden, New Jersey: Thomas Nelson & Sons, 1968.

Periodicals
General
For club publications, check the Organizations for Collectors.

Antique Bottle World
Columbus, Ohio.

Bottle News
Kermit, Texas.

The Crown Point, Newsletter of Lightning Rod Collectors
Las Vegas, Nevada.

Font and Flue
Pattonsburg, Missouri.

Fruit Jar Newsletter
West Orange, New Jersey.

Hobbies, The Magazine for Collectors
Chicago, Illinois.

Old Bottle Magazine
Bend, Oregon.

Index

Numbers refer to entries.

Staff

Prepared and produced by Chanticleer Press, Inc.
Publisher: Paul Steiner
Editor-in-Chief: Gudrun Buettner
Managing Editor: Susan Costello
Project Editor: Jane Opper
Assistant Editor: Lori Renn
Art Director: Carol Nehring
Art Assistants: Ayn Svoboda and Karen Wollman
Production: Helga Lose, Amy Roche, and Alex von Hoffman
Picture Library: Edward Douglas
Drawings: Mary Jane Spring
Symbols: Paul Singer
Design: Massimo Vignelli

The Knopf Collectors' Guides to American Antiques

Also available in this unique full-color format:

Glass 1
Tableware, Bowls & Vases
by Jane Shadel Spillman

Dolls
by Wendy Lavitt

Folk Art
Paintings, Sculpture & Country Objects
by Robert Bishop and Judith Reiter Weissman

Furniture 1
Chairs, Tables, Sofas & Beds
by Marvin D. Schwartz

Furniture 2
Chests, Cupboards, Desks & Other Pieces
by William C. Ketchum, Jr.

Pottery & Porcelain
by William C. Ketchum, Jr.

Quilts
With Coverlets, Rugs & Samplers
by Robert Bishop